Twisted-Stitch Knitting

Traditional Patterns & Garments from the Styrian Enns Valley

Maria Erlbacher

first published in 1982 by the Castle at Trautenfels, Austria
original title, *Überlieferte Strickmuster, Aus Dem Steirischen Ennstal*

English edition published by Schoolhouse Press, 2009
assistance from Wolfgang Otte at *Landesmuseum Joanneum, Landschaftsmuseum, Schloss Trautenfels,*
and Georg Sieberer, our on-site translator in Austria

English translation, Char Dickte
additional help with technique, Kim Hughes & Ilse Sonner

edited and arranged by Amy Detjen and Meg Swansen
proofreaders: Amy Detjen, Kathy Erickson, Tami Schiferl, Joyce Williams

all color photographs by Meg Swansen

Schoolhouse Press

Pittsville, WI 54466

www.schoolhousepress.com

ISBN 13: 978-0-942018-30-1

Library of Congress Control Number: 2009931106

Twisted-Stitch Knitting

Table of Contents

Forward

Herein you will find a style of folk art that has been passed down through generations of knitters since the 18th century, especially in the Enns Valley and the Aus Lake Area (Ausseerland). Many residents of this area own some of the preserved knitted patterns that are a treasure trove of what is called locally, "peasant knitting". These swatches are taken out and studied when looking for suitable motifs for stockings, vests or sweaters for special occasions.

To a large extent this book was made possible by Mrs. Thekla Zeiler, a very prolific knitter, who lived in the Sölk Valley (Sölktal) and to whose memory Mrs. Erlbacher dedicated this book. Through her knitting lessons, these patterns were guarded and taught to many women and children after the second world war. Around 150 different motifs were passed on through Thekla Zeiler in this way.

When Mrs. Maria Erlbacher (who, in later years, became a member of the school board) was a young teacher in the lower valley near Schladming, she discovered one of Thekla Zeiler's pattern samplers and reproduced the motifs, creating many beautiful sweaters and stockings.

Around 1975, Mrs. Erlbacher started to teach knitting in the Gröbming and Schladming high schools - and she was sought after as a knitting teacher in the Enns Valley and far beyond. She taught classes at the Castle at Trautenfels (Schloss Trautenfels) and many women who learned to knit these intricate patterns formed a group that met on a regular basis at the castle.

Mrs. Erlbacher based her chart symbols and graphs on those used by Thelka Zeiler and Mrs. Hildegard Rieger in her 1944 book, *Deutsche Strickkunst: ein Arbeitsheft.*

The Landschaftsmuseum in the Schloss Trautenfels - who originally published the 3 booklets - is indebted to Mrs. Erlbacher for her preservation of these ancient patterns.

Dr. Volker Hänsel

Preface

The spring of 1982 saw the publication of the first of three booklets, called *Traditional Knitting Patterns from the Styrian Enns Valley* from the Landschaftsmuseum at Castle Trautenfels. The second book was published in late fall of 1982. We were delighted at the reception these patterns received not only in the Ennstal, but also in other parts of the country. The enthusiasm and delight that knitters showed for the first two volumes encouraged us to publish a third volume which contained 53 additional charts. Thirty of these are from the estate of Frau Thekla Zeiler, the rest are a compilation of patterns passed down from other families residing in the Ennstal and Ausseerland.

The descriptions of how to use these patterns will certainly be very useful to you, but they do not guarantee that your results will be perfect. A lot depends on the way you knit and the yarn and needles you use. Because of this we do ask you always to make a sample swatch to determine your exact gauge. Only this way can you be sure to figure out exactly how many stitches you need to cast on. It pays to take this extra care so that your finished garment turns out perfectly.

We are sure that you will be able to put together your own creations by using the charts and basic directions in this book, and thereby help this type of folk art to survive and flourish.

We would like to thank Frau Erna Brunner, who was always ready to help with the knitting - and to acknowledge Frau Anni Gruber for knitting some of the garments.

Maria Erlbacher

Thekla Zeiler

Mrs. Thekla Zeiler (1883 - 1960) worked from pattern samplers created by other knitters before her and taught the techniques of Twisted-Stitch knitting to a new generation. Through her, the treasured collection of patterns existing in the Enns Valley was enriched immeasurably.

Mrs. Zeiler had worked as a farmhand for her relatives and later on as day-laborer. In 1929 she began to knit on a more professional level and in 1934 worked for the Graz Museum of Folk Art. Between 1935 - 1939 she was a ski instructor in New York. In 1943 she began teaching Twisted-Stitch knitting classes in the winter months and in one of her letters, she described teaching dozens of courses in a variety of towns, among which were Ramsau, Untertal, Klaus, Birnberg, Haus, Bruggen, Groebming, Mitterberg, Kleinsoelg, Irdning und Donnersbach.

We owe her a huge debt of gratitude for the wealth of patterns and graphs she left for us. We want to take care of the legacy left by her and feel that it is our duty to share this great knowledge with other interested knitters.

Techniques

This type of knitting is fairly simple for any interested knitter. Knit stitches are worked into the back loop, producing twisted stitches which are more pronounced. A twisted knit stitch is referred to as **k1b** (knit one back). Thus, k2b means knit 1 back, knit 1 back. Unless you work 'flat', a plain knit stitch is rare; nearly all knit stitches are twisted.

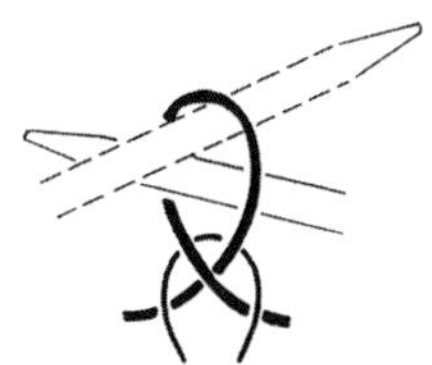
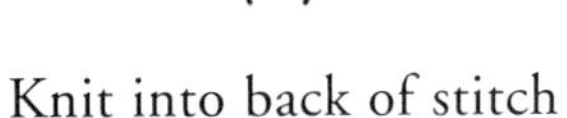

Knit into back of stitch

Twisted stitches

Motifs are created by crossing twisted knit stitches to the left or right over other stitches. These stitches can travel over purls or over other twisted knit stitches.

All graphs and pictures show the **front** of the knitting and you will note that the travelling stitches are worked **every** round/row.

Circular: When knitting in the round, the front of the work always faces you and each stitch is worked as shown on the chart. (*Editor's Note: Although instructions for the vests and sweaters in this book are for flat pieces worked back and forth, you may re-design them to be knitted in the round.)*

Flat: When working back and forth, k1b on the front of the work becomes p1b on the other side; travelling stitches and decreases must also be reversed.

Editor's Note: Occasionally, after a stitch has been travelled-over, you may find it is altered: a purl might become a knit, or a knit become a purl (example: Motif #52); remain alert.

Legend:

8 Knit 1 back (k1b, a twisted knit stitch)
– Purl
O Knit
X Knit 2 together
2 Purl 2 together
V Knit 2 together through the back

Ŧ Pick up 1 purled stitch
8̧ Pick up 1 knit stitch- twisted
• Vertical repeat of pattern
(Denoted by dots at start and end)

Abbreviations:

R	Rows
M	Stitch(es)
RM	Edgestitch(es)
gl	all knit
verk	backwards
verschr	twisted
li	purl
re	knit

RT = Right Twist (see pages 4, 5)
LT = Left Twist (see pages 4, 5)
RT2/1 = Right Twist over 2 sts over 1 stitch (see page 6)
RT2/2 = Right Twist, 2 sts over 2 sts (see page 7)
LT2/1 = Left Twist, 2 sts over 1 stitch (see page 6)
LT2/2 = Left Twist, 2 sts over 2 sts (see page 7)
Diagonal Arrow pointing either left or right, tells you the direction the travelling stitch will take.
A **Vertical Line** divides the sts of a cable (see #5, page 13)
Dotted Lines around 1 (#65), **2** (#19), **or 4** (#35) **sts** = those sts remain in their original position; adjacent stitches travel over them.
RM = slip last stitch p'wise to right-hand needle, turn. Take wool between needles to back (around the base of the slipped stitch) and knit. This gives a pretty, knot-like appearance to the edge (see page 146).

How to Read the Charts

Charts are always read from **right** to **left** (unless you work 'flat'; see p8). When learning this technique, it helps to knit in the round on a sample cap or sock, so the front of the work always faces you; no 'purling back'.

The diagonal arrow shows the direction of the travelling stitch and is positioned **below** the action. The position of the stitches on any row shows how they appear **after** being travelled.

These pages show examples of the most commonly used crossings. There are anomolies, such as the sleeve on pp182-183) where a twisted stitch crosses over 2 purls.

Example 1. Crossing k1b over p1

Many charts have you cross a twisted knit stitch over a purl to the left or right, as shown below.

8 – ↖ – 8 **LT**: k1b crosses over p **to the left**	– 8 ↗ 8 – **RT**: k1b crosses over p **to the right**

LT with cable needle: Slip twisted knit stitch onto cable needle and hold in front. P1, then k1b from cable needle.

RT with cable needle: Slip purl stitch onto cable needle and hold in back. K1b, then purl stitch from cable needle.

LT without cable needle: Slip 2 stitches to right-hand needle (twisted knit and purl). From the front, insert left-hand needle into twisted knit. Slide the right-hand needle out, letting the purl stitch fall free for a moment. Pick it up again from the back with right-hand needle, replace to left-hand needle and p1, k1b.

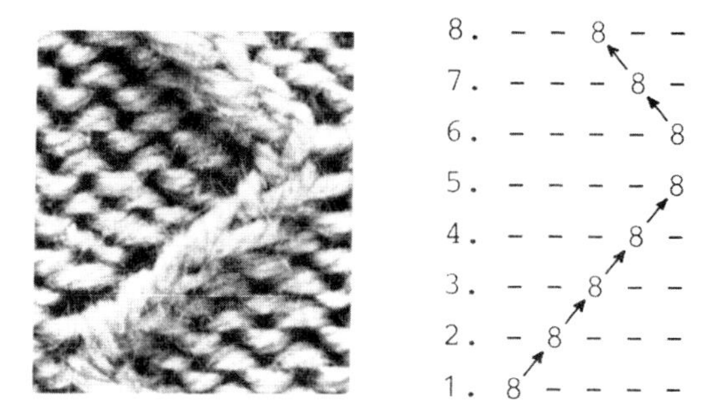

RT without cable needle: Slip 2 stitches to right-hand needle (p and twisted knit). From the back, insert left-hand needle into p stitch. Slide the right-hand needle out, letting the twisted knit stitch fall free for a moment. From the front, pick it up again with right-hand needle; replace to left-hand needle and k1b, p1.

Sample: *Single Alpine Path* motif #16, worked over 5 sts. Here is a verbal description of the above chart.

1. p4, k1b.
2. p3, rt.
3. p2, rt, p1.
4. p1, rt, p2.
5. rt, p3.
6. k1b, p4 (no arrow).
7. lt, p3.
8. p1, lt, p2.

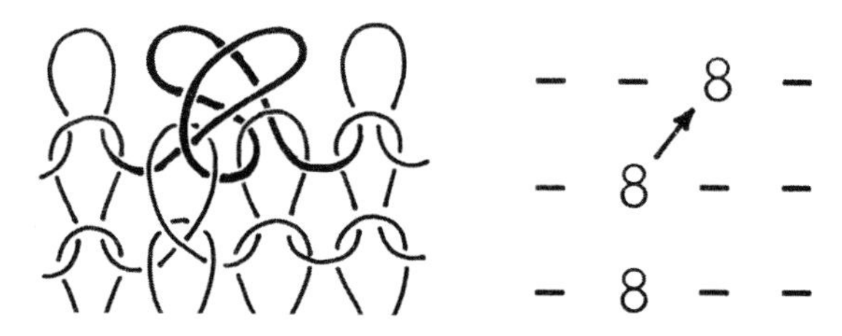

An illustration of a right twist (rt), twisted knit over purl.

Example 2. Crossing k1b over k1b

In this example, a twisted knit stitch is crossed over another twisted knit stitch to left or right as shown below.

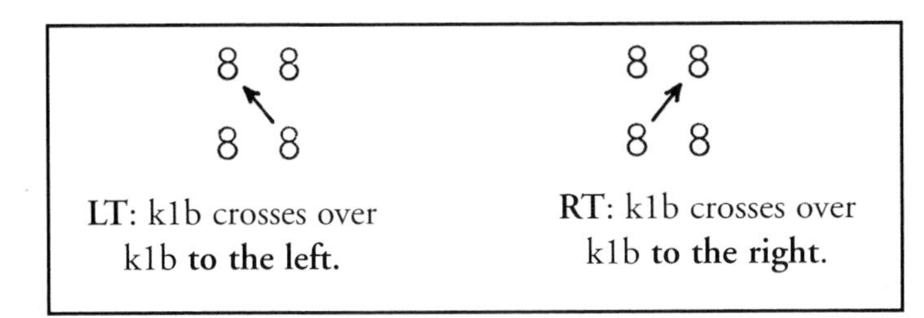

8 8
8 8
LT: k1b crosses over
k1b to the left.
8 8
8 8
RT: k1b crosses over
k1b to the right.

LT with cable needle: Slip first stitch onto cable needle and hold in front. K1b, then k1b from cable needle.

RT with cable needle: Slip first stitch onto cable needle and hold in back. K1b, then k1b from cable needle.

LT without cable needle: Slip 2 stitches to right-hand needle (both k1b). From the front, insert left-hand needle into first slipped st. Slide the right-hand needle out, letting the other stitch fall free for a moment. Pick it up again from the back with right-hand needle, replace to left-hand needle and k1b, k1b.

RT without cable needle: Slip 2 stitches to right-hand needle (both k1b). From the back, insert left-hand needle into first slipped stitch. Slide the right-hand needle out, letting second st fall free for a moment. From the front, pick it up again with right-hand needle; replace to left-hand needle and k1b, k1b.

```
8.  8 - - 8 8 - - 8
7.  8 - - 8 8 - - 8
6.  - 8 8 - - 8 8 -
5.  - 8 8 - - 8 8-
4.  8 - - 8 8 - - 8
3.  8 - - 8 8 - - 8
2.  - 8 8 - - 8 8 -
1.  - 8 8 - - 8 8 -
```

Sample: *Burning Love* motif #42, worked over 8 sts. Here is a verbal description of the above chart.

1. p1, k2b, p2, k2b, p1.
2. p1, rt, p2, rt, p1.
3. rt, lt, rt, lt.
4. k1b, p2, lt, p2, k1b.
5. lt, rt, lt, rt.
6. p1, rt, p2, rt, p1.
7. rt, lt, rt, lt.
8. k1b, p2, lt, p2, k1b.

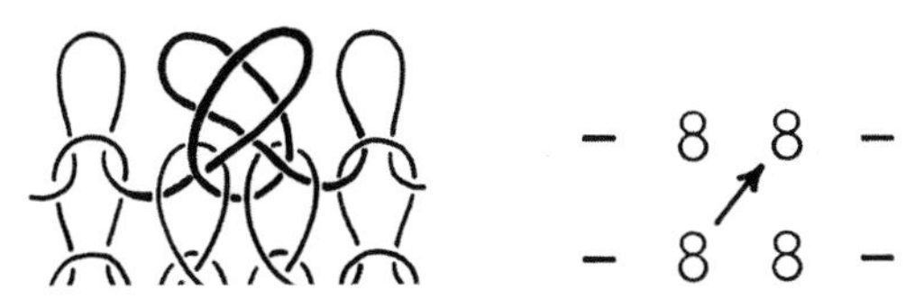

An illustration of a right twist (rt), k1b over k1b.

Example 3. Crossing k2b over p

In this example, cross 2 twisted knit stitches over a purl stitch to left or right as shown below.

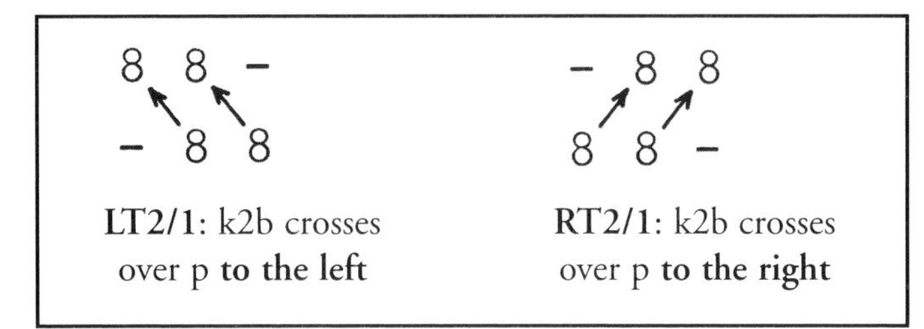

LT2/1: k2b crosses over p **to the left**

RT2/1: k2b crosses over p **to the right**

LT2/1 with cable needle: Slip 2 twisted knit sts onto cable needle and hold in front. P1, then k2b from cable needle.

RT2/1 with cable needle: Slip purl stitch onto cable needle and hold in back. K2b, then purl the stitch from cable needle.

LT2/1 without cable needle: Slip 3 stitches to right-hand needle (2 twisted k stitches and p). From the front, insert left-hand needle into 2 twisted k stitches. Slide the right-hand needle out, letting the p stitch fall free for a moment. From the back, pick it up again with right-hand needle, replace to left-hand needle and p1, k2b.

RT2/1 without cable needle: Slip 3 stitches to right-hand needle (p and 2 twisted k stitches). From the back, insert left-hand needle into p stitch. Slide the right-hand needle out, letting the 2 twisted knit stitches fall free for a moment. From the front, pick them up again with right-hand needle; replace to left-hand needle and k2b, p1.

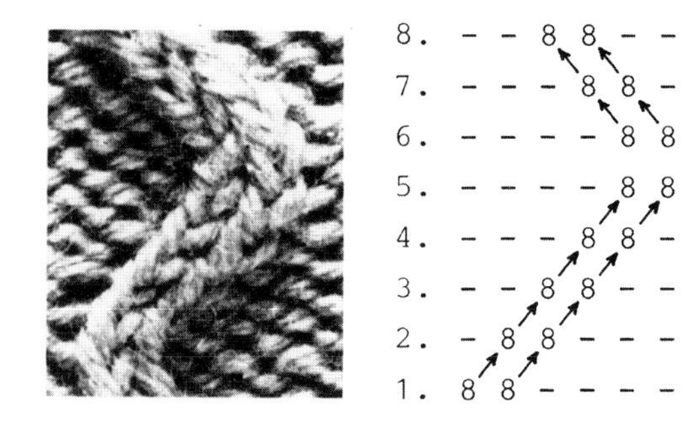

Sample: *Alpine Path* motif #8, worked over 6 sts. Here is a verbal description of the above chart.

1. p4, k2b.
2. p3, rt2/1.
3. p2, rt2/1, p1.
4. p1, rt2/1, p2.
5. rt2/1, p3.
6. k2b, p4.
7. lt2/1, p3.
8. p1, lt2/1, p2.

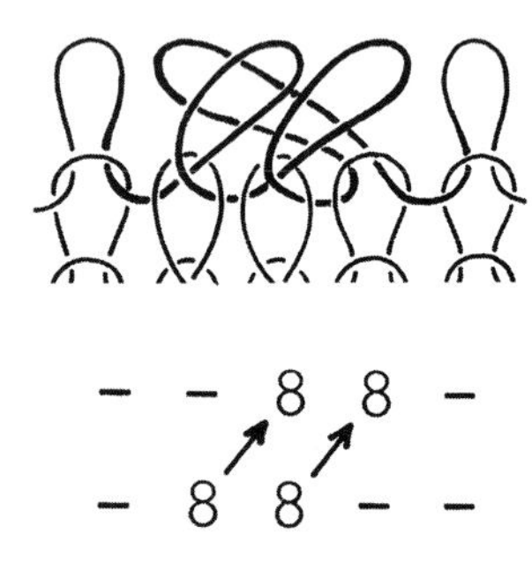

An illustration of k2b over p (rt2/1).

Example 4. Crossing k2b over k2b

Working a 4-stitch cable: This is similar to Example 2, but you will cable 2 twisted stitches over 2 twisted stitches. The vertical bar shows the division of sts to be cabled; the arrow shows the direction of the cable.

```
 <-----------------         ----------------->
  8  8 | 8  8                8  8 | 8  8
 ------+-------             ------+-------
  8  8   8  8                8  8   8  8
```

k2b crosses over k2b **to the left**	k2b crosses over k2b **to the right**

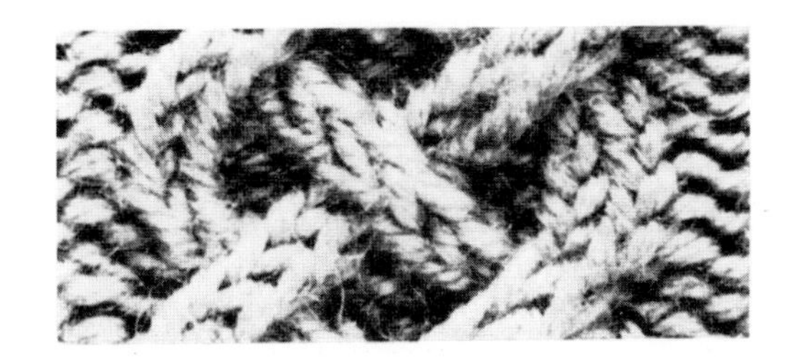

```
6.  8 8 - - 8 8 - - 8 8 - - 8 8
5.  8 8 - - - 8 8|8 8 - - - 8 8
4.  8 8 - - - 8 8 8 8 - - - 8 8
3.  8 8 - - 8 8 - - 8 8 - - 8 8
2.  - 8 8|8 8 - - - - 8 8|8 8 -
1.  - 8 8 8 8 - - - - 8 8 8 8 -
```

LT2/2 with cable needle: Slip 2 twisted stitches onto cable needle and hold in front. K2b, then k2b from cable needle.

RT2/2 with cable needle: Slip 2 twisted stitches onto cable needle and hold in back. K2b, then k2b from cable needle.

LT2/2 without cable needle: Slip 4 twisted k stitches to right-hand needle. From the front, insert left-hand needle into 2 twisted k stitches on the right. Slide right-hand needle out, letting the other k2b fall free for a moment. From the back, pick them up again with right-hand needle, replace to left-hand needle and k2b, k2b.

RT2/2 without cable needle: Slip 4 twisted k stitches to right-hand needle. From the back, insert left-hand needle into 2 twisted k stitches on the right. Slide right-hand needle out, letting the other 2 twisted sts fall free for a moment. From the front, pick them up again with right-hand needle; replace to left-hand needle and k2b, k2b.

Sample: *Quadruple Braid* motif #56, worked over 14 sts. Here is a verbal description of the above chart.

1. p1, k4b, p4, k4b, p1.
2. p1, rt2/2, p4, rt2/2, p1.
3. rt2/1, lt2/1, rt2/1, lt2/1 (see Example 3).
4. k2b, p2, lt2/1, rt2/1, p2, k2b.
5. k2b, p3, lt2/2, p3, k2b.
6. k2b, p2, rt2/1, lt2/1, p2, k2b.

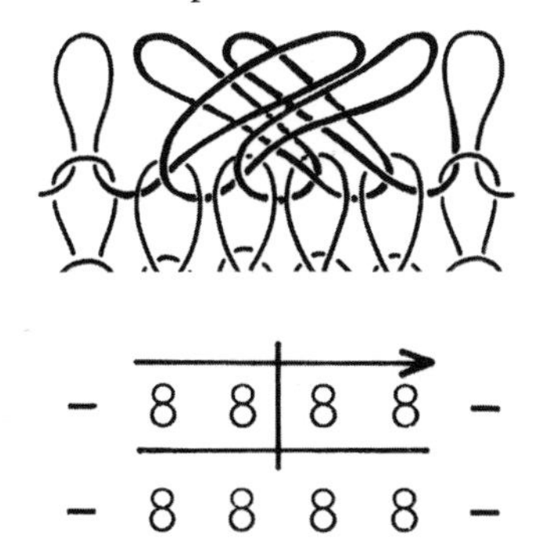

An illustration of k2b over k2b (rt2/2);

```
RM - 8 - - 8 8 - - 8 - - - 8 8 - - 8 8 - - - 8 - 8 - - 8 - 8 - RM
RM - 8 - - 8 8 - - 8 - - 8 - - 8 8 - - 8 - - - 8 8 - - 8 8 - - RM
RM - 8 - - 8 8 - - 8 - - 8 - - 8 8 - - 8 - - - 8 8 - - 8 8 - - RM
RM - - 8 - 8 8 - 8 - - - - 8 8 - - 8 8 - - - 8 - - 8 8 - - 8 - RM
RM - - 8 8 8 8 8 8 - - - - 8 8 - - 8 8 - - - 8 - - 8 8 - - 8 - RM
RM - 8 - - 8 8 - - 8 - - 8 - - 8 8 - - 8 - - - 8 8 - - 8 8 - - RM
RM - 8 - - 8 8 - - 8 - - 8 - - 8 8 - - 8 - - - 8 8 - - 8 8 - - RM
RM - 8 - - 8 8 - - 8 - - - 8 8 - - 8 8 - - - 8 - - 8 8 - - 8 - RM
RM - 8 - - 8 8 - - 8 - - - 8 8 - - 8 8 - - - 8 - - 8 8 - - 8 - RM
RM - - 8 - 8 8 - 8 - - - 8 - - 8 8 - - 8 - - - 8 8 - - 8 8 - - RM
RM - - 8 8 8 8 8 8 - - - 8 - - 8 8 - - 8 - - - 8 8 - - 8 8 - - RM
RM - 8 - - 8 8 - - 8 - - - 8 8 - - 8 8 - - - 8 - 8 - - 8 - 8 - RM
RM - 8 - - 8 8 - - 8 - - - 8 8 - - 8 8 - - - 8 - 8 - - 8 - 8 - RM
RM - 8 - - 8 8 - - 8 - - 8 - - 8 8 - - 8 - - 8 - 8 - - 8 - 8 - RM
RM - 8 - - 8 8 - - 8 - - 8 - - 8 8 - - 8 - - 8 - 8 - - 8 - 8 - RM
RM - - 8 - 8 8 - 8 - - - - 8 8 - - 8 8 - - - - 8 8 - - 8 8 - - RM
RM - - 8 8 8 8 8 8 - - - - 8 8 - - 8 8 - - - - 8 8 - - 8 8 - - RM
RM - 8 - - 8 8 - - 8 - - 8 - - 8 8 - - 8 - - 8 - - 8 8 - - 8 - RM
RM - 8 - - 8 8 - - 8 - - 8 - - 8 8 - - 8 - - 8 - - 8 8 - - 8 - RM
RM - 8 - - 8 8 - - 8 - - - 8 8 - - 8 8 - - - - 8 8 - - 8 8 - - RM
RM - 8 - - 8 8 - - 8 - - - 8 8 - - 8 8 - - - - 8 8 - - 8 8 - - RM
RM - - 8 - 8 8 - 8 - - - 8 - - 8 8 - - 8 - - 8 - - 8 8 - - 8 - RM
RM - - 8 8 8 8 8 8 - - - 8 - - 8 8 - - 8 - - 8 - - 8 8 - - 8 - RM
RM - 8 - - 8 8 - - 8 - - - 8 8 - - 8 8 - - - - 8 8 - - 8 8 - - RM
RM - 8 - - 8 8 - - 8 - - - 8 8 - - 8 8 - - - - 8 8 - - 8 8 - - RM
```

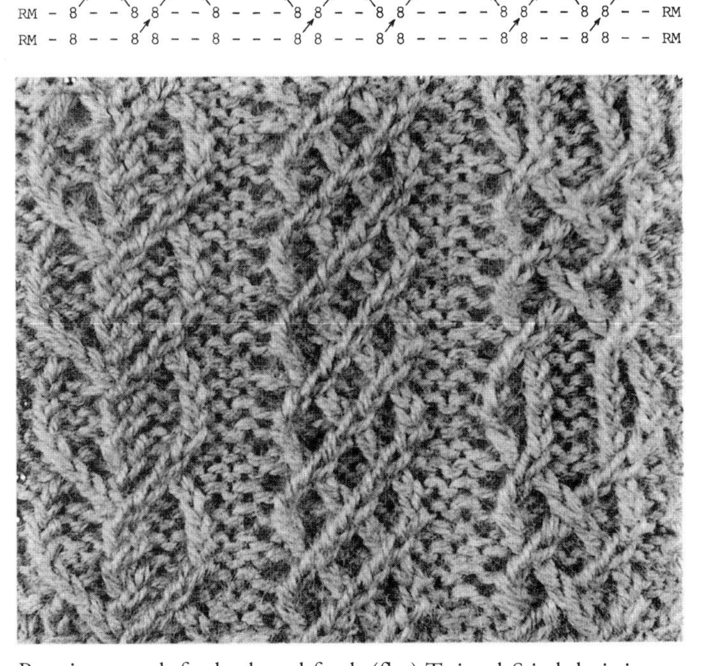

Practice swatch for back and forth (flat) Twisted-Stitch knitting.

Twisted-Stitch worked back and forth.

When knitting a flat piece, begin the chart on the right side of the bottom row. This is the front of your piece. On the return (back) row the chart is read from left to the right, using row 2. Continue in this manner until the piece is completed.

The twisted knit stitches on the front are twisted purls on the back, and the purl stitches on the front are plain knit on the back.

The crossed stitches must be crossed, even when working the return rows on the inside of the knitting. Stitches that were purled on the outside, are knitted plain (not twisted) on the inside. But twisted knit stitches on the outside must be twisted purl stitches on the inside. There are two ways to do this.

a) Pick up the stitch with the right needle, twist it and return it to the left needle. Purl it as always.

b) Leave stitch on the left needle, but purl it through the back loop (wool forward, insert tip of right needle - from left-to-right- through back of stitch; purl).

This back and forth variation - with or without a cable needle - needs to be practiced before attempting to do a large piece.

Return row:

a) This is how to knit it	o + + o o + + o
b) This is what you see on the front side	- 8 8 - - 8 8 –

o = knit
+ = twisted purl

We began to import Maria Erlbacher's books in the 1980s, and included a translation sheet with each set. We leaned upon technical notes kindly supplied by Kim Hughes and Ilse Sonner, and I adopted their recommended method of re-positioning travelling stitches on the left-hand needle before working them.

Over the years, I have devised a few methods which you might find useful.

When re-positioning stitches in anticipation of travelling:

- if the last stitch replaced to the left-hand needle is a purl, duck under the working wool before picking it up to place on the left needle. That way the working wool is in front, ready to purl.

- if the last stitch replaced to the left-hand needle is a knit, do not replace it; leave it on the right-hand needle, insert the tip of the left needle into the front and knit (twisted).

When blocking a swatch you have great leeway in altering the width. Stretched horizontally, it can result in extra inches of width, but will flatten the motifs. Just gently patting the wet swatch will result in a more pronounced topography, but narrower width. Experiment to achieve the results you like, then take a gauge-reading. Keep the blocked swatch in your knitting bag to remind you of the finished appearance.

This charting system is quite unique, and if it befuddles you at first, study the photographs to help find your way - they reveal so much. With practice, the charts will become clearer.

Schoolhouse Press is pleased to reprint this series (shown on the cover), which we have amalgamated into a single volume. Georg Sieberer was a great help as our translator when my sister, Lloie, and I met the author and Wolfgang Otte, at Schloss Trautenfels, in 2006.

Char Dickte patiently and skillfully translated all three books into English for us.

Meg Swansen, 2009

cm	**inches**
1.00	0.39
10.00	3.94
20.00	7.87
30.00	11.81
40.00	15.75
50.00	19.69
60.00	23.62
70.00	27.56
80.00	31.50
90.00	35.43
100.00	39.37

mm	**inches**
12	1/2
13	1/2
19	3/4
25	1
31	1 1/4
32	1 1/4
38	1/2
51	2

grams	**ounces**
100	3.5
125	4.4
150	5.3
175	6.2
200	7.1
250	8.8
300	10.6
500	17.6
750	26.5
1000	35.3

needle sizes

(mm)	(US)
2.0	0
2.25	1
2.75	2
3.0	-
3.25	3
3.5	4
3.75	5
4.0	6
4.5	7
5.0	8
5.5	9
6.0	10
6.5	10-1/2

Most of the German/US sweater-size conversion charts we found on the Internet varied slightly from each other.

We recommend you rely on a good (blocked) swatch, followed by calculating your Gauge and Measurement. Adding or subtracting small motifs can get you to the stitch-count you need.

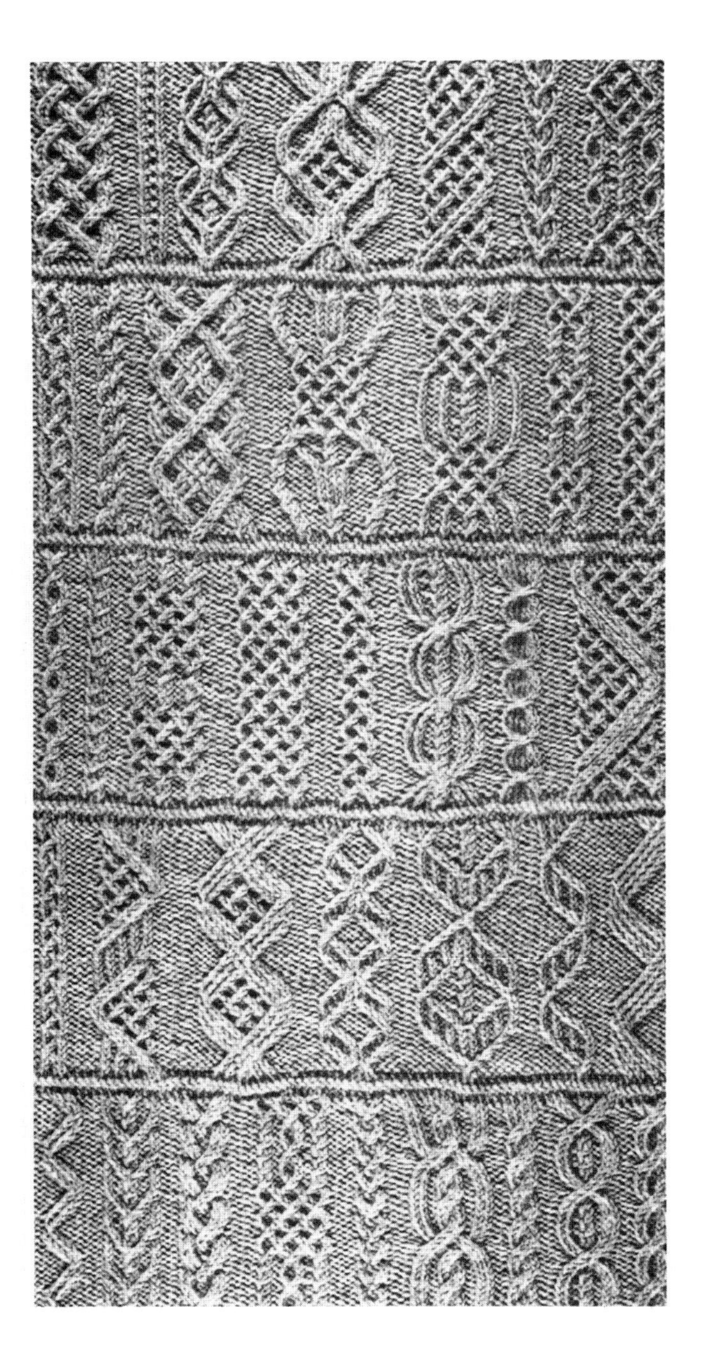

Originally, samplers such as these were knitted by Thekla Zeiler and others, as notebooks for their collections of motifs. This was a way to preserve patterns they had designed themselves as well as keep track of motifs learned from other knitters.

The author knitted these samplers by working them in the round with 12 knit stitches at the beginning. When done, they were cut open down the center of the 12 stitches and 6-stitch facings were tacked down along each selvedge.

It is best to work Twisted Stitch motifs firmly and use a light-colored, tightly spun and plied, medium-weight wool. This type of wool shows the patterns to their best advantage and a pale color makes it easier to 'read' the designs as you knit.

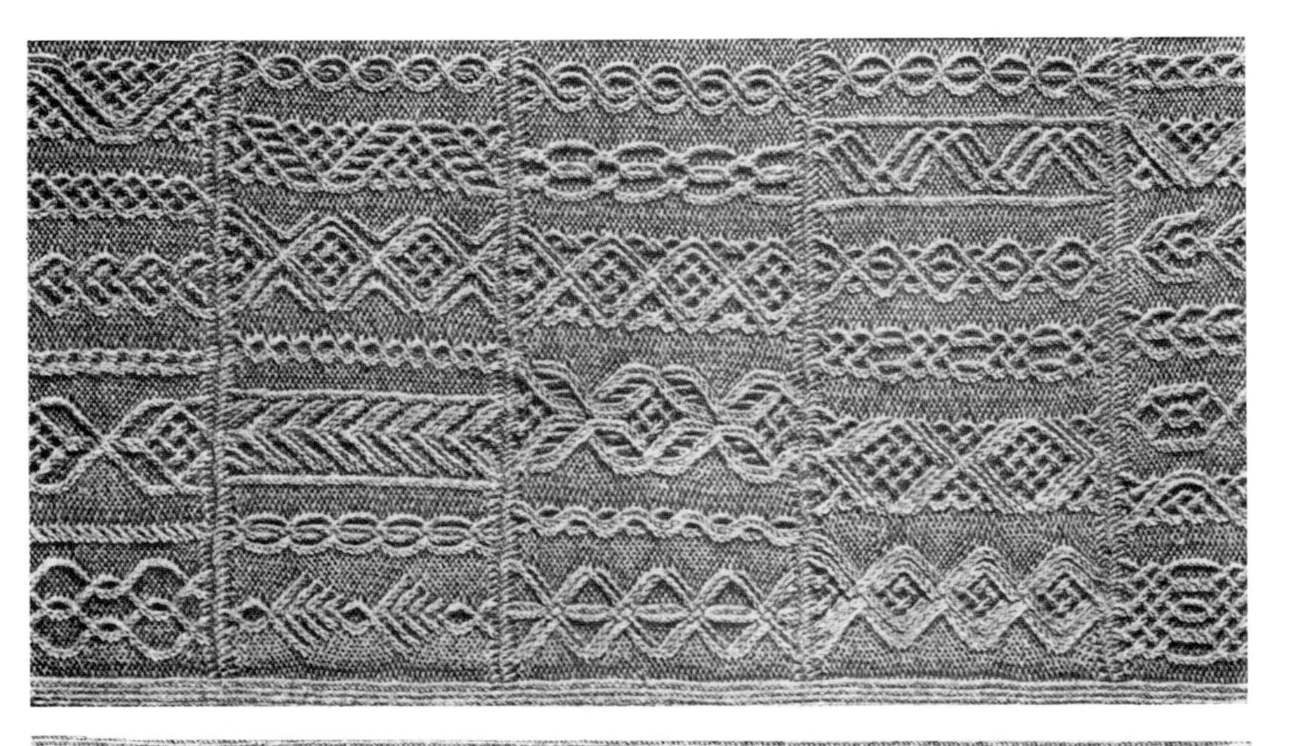

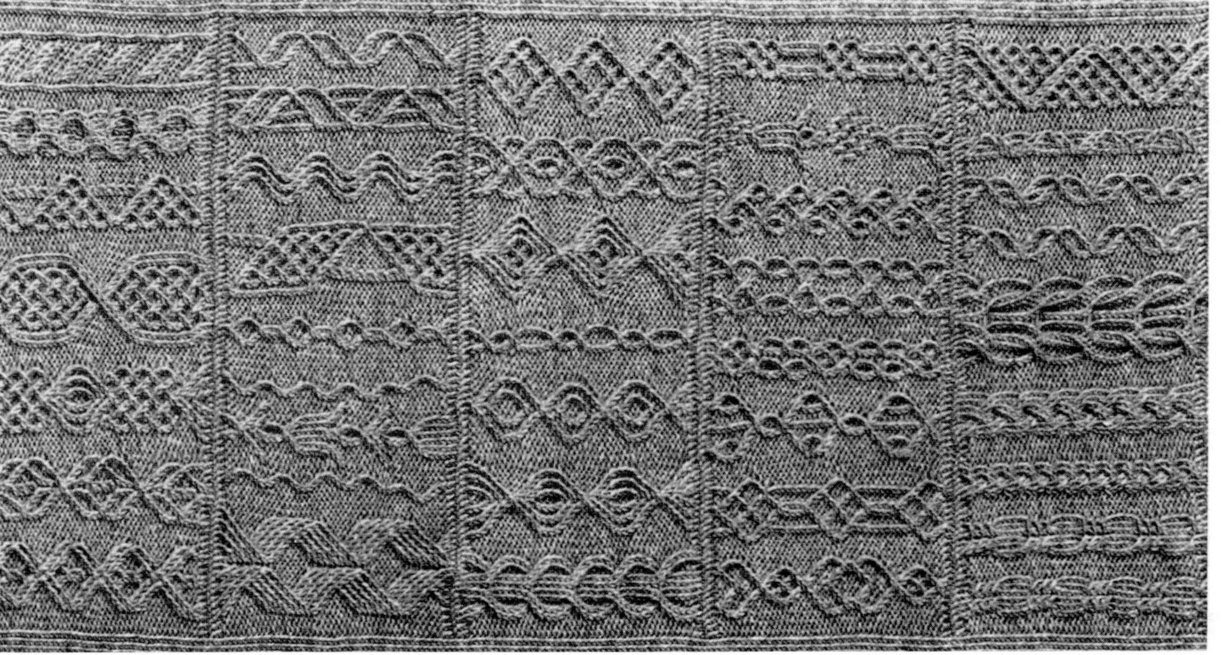

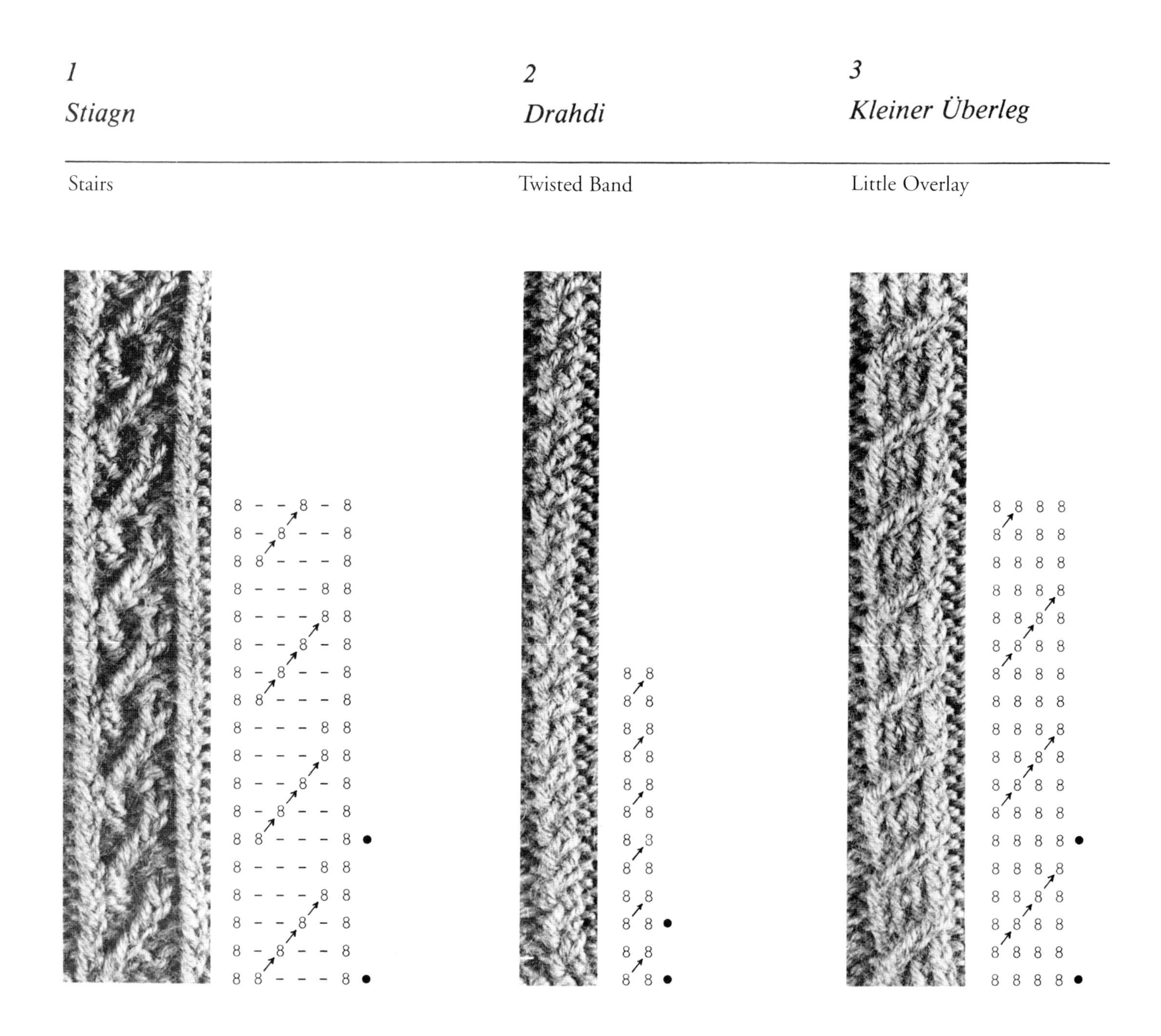

1

Stiagn

Stairs

2

Drahdi

Twisted Band

3

Kleiner Überleg

Little Overlay

4
Großer Überleg

Big Overlay

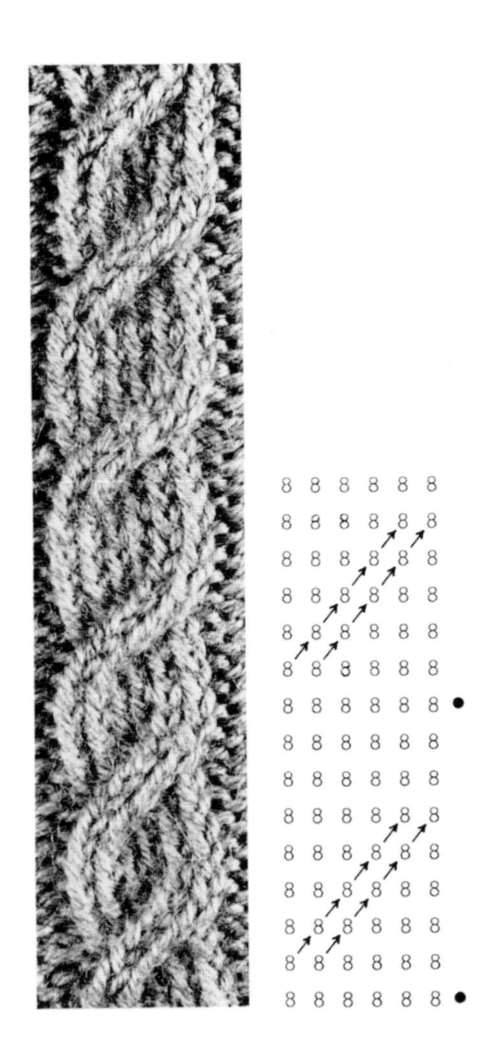

```
8 8 8 8 8 8
8 8 8 8 8 8
8 8 8 8 8 8
8 8 8 8 8 8
8 8 8 8 8 8
8 8 8 8 8 8
8 8 8 8 8 8 •
8 8 8 8 8 8
8 8 8 8 8 8
8 8 8 8 8 8
8 8 8 8 8 8
8 8 8 8 8 8
8 8 8 8 8 8
8 8 8 8 8 8
8 8 8 8 8 8 •
```

5
Großer Doppelüberleg

Big Double Overlay

```
8 8 8 8 8 8 8 8 8 8 8 8
8 8 8 8 8 8 8 8 8 8 8 8
8 8 8 8 8 8 8 8 8 8 8 8
8 8 8 8 8 8 8 8 8 8 8 8
8 8 8 8 8 8 8 8 8 8 8 8
8 8 8 8 8 8 8 8 8 8 8 8
8 8 8 8 8 8 8 8 8 8 8 8
8 8 8 8 8 8 8 8 8 8 8 8
8 8 8 8 8 8 8 8 8 8 8 8
8 8 8 8 8 8 8 8 8 8 8 8
8 8 8 8 8 8 8 8 8 8 8 8
8 8 8 8 8 8 8 8 8 8 8 8 •
8 8 8 8 8 8 8 8 8 8 8 8
8 8 8 8 8 8 8 8 8 8 8 8
8 8 8 8 8 8 8 8 8 8 8 8
8 8 8 8 8 8 8 8 8 8 8 8
8 8 8 8 8 8 8 8 8 8 8 8
8 8 8 8 8 8 8 8 8 8 8 8 •
```

6
Verzwicktes Dreieck

Distorted Triangle

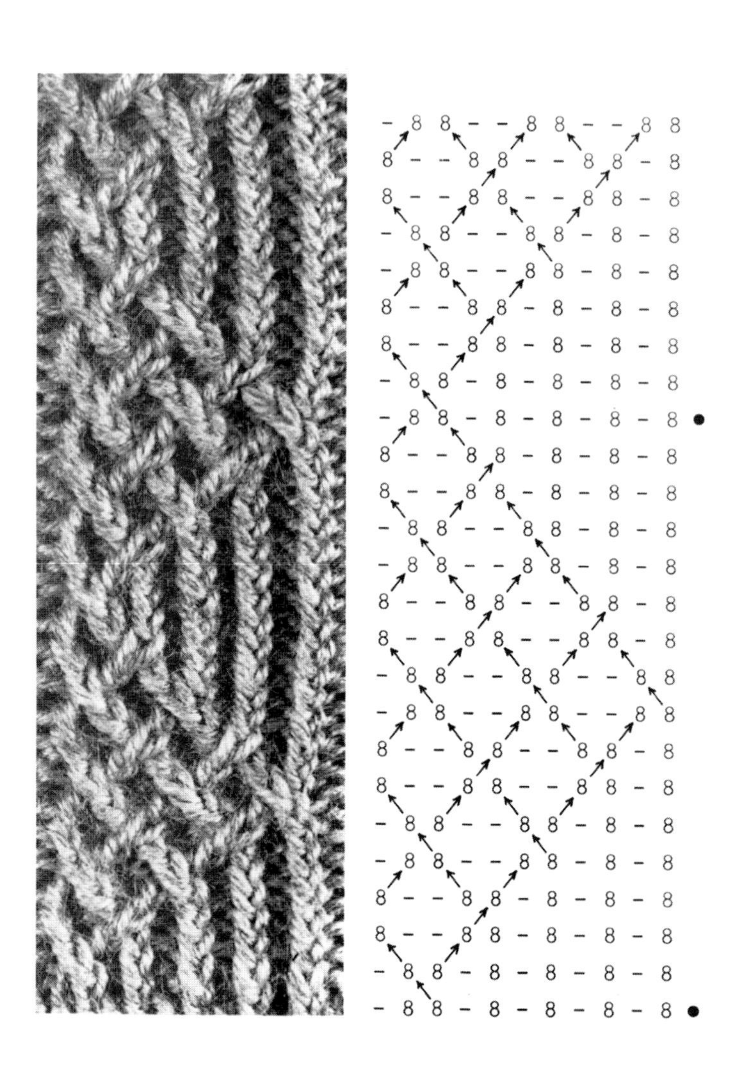

7
Nullenzwickel

Zero Insert, #1

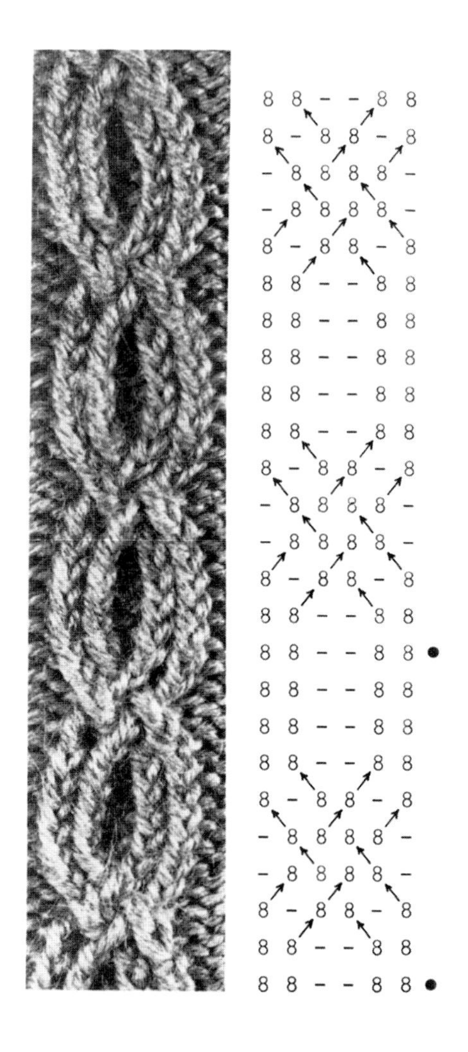

8 *Almweg*

Alpine Path

"Alm" is an Alpine mountain meadow where cows graze all summer long. They are watched over by a "Sennerin", usually a young woman, who spends the summer with them.

```
- - 8 8 - -
- 8 8 - - -
8 8 - - - -
8 8 - - - -
- 8 8 - - -
- - 8 8 - -
- - - 8 8 -
- - - - 8 8 •
- - - - 8 8
- - - 8 8 -
- - 8 8 - -
- 8 8 - - -
8 8 - - - -
8 8 - - - -
- 8 8 - - -
- - 8 8 - -
- - - 8 8 -
- - - - 8 8 •
```

9 *Tulipan*

Tulips

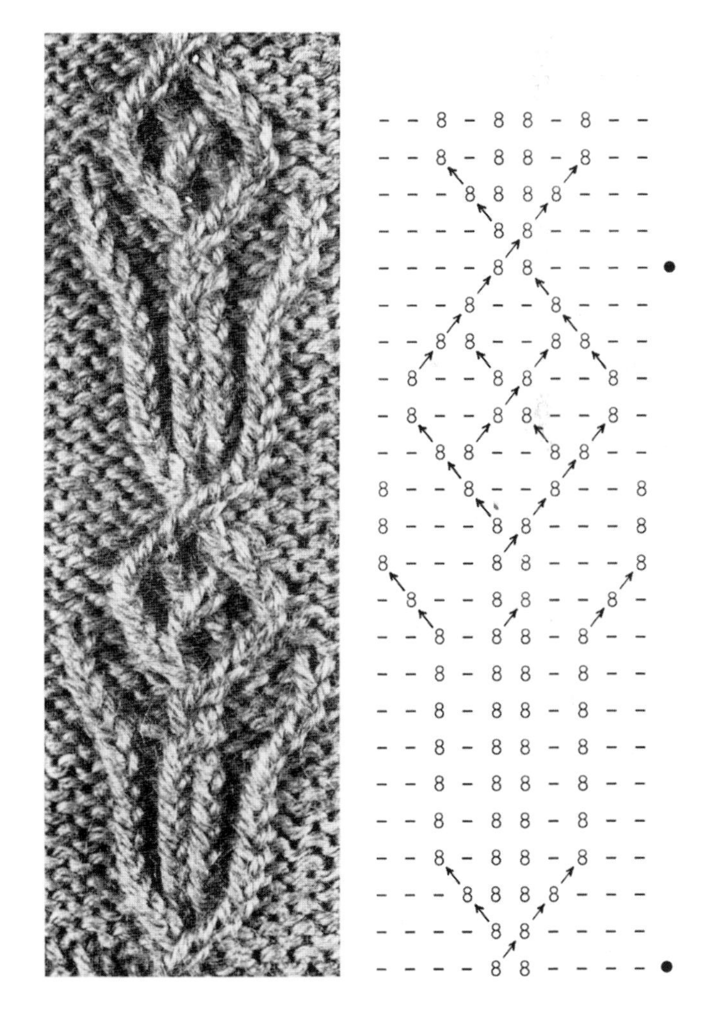

10
Almwegketterl

Alpine Path Necklace or Chain

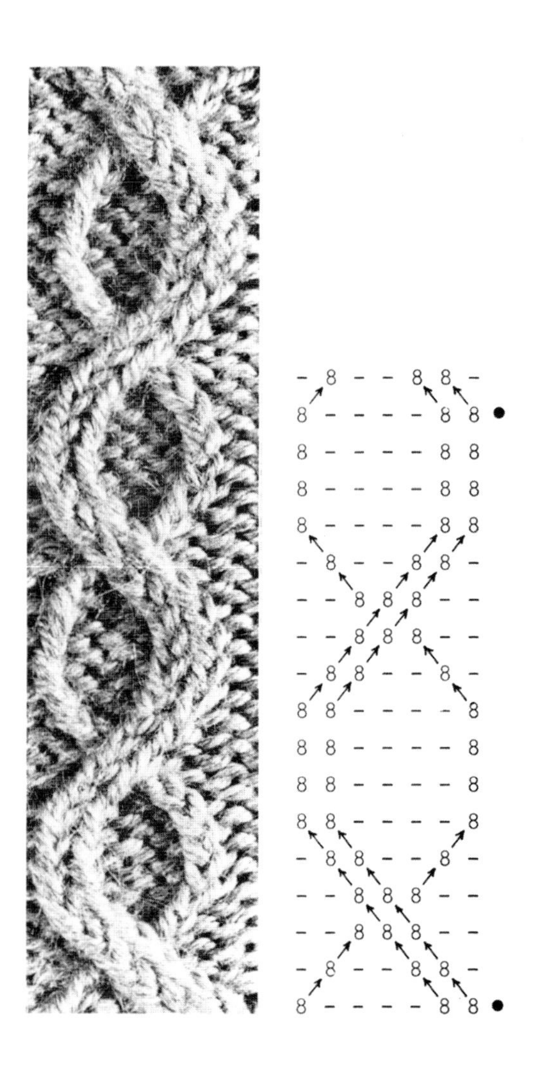

11
Doppelzentimeterband

Double Measuring Tape

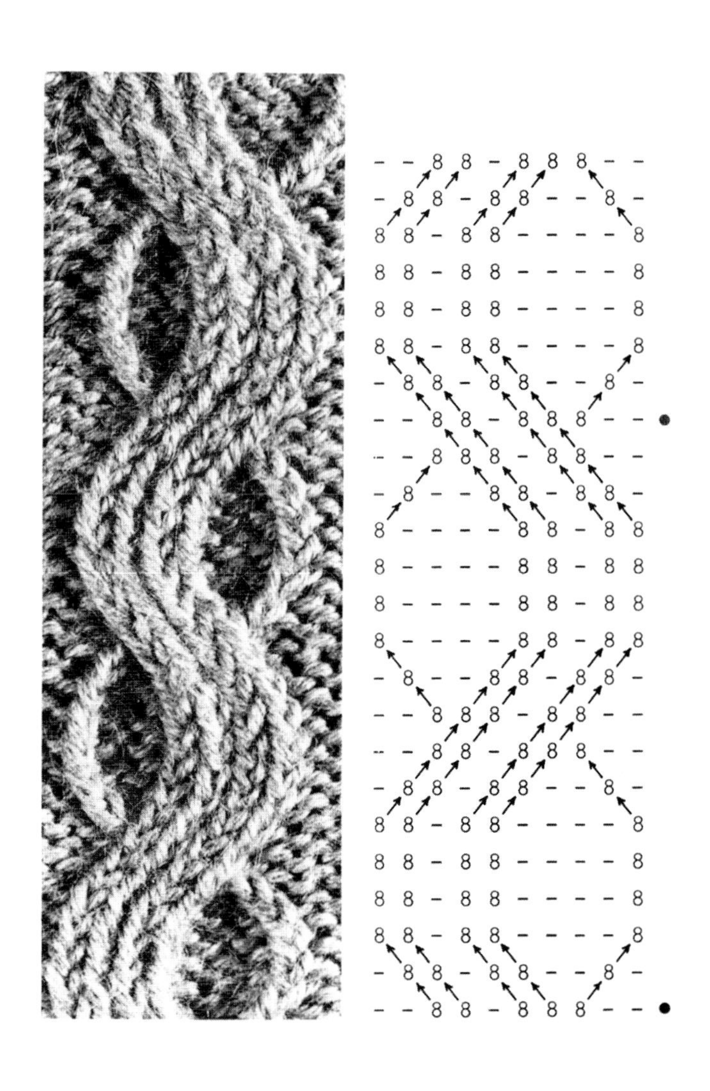

12
Kleines Fenster

Little Window

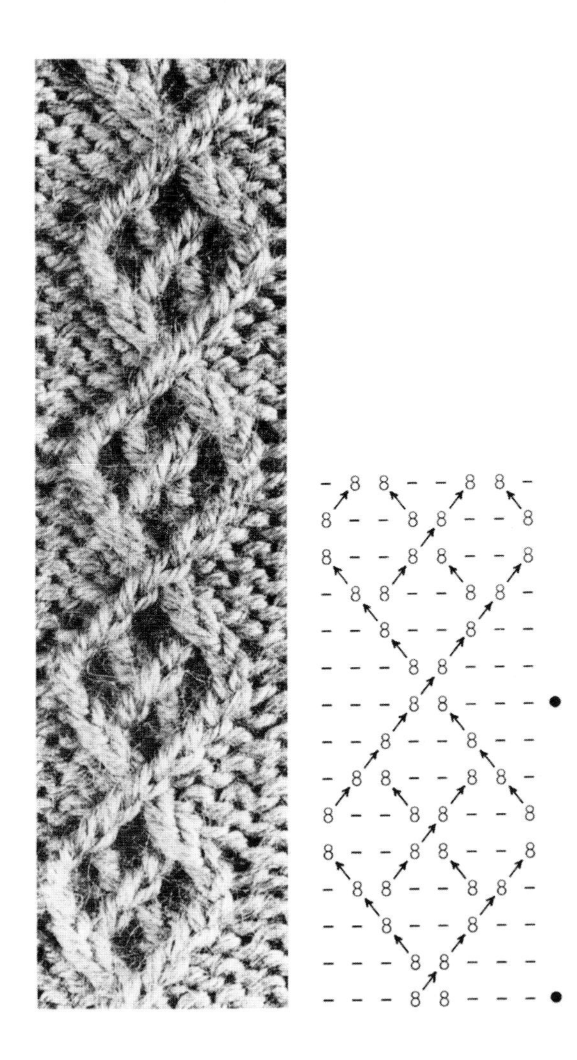

13
Stoaniger Almweg

Rocky Alpine Path

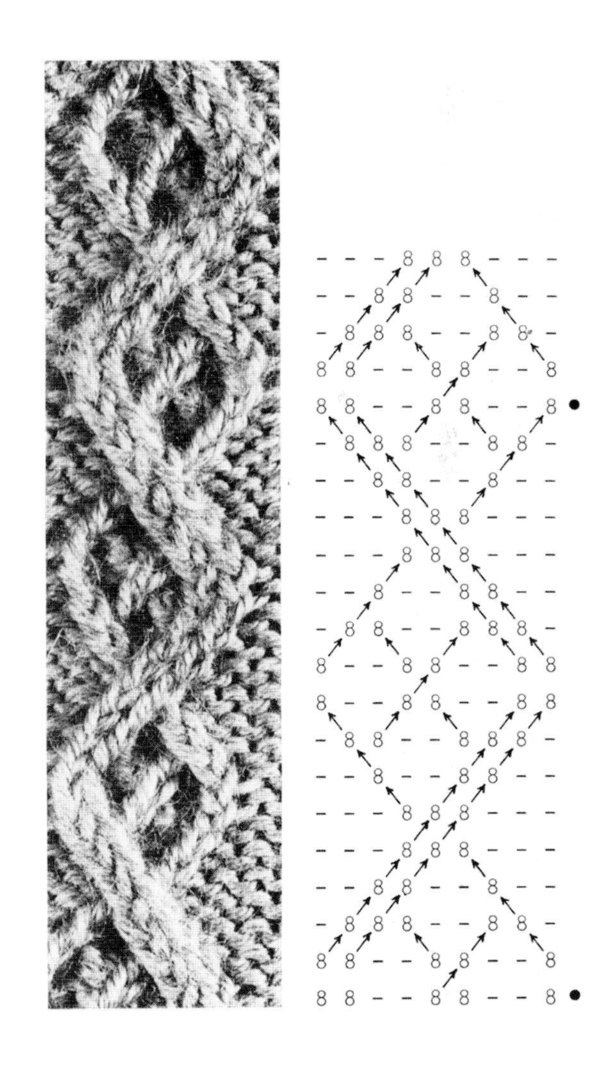

14
Doppeltes Almwegerl

Double Alpine Path

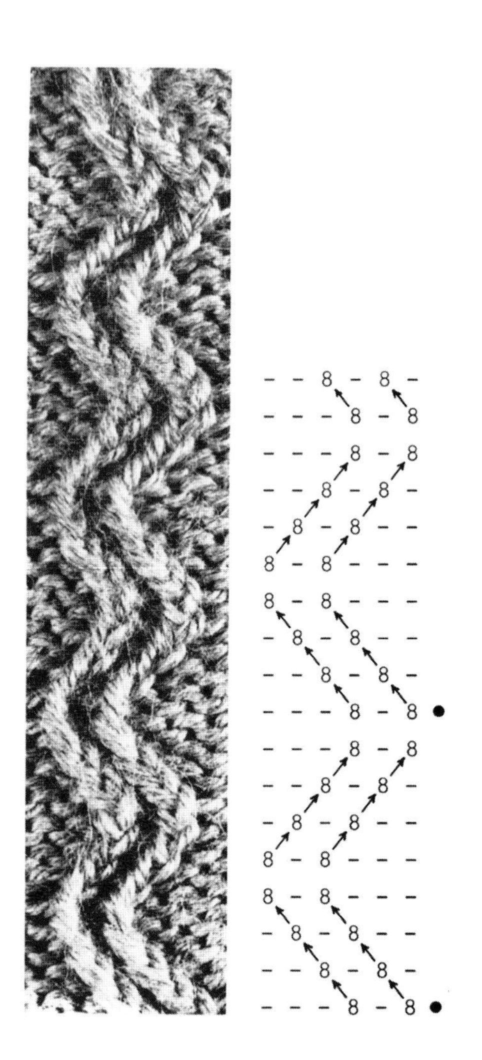

```
- - 8 - 8 -
- - - 8 - 8
- - - 8 - 8
- - 8 - 8 -
- 8 - 8 - -
8 - 8 - - -
8 - 8 - - -
- 8 - 8 - -
- - 8 - 8 -
- - - 8 - 8 ●
- - - 8 - 8
- - 8 - 8 -
- 8 - 8 - -
8 - 8 - - -
8 - 8 - - -
- 8 - 8 - -
- - 8 - 8 -
- - - 8 - 8 ●
```

15
Fischgräten

Fish Bones, #1

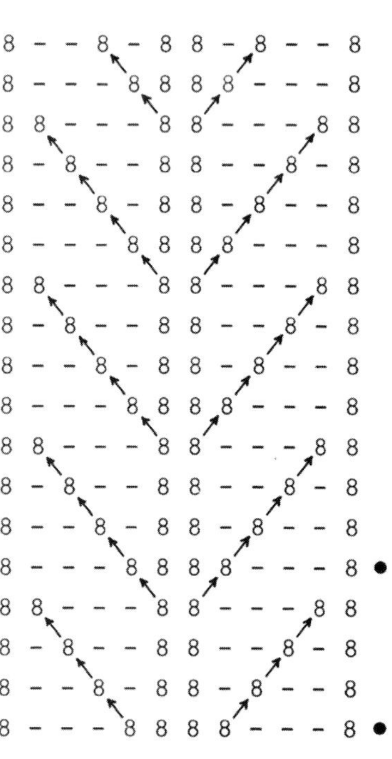

16

Einfaches Almwegerl

Single Alpine Path

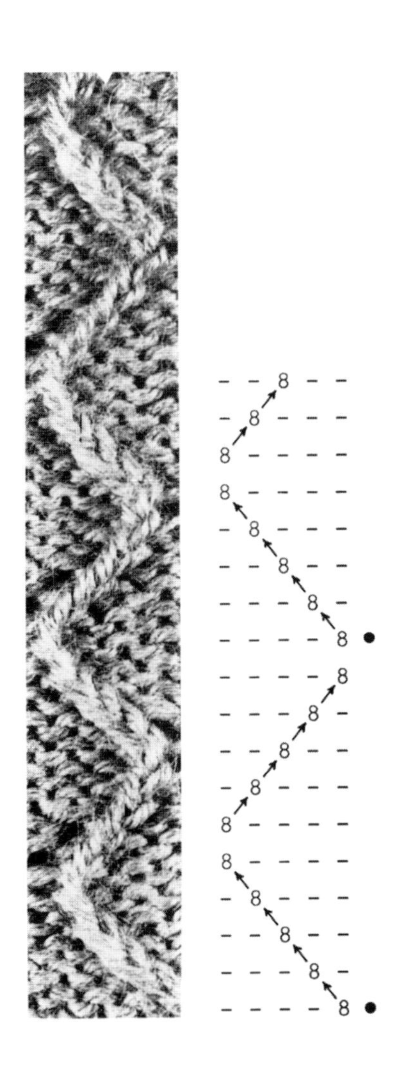

17

Viereckkette mit Fenster

Square Chain with Windows

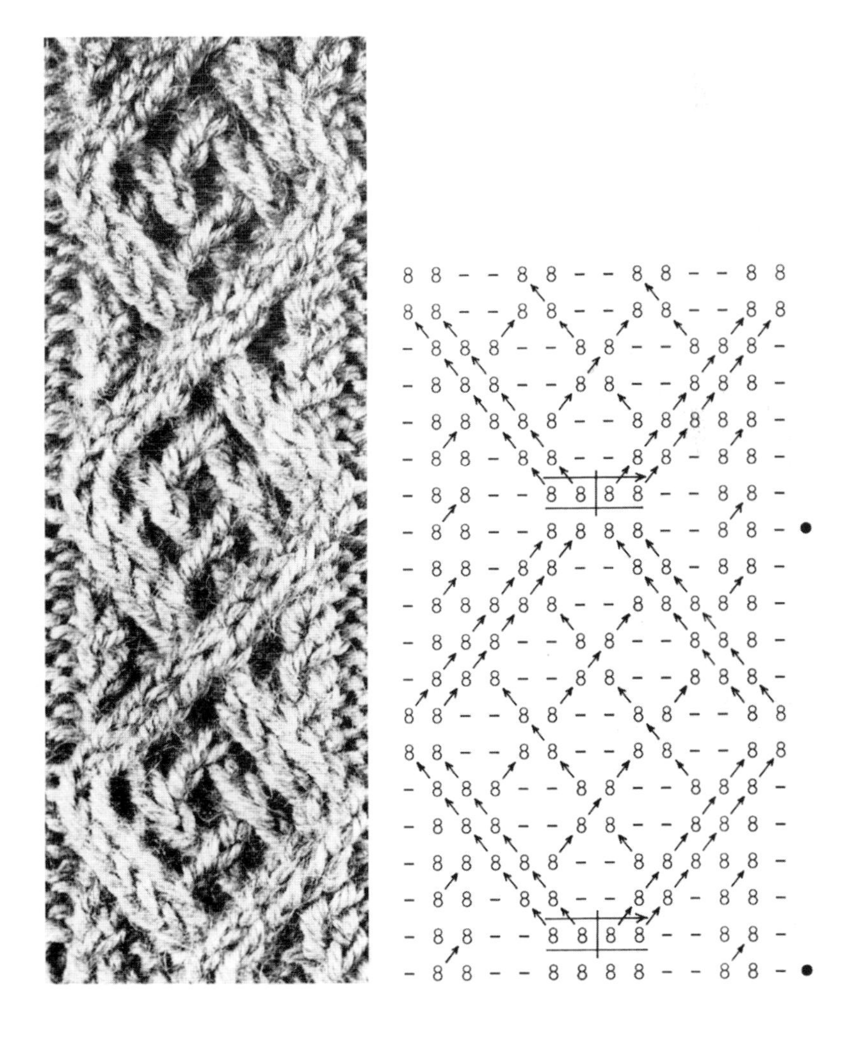

18
Doppelnull

Double Zero

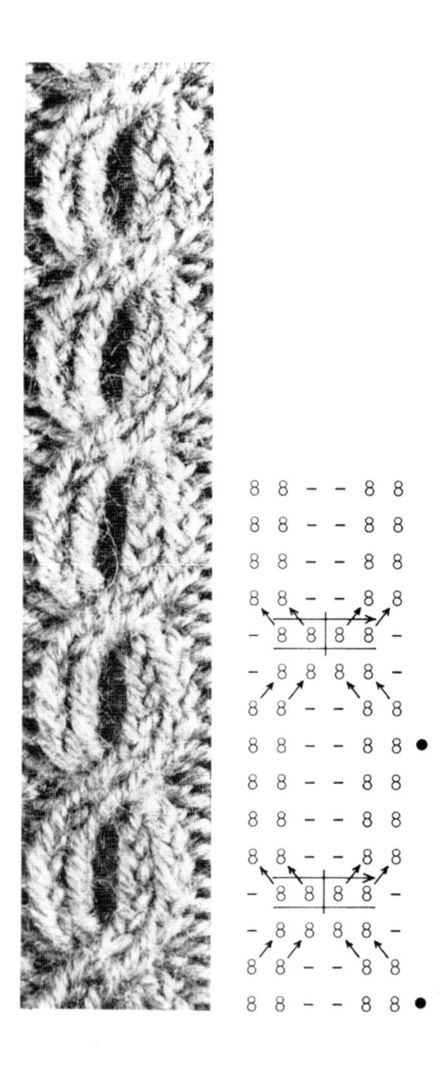

19
Doppelnullen mit Drahdi

Double Zero with Twisted Band

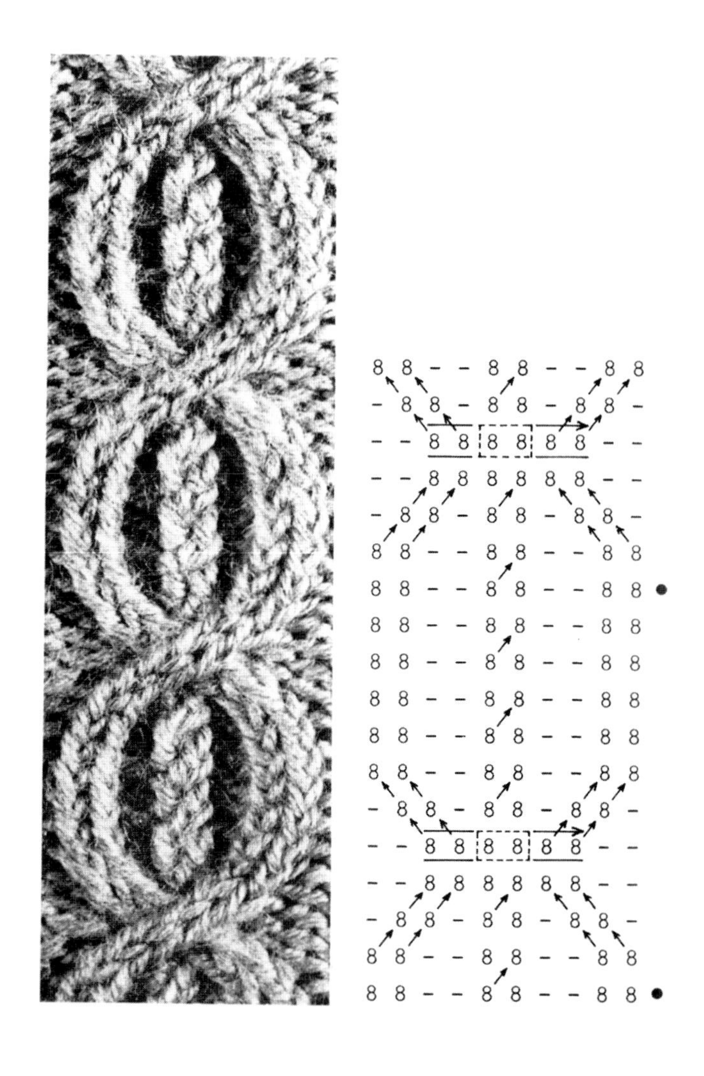

20
Kleiner Zopf

Little Braid

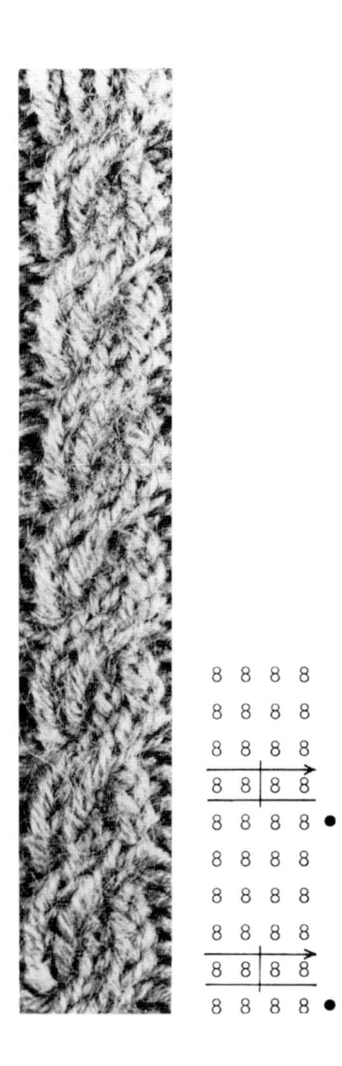

21
Nullenzopf

Zeros with Braid

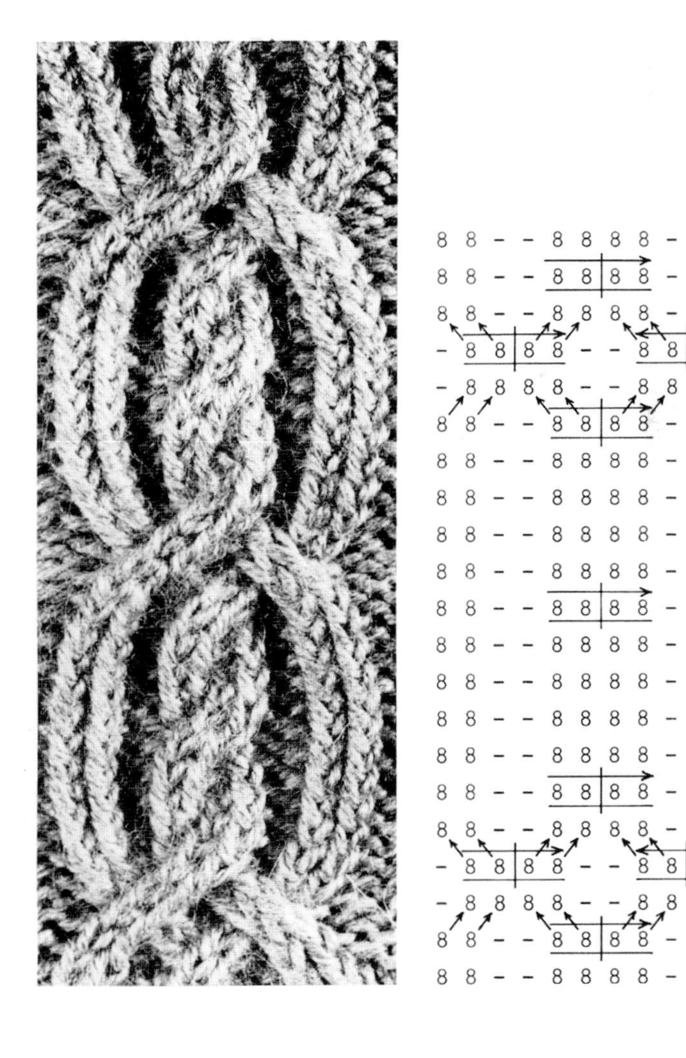

22
Offenes einfaches Ketterl

Open Single Chain

```
- 8 8 -
8 8 8 8
8 - - 8
8 - - 8
- 8 8 -
8 8 8 8
8 - - 8
8 - - 8
- 8 8 -
8 8 8 8
8 - - 8
8 - - 8
- 8 8 -
8 8 8 8 •
8 - - 8
8 - - 8
- 8 8 -
8 8 8 8 •
```

23
Stücklkette

Chain in Pieces

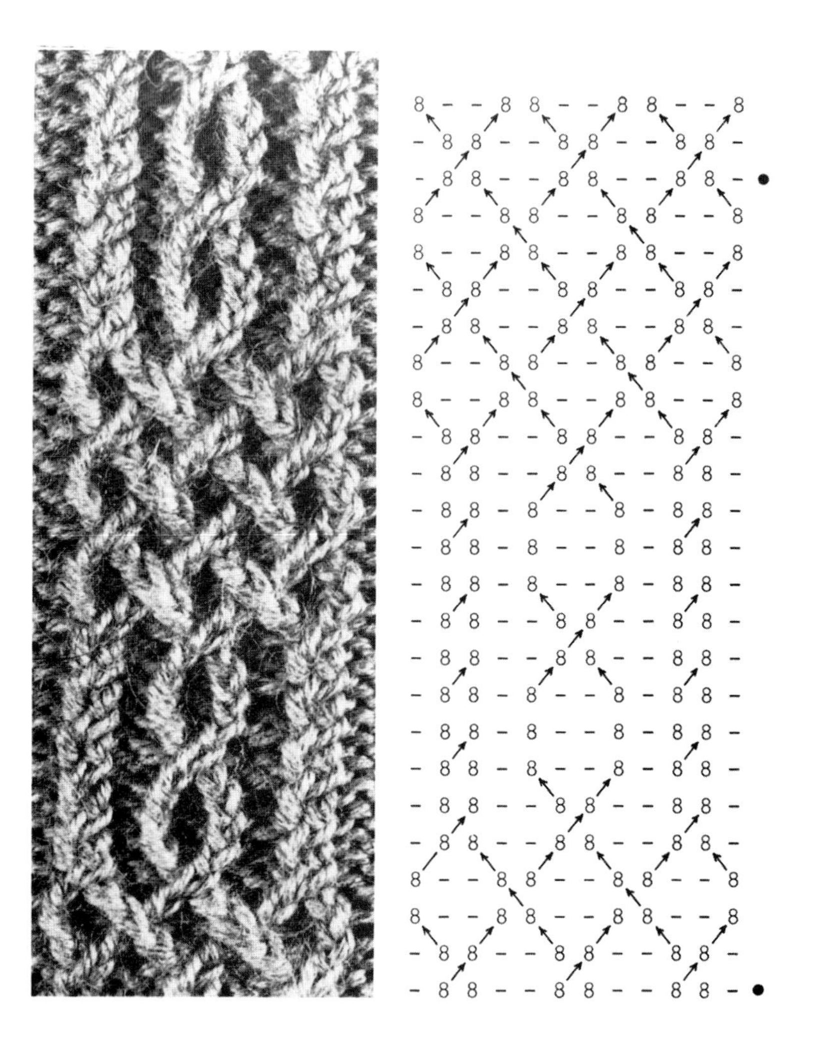

24

Offenes Doppelketterl

Open Double Little-Chain

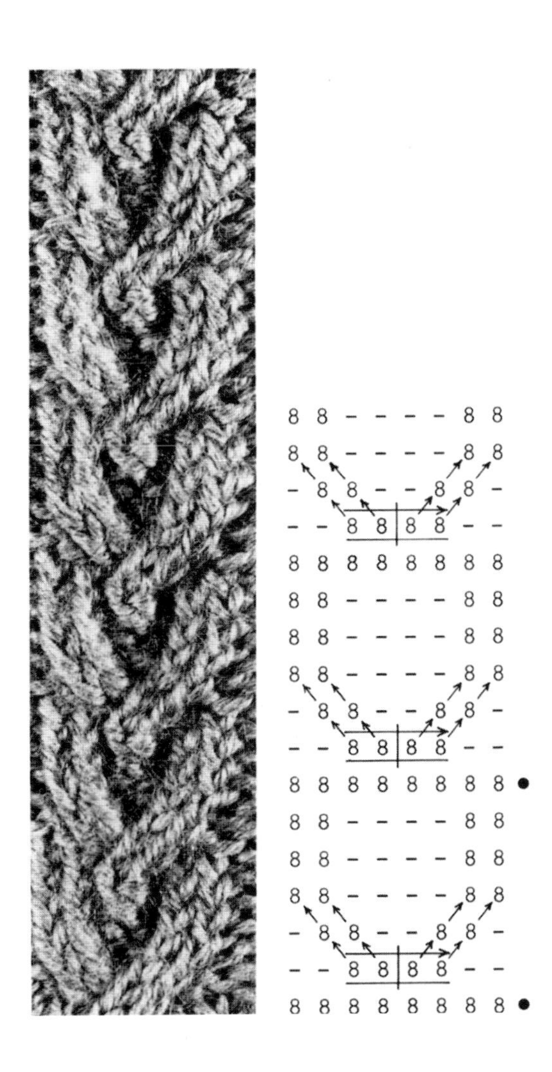

25

Kornähre

Ear of Wheat, #1

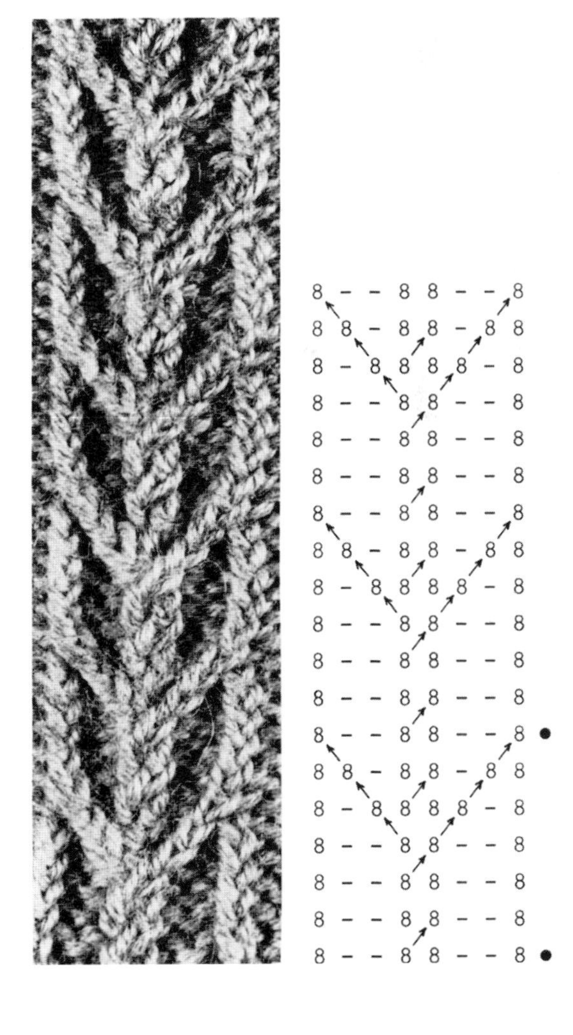

26
Vierfaches Band

Four-Ply Band

27
Zentimeterband

Centimeter Measuring Tape

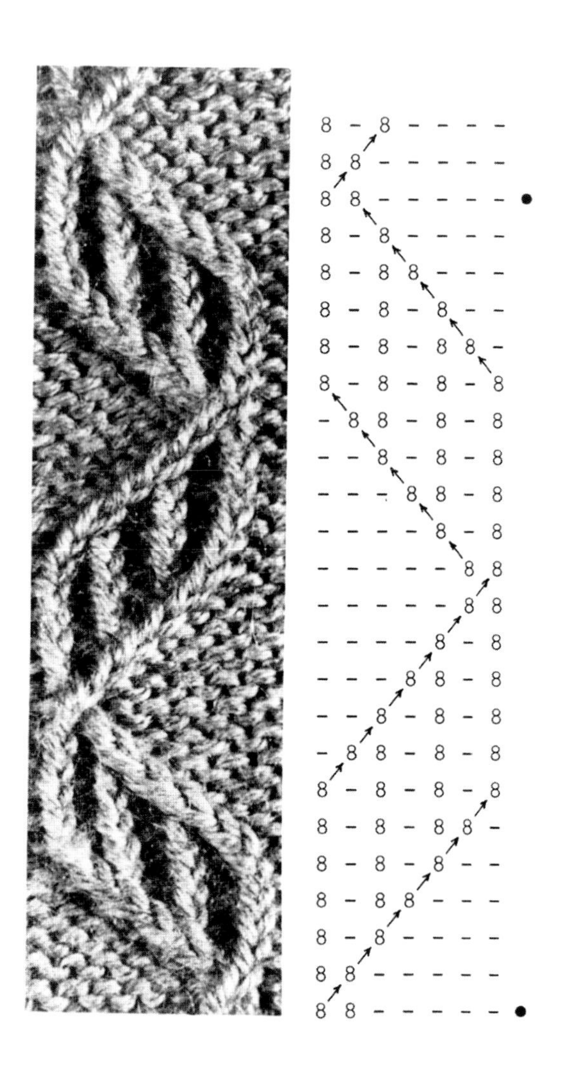

28
Untertaler Model

Lower Valley Pattern

29

Zweifaches Band

Double Band

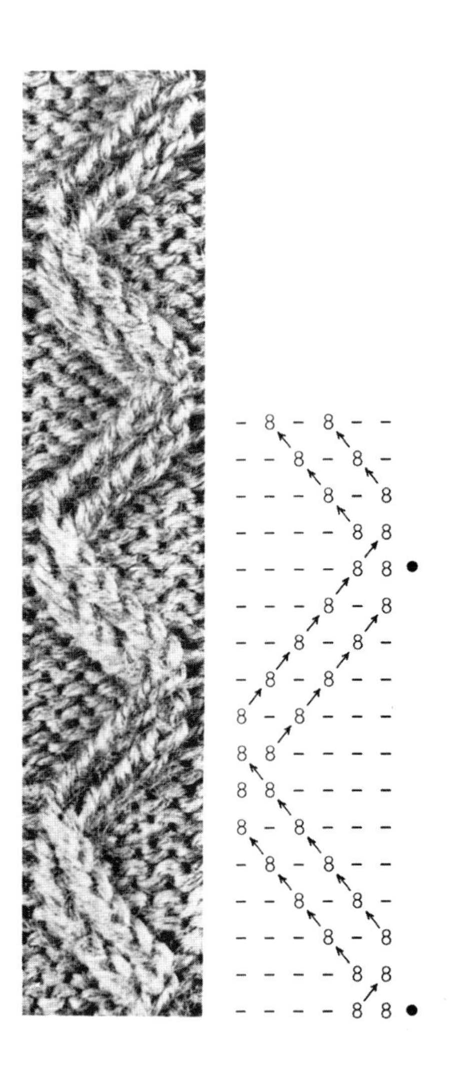

30

Kleeblatt

Clover Leaf, #1

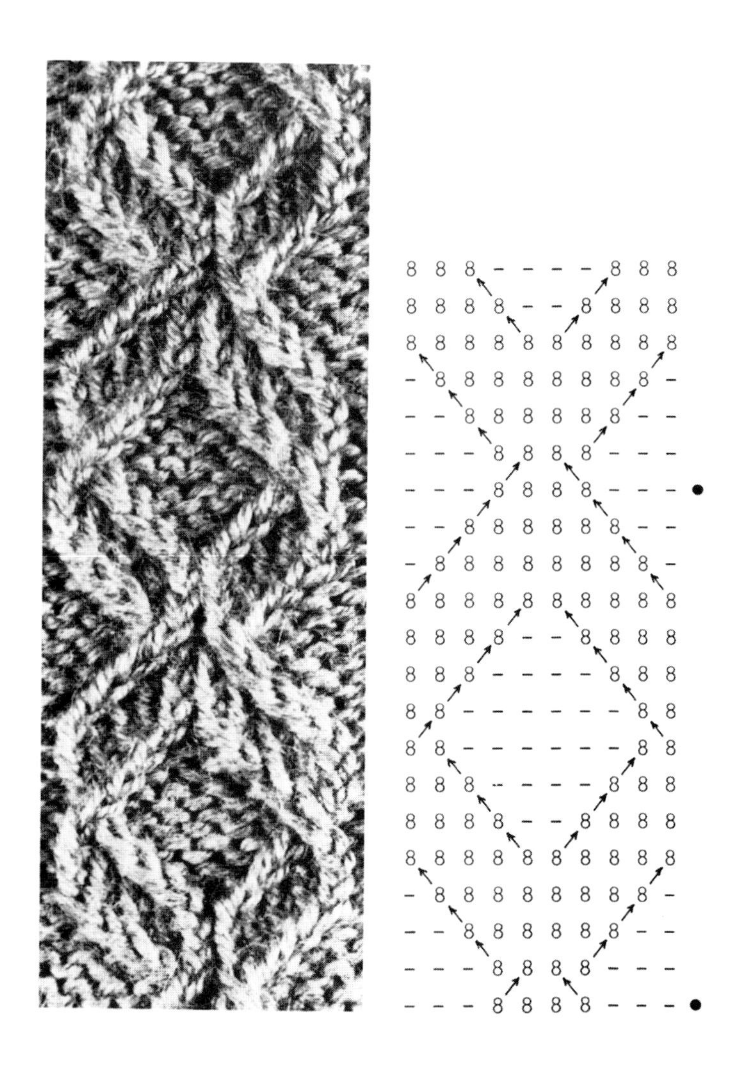

31
Dreifaches Band mit Fenster

Triple Band with Windows

32

Almweg mit Stangen

Alpine Path with Bars

33

Almweg mit Dreieck

Alpine Path with Triangles

34
Dreimaschenüberzug

Three-Stitch Crossover

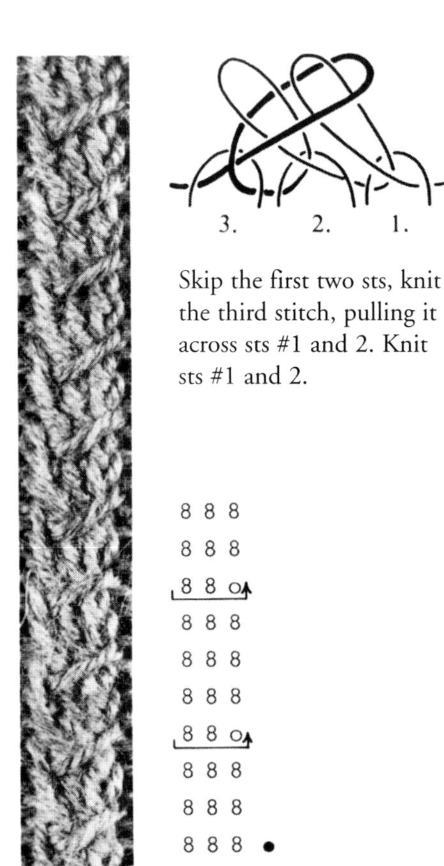

Skip the first two sts, knit the third stitch, pulling it across sts #1 and 2. Knit sts #1 and 2.

35
Butterschüsserl oder Ramsauer Model

Butter Bowl

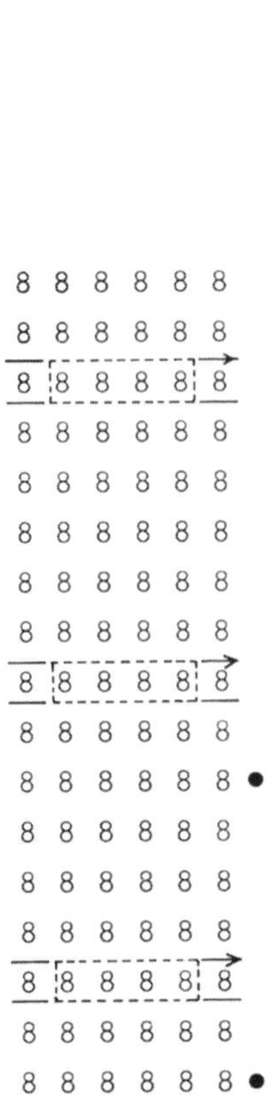

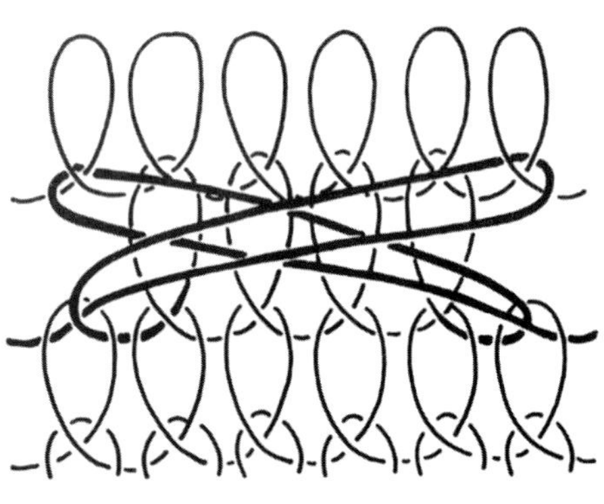

4.	8	8	8	8	8	8
3.	8	8	8	8	8	8
2.	8	8	8	8	8	8
1.	8	8	8	8	8	8

The cross-over is in row 3. Only the 2 outside sts (#1 & #6) are crossed. Pick up stitch #1 with your R needle. Do not knit it. Pick up sts #2, 3, 4 and 5 with a spare needle, and hold behind your work. Cross stitch #6 and #1 so they lean to the right. Knit stitch #6, knit the 4 middle sts, then knit stitch #1. Make sure the 4 middle sts are under the cross made by stitch #1 and #6.

36

Stangennullen

Bar with Zeros, #1

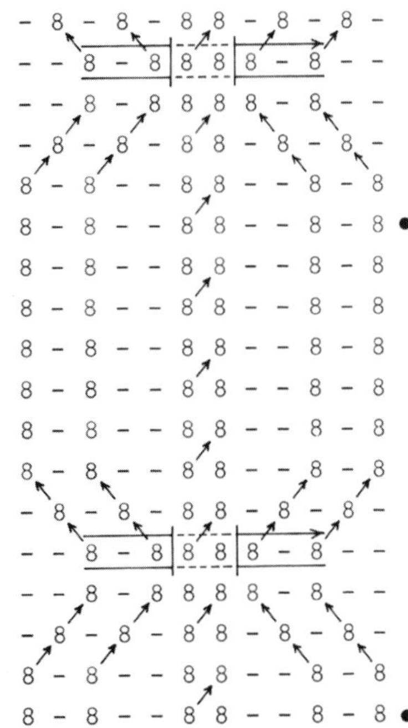

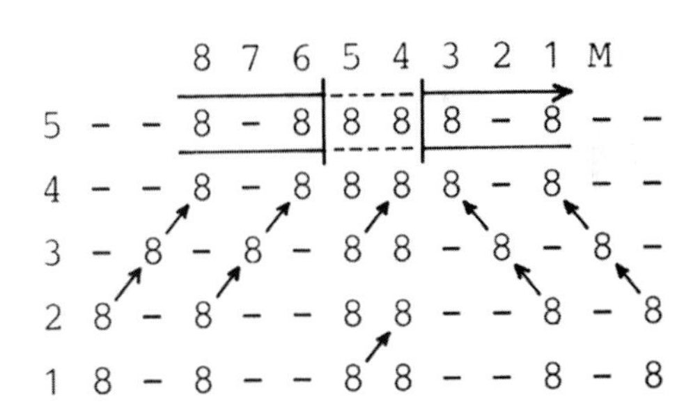

Row 5 has the cross. Use an extra needle (or two) for this maneuver. Pick up sts #1, 2 and 3 with the 1st extra needle and hold it behind your work. Pick up sts #4 and 5 with the second extra needle and hold it in front of your work. Work sts #6, 7 and 8 following the chart. Now knit the two sts from the second extra needle and finish by knitting sts #1, 2 and 3 from the first extra needle.

37
Zopf

Braid, #1

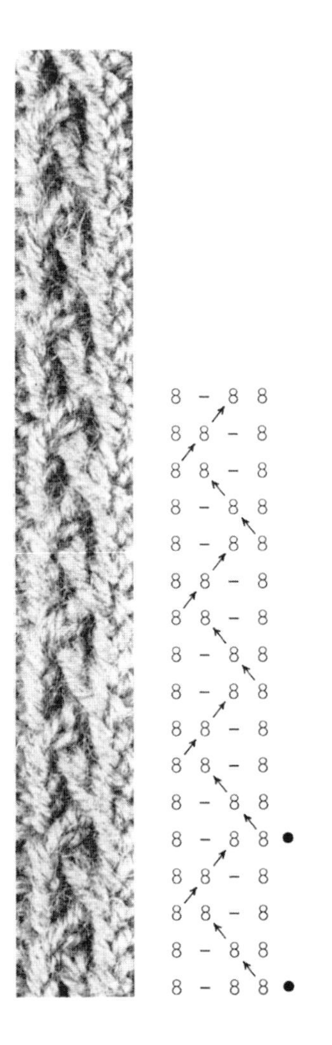

38
Vergessene Liab

Forgotten Love, #1

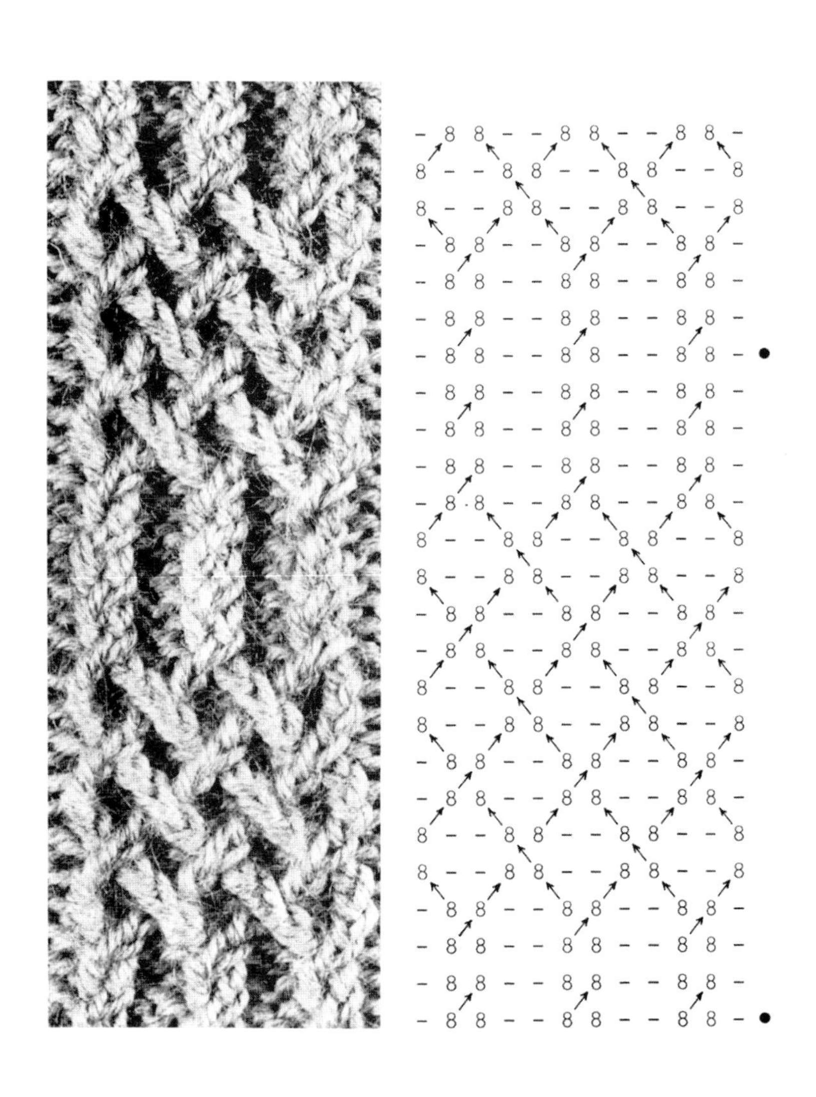

39
Dreifaches Ketterl

Triple Little-Chain

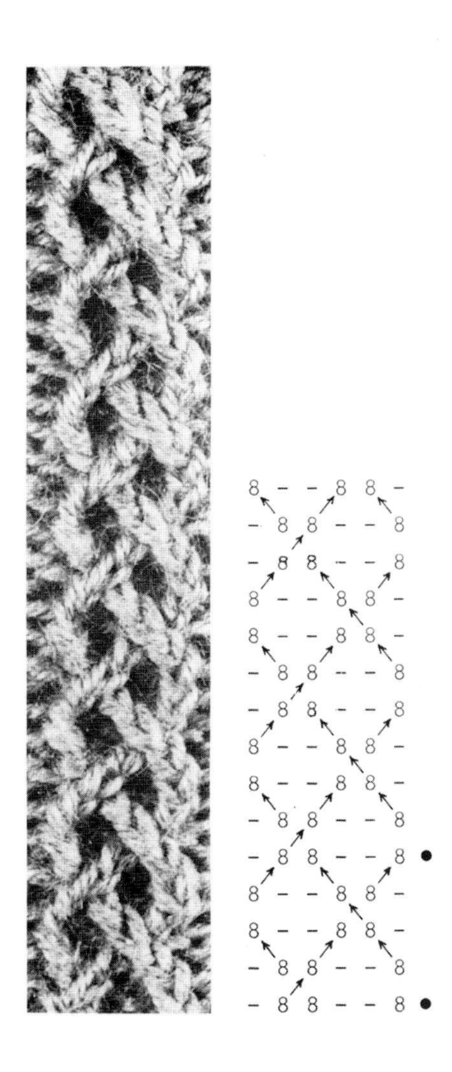

40
Brennende Liab

Burning Love (wide)

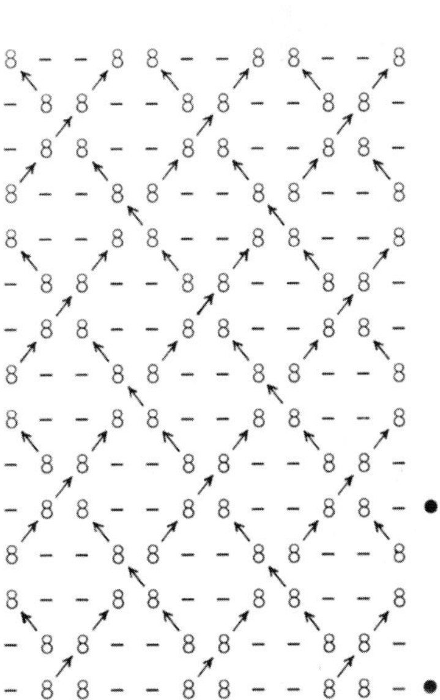

41
Vergessene Liab

Forgotten Love, #2

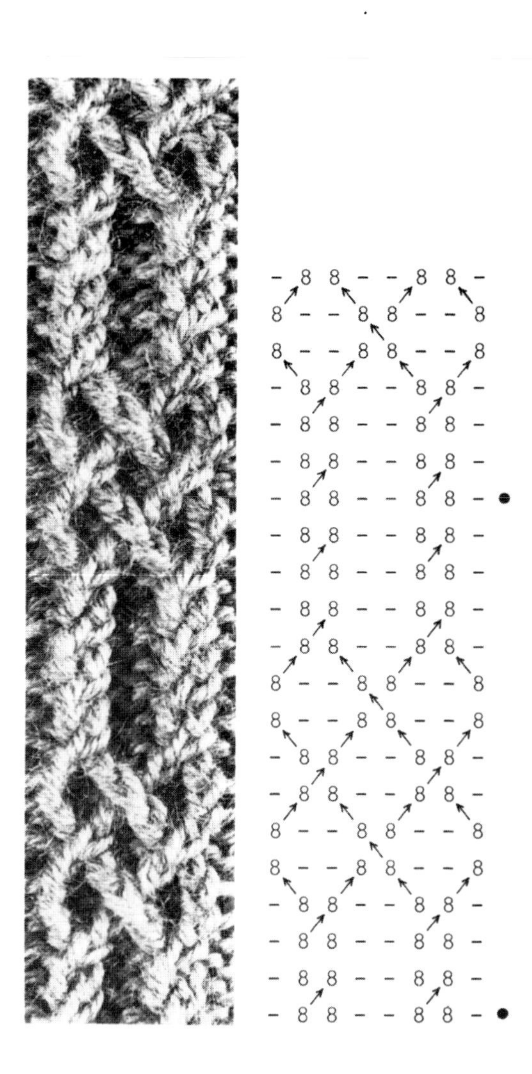

42
Brennende Liab

Burning Love (narrow)

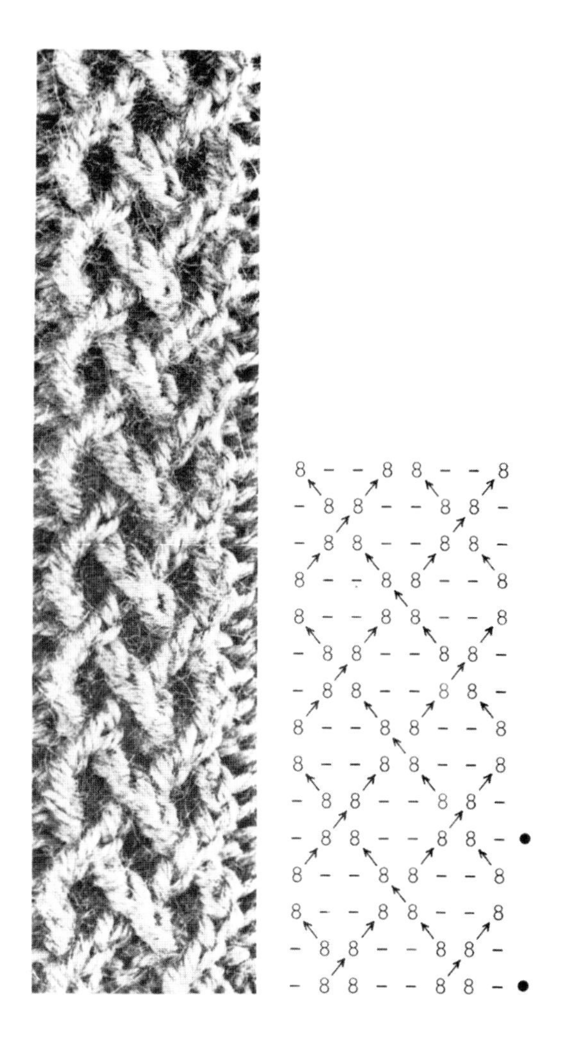

43

Nullenzwickel mit Drahdi

Zero Gusset with Twisted Band

44

Kettentulipan

Tulip Chains

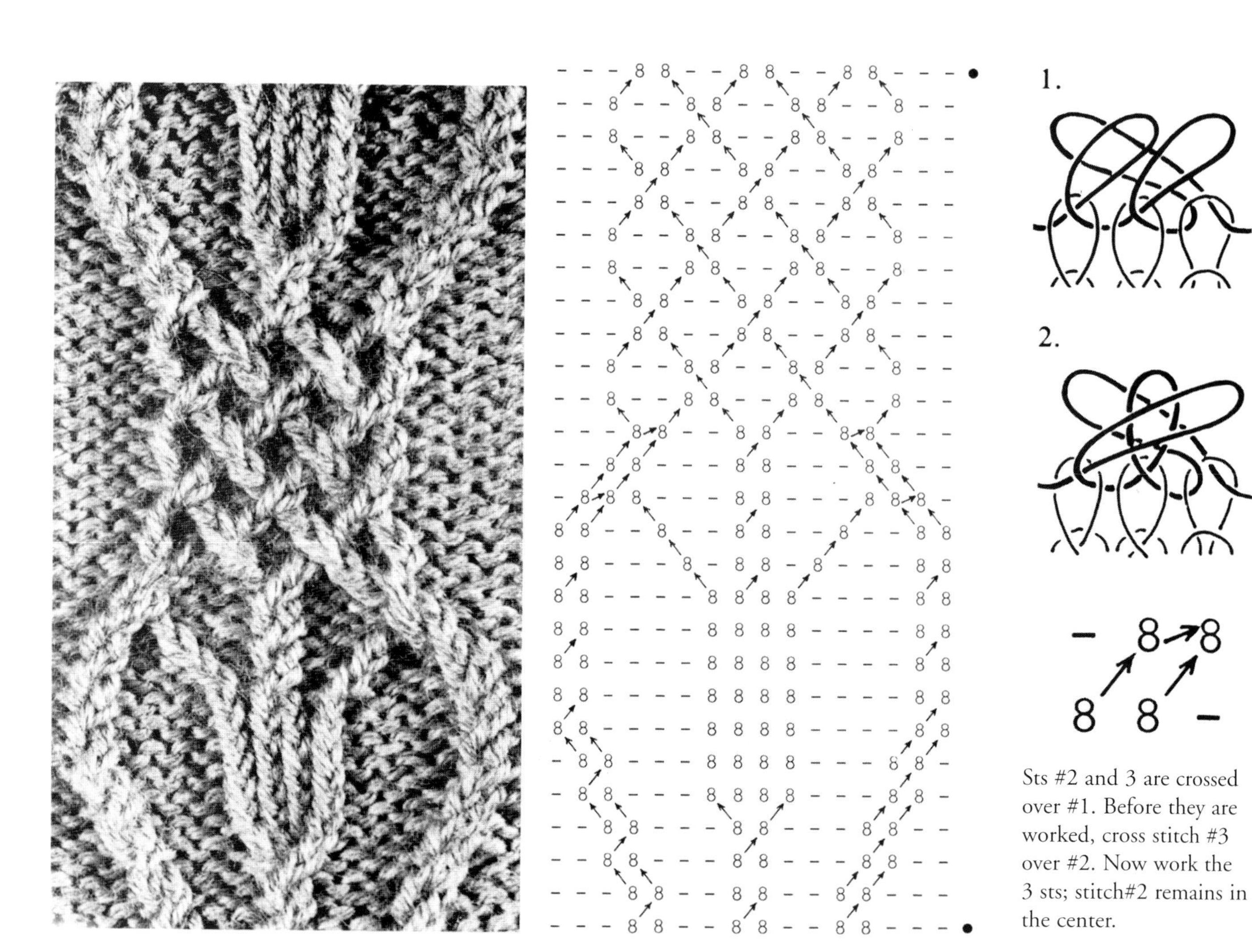

Sts #2 and 3 are crossed over #1. Before they are worked, cross stitch #3 over #2. Now work the 3 sts; stitch#2 remains in the center.

45

Dreifaches Band mit Viereck

Triple Band with Squares

46
Kleines Viereckketterl

Little Square Chains

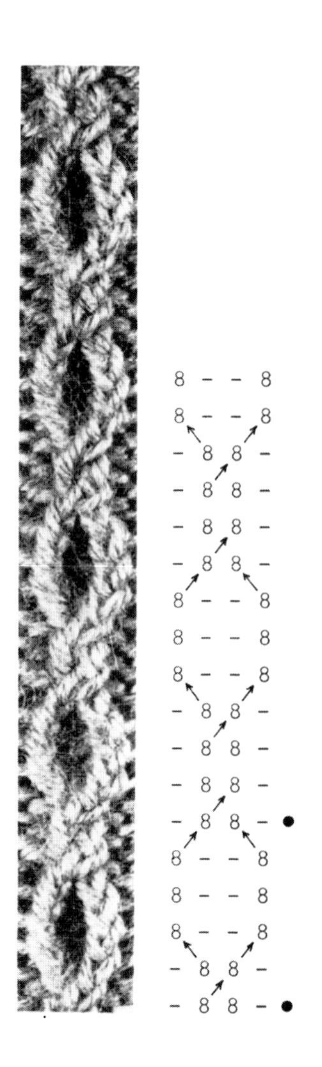

47
Drahdifenster

Twisted Band with Windows

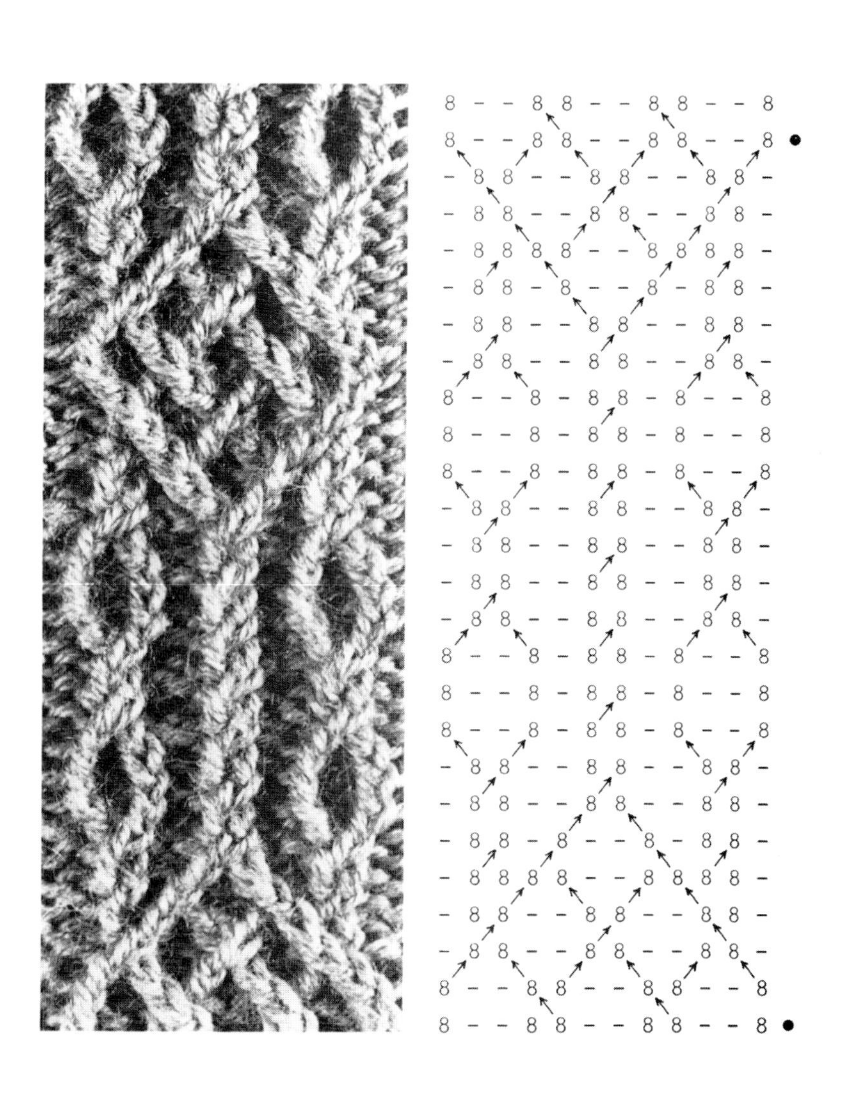

48

Zweifache Kette

Double Chain, #1

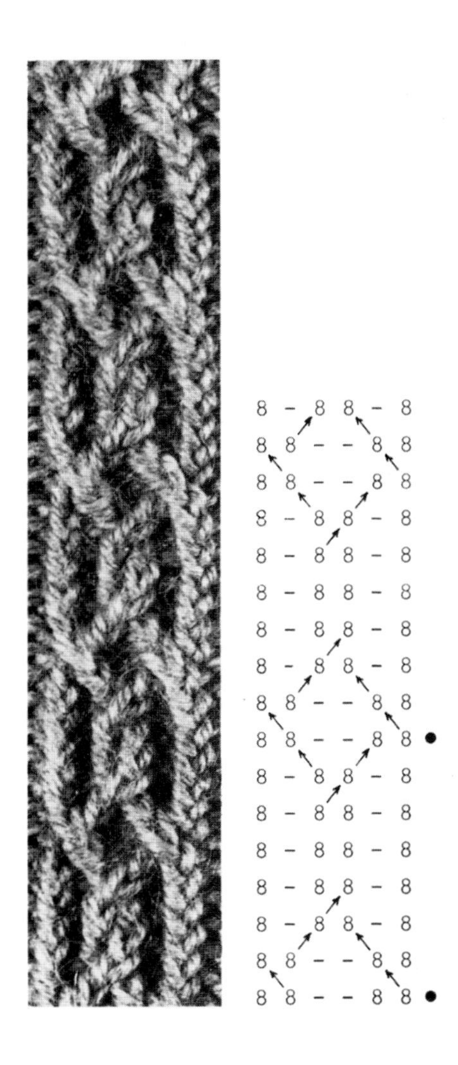

49

Sechsfache Streifenkette

Sixfold Stripe Chain

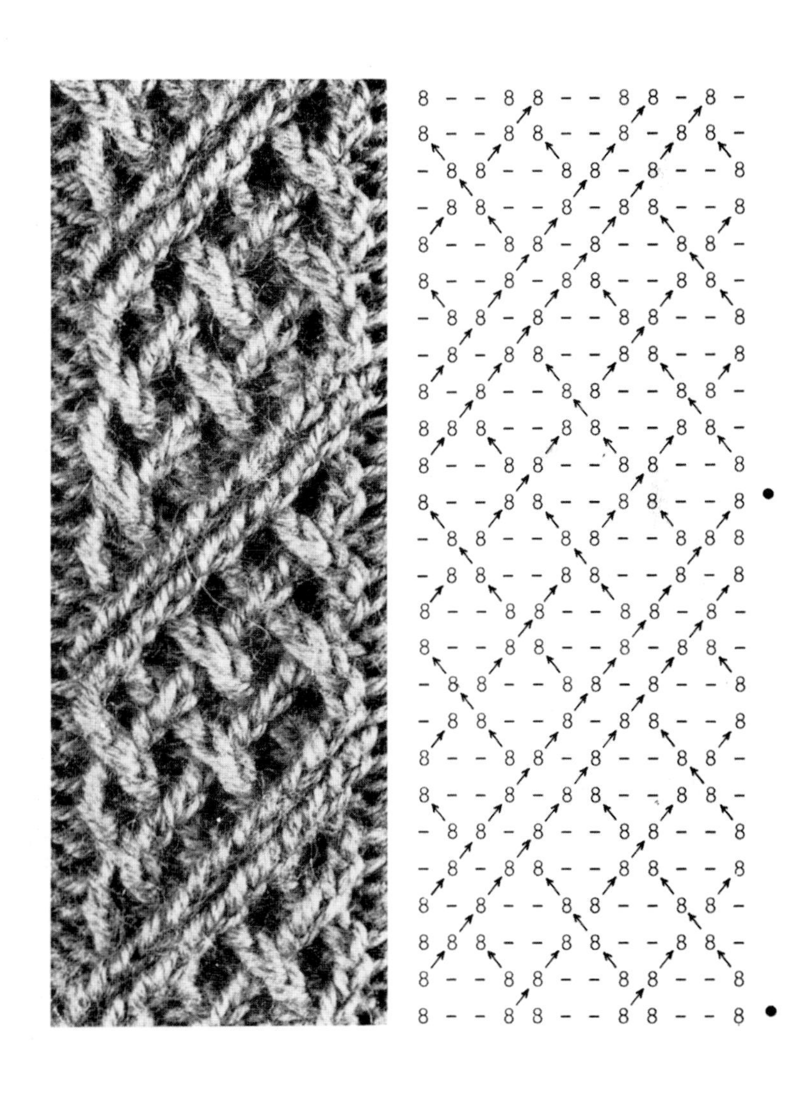

50
Offenes Drahdiketterl

Open Twisted Band Chain

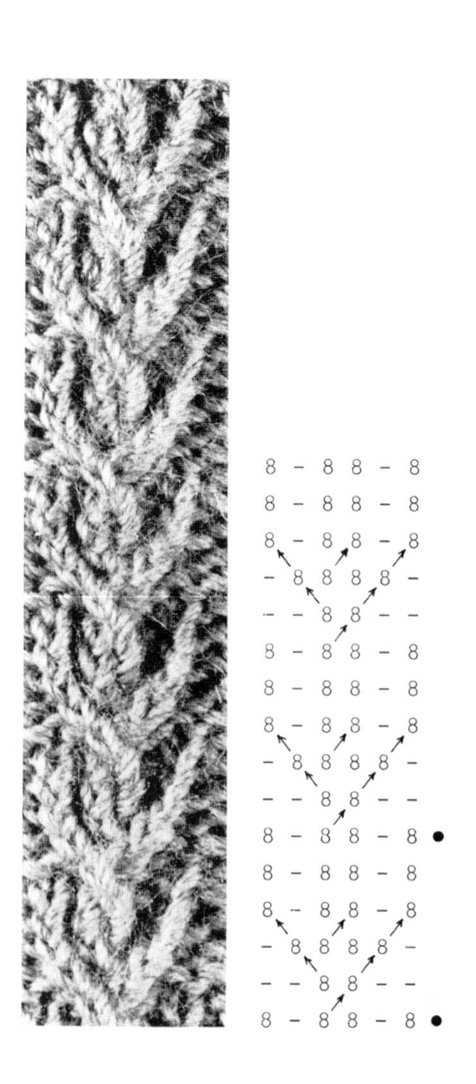

51
Kleeblatt

Clover Leaf, #2

52
Spinnerin

Woman Spinner, #1

53

Schlußketterl

Lock Little-Chain

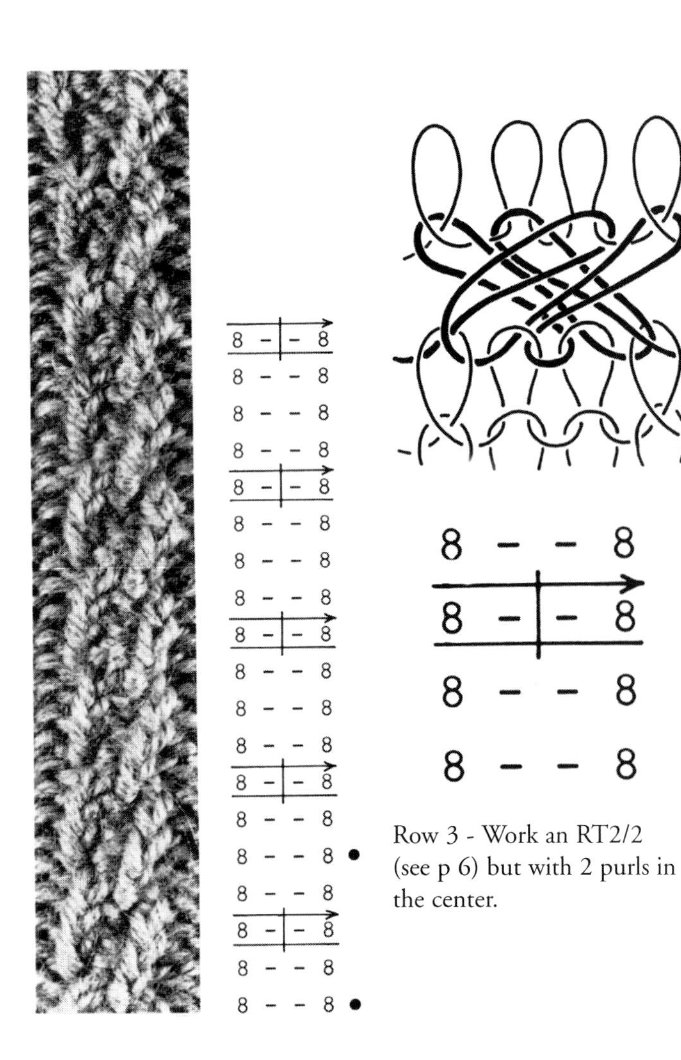

8	- |	-	8 →	
8	-	-	8	
8	-	-	8	
8	-	-	8	
8	- |	-	8 →	
8	-	-	8	
8	-	-	8	
8	-	-	8	
8	- |	-	8 →	
8	-	-	8	
8	-	-	8	
8	-	-	8	
8	- |	-	8 →	
8	-	-	8	
8	-	-	8	•
8	-	-	8	
8	- |	-	8 →	
8	-	-	8	
8	-	-	8	•

8	-	-	8
8	- |	-	8 →
8	-	-	8
8	-	-	8

Row 3 - Work an RT2/2 (see p 6) but with 2 purls in the center.

54

Doppelzopf

Double Braid, #1

This pattern consists of two braids (cables) next to each other. The vertical line in the center of the chart shows where the braids are separated.

8	8	8	8 |	8	8	8	8	
8	8	8	8 |	8	8	8	8	
8	8	8	8 |	8	8	8	8	
8	8 |	8	8 → |	← 8	8 |	8	8	
8	8	8	8 |	8	8	8	8	
8	8	8	8 |	8	8	8	8	•
8	8	8	8 |	8	8	8	8	
8	8	8	8 |	8	8	8	8	
8	8	8	8 |	8	8	8	8	
8	8 |	8	8 → |	← 8	8 |	8	8	
8	8	8	8 |	8	8	8	8	
8	8	8	8 |	8	8	8	8	•

55
Woazkörndl

Wheat Grain

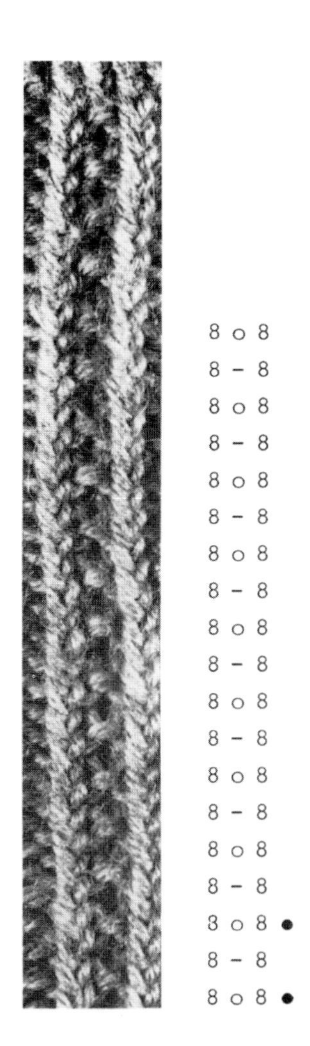

```
8 o 8
8 - 8
8 o 8
8 - 8
8 o 8
8 - 8
8 o 8
8 - 8
8 o 8
8 - 8
8 o 8
8 - 8
8 o 8
8 - 8
8 o 8
8 - 8
8 o 8 •
8 - 8
8 o 8 •
```

56
Vierfacher Zopf

Quadruple Braid

```
8 8 - - - 8 8|8 8 - - - 8 8
8 8 - - - 8 8 8 8 - - - 8 8
8 8 - - 8 8 - - 8 8 - - 8 8
- 8 8|8 8 - - - - 8 8|8 8 -
- 8 8 8 8 - - - - 8 8 8 8 -
8 8 - - 8 8 - - 8 8 - - 8 8
8 8 - - - 8 8|8 8 - - - 8 8
8 8 - - - 8 8 8 8 - - - 8 8
8 8 - - 8 8 - - 8 8 - - 8 8
- 8 8|8 8 - - - - 8 8|8 8 -
- 8 8 8 8 - - - - 8 8 8 8 - •
8 8 - - 8 8 - - 8 8 - - 8 8
8 8 - - - 8 8|8 8 - - - 8 8
8 8 - - - 8 8 8 8 - - - 8 8
8 8 - - 8 8 - - 8 8 - - 8 8
- 8 8|8 8 - - - - 8 8|8 8 -
- 8 8 8 8 - - - - 8 8 8 8 - •
```

57
Kleines Ketterl

Small Chain, #1

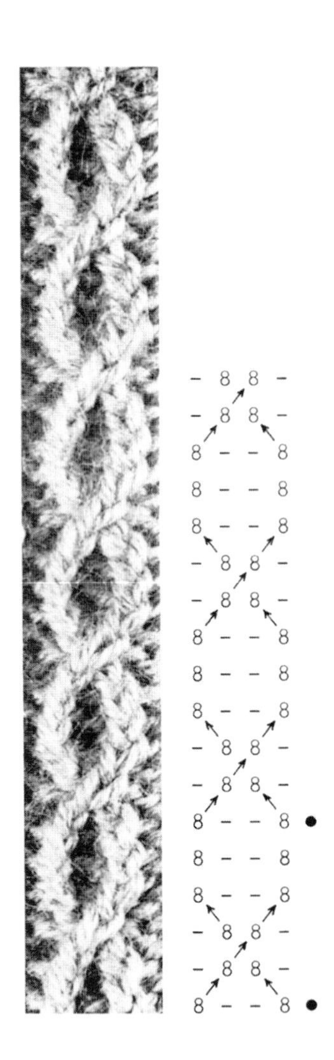

58
Ketterlzopf

Braided Chain

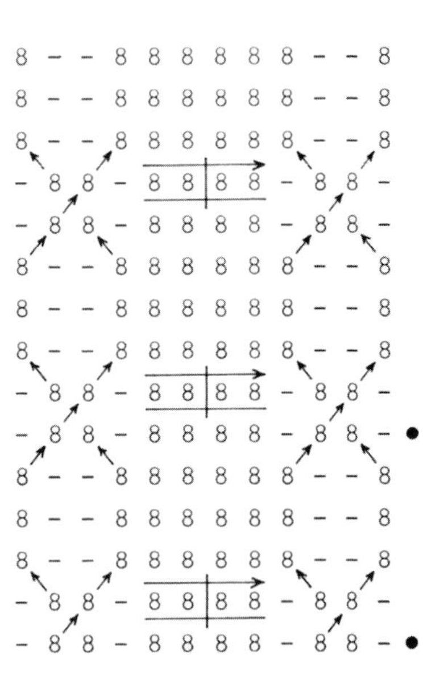

59

Kreuzketterl

Crossed Chain

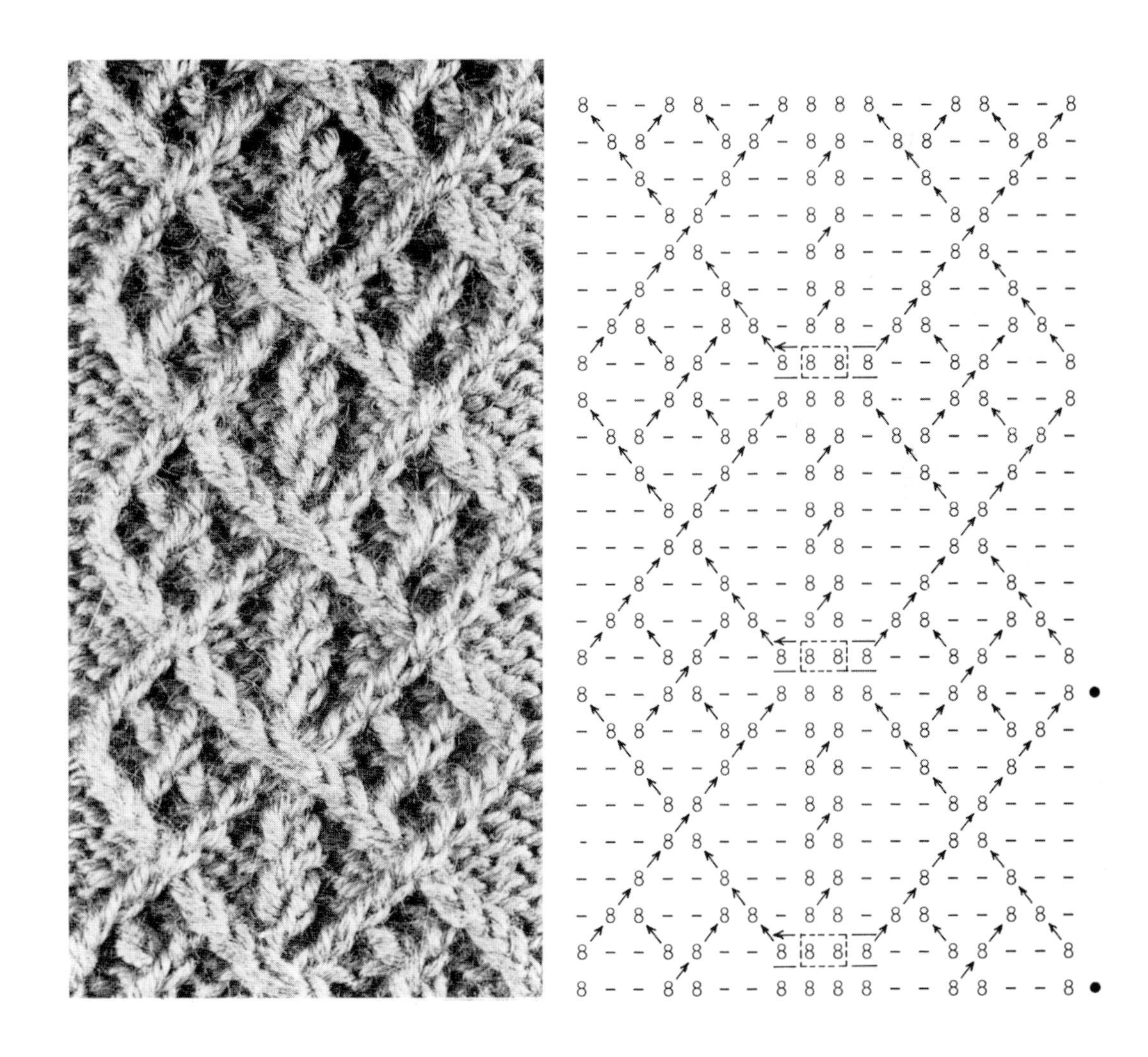

60
Zweifache Kette

Double Chain, #2

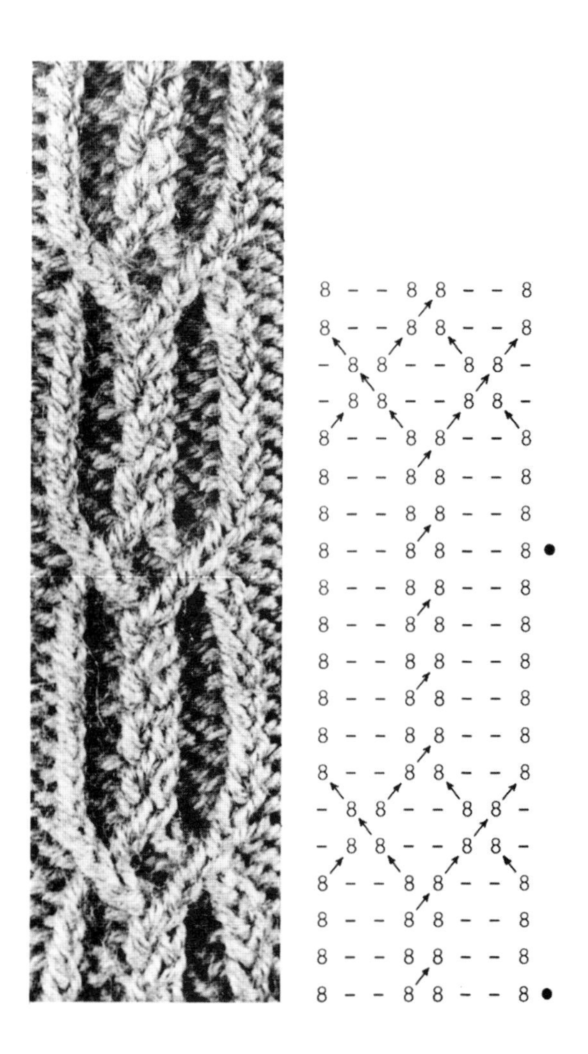

61
Kleeblatt

Clover Leaf, #3

62

Nullenzwickel

Zeros Insert, #2

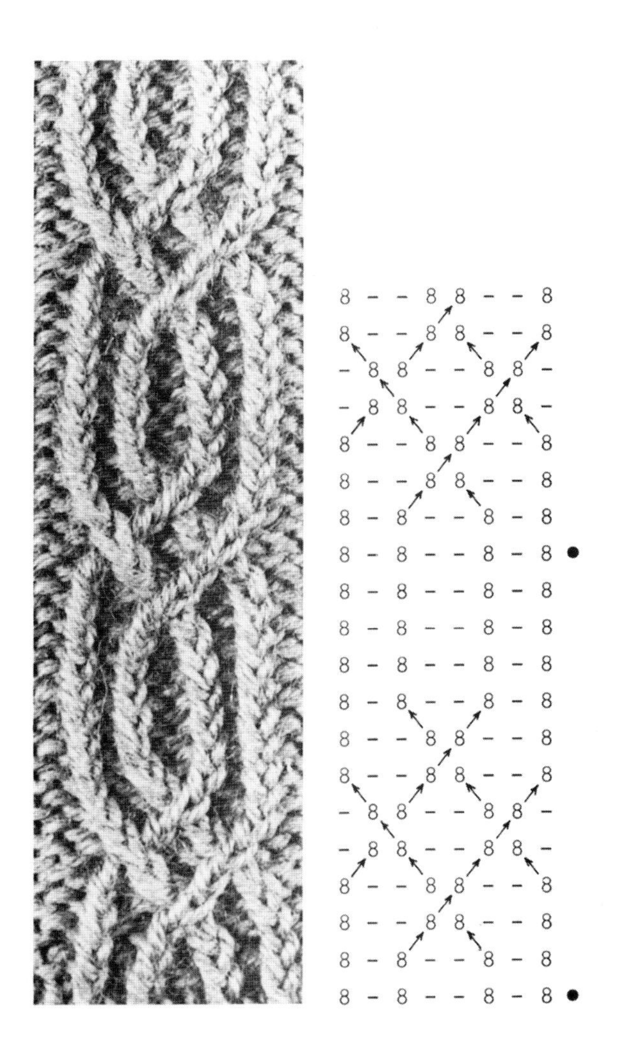

63

Nullen mit Fenster

Zeros with Window, #1

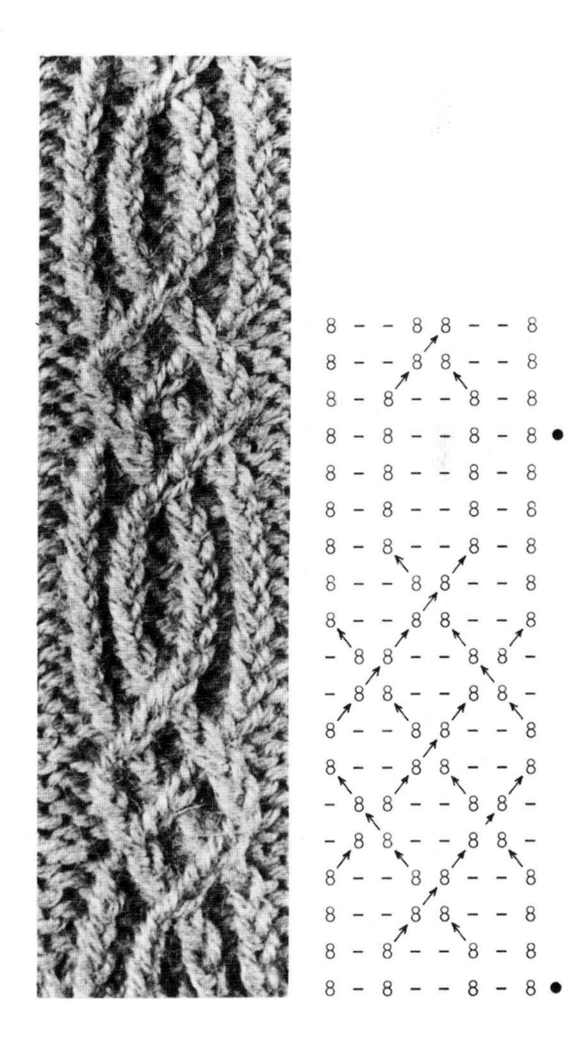

64

Großes Fenster

Large Window

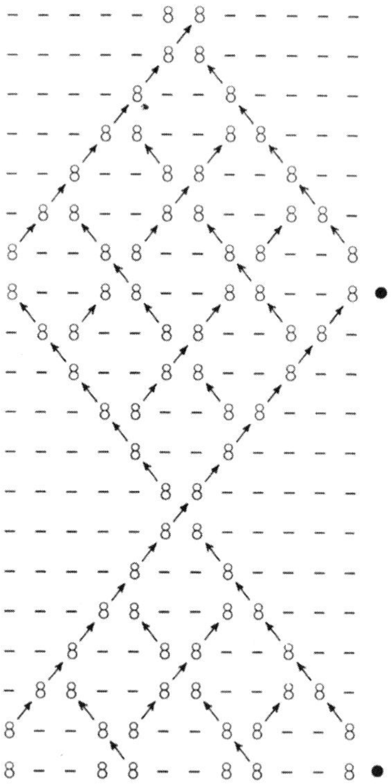

65

Kleines Durchschlupfketterl

Small Slip-Through Chain

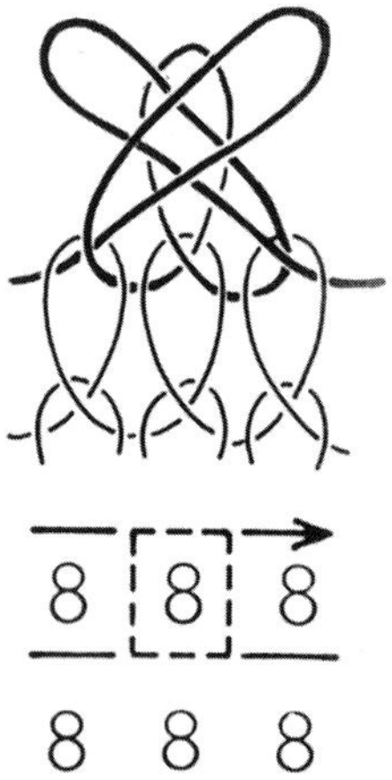

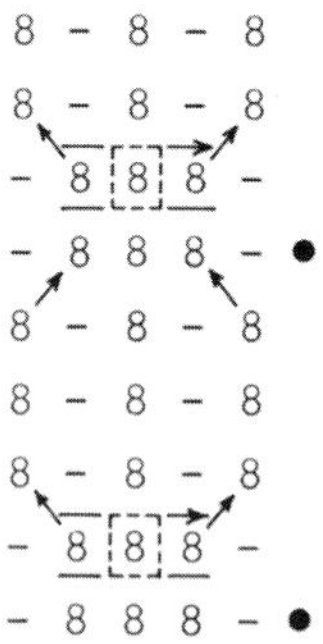

66
Almweg mit Dreieck und Stangen

Alpine Path with Triangles and Bars

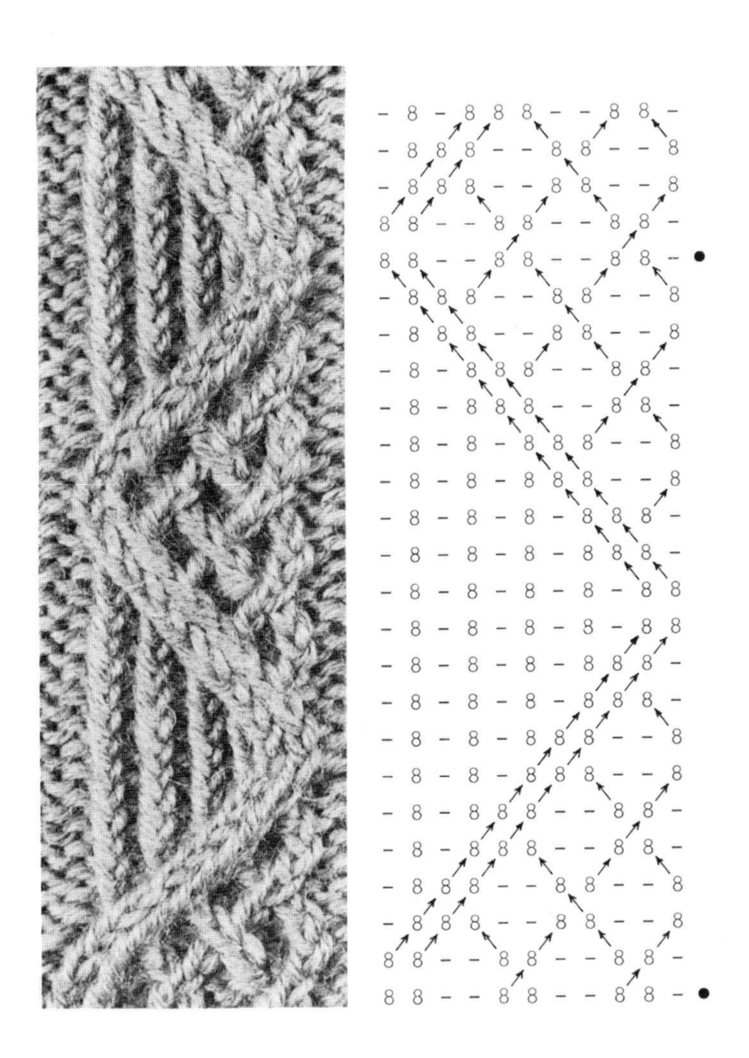

67
Drahdikette

Twisted Band with Chain

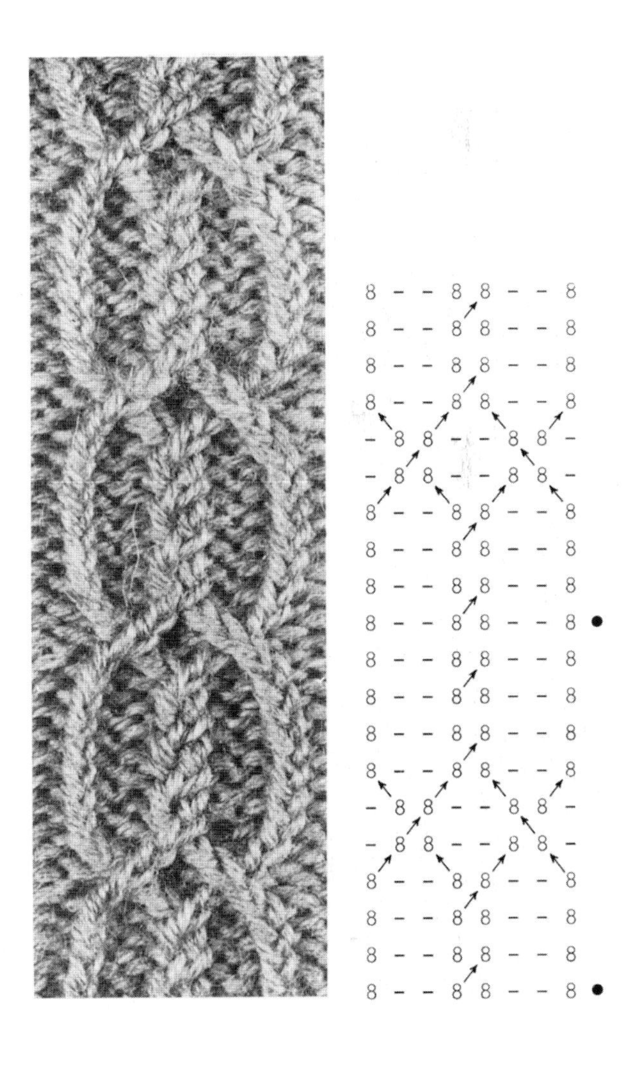

68
Doppelalmweg mit Fenster

Double Alpine Path with Window

69
Einfacher Obenauf

Simple On-Top Stitch

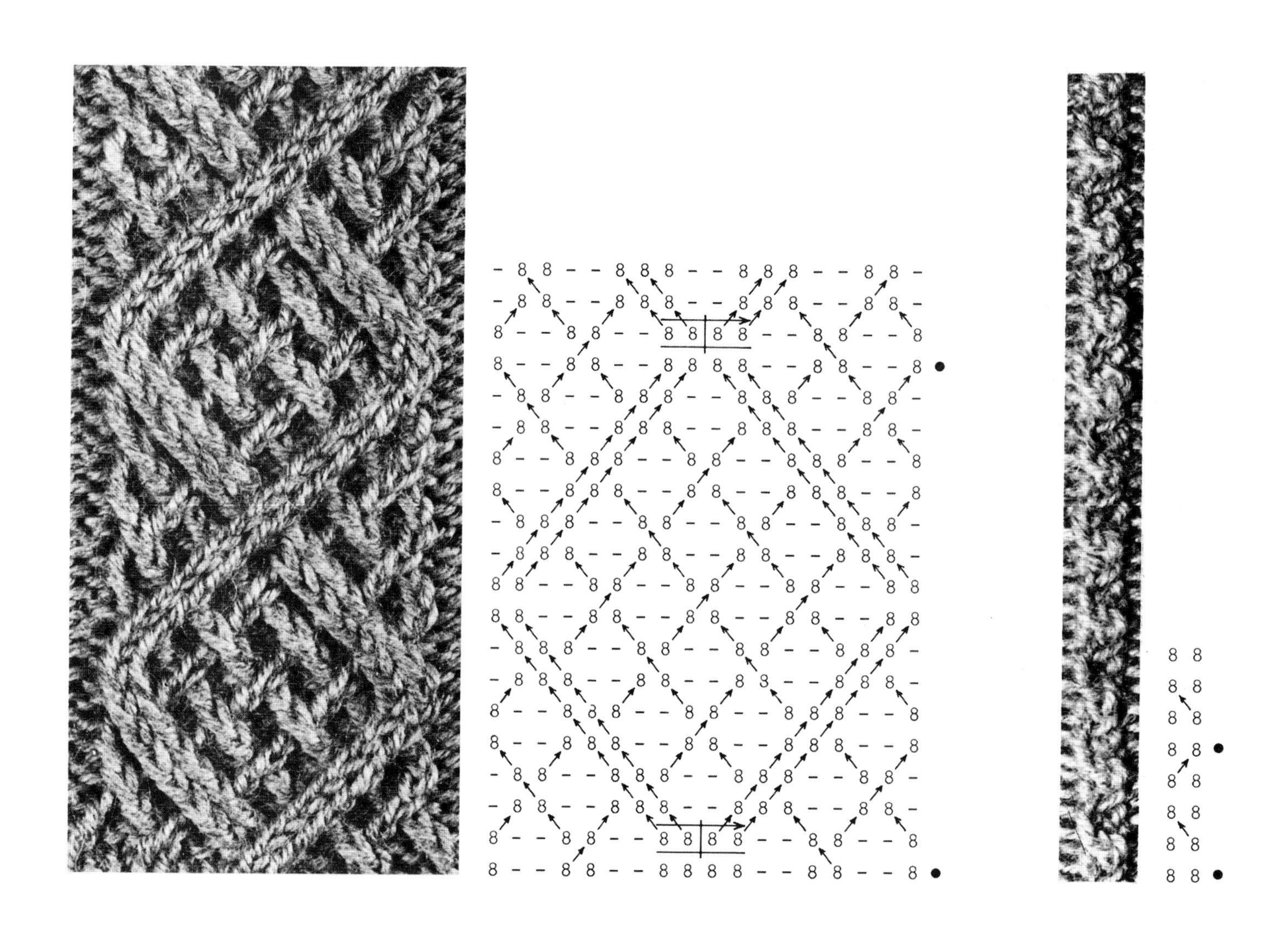

70
Ennstaler Model

Enns Valley Pattern

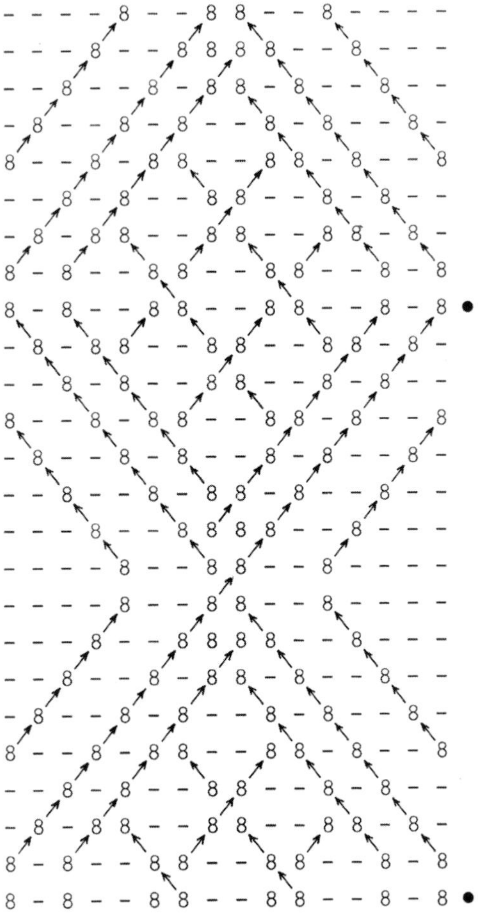

71
Schmaler Bandmodel

Small Band Pattern

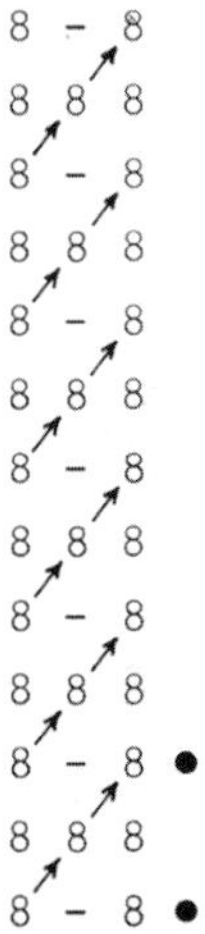

72
Drahdinull

Twisted Band with Zeros

73
Sechsfache Drahdikette

Sixfold Twisted Band Chain

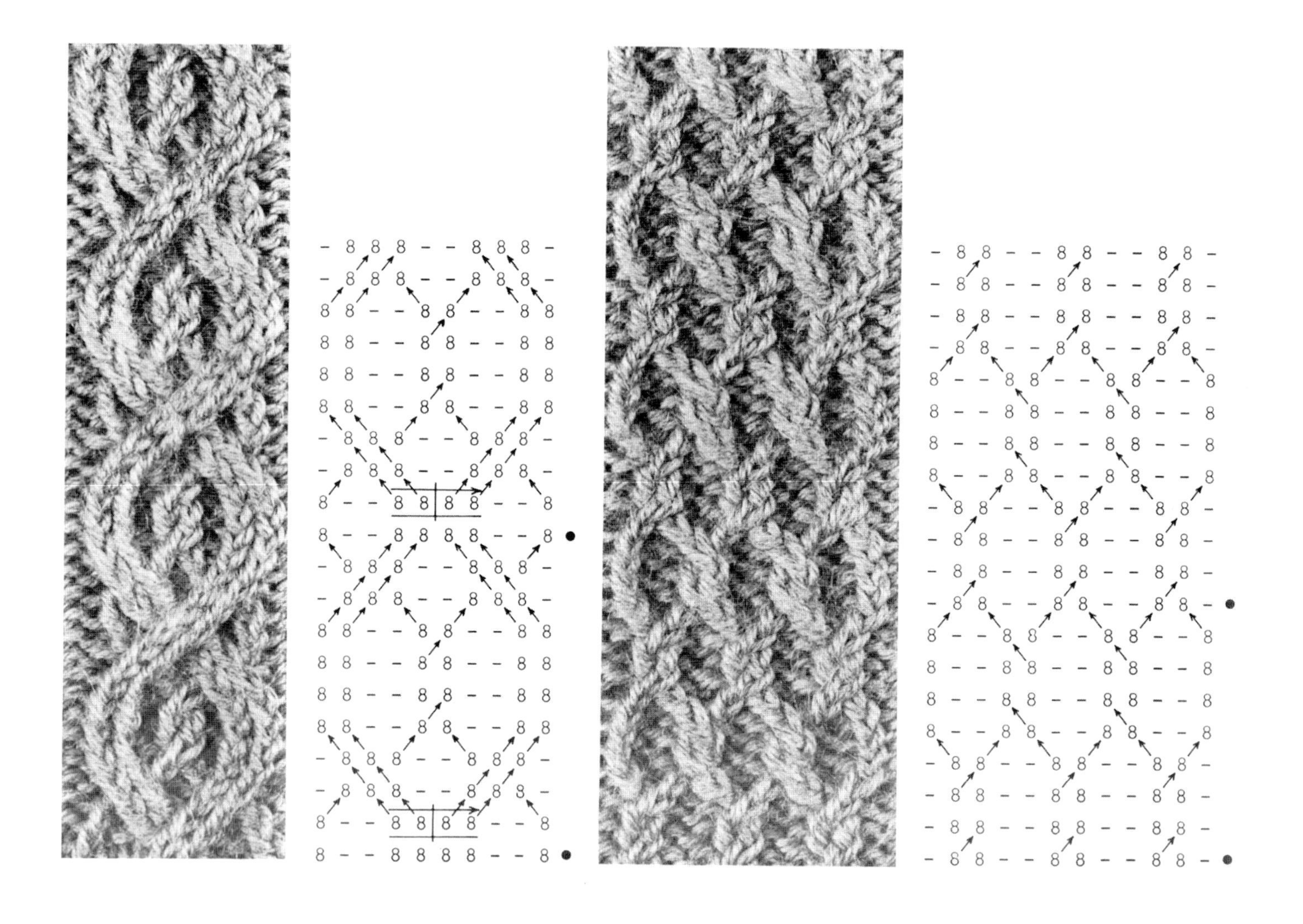

74

Bandmodel

Band Stitch, #1

75

Großes Doppelketterl mit Drahdi

Large Double Chain with Twisted Band

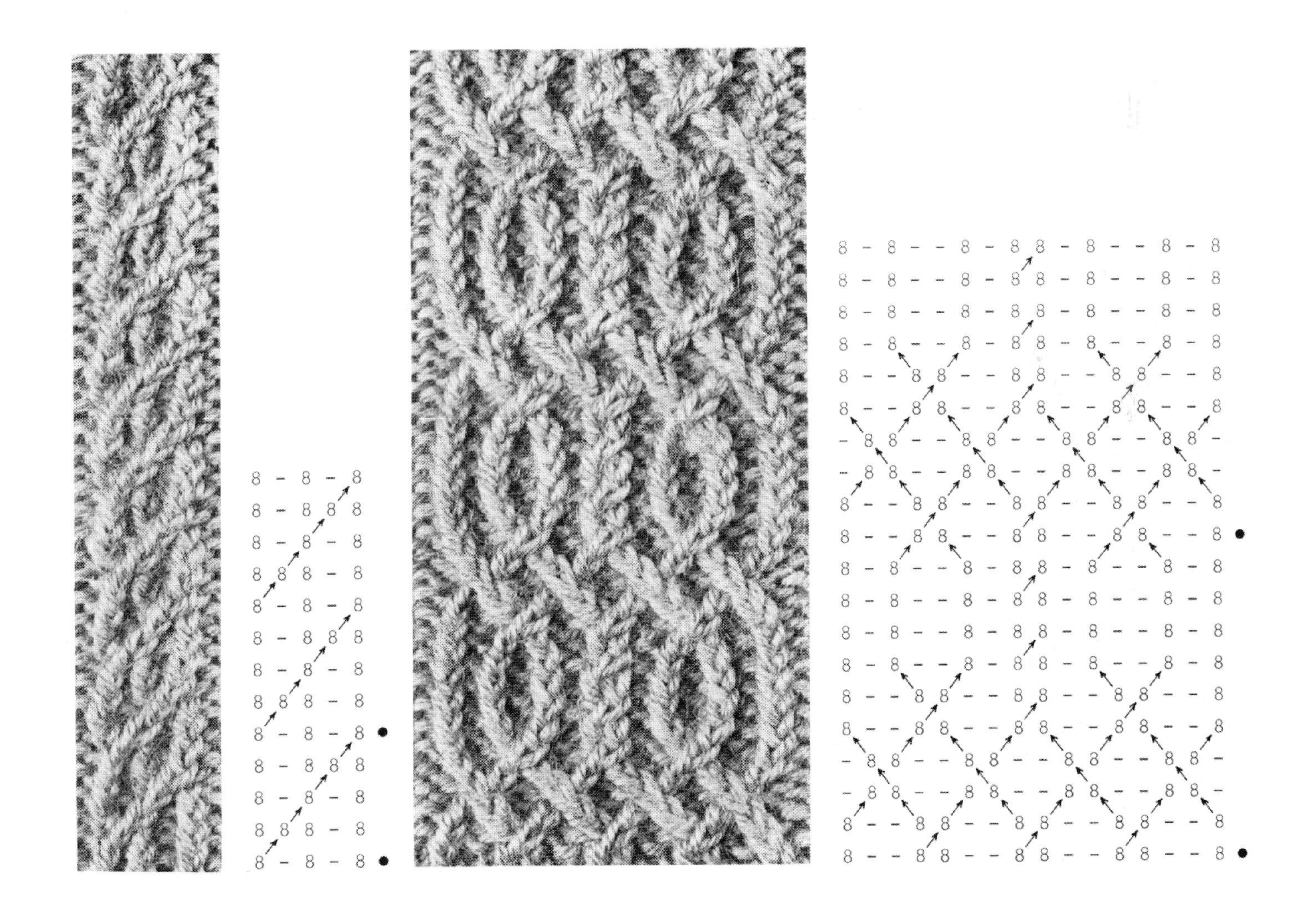

76
Klausner Model

Klausner Pattern

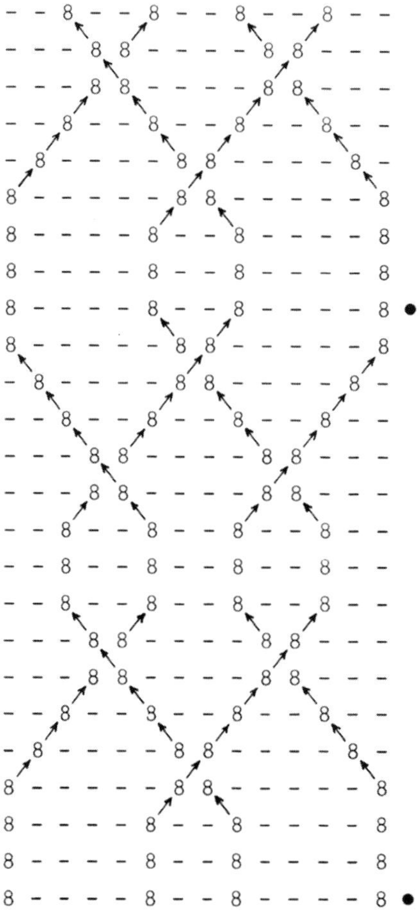

77
Drahdiketterl

Twisted Band Chain

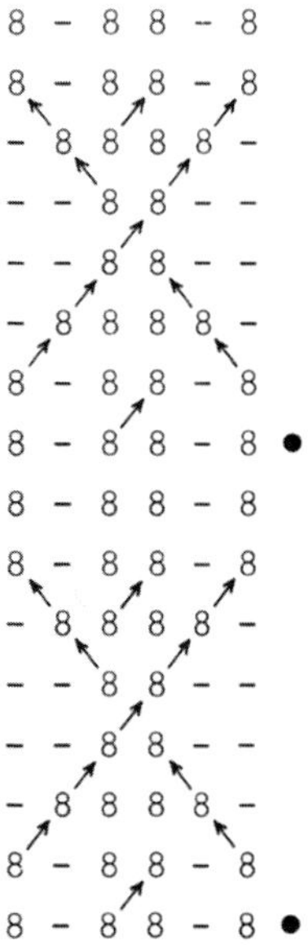

78
Sonnberger Model

Sunny Mountain Pattern

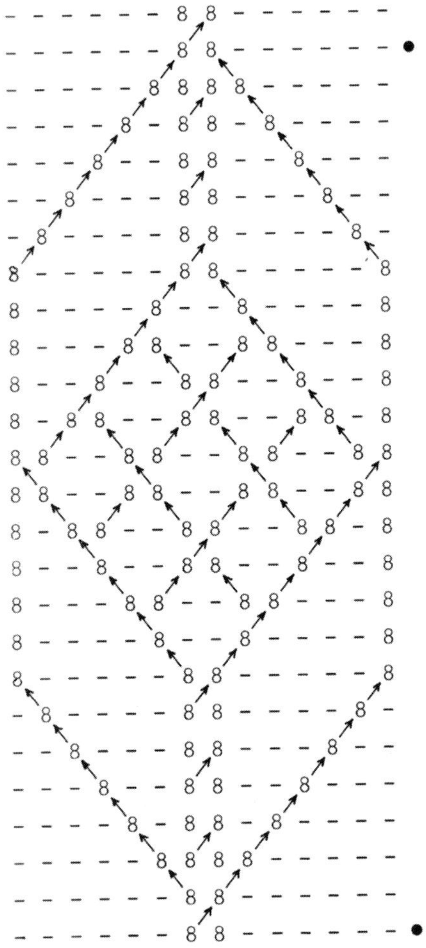

79
Kleiner doppelter Obenauf

Small Double-Top Stitch

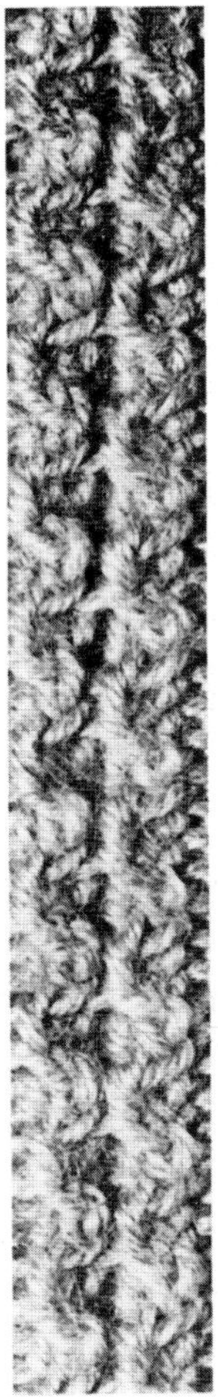

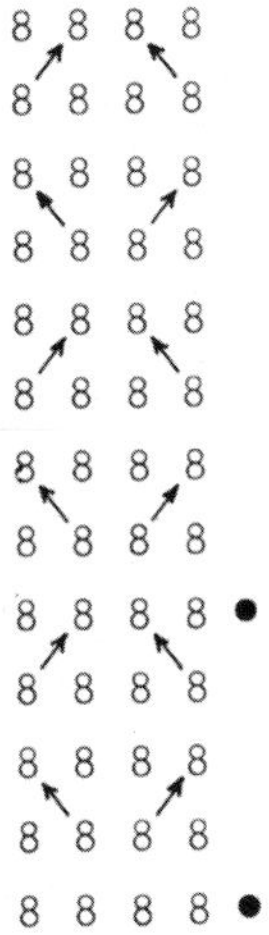

80
Herz

Heart

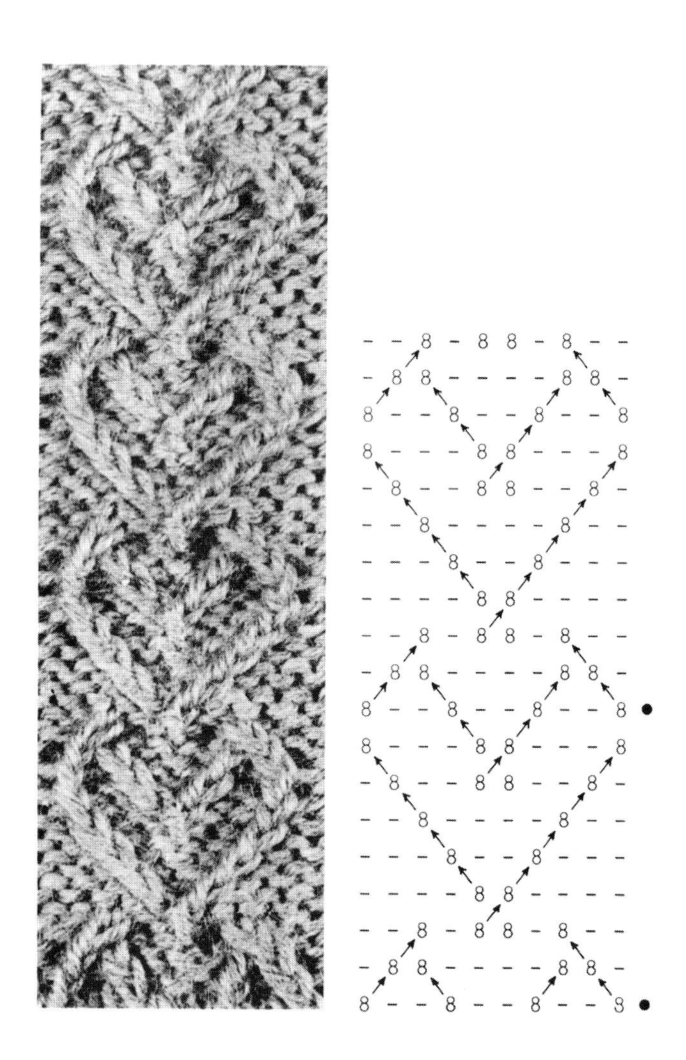

81
Bodenketterl

Basic Chain

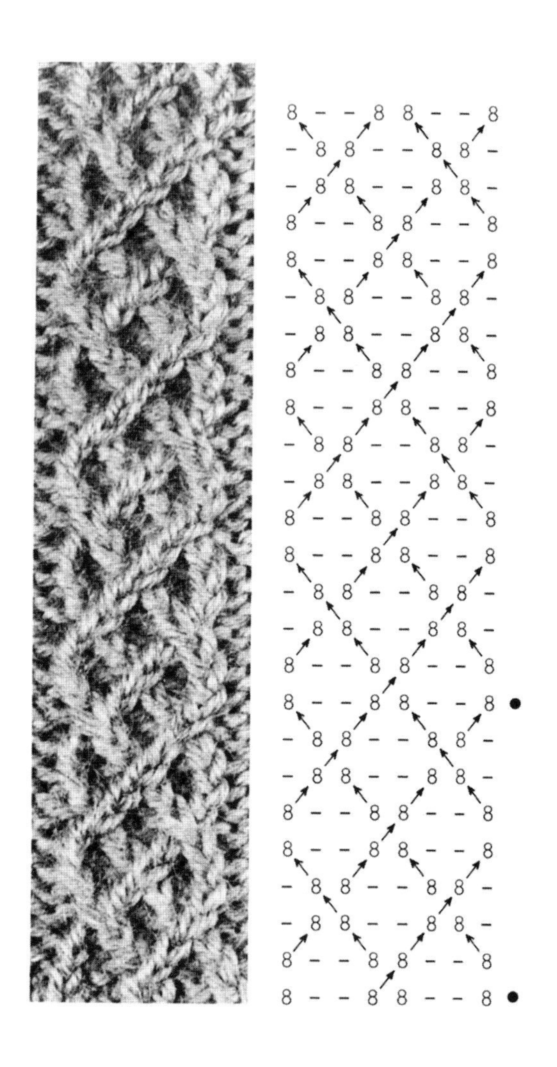

82
Baum

Tree

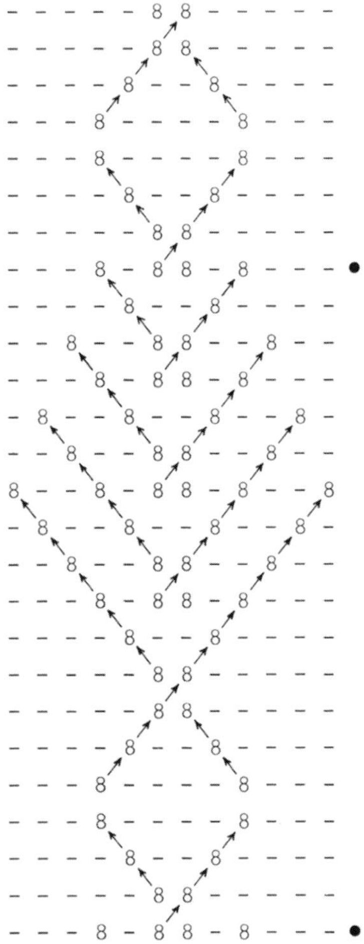

83
Kleines Nullerl

Little Zeros

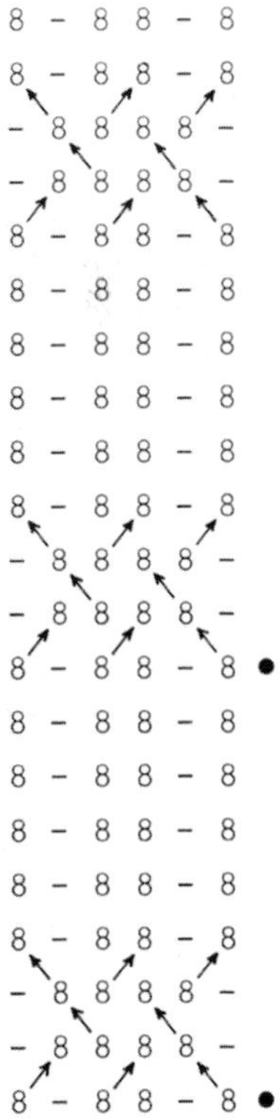

84
Jagersteig

Hunter's Path

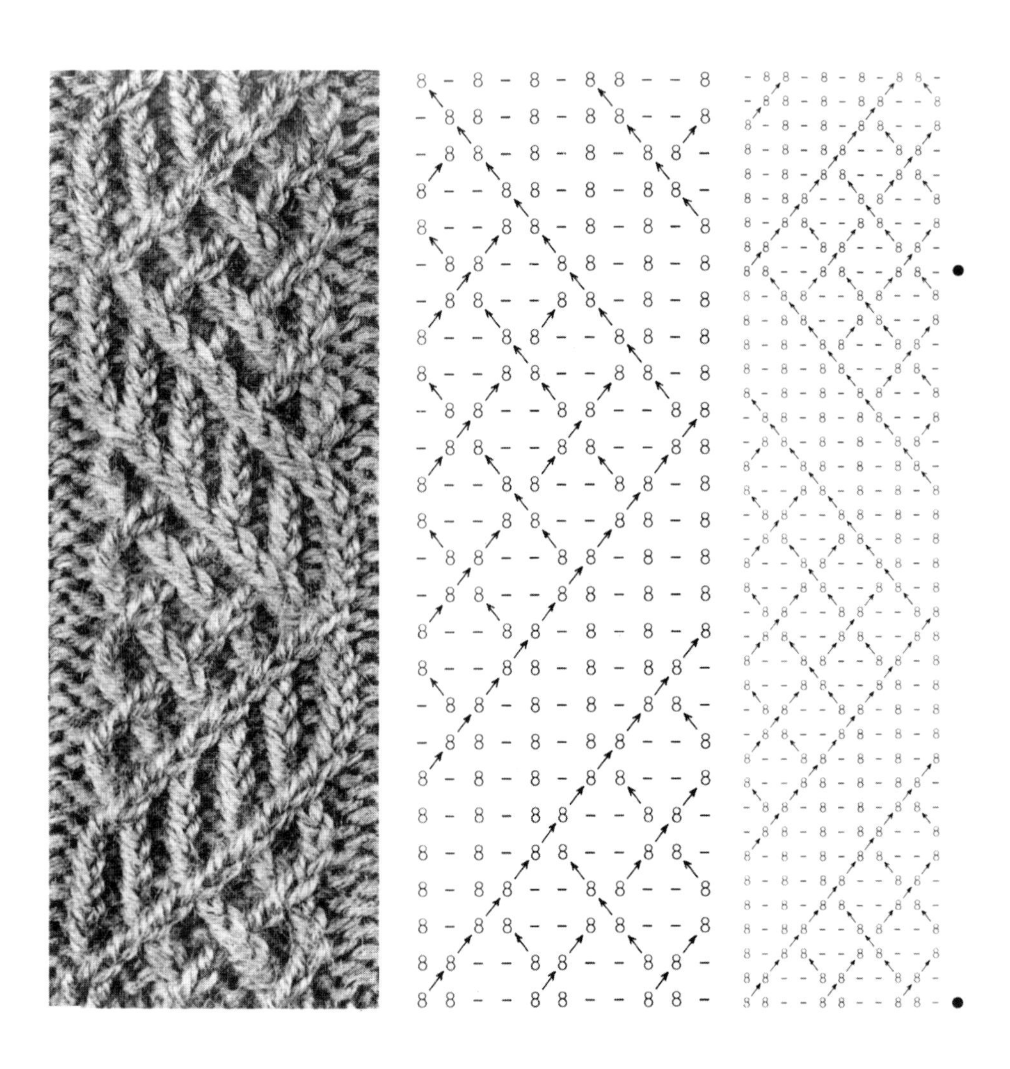

85

Seewigtaler Model

Seewigtaler Pattern

86
Doppelte Fischgräte

Double Fish Bone

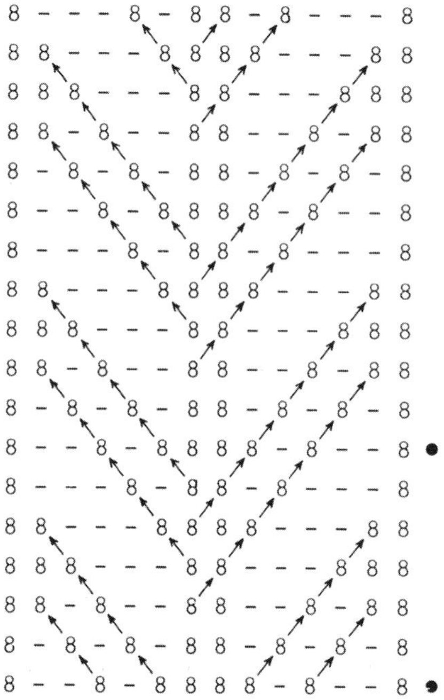

87
Glattes Ketterl

Smooth Chain

See helpful drawing on chart #65.

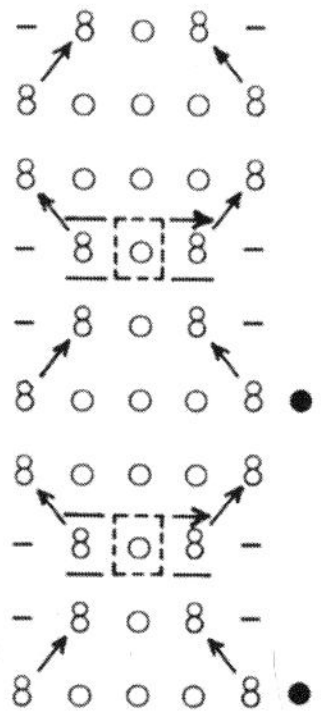

88
Hexnhaxn

Witch's Legs

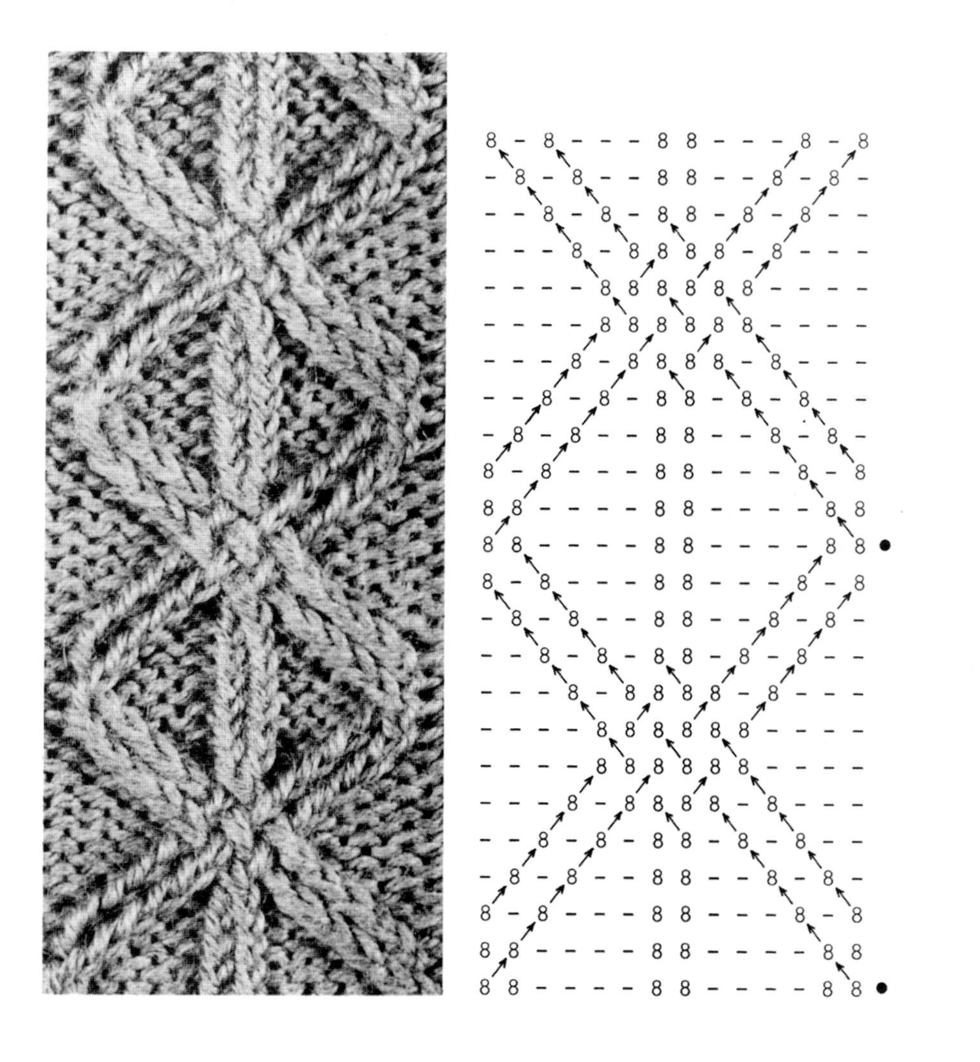

89
Zentimeterband

Centimeter Tape

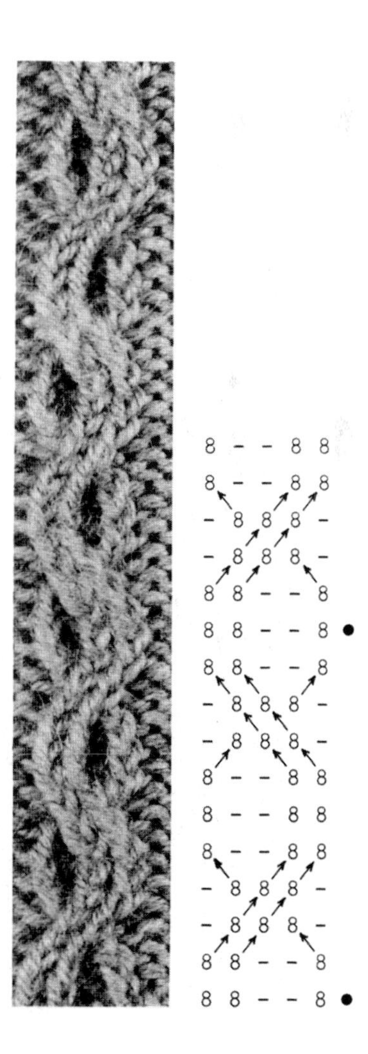

90
Spinnerin

Woman Spinner, #2

91
Großes Ketterl mit Drahdi

Large Chain with Twisted Bands

92
Doppelkette mit Drahdi

Double Chain with Twisted Bands

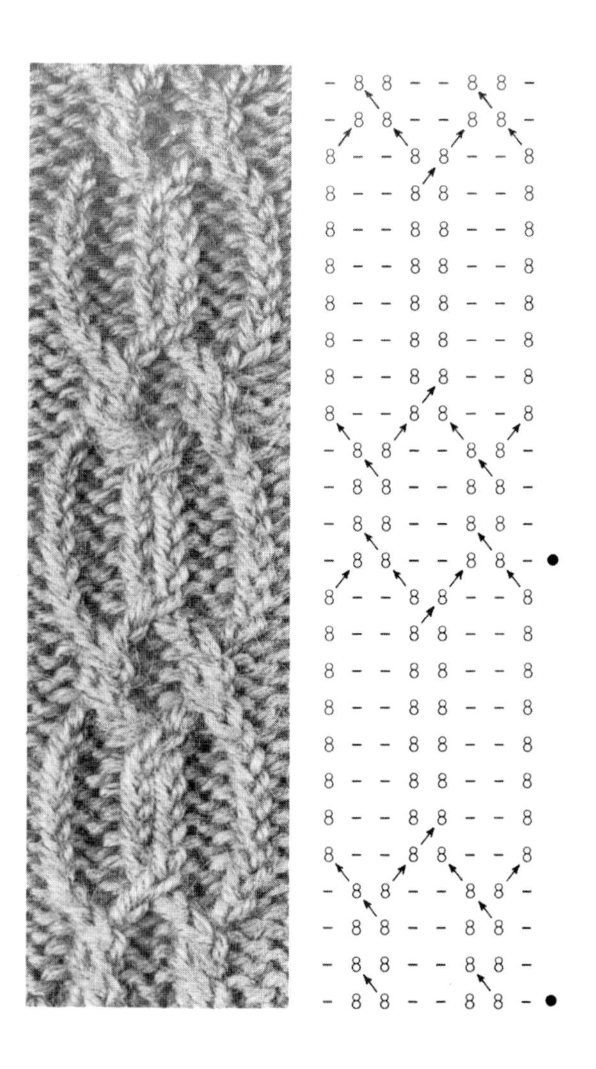

93
Doppelketterl

Double Chain, #3

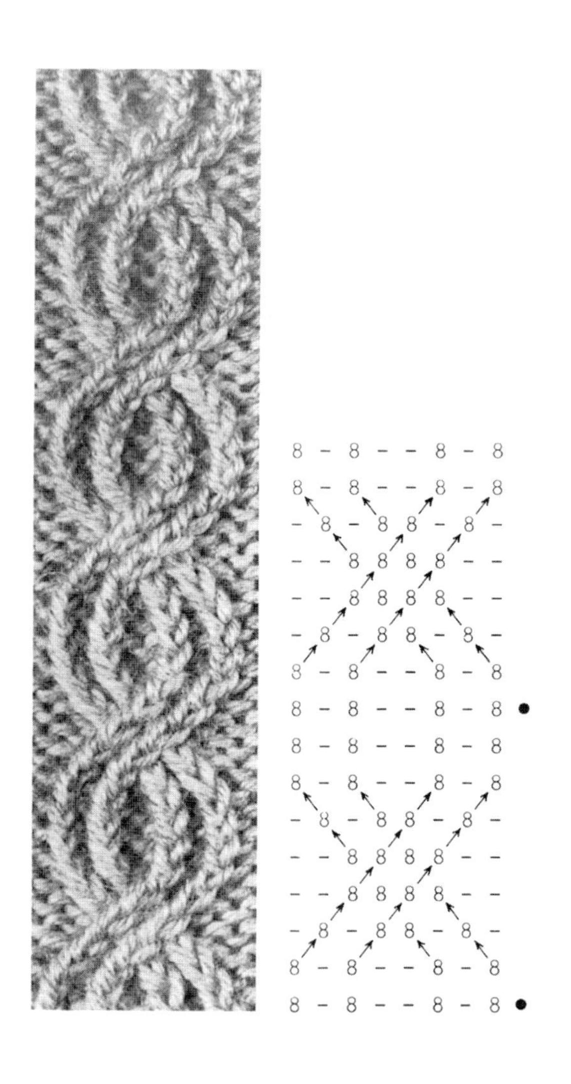

94
Vergessene Liab

Forgotten Love, #3

95
Salzburger Model

Salzburg Pattern, #1

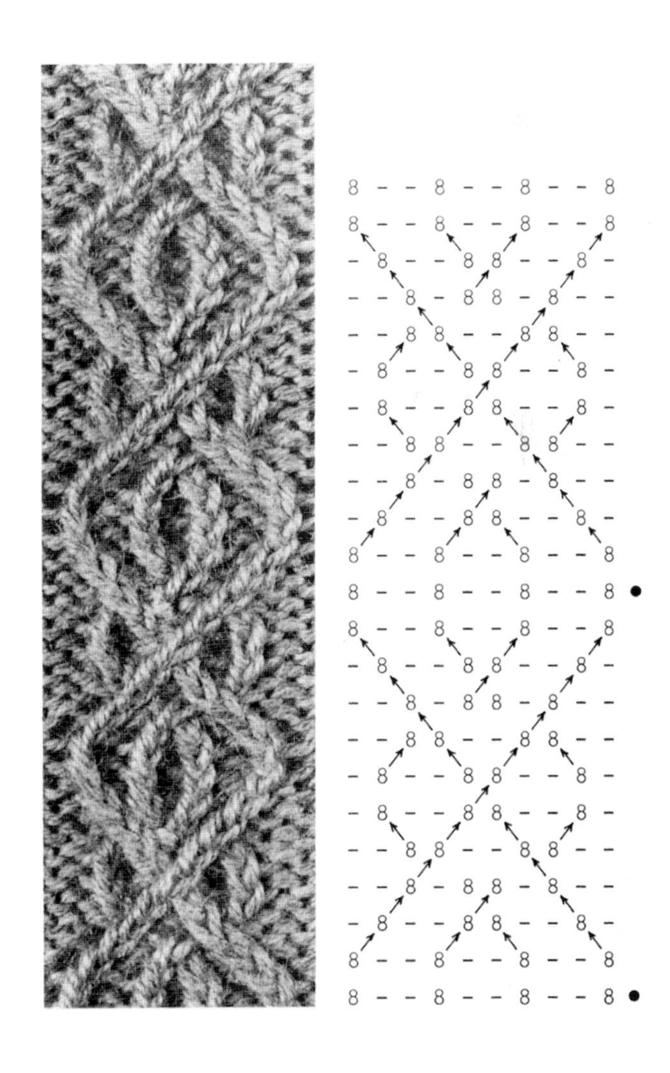

96

Kreuzband

Crossing Ribbons

97

Bandzwickel

Ribbon Insert

98
Weitband

Wide Band

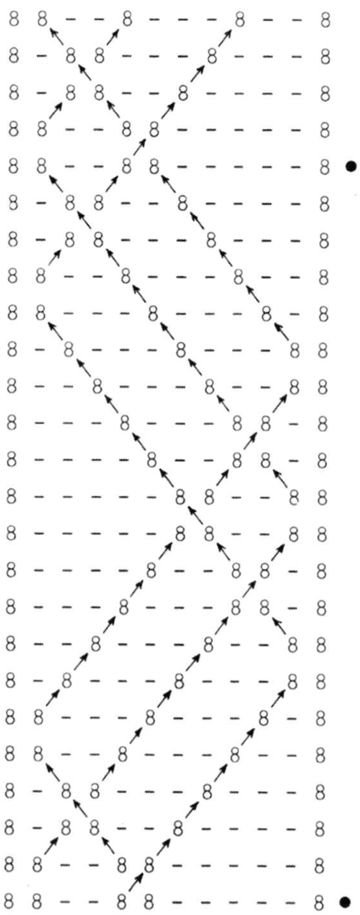

99
Großes Durchschlupfketterl

Large Slip-Through Chain

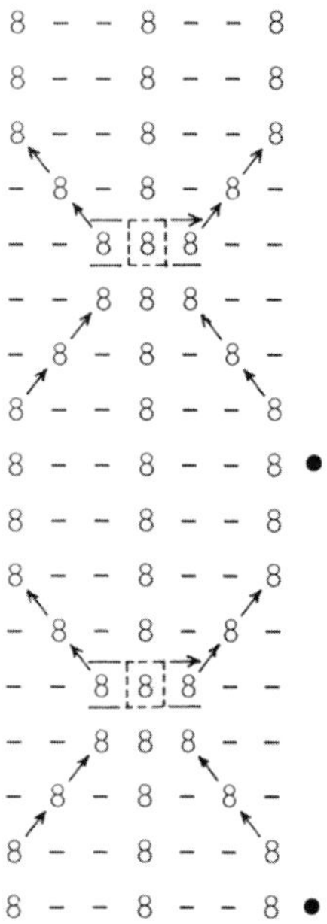

100
Dreifaches Ketterl mit Almweg

Triple Chain with Alpine Path

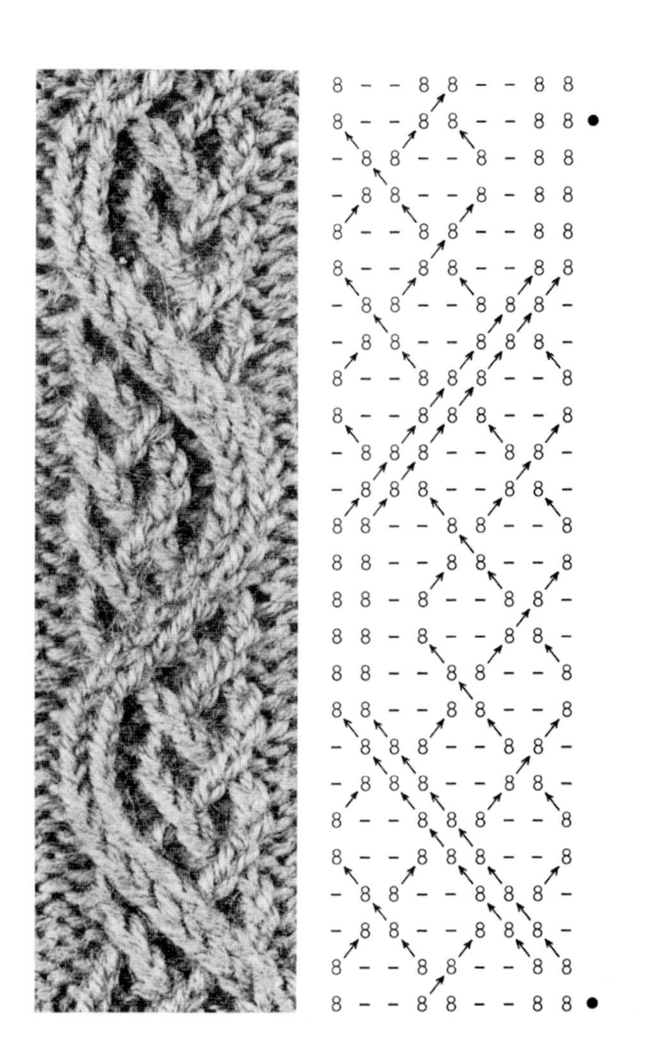

101
Untertaler Strumpfmodel

Stocking Pattern from Untertal

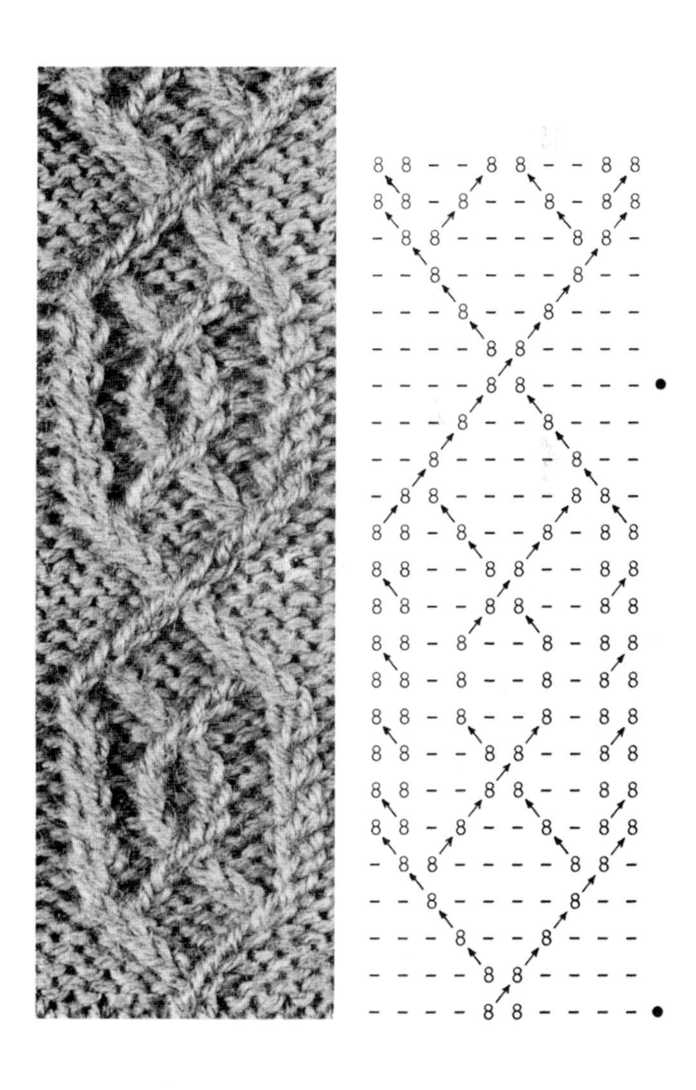

102
Kornähre

Ear of Wheat, #2

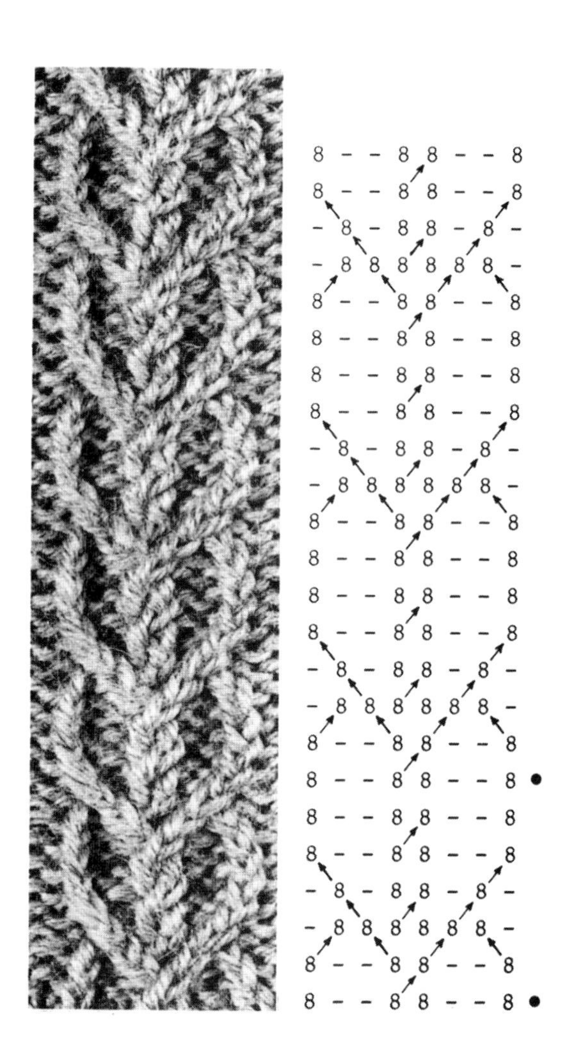

103
Tulpe

Tulip

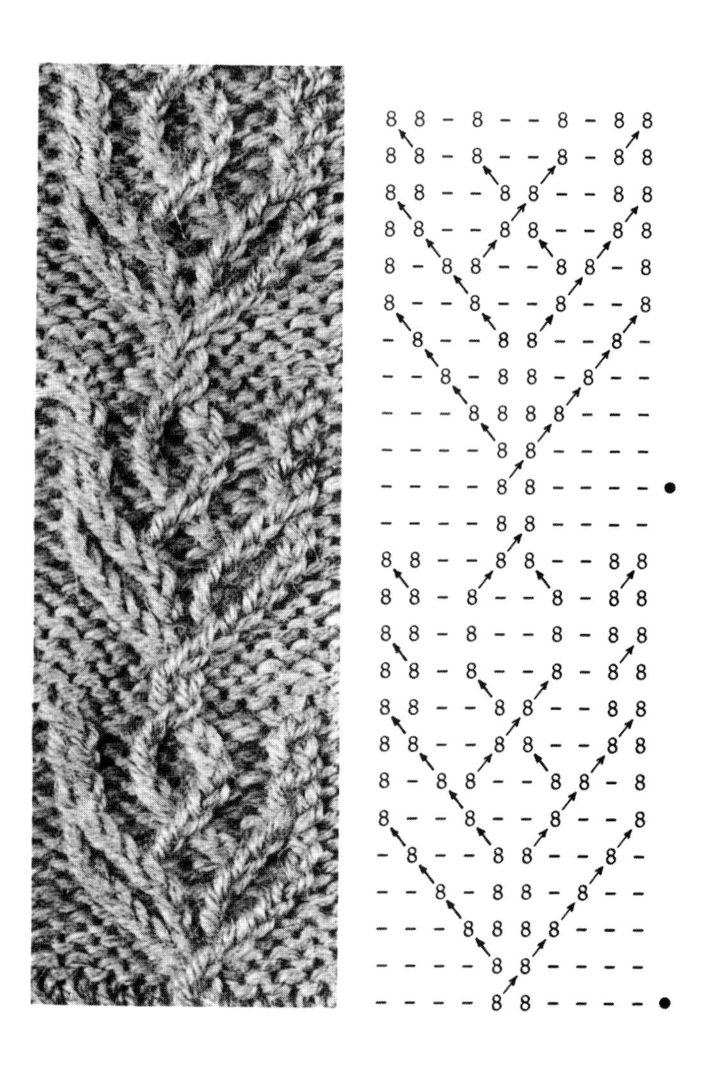

104
Hauser Model

Hauser Pattern

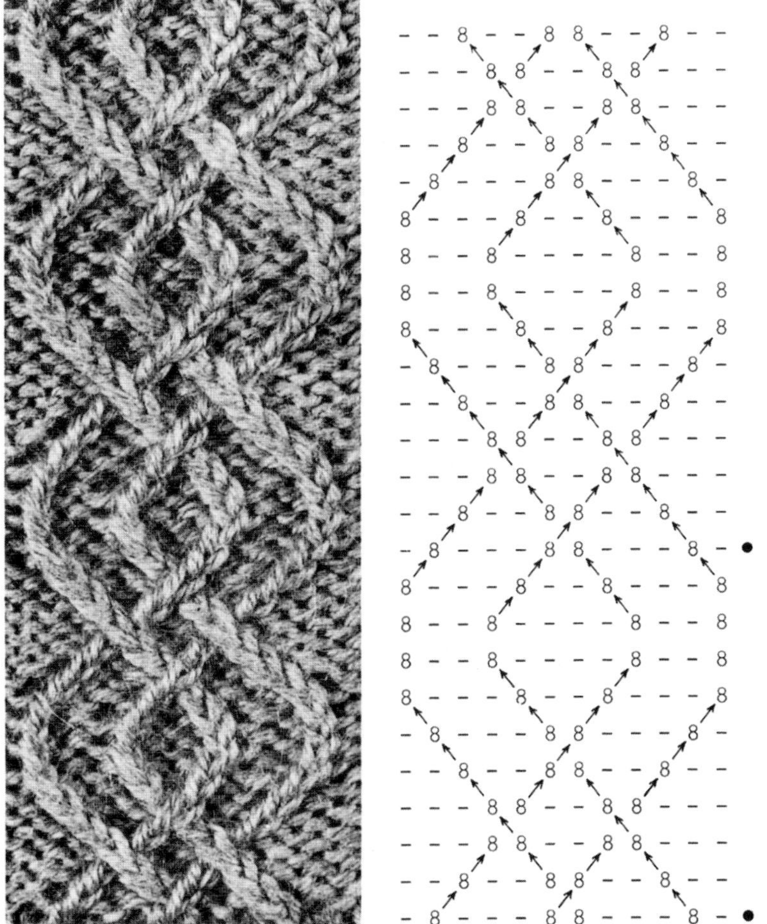

105
Bandmodel

Band Stitch, #2

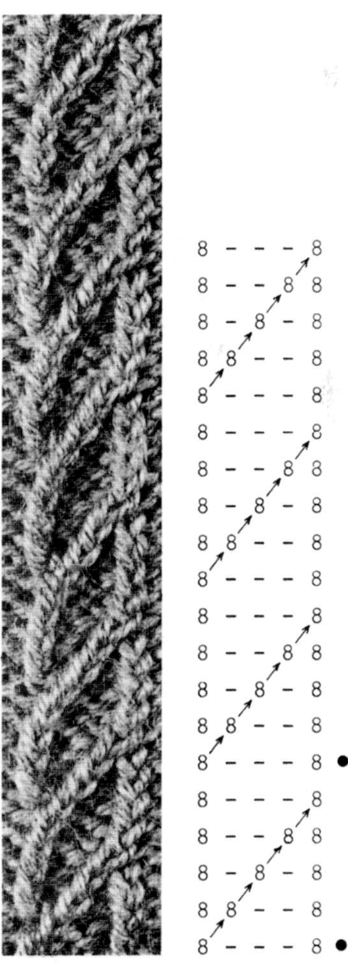

106
Dreifacher Zopf

Triple Braid

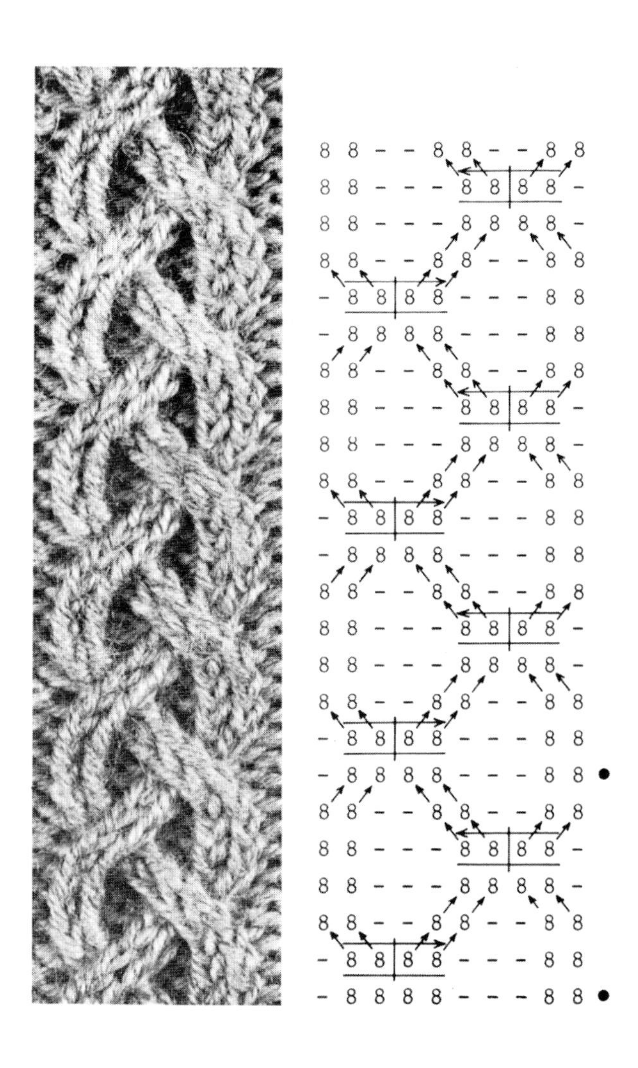

107
Vierfache Drahdikette

Quadruple Twisted Ribbon Chain

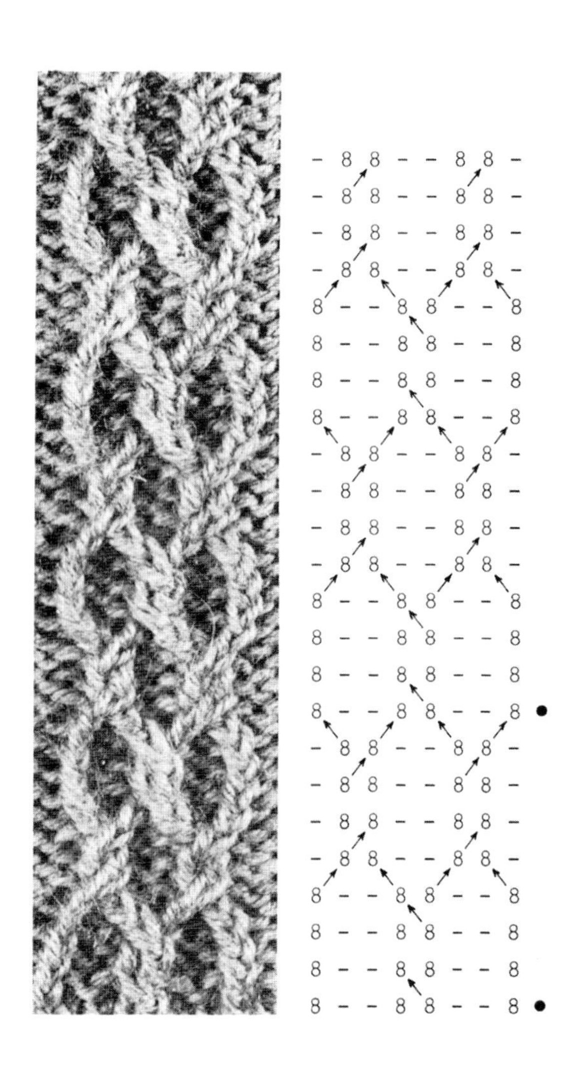

108
Gumpentaler Model

Gumpen Valley Pattern

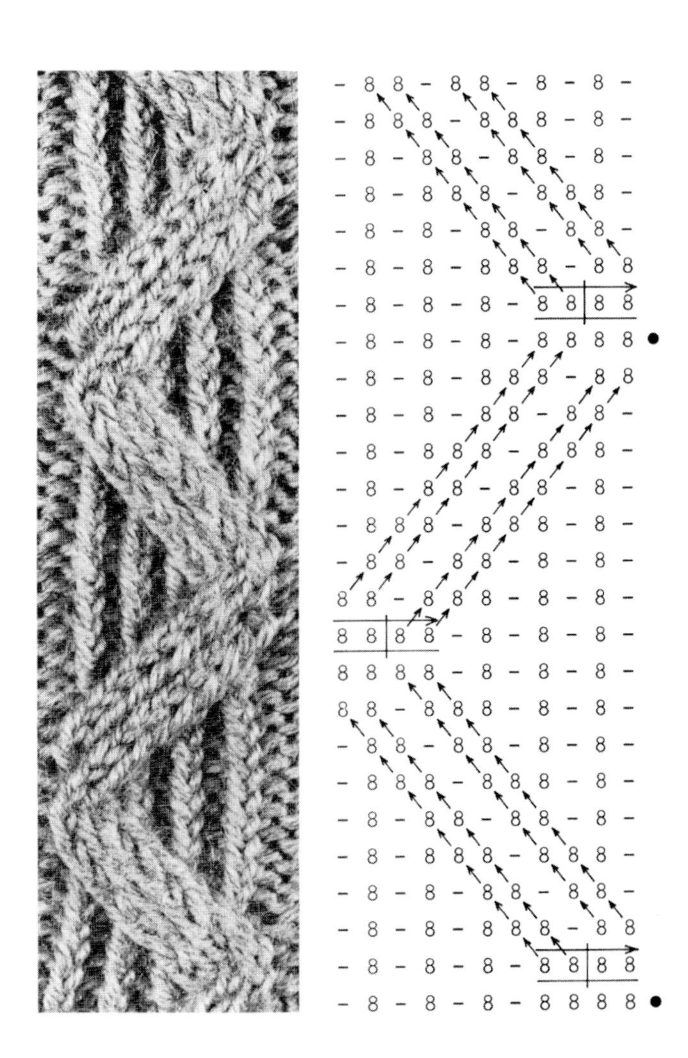

109
Ennslinger Model

Ennsling Pattern

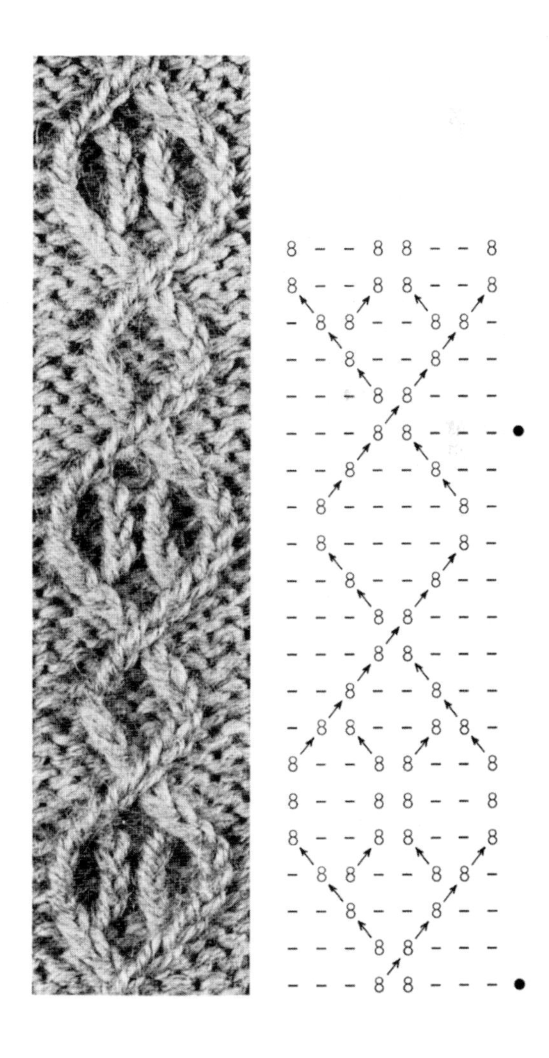

110
Sölkner Model

Sölken Pattern

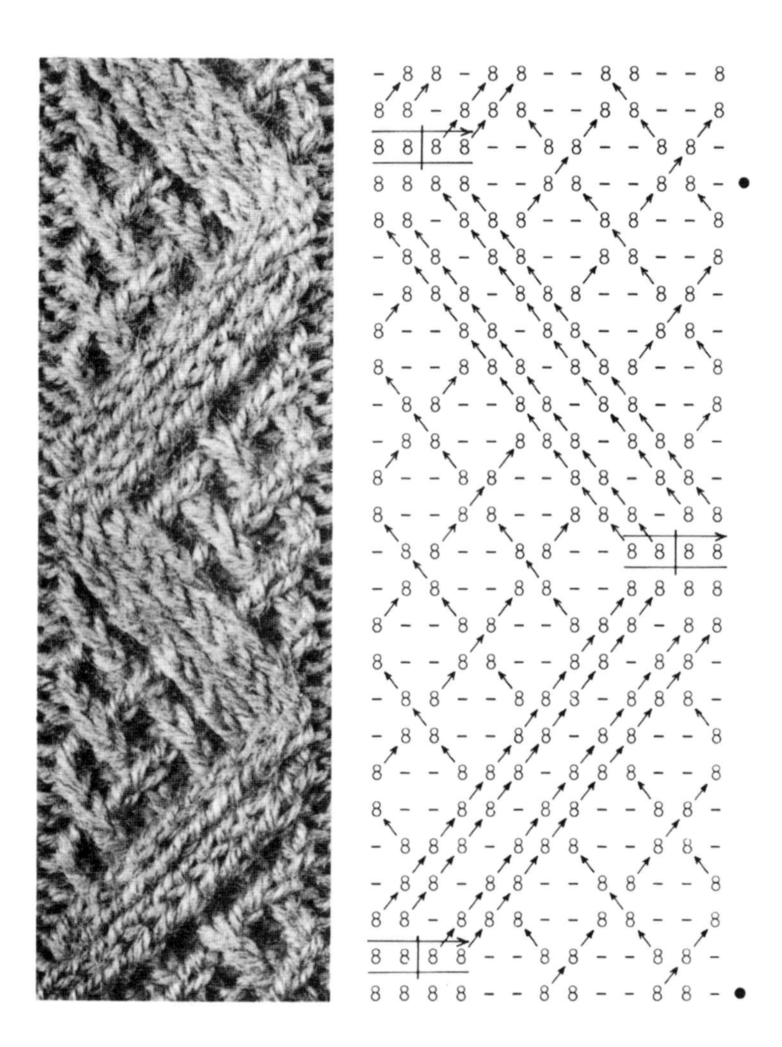

111
Zopf

Braid, #2

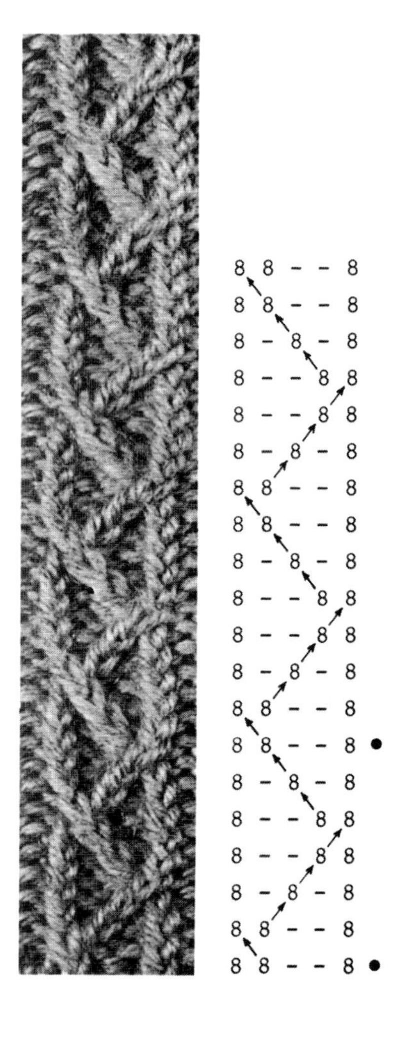

112
Offene Liab

Open Love

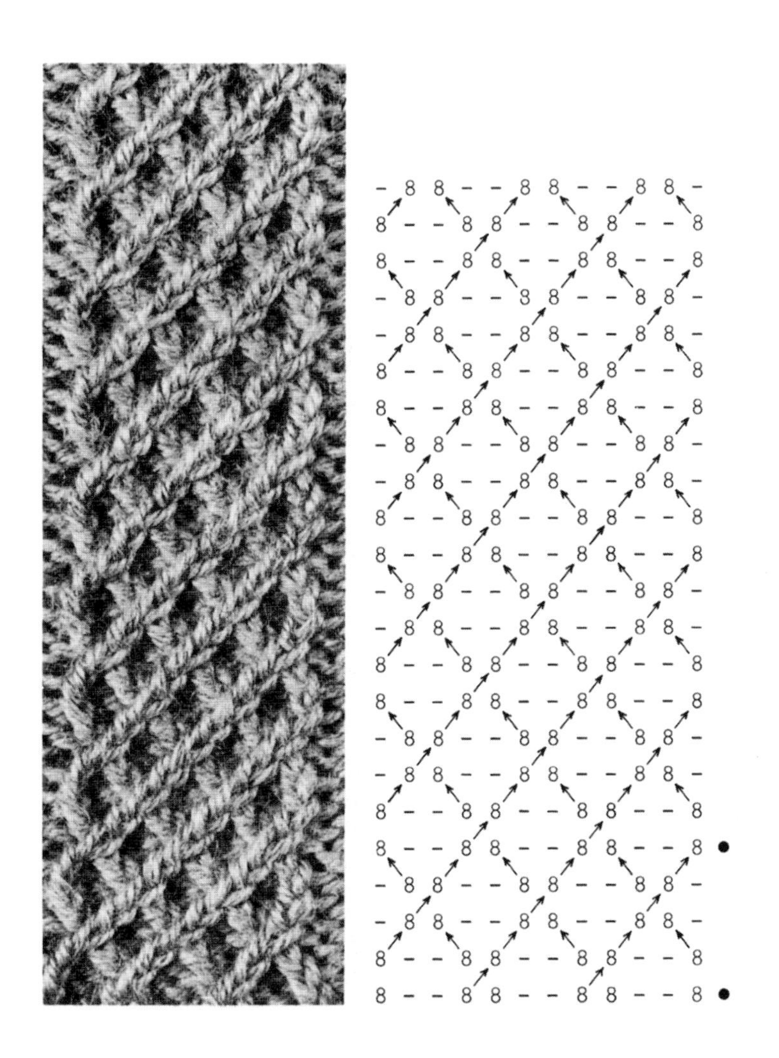

113
Hahntritt

Rooster Steps

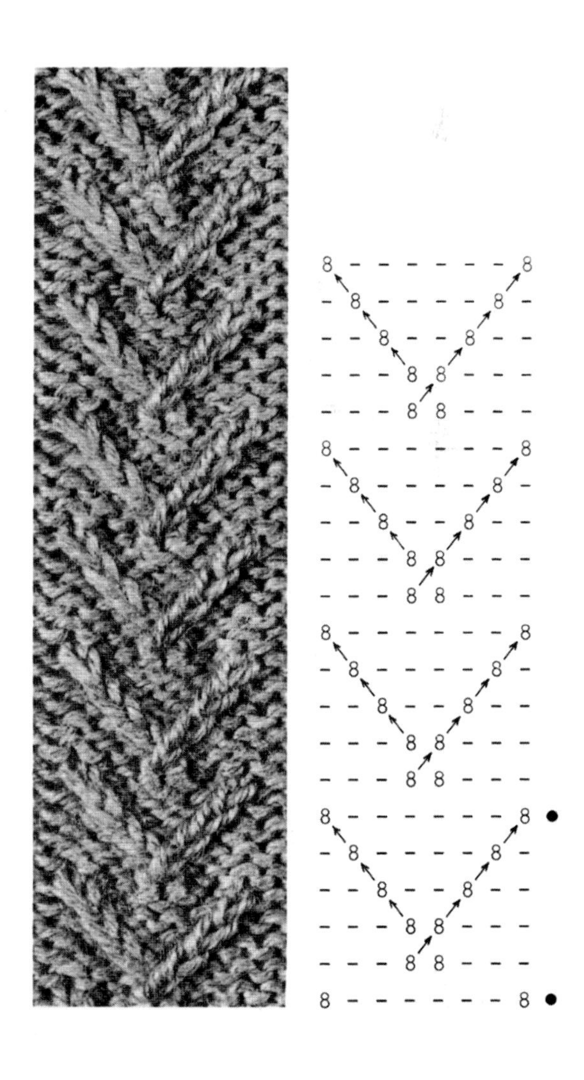

114
Bäumchen

Little Tree

115
Tulpenketterl mit Fenster

Tulip Chain with Window

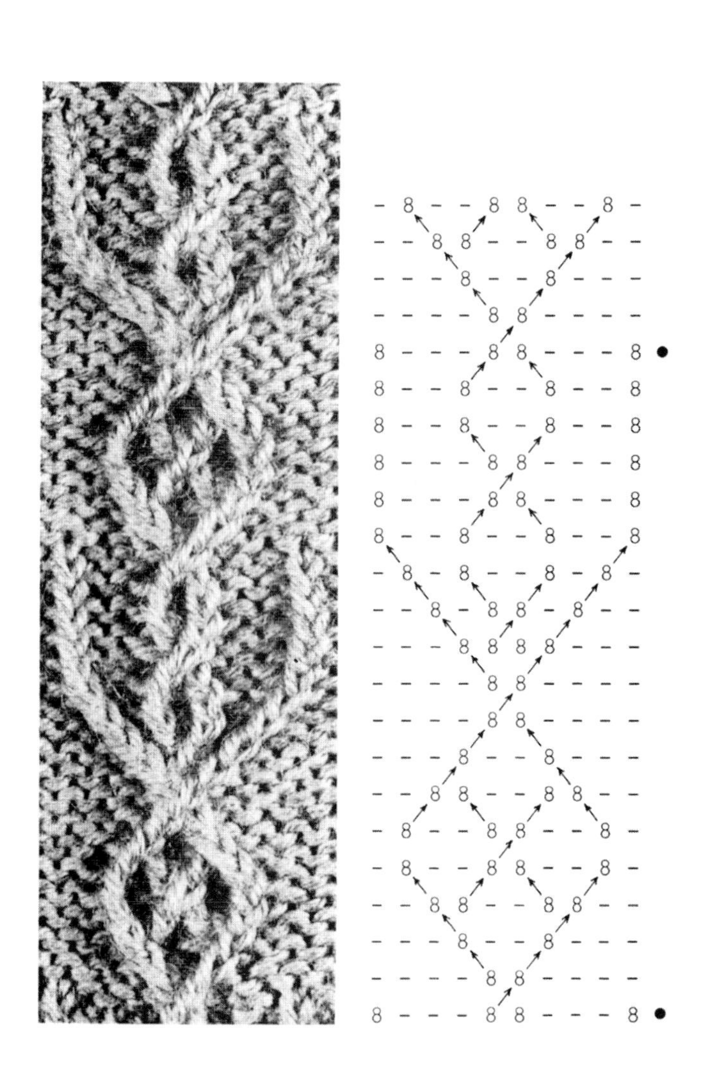

116
Doppelviereck mit Drahdi

Double Square with Twisted Band

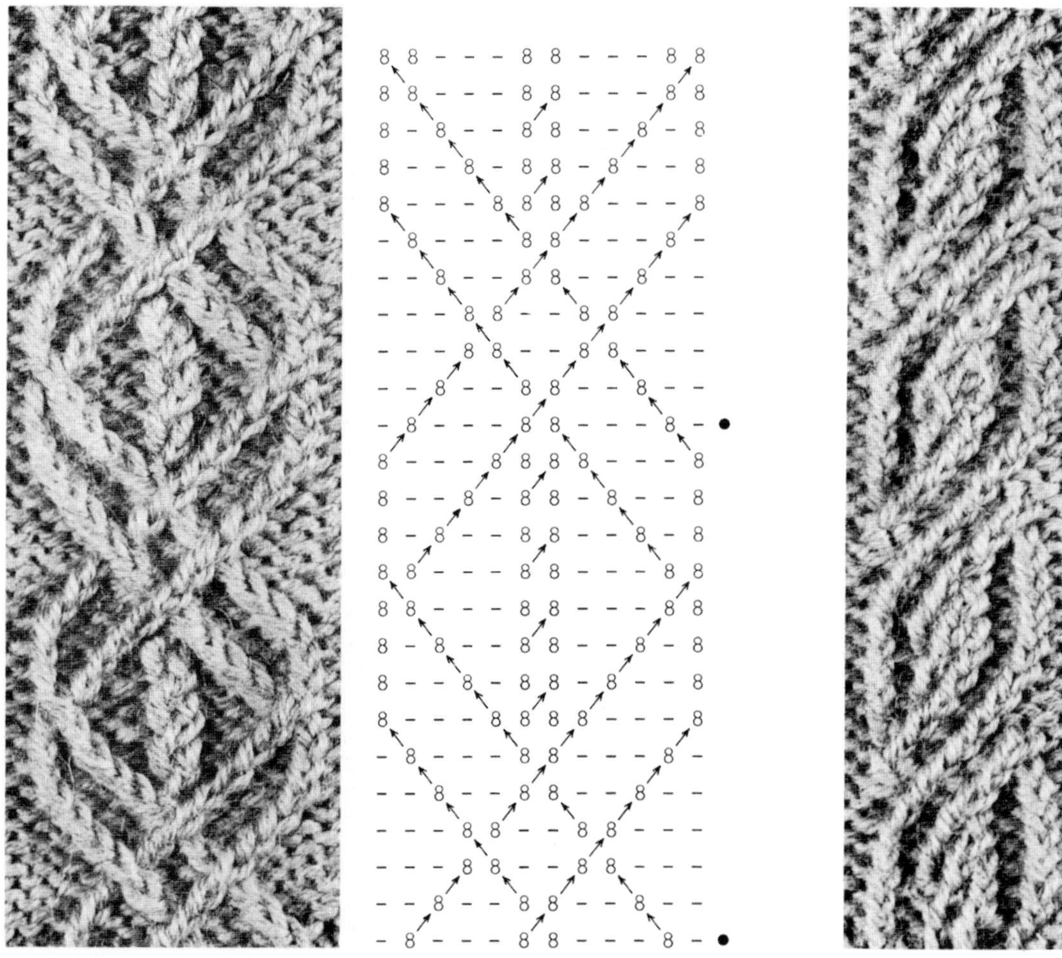

117
Schlangenmodel

Snake Pattern

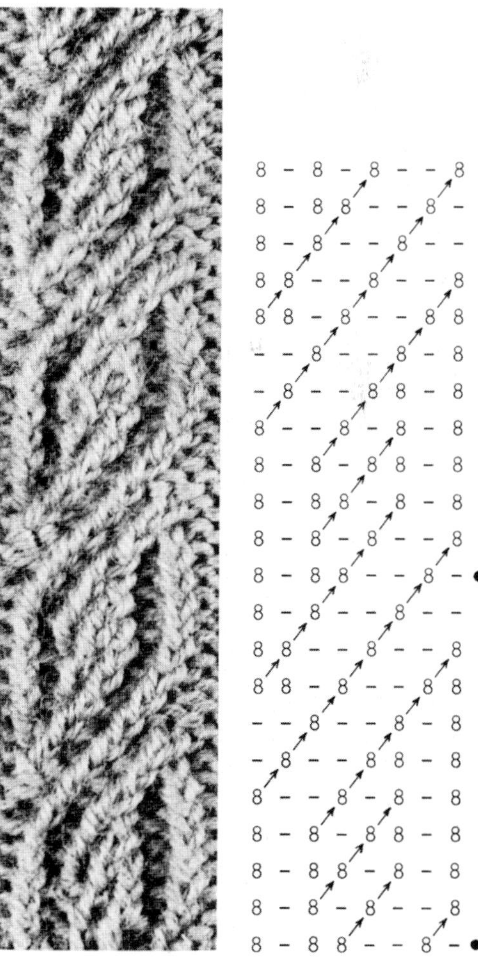

118
Weißenbacher Model

Weissenbach Pattern

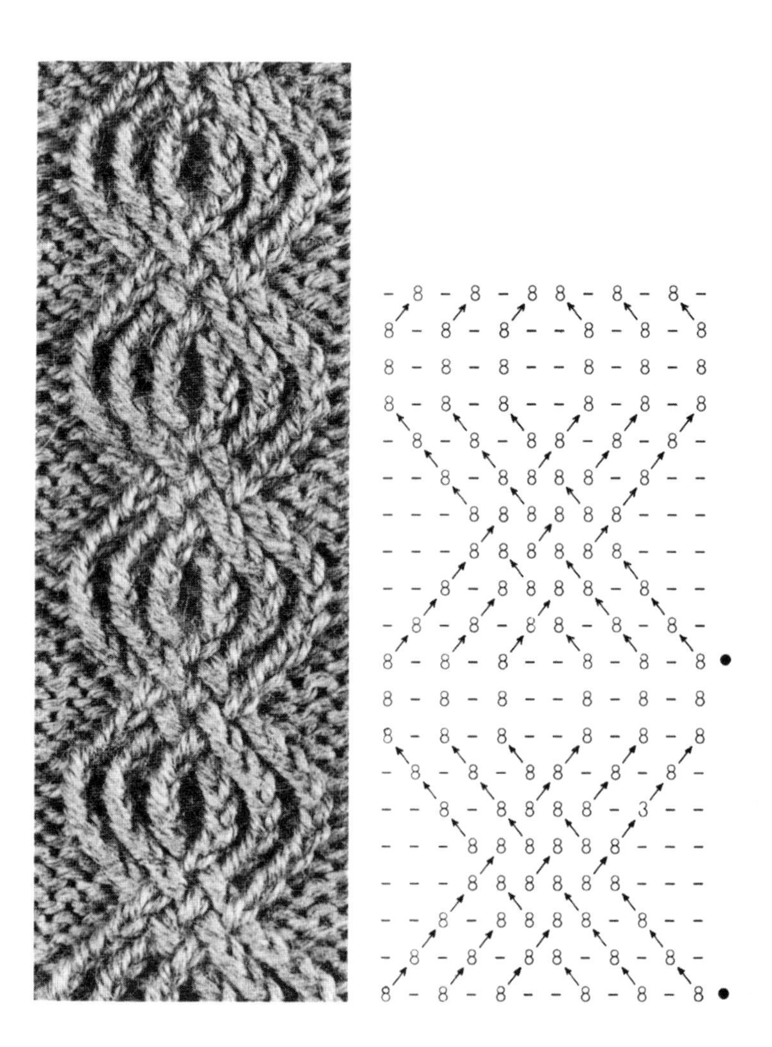

119
Kleines Doppelzopferl

Small Double Braid

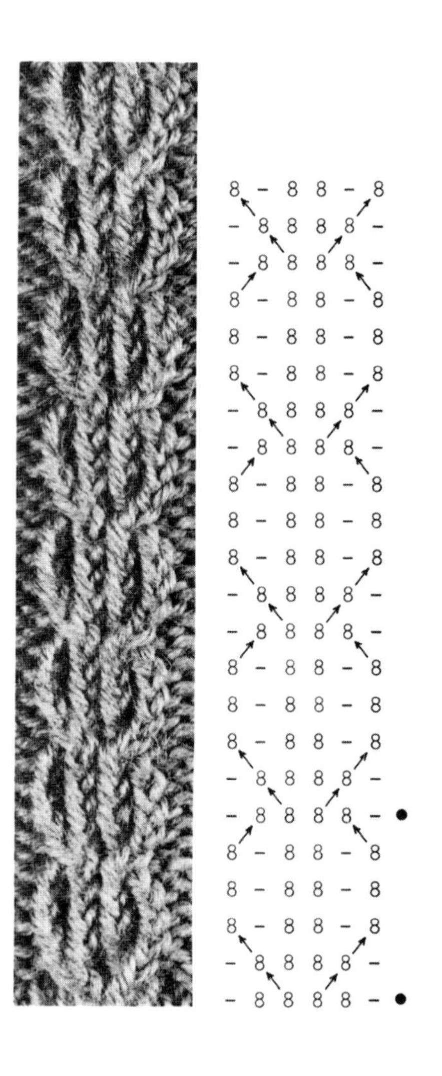

120
Stangennullen

Bar with Zeros, #2

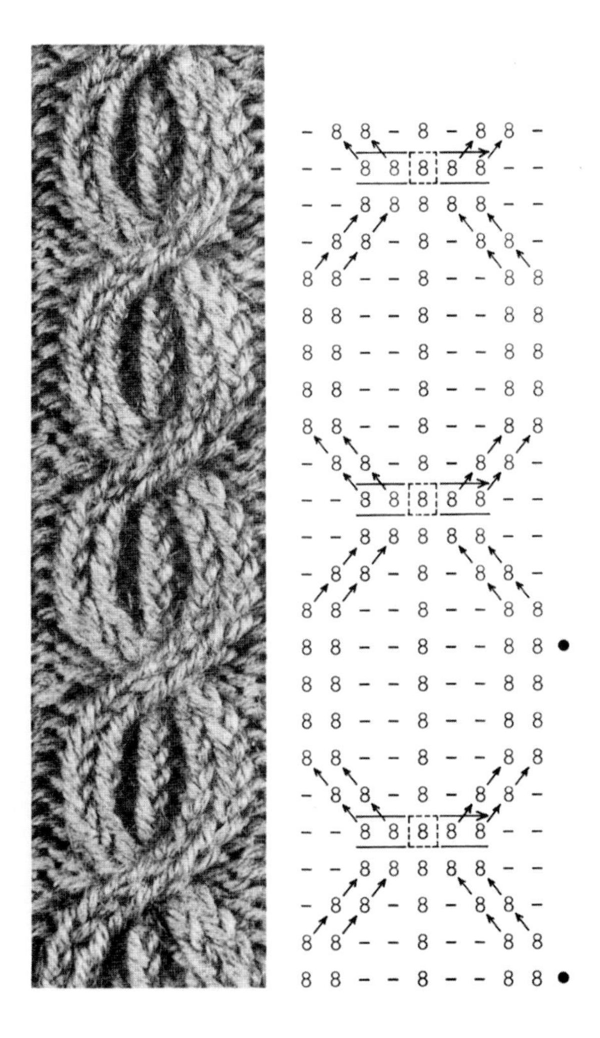

121
Ketterlfenster

Chain of Windows

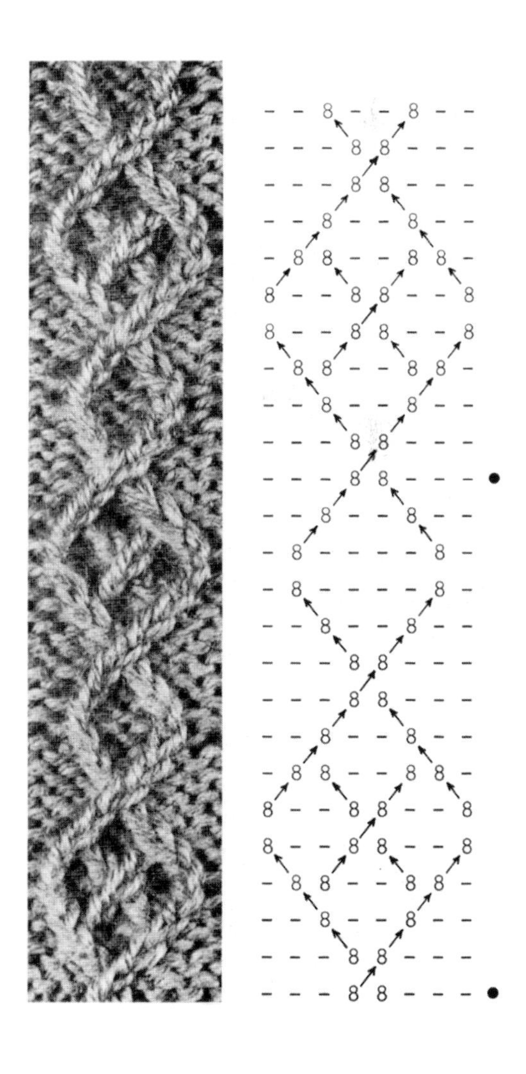

122
Dreieck

Triangle

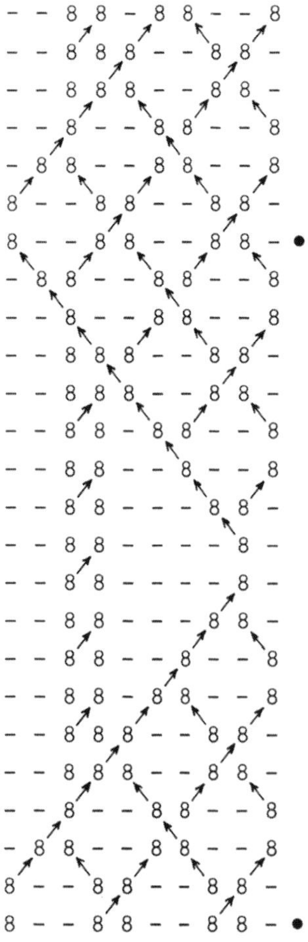

123
Kleeblatt

Clover Leaf, #4

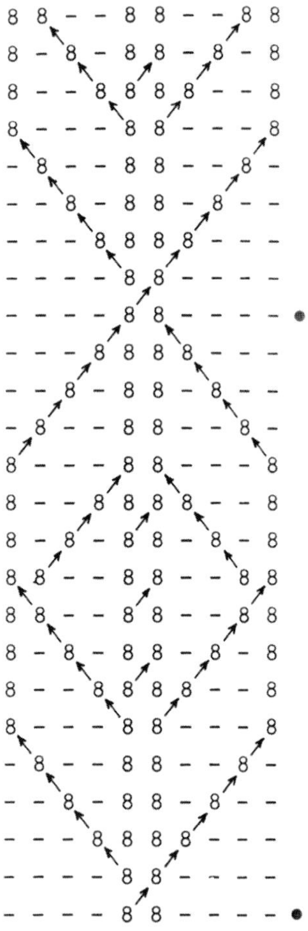

124
Kleines Doppelband mit Drahdi

Small Double Ribbon with Twisted Band

125
Doppelstiege

Double Stairs

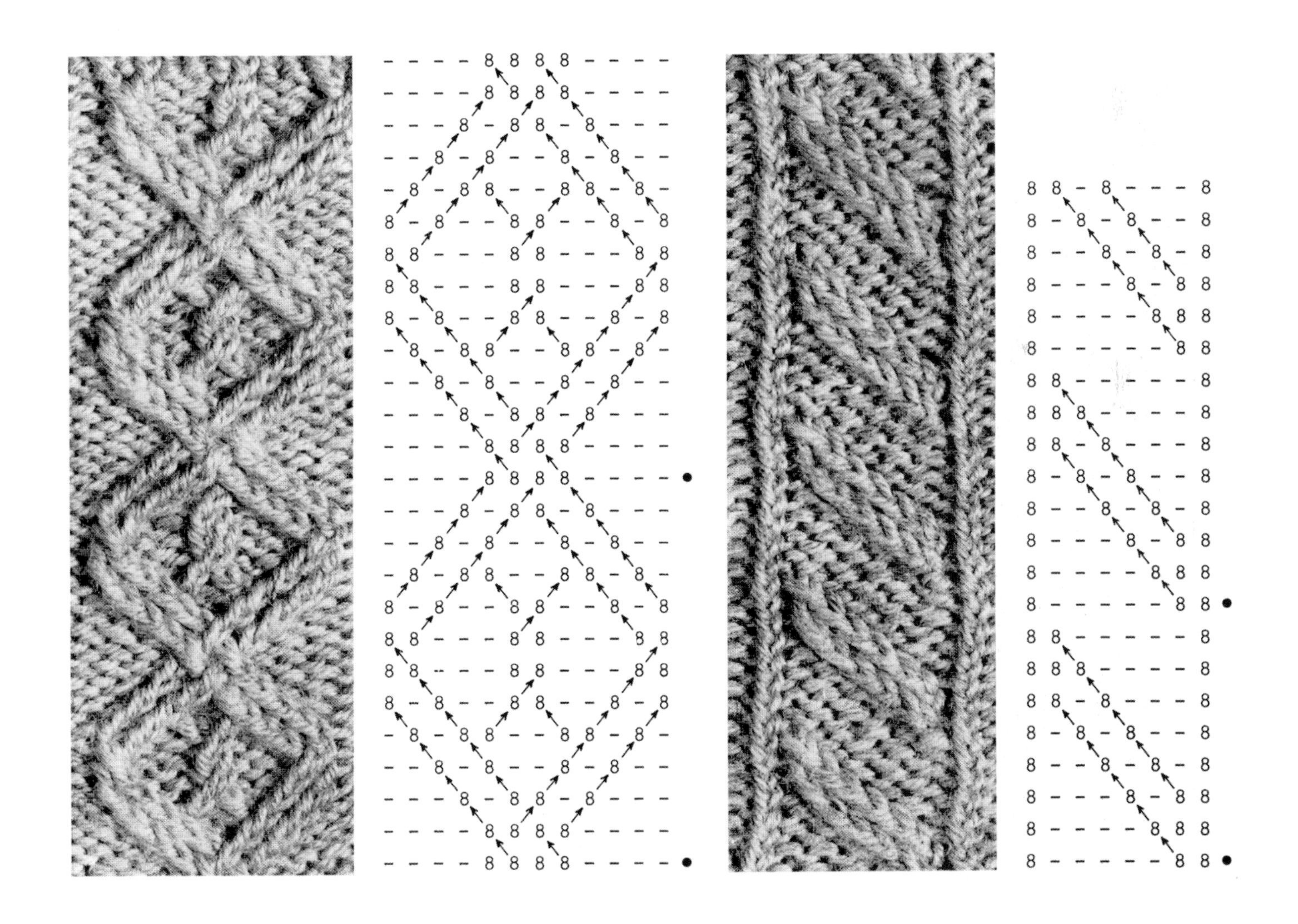

126
Traum

Dream

127
Großer Obenauf

Large Top Stitch

128
Stücklkette mit Zwetschkenkern

Pieced Chain with Plum Pit

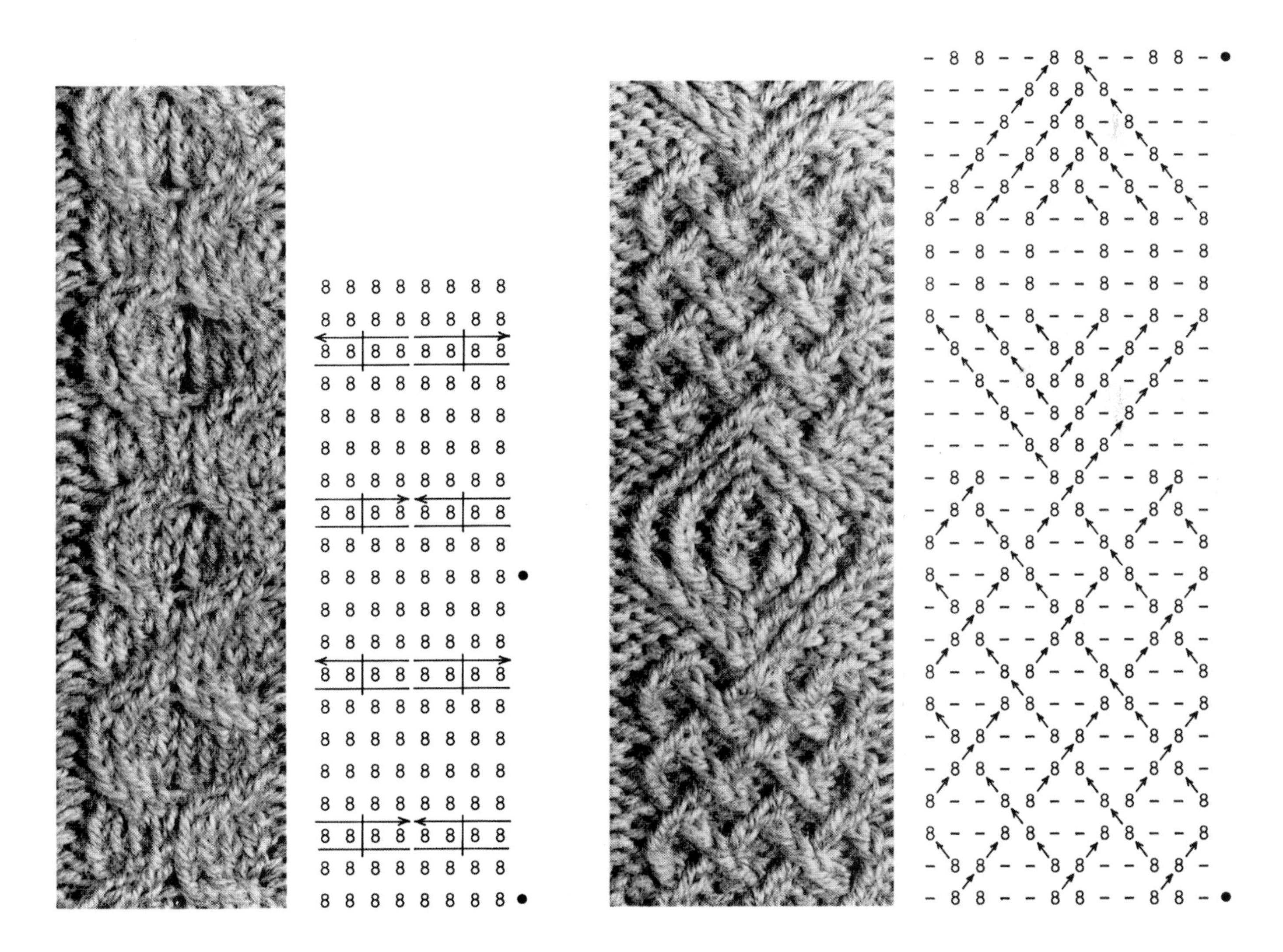

129
Fünffaches Doppelband

Quintuple Double Band

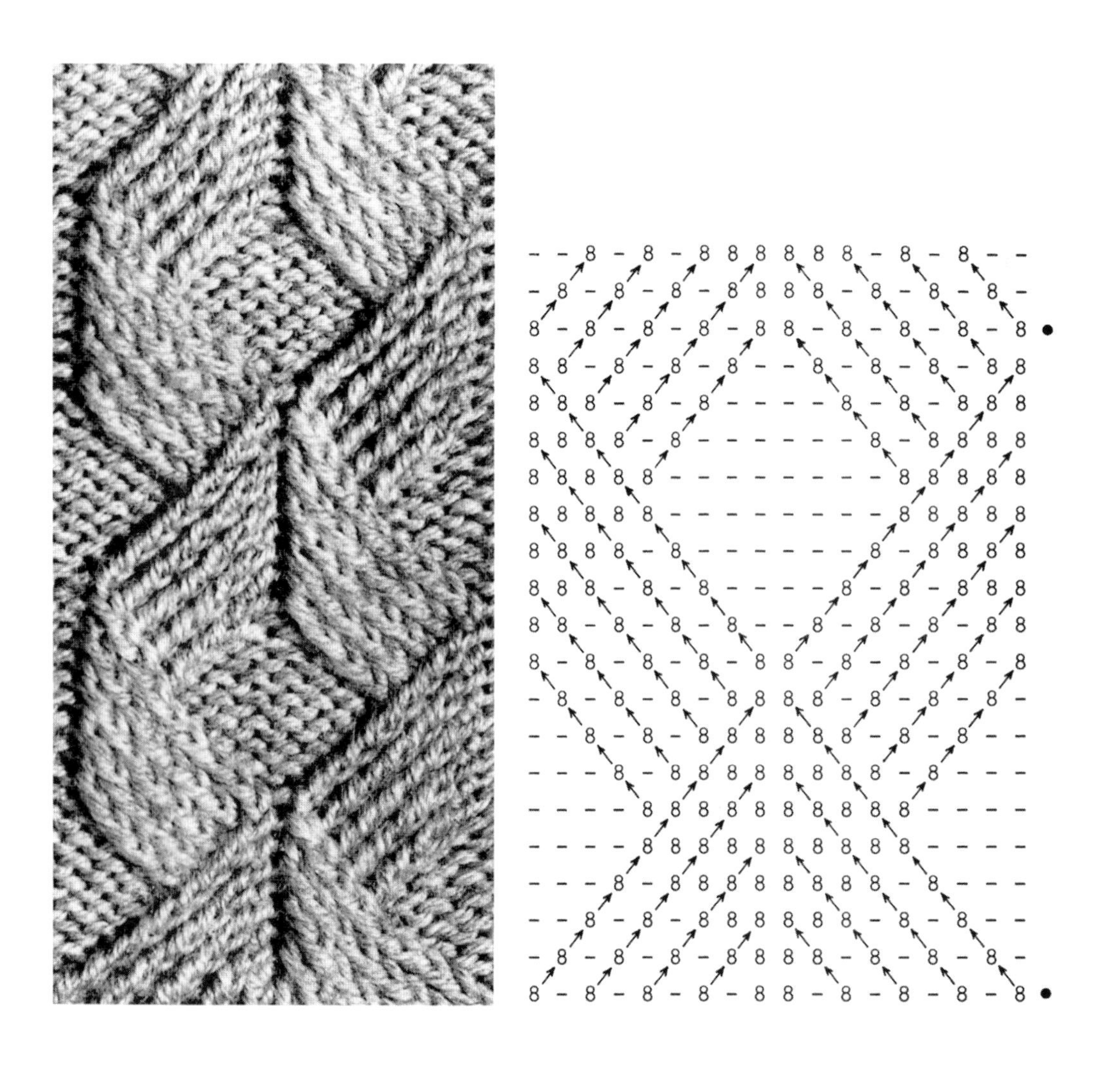

130
Tulipan mit Bäumchen

Tulips with Small Tree

131
Kettenband

Chain Band

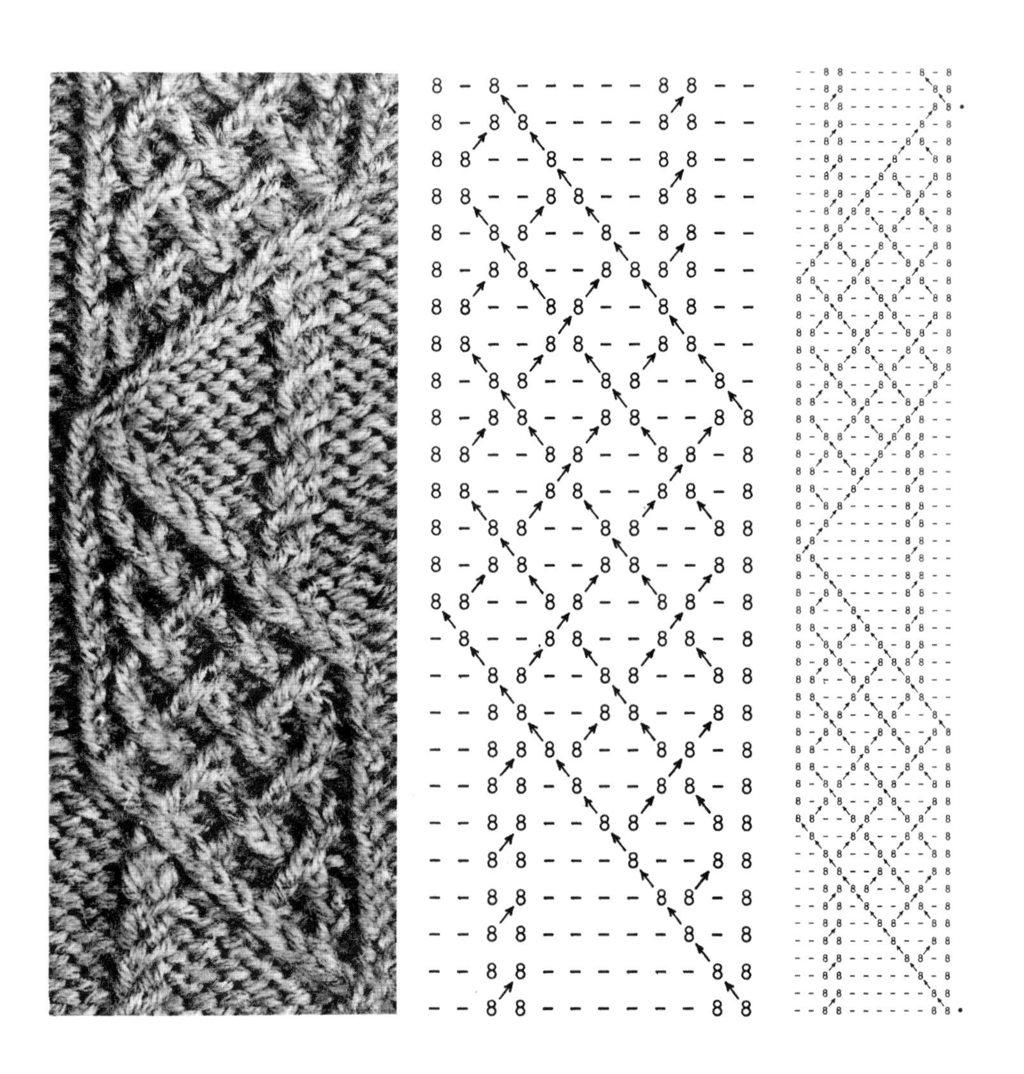

132
Kette

Chain

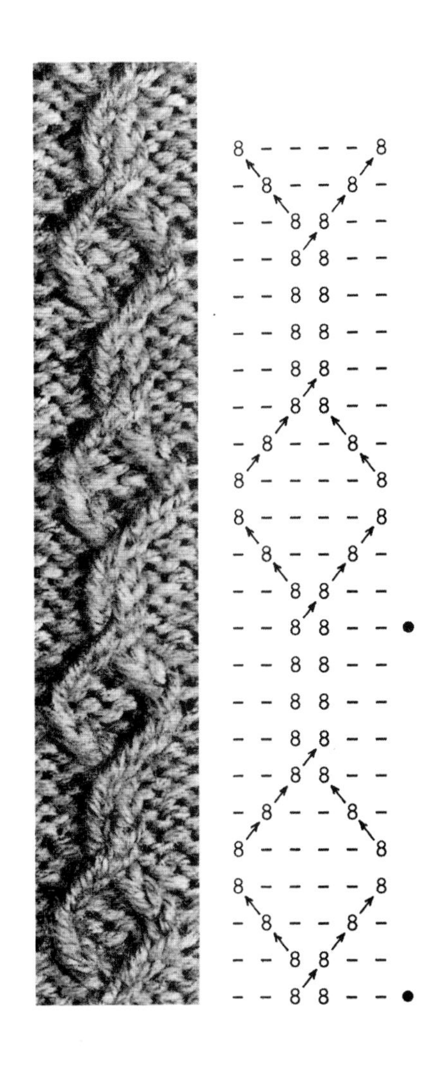

133
Dreifaches Almwegerl

Triple Small Alpine Path

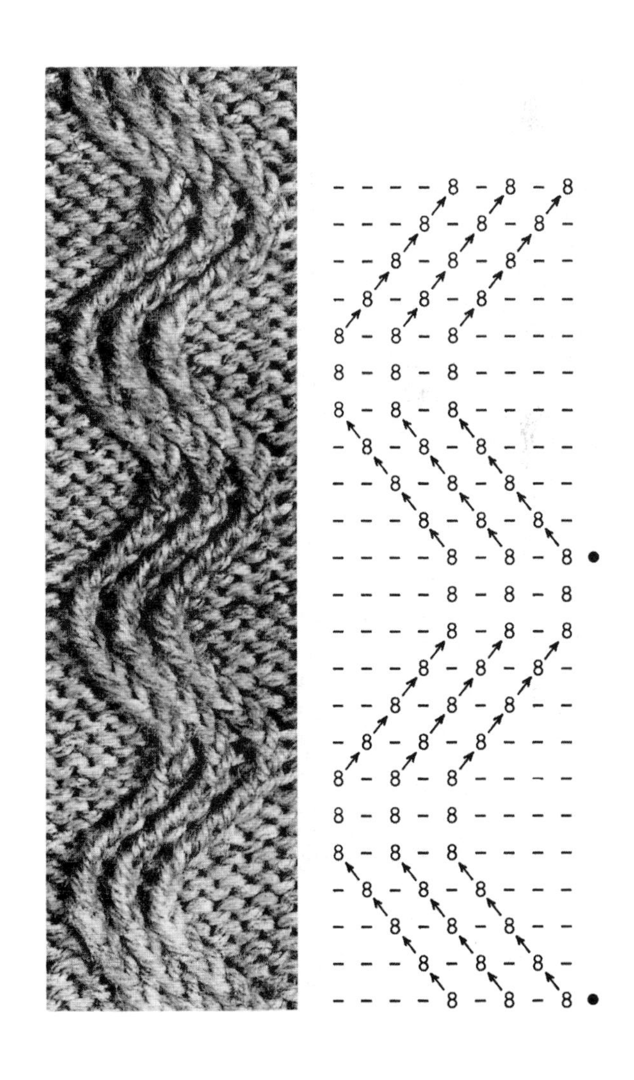

134
Zwetschkenkern mit Fenster

Plum Pit with Windows

135
Doppelzopf

Double Braid, #2

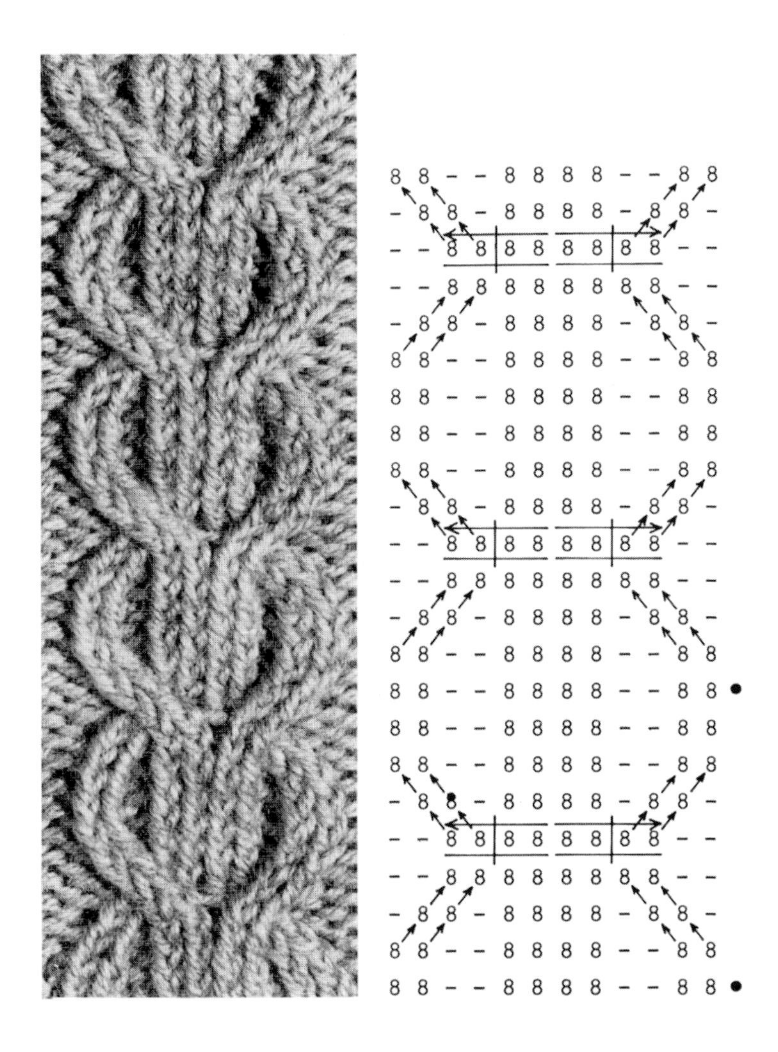

136
Zopfstreifen

Braid Stripe, #1

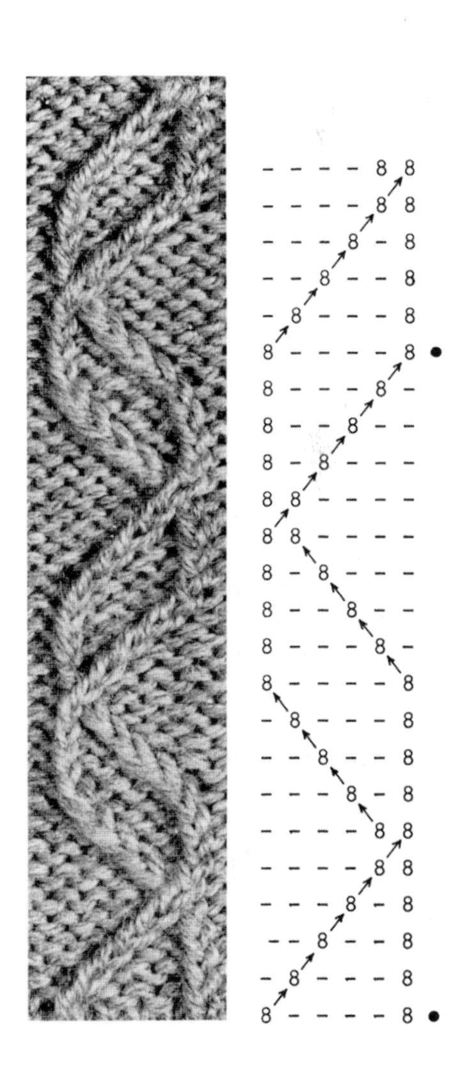

137
Doppelviereck

Double Square

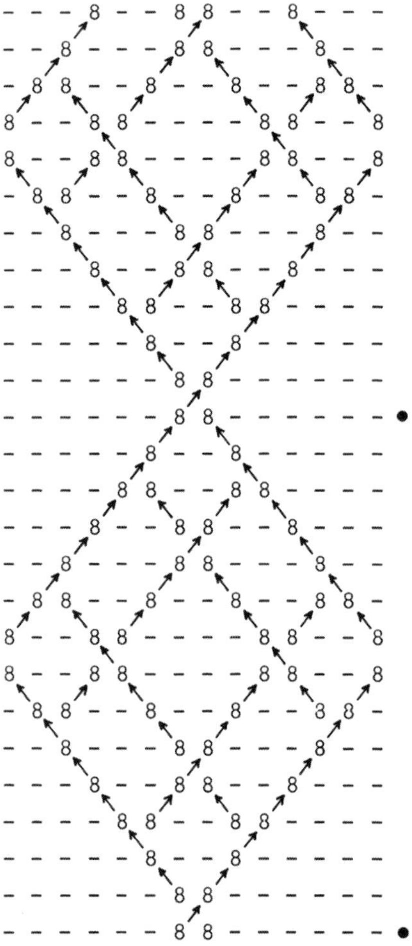

138
Zopfstreifen

Braid Stripe, #2

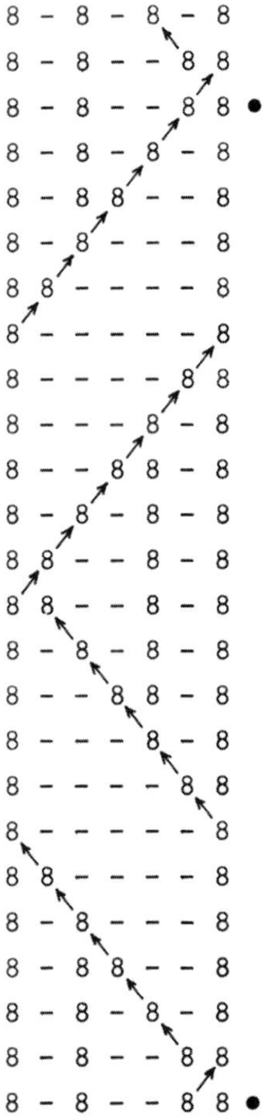

139
Salzburger Model

Salzburg Pattern, #2

140
Donnersbacher Strumpfmodel

Thunder River Stocking Pattern

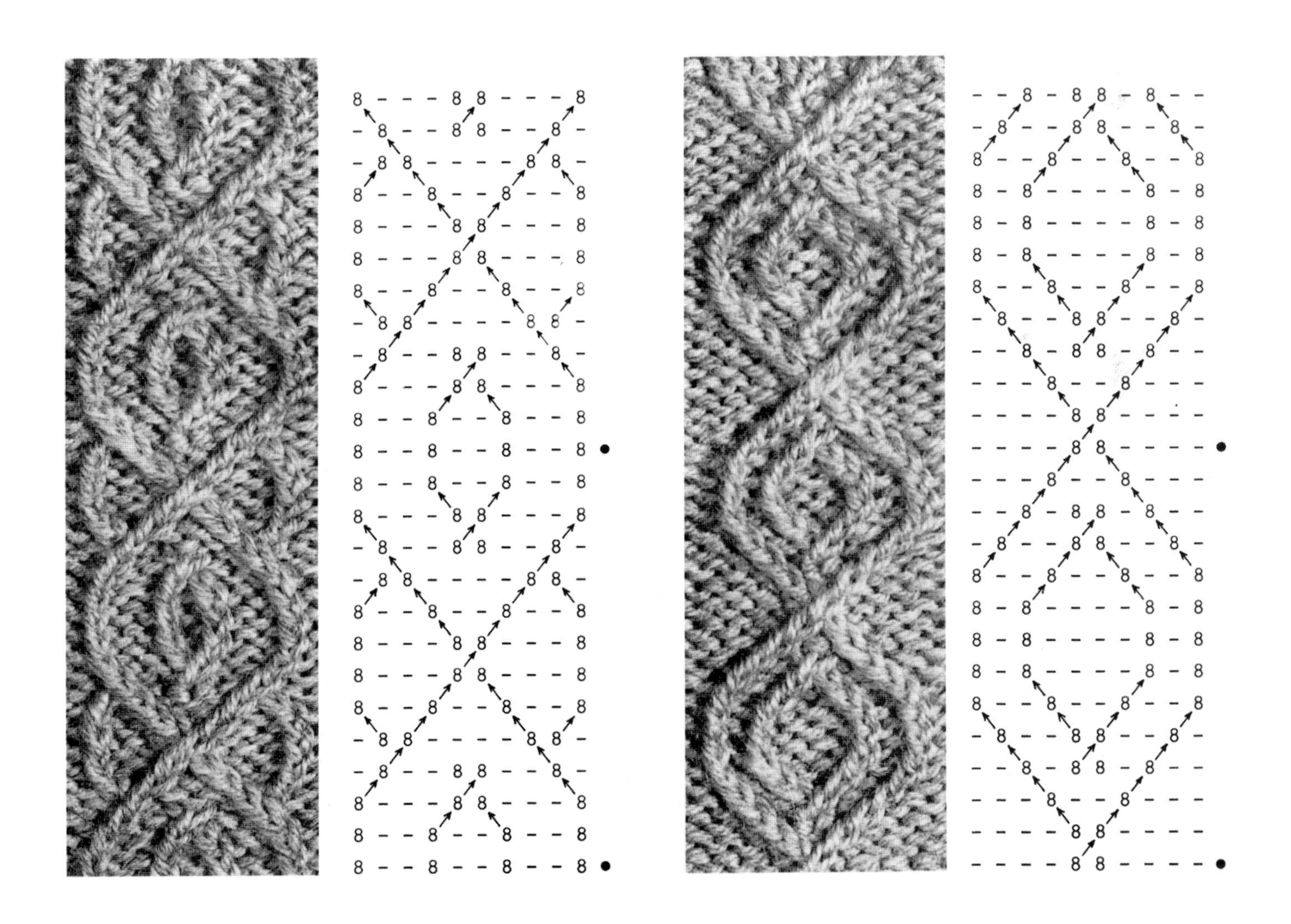

141
Ketterl

Small Chain, #2

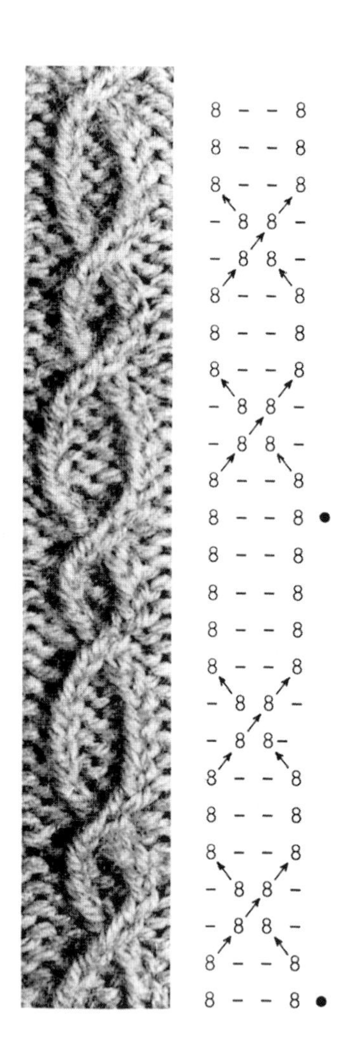

142
Zwetschkenkern

Plum Pit

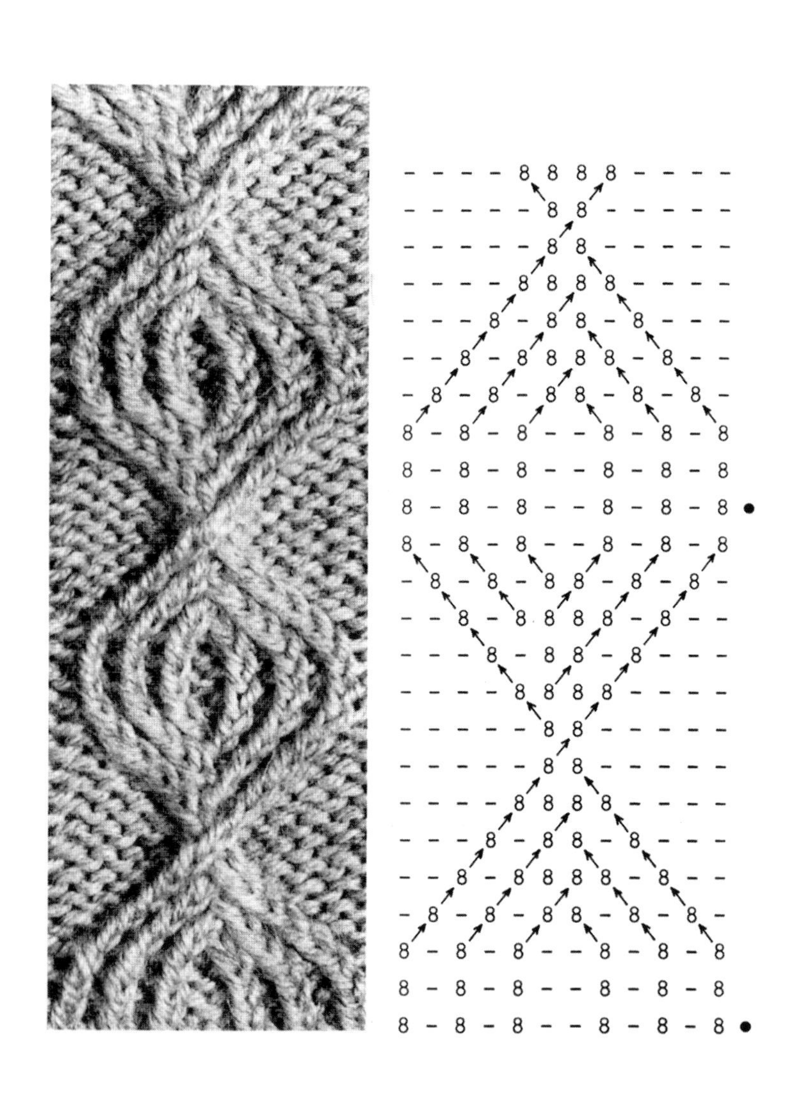

143
Tulpenmuster

Tulip Pattern, #3

144
Großes Doppelketterl

Large Double Chain

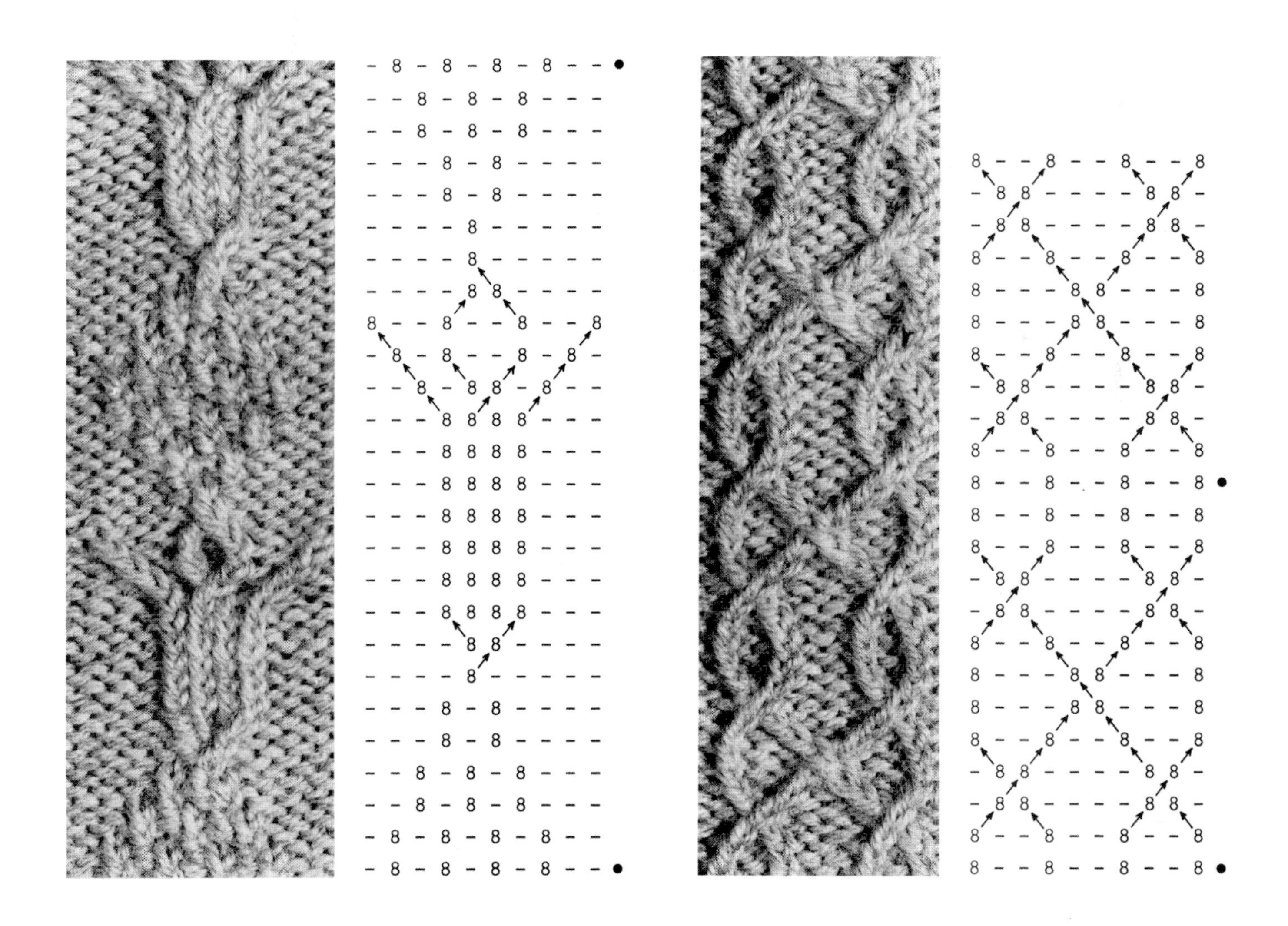

145
Blatt

Leaf

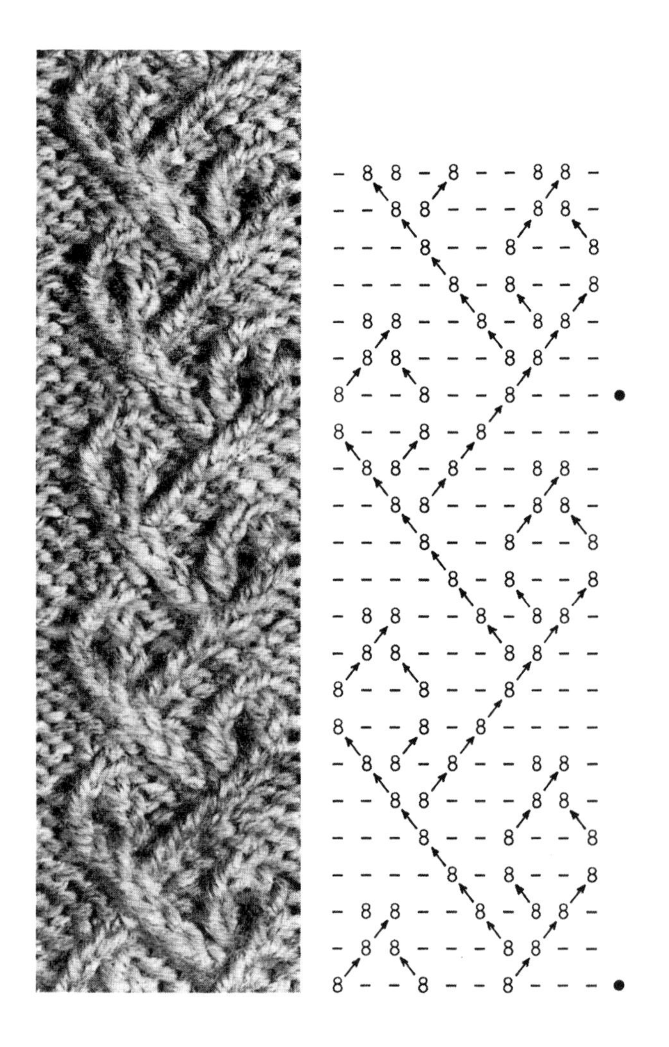

146
Vergessene Liab

Forgotten Love, #4

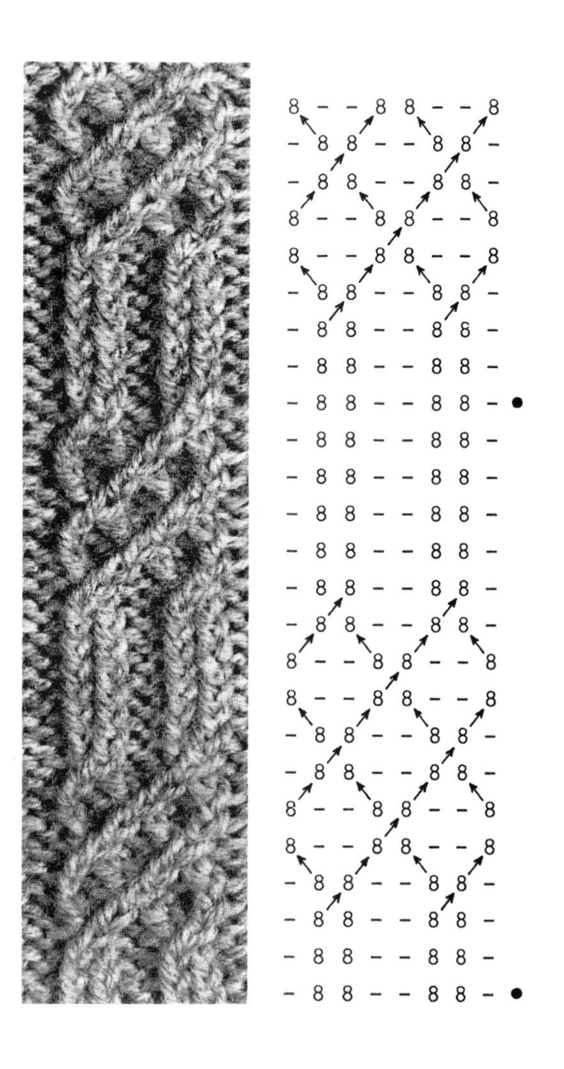

147
Streifenviereck

Striped Squares

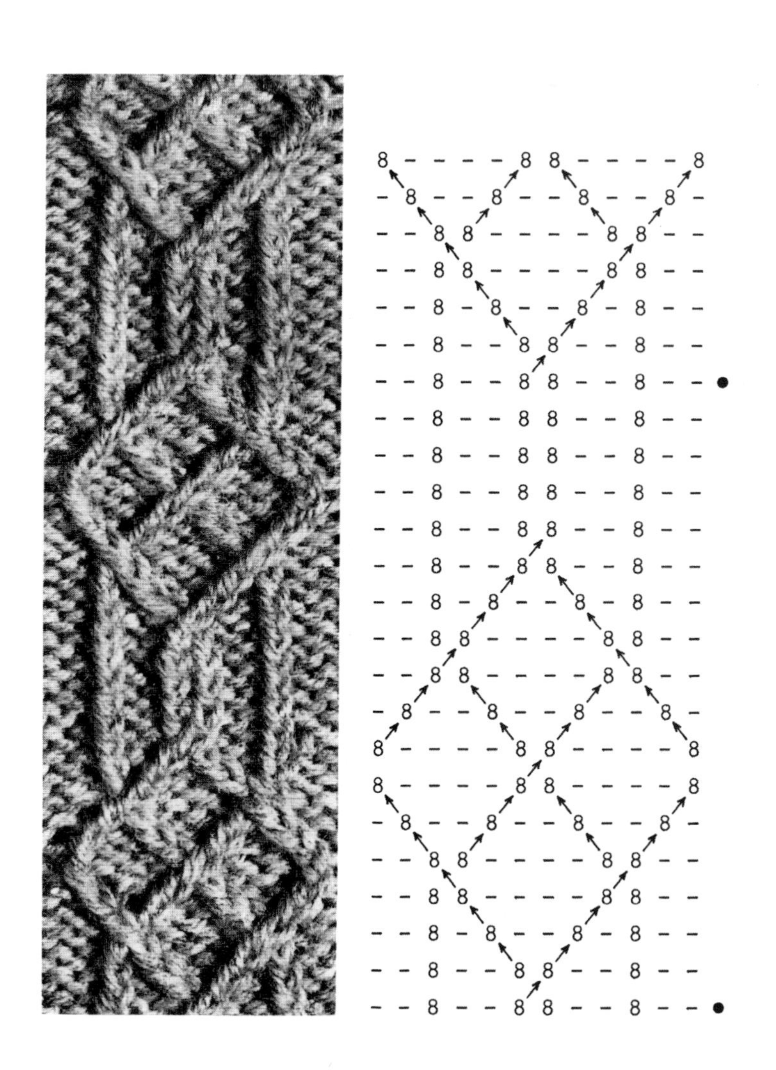

148
Doppelketterl mit Fensterl

Double Chain with Small Windows

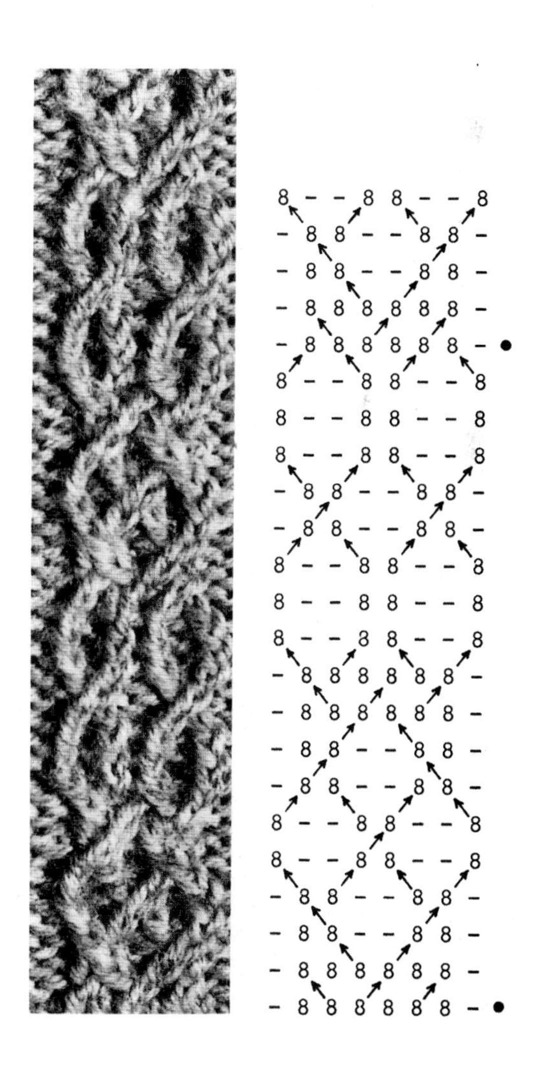

149
Murtaler Model

Mur Valley Pattern

150
Glatter Zopfstreifen

Knit Braided Stripe

Pick up the first stitch, and put the second (center) stitch on a spare needle, hold behind your work.

Cross the first and third stitch in the direction of the arrow, and knit them in the following order:
- third stitch
- second stitch from the spare needle and
- first stitch.

151
Doppelherz mit Fenster

Double Heart with Window

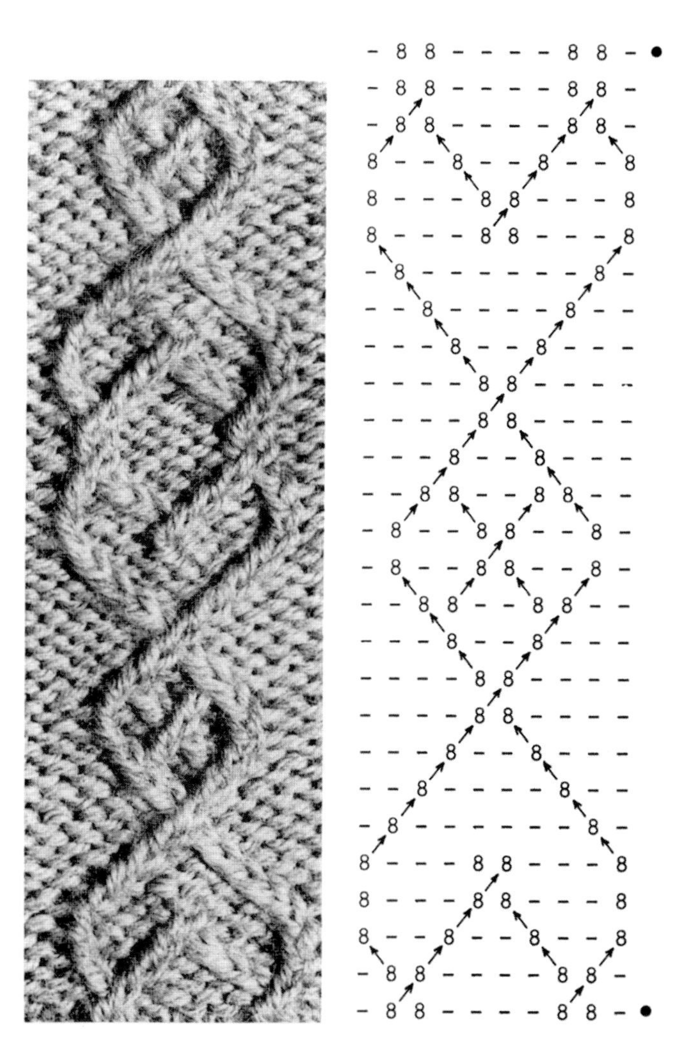

152
Kleiner Zopfstreifen

Small Braid Stripe, #1

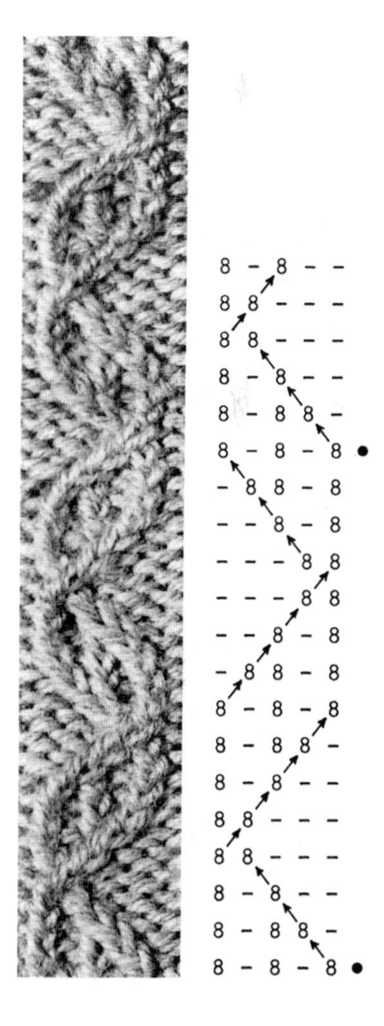

153
Kleiner Zopfstreifen

Small Braid Stripe, #2

154
Offene Liab mit Almweg

Open Love with Alpine Path

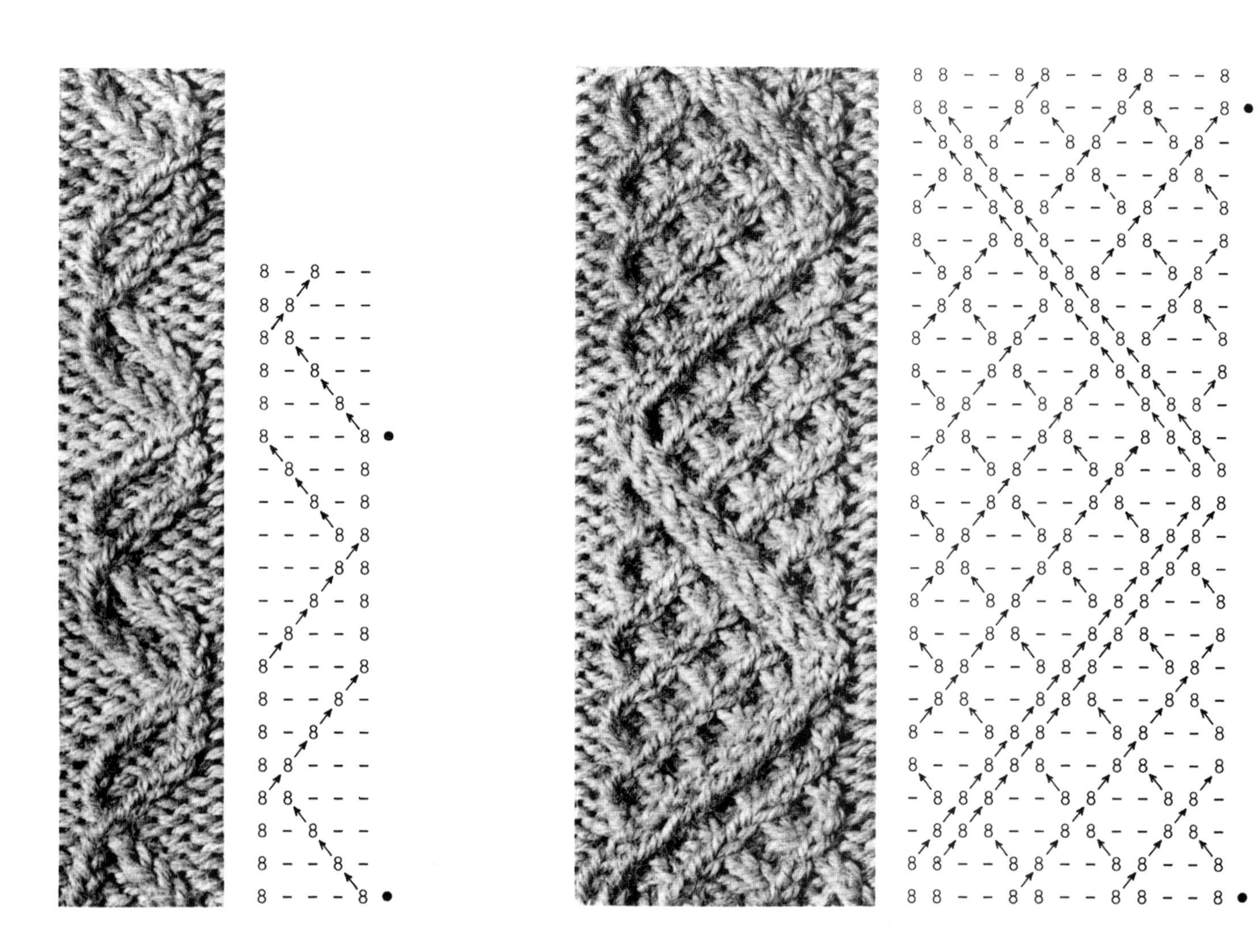

155
Doppelzopf

Double Braid, #3

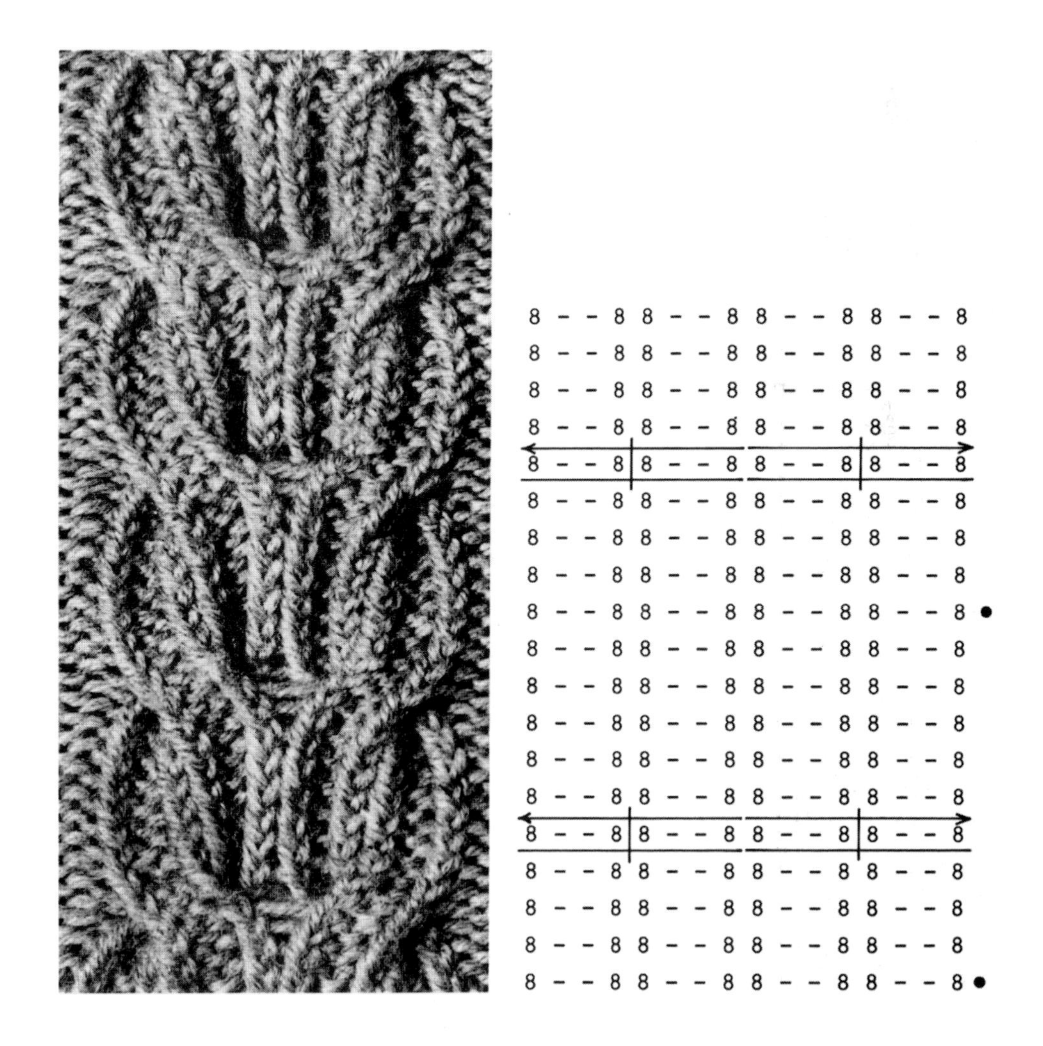

156
Versetzter dreifacher Zopf

Staggered Triple Braid

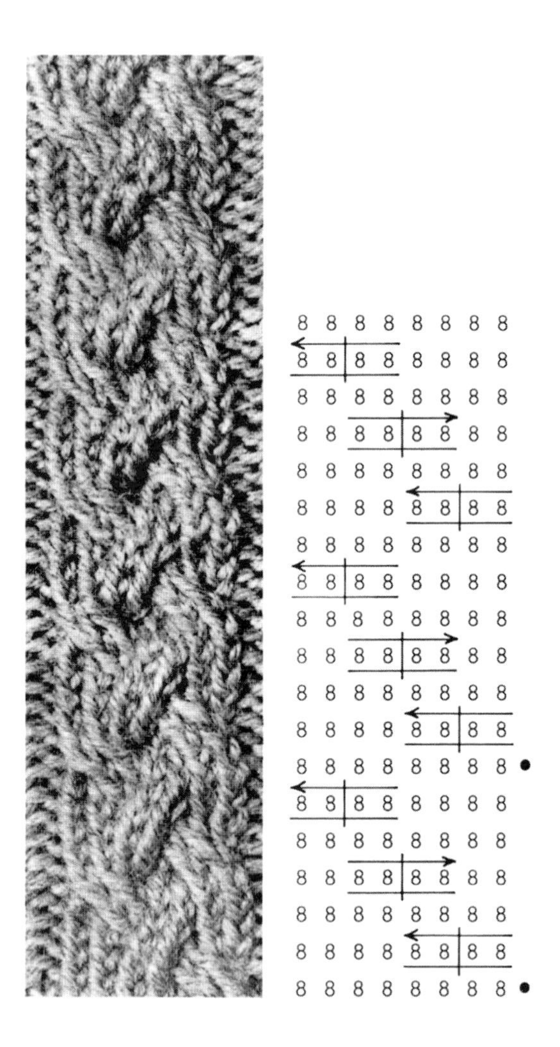

157
Zopfmodel

Braid Pattern

Braids are normally worked over an even number of sts, but these braids have an uneven number. When crossing the sts, one stitch is lifted over two.

158

Doppelseitiger Überzug

Double-Sided Crossover

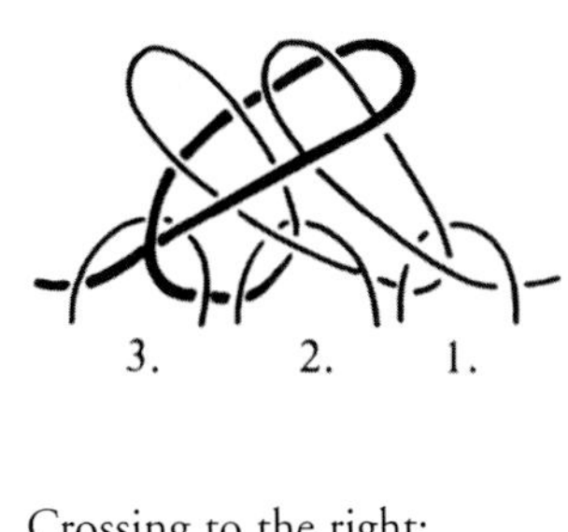

Crossing to the right:
Leave sts #1 and 2 on left needle. Use right needle to stretch stitch #3 over sts #1 and 2. Work all 3 stitches (see drawing).

Crossing to the left:
Slip sts #1, 2 and 3 to the right needle without knitting them. Use left needle to stretch stitch #1 over sts #2 and 3. Slip all 3 back to the left needle and work them in the following order - #2, 3 and 1.

159

Versetzter Zopf

Uneven Braid

8 8 8 8 8 8
8 8 8 8 8 8
8 8 8 8 8 8
8 8 8 8 8 8
8 8 8 8 8 8
8 8 8 8 8 8
8 8 8 8 8 8
8 8 8 8 8 8
8 8 8 8 8 8
8 8 8 8 8 8
8 8 8 8 8 8
8 8 8 8 8 8
8 8 8 8 8 8
8 8 8 8 8 8
8 8 8 8 8 8 •
8 8 8 8 8 8
8 8 8 8 8 8
8 8 8 8 8 8
8 8 8 8 8 8 •

160
Ein Ausseer Stutzenmodel

Ausseer Stocking Pattern, #1

161
Fischgräten

Fish Bones, #2

162
Woazkörndl

Small Wheat Grain

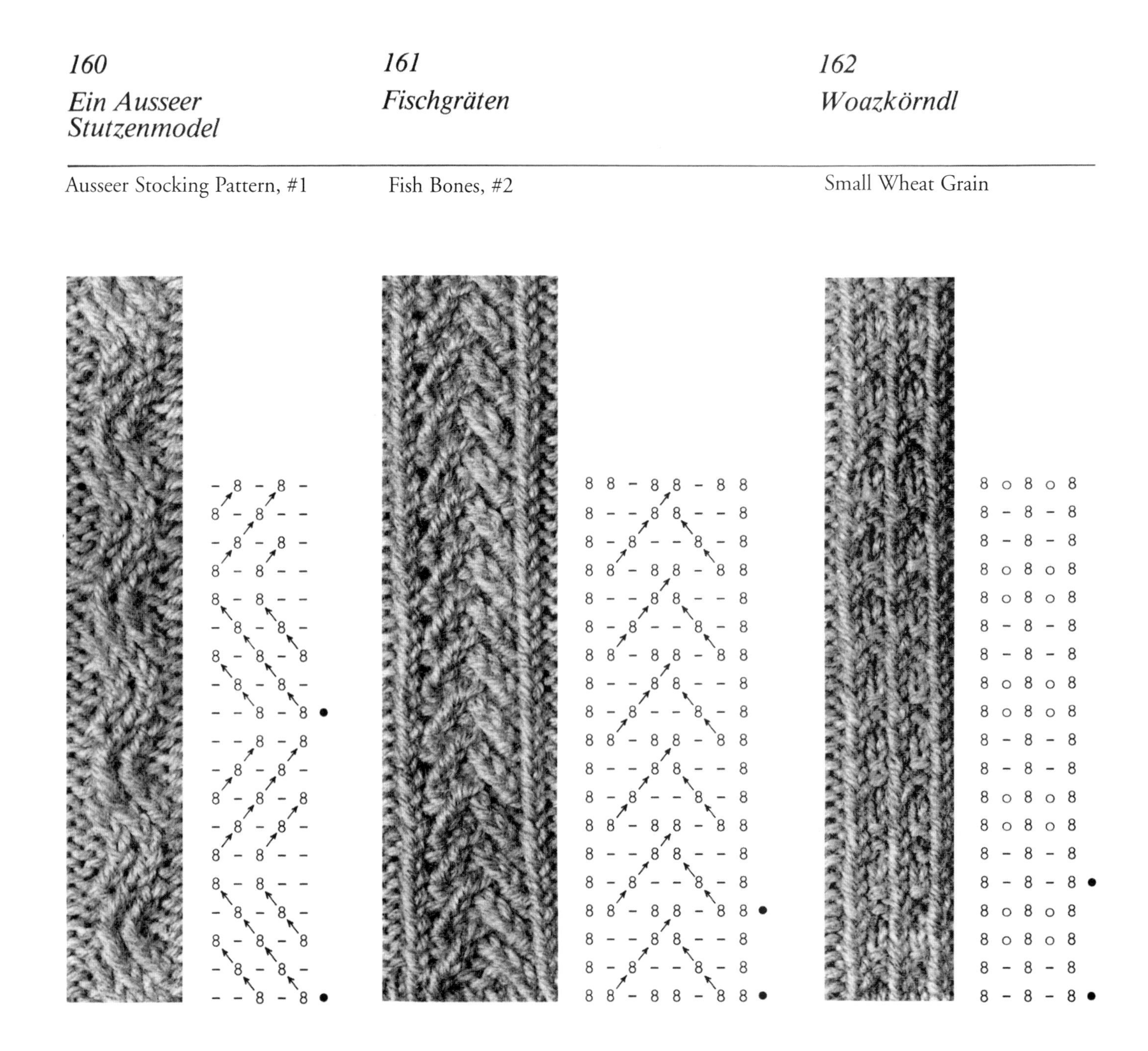

163
Zwetschkenkern und Kreuzerl

Plum Pit and Small Crosses

164
Glöckerl

Little Bell

165
Ein Ausseer Stutzenmodel

Ausseer Stocking Pattern, #2

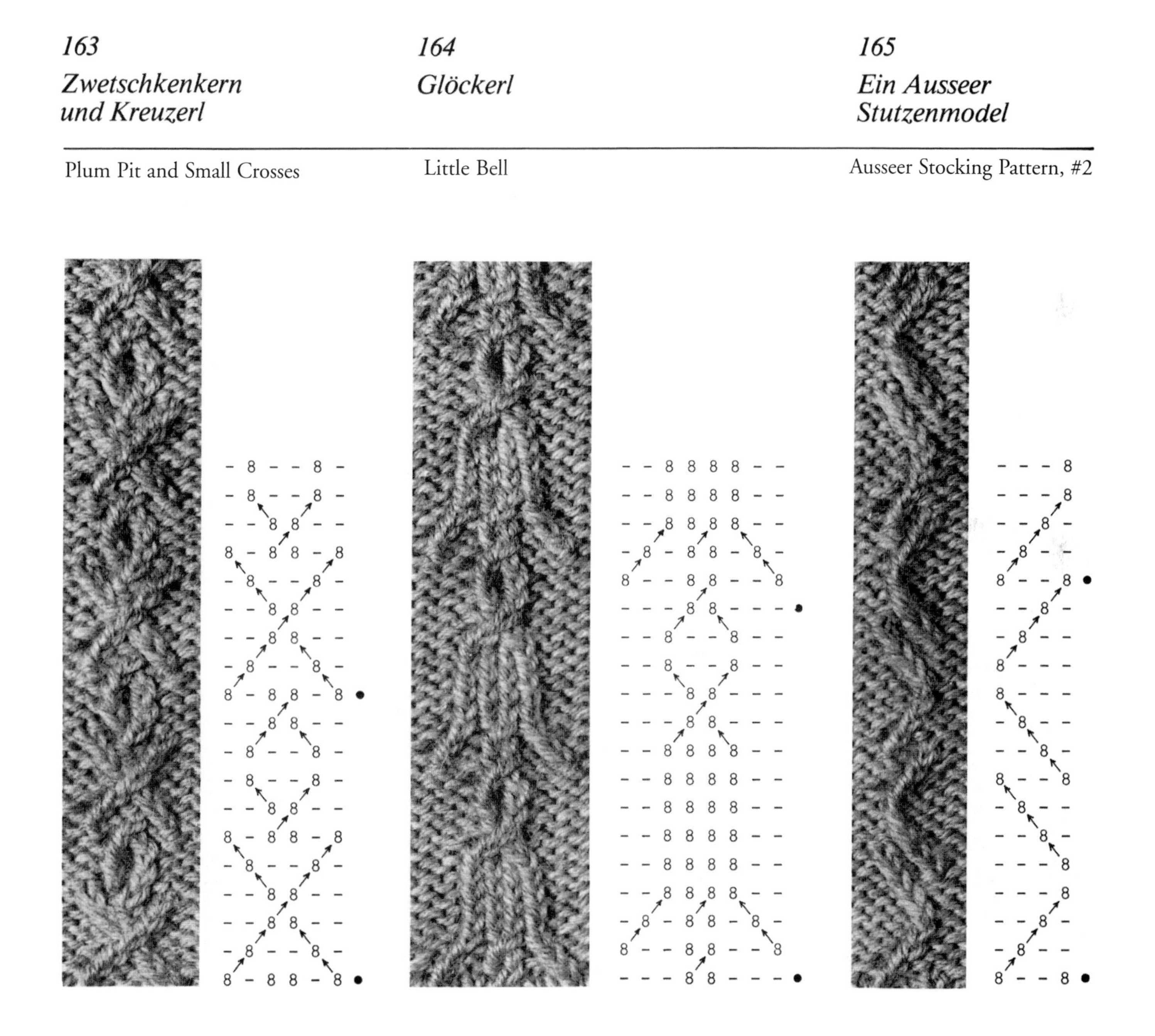

166
Doppelkette

Double Chain, #4

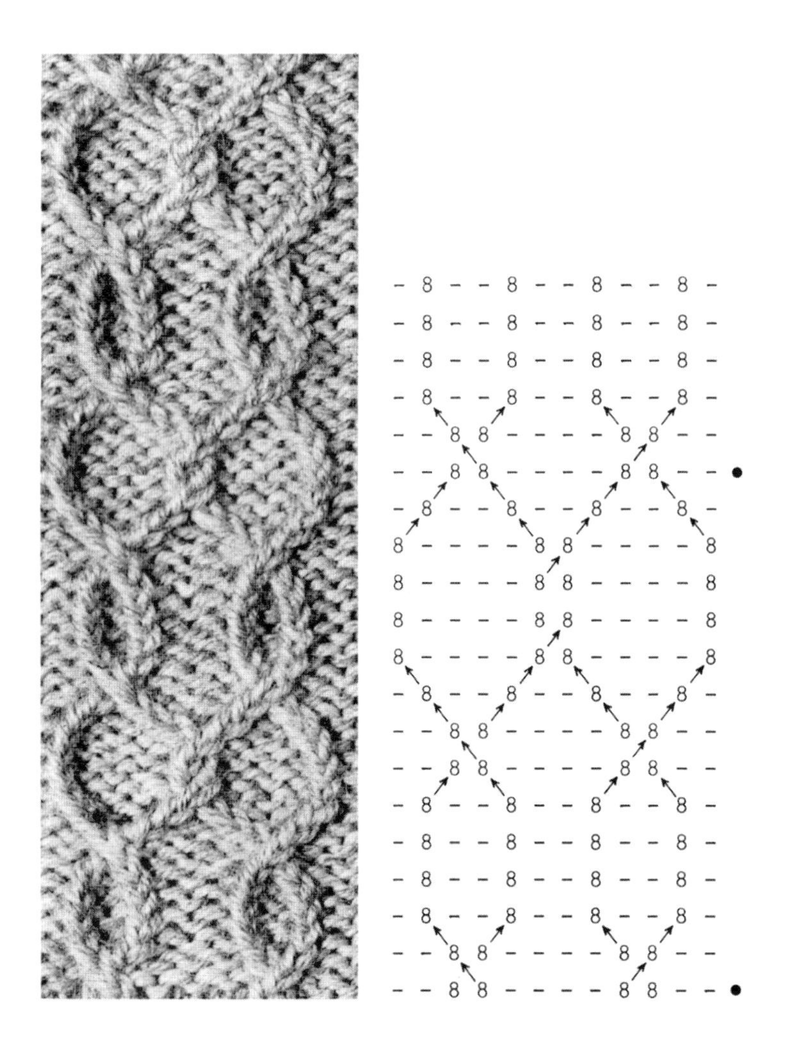

167
Fischgräten

Fish Bones, #3

```
8 8 – – 8 – – 8 8
8 – – 8 8 8 – – 8
8 – 8 – 8 – 8 – 8
8 8 – – 8 – – 8 8
8 – – 8 8 8 – – 8
8 – 8 – 8 – 8 – 8
8 8 – – 8 – – 8 8
8 – – 8 8 8 – – 8
8 – 8 – 8 – 8 – 8
8 8 – – 8 – – 8 8
8 – – 8 8 8 – – 8
8 – 8 – 8 – 8 – 8
8 8 – – 8 – – 8 8
8 – – 8 8 8 – – 8
8 – 8 – 8 – 8 – 8
8 8 – – 8 – – 8 8 •
8 – – 8 8 8 – – 8
8 – 8 – 8 – 8 – 8
8 8 – – 8 – – 8 8 •
```

168
Zopf

Braid, #3

```
8 8 8 8 8 8
8 8 8|8 8 8 →
8 8 8 8 8 8
8 8 8 8 8 8
8 8 8 8 8 8
8 8 8|8 8 8 →
8 8 8 8 8 8
8 8 8 8 8 8 •
8 8 8 8 8 8
8 8 8 8 8 8
8 8 8 8 8 8
8 8 8 8 8 8
8 8 8 8 8 8
8 8 8|8 8 8 →
8 8 8 8 8 8
8 8 8 8 8 8
8 8 8 8 8 8
8 8 8|8 8 8 →
8 8 8 8 8 8
8 8 8 8 8 8 •
```

169
Verschlungene Kette

Interlaced Chain

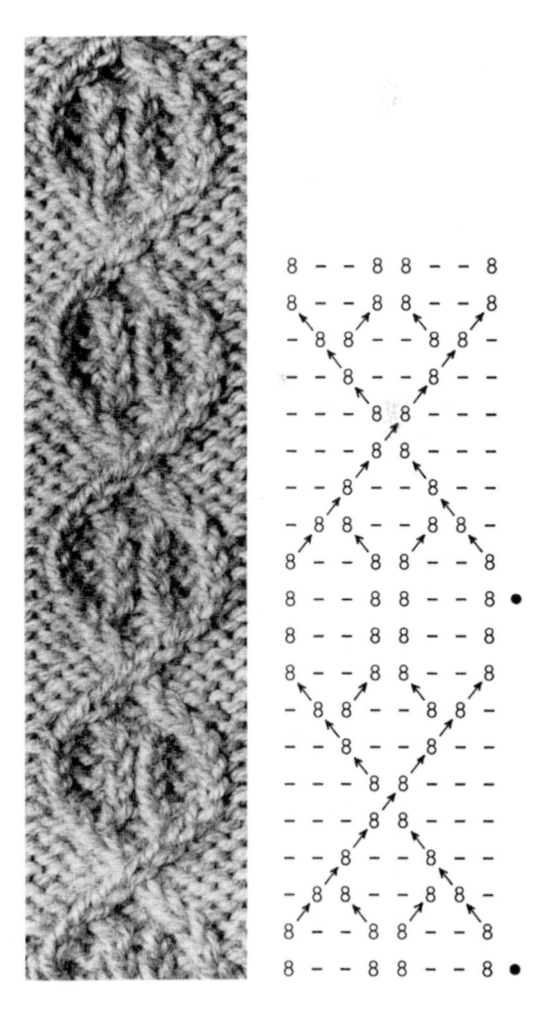

170
Nullen mit Fenster

Zeros with Window, #2

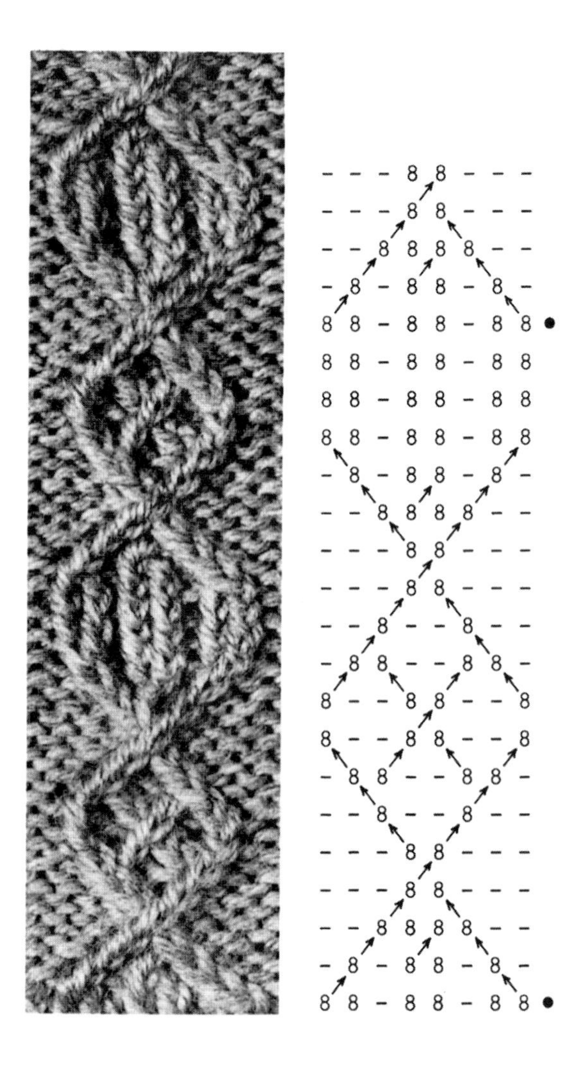

171
Nullen mit Fenster

Zeros with Window, #3

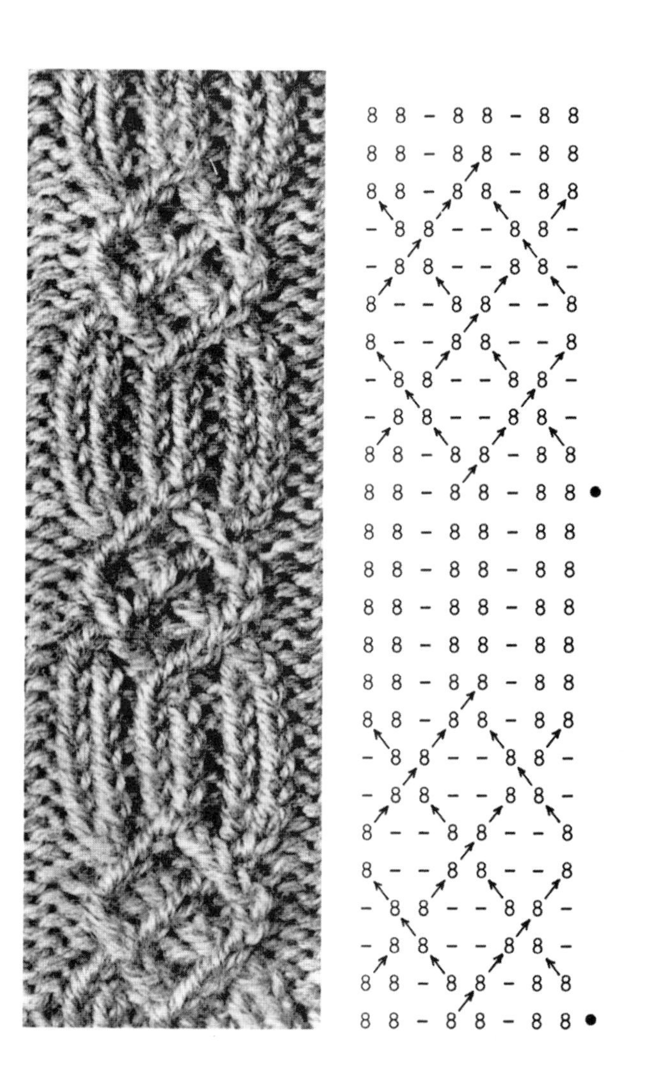

172
Fischgräten mit Ketterl

Fish Bones with Small Chain , #1

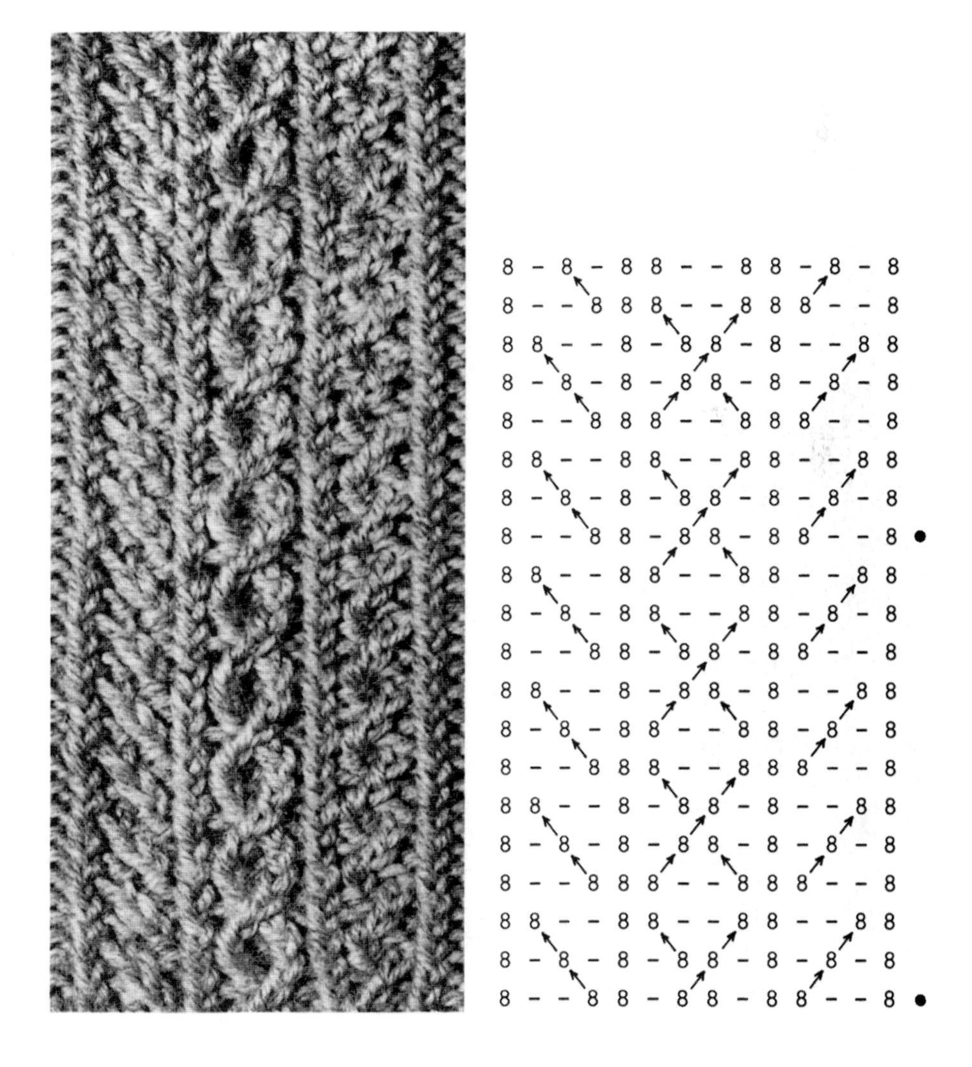

173
Brennende Liab im Dreieck

Burning Love in a Triangle

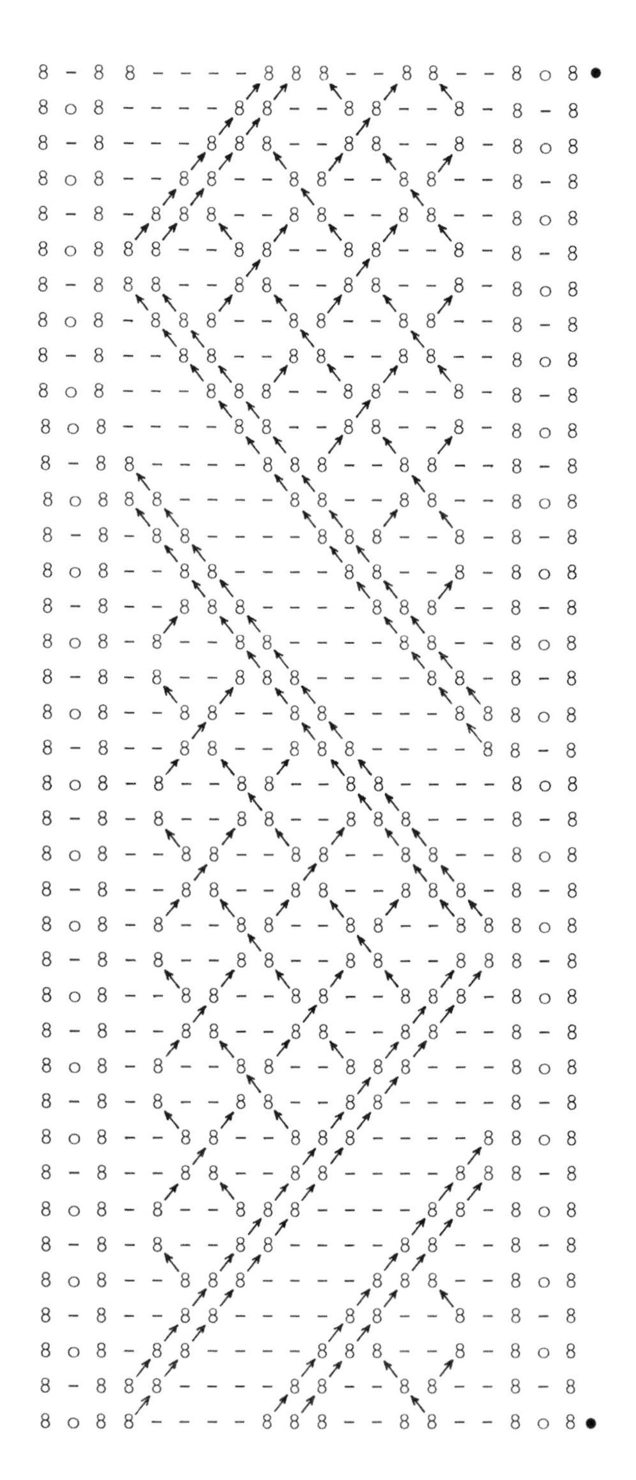

174
Fischgräten und Ketterl

Fish Bones and Small Chain, #2

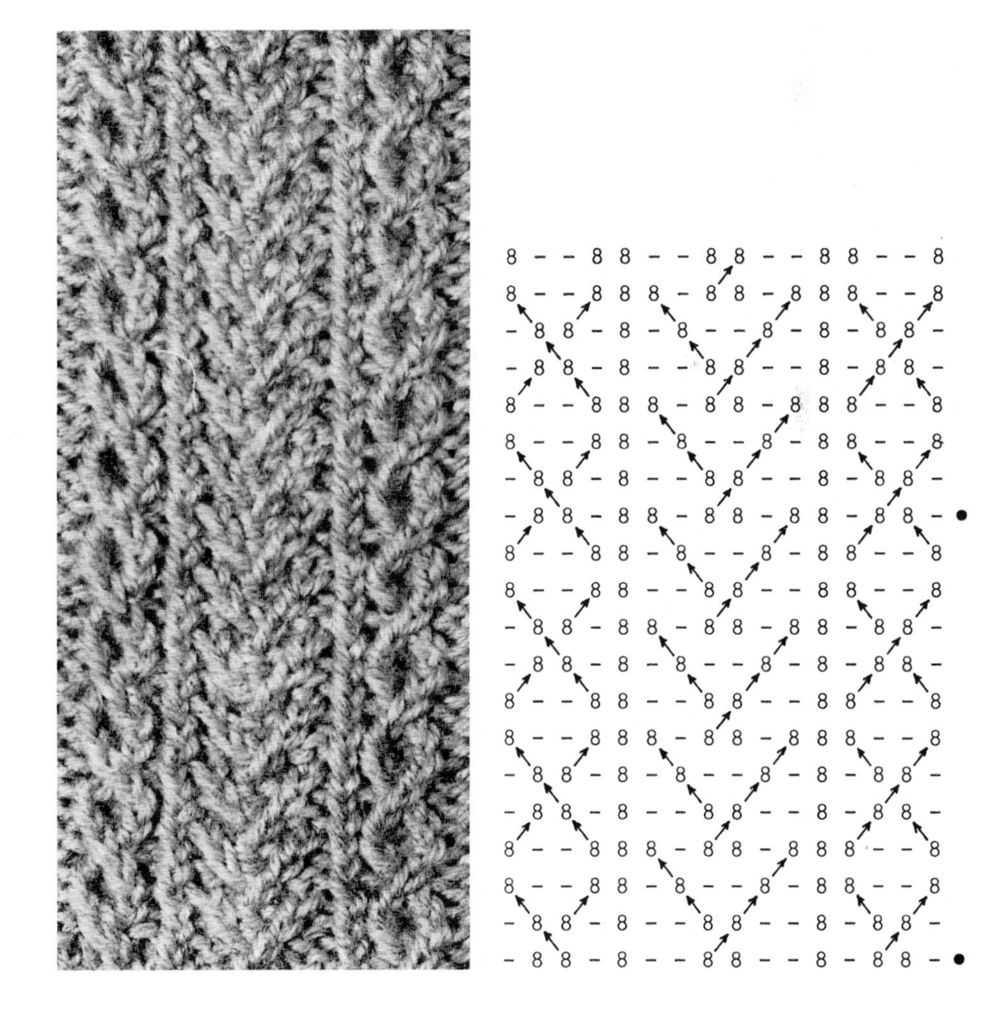

Stockings

General Notes on Stockings

This is a good way to start knitting a sampler. Don't worry, it will not be that hard! All of your stitches will be on 4 or 5 double pointed *(or 2 circular)* needles and you will knit round and round. You can always see and read your pattern as the front of the work faces you all the time; you never have to work stitches from the back of the fabric.

In the courses that I teach to enthusiastic and interested knitters, I often hear that someone saw an exceptionally beautiful stocking with an extraordinary knitted calf gusset. Men love to wear these stockings with their knickers, as the band around the lower edge of knickers is right where the top of the stocking starts. It is the perfect accessory, and we can show off our knitting skills with these hand made items.

Around 1780, beautifully knitted wool stockings in the Enns Valley and the Auseerland were primarily white, grey, blue and green, and part of the native garb.

Pictures and paintings of regional costumes of that time show us that certain patterns, i.e. The Braid (*der Zopf*), Burning Love (*Brennende Liab*) or the Plain Chain (*Einfache Ketterl*), are well liked and often repeated. Such memorable patterns surely were passed from village to village, valley to valley and over the borders to neighboring countries. Imaginative and resourceful knitters were able to enrich their collection of patterns in that way.

Well- it's time to begin knitting our stockings. There are two parts to designing a stocking.

1. The order in which the patterns are knitted.

2. The patterns in the calf gusset.

My advice to you is to use the examples in this book for your first attempts. After that you will be able to pick out any other patterns you like, arrange them in your own way and make the stockings your own creation.

This will be fun!

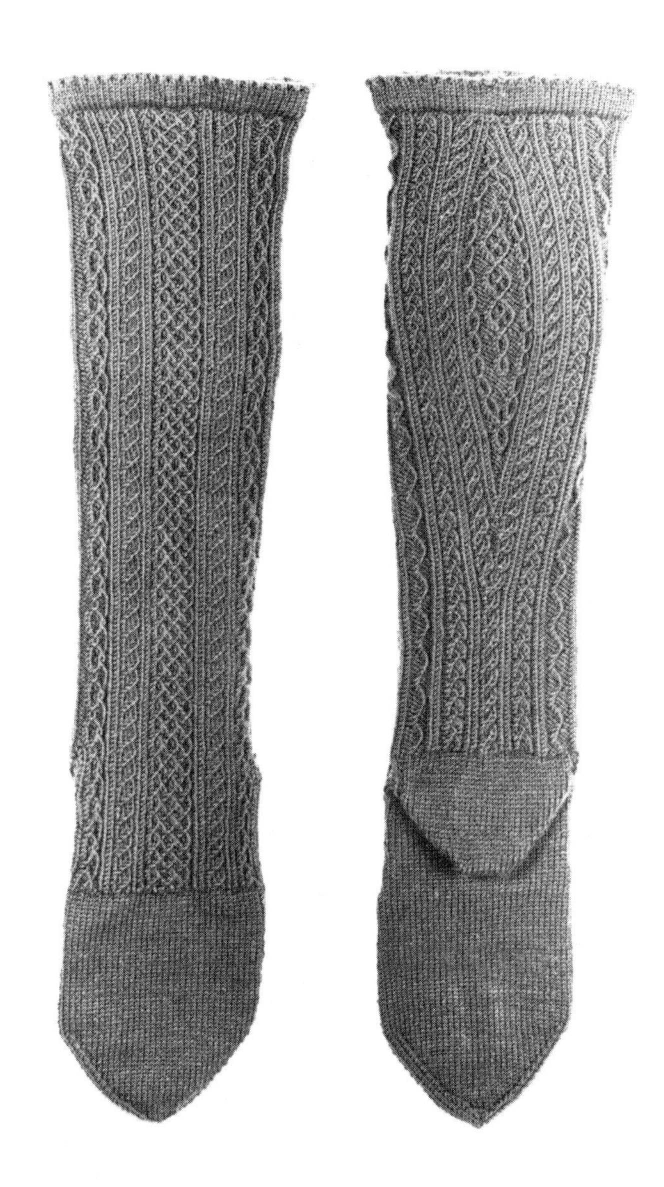

Stutzen*: There really is no English translation for this word; they are men's stockings specifically designed to be worn with Lederhosen.*

Materials: 250- 300 grams of wool; a set of 1.25 mm to 2.5 mm needles, depending upon your gauge.

Ribbing: Cast on 92 sts and divide evenly on 4 needles. Knit 8 rounds. Row 9: Picot edging (called, "Mouse Tooth" in German) - *k2 tog, YO* to the end of the round. Knit 8 more rounds.

Next round: Fold work along the round of holes and knit together the loop from your first cast- on stitch with your first stitch. Continue with the second and all the way to the end of the round. (Leave an opening for the elastic.)

Leg of the stocking: Look through the following examples and pick out your patterns plus one for the calf gusset. Count how many stitches are used for your patterns, and increase as needed when doing your first row. Start your pattern at the lower right of your chart; continue, stitch for stitch, row to row, just as in the charts. When you are done with the calf gusset, work to the ankle. At this time your knitting should measure about 38- 40 cm. Knit the heel of your choice.

The top of the foot is knitted in pattern for about 8- 10 cm long and the rest of the foot is worked in plain stocking stitch. Reduce the number of stitches, as the patterned section pulls in more than plain knitting.

After decreasing the gusset to the wanted number of stitches, knit the foot as long as needed, then decrease for the toe. When the stockings are done, lay them flat, cover with a damp cloth and let them dry. Don't forget to put elastic around the top.

Please note: Charts for the individual patterns consist of different numbers of vertical repeats; please be careful to knit each pattern for the specified number of rounds. The charts are marked with a pair of dots on the right-hand side; these indicate one vertical repeat.

Practical tips

Before beginning any of the patterns, please read the following tips carefully, take a good look at the drawings that show how the stitches are done and practice.

Choosing your yarn: Use either pure sheep's wool or a yarn that is made for knitting stockings. It should be suitable for knitting with size 1.25- 2 mm needles. The wool should be strong and have a firm twist. The more twist in the thread, the better you will be able to see the stitch patterns. When you are using 100% wool, it is advisable to use the thread that is sold for use in reinforcing the fabric, along with the wool, when knitting the heels and toes.

For women's stockings that will be worn with a Dirndl, a cotton yarn would be more suitable. This is available in several thicknesses. Use a yarn that will work well when knitted with size 1.25- 2.5 mm needles.

Wool amounts: Men's Stutzen about 250- 300 grams; Boy's Stutzen (depending on age) 100- 200 grams; Women's knee stockings require 200- 250 grams.

The 4 parts of a man's stocking:

1. The border (ribbing)
2. The calf gusset (calf shaping plus the ankle)
3. The heel
4. The foot (instep and sole) and the toe.

Women's knee socks: These are very similar to men's Stutzen; the difference consists of the calf being shaped not by increases and decreases, but only by decreases.

Knitting *Stutzen* following a pattern: I recommend that you follow the pattern exactly as written for your first pair of stockings. After completing this test piece, it will be easy to substitute your favorite stitch patterns. An old "rule" states, that *Stutzen* or stockings should contain 5 to 7 different stitch patterns.

Ribbing: Cast on the required number of stitches given in the patterns. Join, being careful not to twist. Divide the stitches on four needles (or a pair of 24" circular needles). Knit 8 rounds in stockinette stitch. The 9th row is the Picot row (k 2 together, YO, repeat to the end of the round). Knit 8 more rounds in stockinette stitch. Fold the fabric along the row of holes, right sides facing out.

Next row: The first cast on loop is knitted together with the first stitch, the second cast on loop with the second stitch and so on until you get to the end of the round. Leave a small opening for elastic to help keep the stocking up.

From calf to heel: Since the calf is larger than the knee, it will require more stitches. Increase by the necessary amount of stitches by knitting the first row without pattern stitches and increasing by the same number of stitches on each needle. Depending on the patterns used, some of the stitches might need to be moved around in the next row.

When the calf is done, the piece is knitted straight, without decreasing, to the heel. The total length for men is between 38 to 44 cm. The ankle part (the straight section between the end of the calf and the beginning of the heel) should measure about 1/3 of the total length. For very large sizes, of course, the calf is longer.

Heel: Half the total stitches will be used for the heel, the other half for the instep. The pattern will be knitted for about 10- 12 cm on the instep of the stocking.

On women's stockings, the pattern on the instep will be worked almost to the tip of the toes. Since the heels are knitted in stockinette stitch, it will be necessary to decrease some stitches in the first heel row. Working with a third needle, the heel is knitted on the two back needles. The normal heel is as follows: *Slip 1, knit across heel. Turn. Slip 1, knit 2, purl across heel to last three stitches, knit 2, purl 1.* Repeat between *s. When the heel flap is tall enough (generally half the number of heel sts = number of heel rows), it is time to turn the heel.

Turn the Heel: Start on a right side row in the middle of the heel, using two of the needles. Divide the stitches of half the heel (one needle) by three. For example: with 18 stitches for half of the heel, knit 5 stitches, knit together the 6th and 7th stitches through the back and turn your work. This creates a small hole. For the next row slip the first stitch, purl to the center of the heel, purl 5 stitches from the other needle, purl together stitches # 6 and 7 and turn your work. Slip the first stitch and knit across to the stitch before the small hole. From now on the stitch before and after the hole are knitted together on a right side row, and purled together on a wrong side row until all of the stitches on both sides of the center stitches are gone.

Foot and Toe: Divide bottom of heel flap stitches evenly onto two needles. Start at center of heel on right side row and knit across stitches to edge of flap, knit into the back of the flap-edge-stitches to create new stitches. To eliminate possible holes between the new stitches and top of the foot, make a new stitch through the space between 2 stitches of the previous round (or twist a loose strand and put it on the needle). Work across the two sock top needles in pattern. Make a new stitch at edge, knit up flap edge stitches and work bottom of flap stitches as on other side.

Gussets: Stitches will now be decreased to the number of you had around the ankle, as follows:

- knit from the first heel needle until 3 stitches remain. Knit together the second and third stitch and knit the last stitch.

- on the fourth needle knit the first stitch, knit together the second and third stitch through the back loops. Knit two rounds between each decrease row.

Keep decreasing in this way until the heel stitches equal the number of instep stitches. When the foot is long enough (measure it on a sock that fits), begin the toe decreases.

Shaped decreases: (fits well for most feet): Decrease at the end of needle #1, beginning of needle #2, at the end of needle #3, and at the beginning of needle #4.

Round 1: Knit needle #1 until 3 stitches remain. Knit 2 together and knit the last stitch. On needle #2, knit 1 and knit the next 2 stitches together through the back. Knit to the end of the needle. Repeat for needles #3 and #4.

Round 2: Knit one round even.

Repeat these two rounds 9 times. After that decrease every round down to 8 stitches. Weave with kitchener stitch.

Finishing: Shape the stockings on a flat surface. Cover with a damp towel and let them dry. Insert elastic in the tops.

this gusset uses motifs #50 and #51

Center Back

▽

```
8 8 - 8 - - 8 - 8 8 - 8 - - - - 8 8 - - 8 8 - - 8
8 8 - 8 - - 8 - 8 8 - - 8 - - - 8 8 - - 8 8 - - 8
8 8 - - 8 8 - - 8 8 - - - 8 - - 8 8 - 8 - - 8 8 -
8 8 - 8 8 8 8 - 8 8 - - - - 8 - 8 8 - 8 - - 8 8 -
8 8 - 8 - - 8 - 8 8 - - - - 8 - 8 8 - 8 - - 8 8 -
8 8 - 8 - - 8 - 8 8 - - - 8 - - 8 8 - 8 - - 8 8 -
8 8 - - 8 8 - - 8 8 - - 8 - - - 8 8 - - 8 8 - - 8
8 8 - 8 8 8 8 - 8 8 - 8 - - - - 8 8 - - 8 8 - - 8
8 8 - 8 - - 8 - 8 8 - 8 - - - - 8 8 - - 8 8 - - 8
8 8 - 8 - - 8 - 8 8 - - 8 - - - 8 8 - - 8 8 - - 8
8 8 - - 8 8 - - 8 8 - - - 8 - - 8 8 - 8 - - 8 8 -
8 8 - 8 8 8 8 - 8 8 - - - - 8 - 8 8 - 8 - - 8 8 -
8 8 - 8 - - 8 - 8 8 - - - - 8 - 8 8 - 8 - - 8 8 -
8 8 - 8 - - 8 - 8 8 - - - 8 - - 8 8 - 8 - - 8 8 -
8 8 - - 8 8 - - 8 8 - - 8 - - - 8 8 - - 8 8 - - 8
8 8 - 8 8 8 8 - 8 8 - 8 - - - - 8 8 - - 8 8 - - 8
```

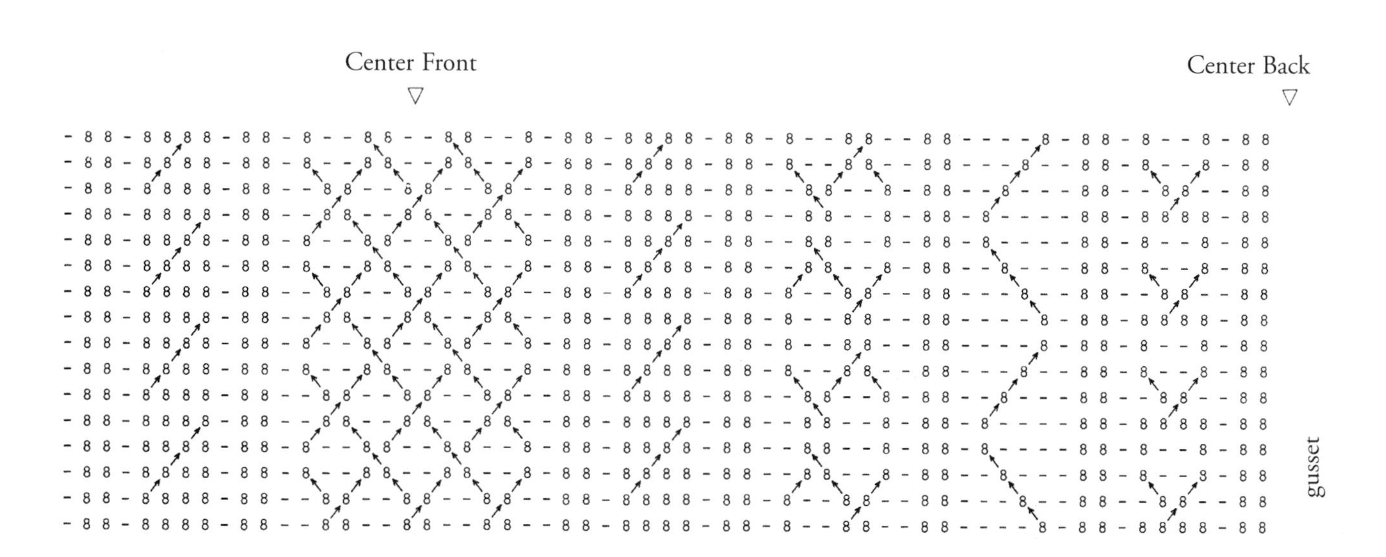
Center Front
Center Back
gusset

Center Back

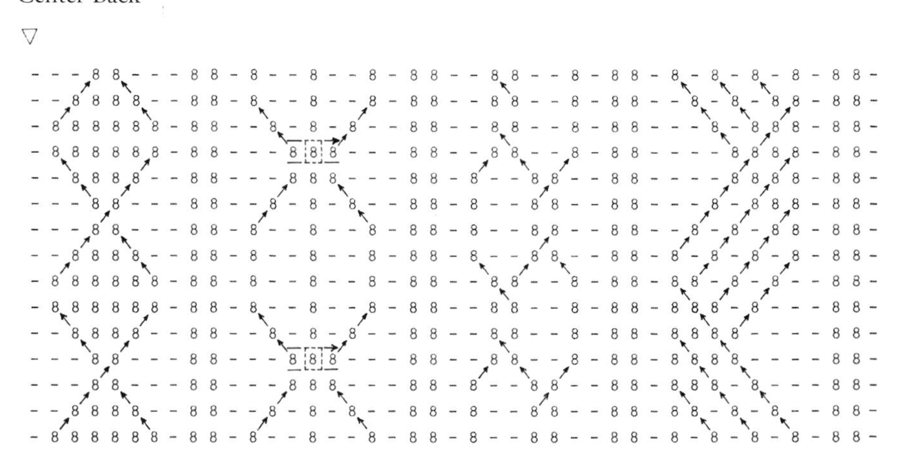

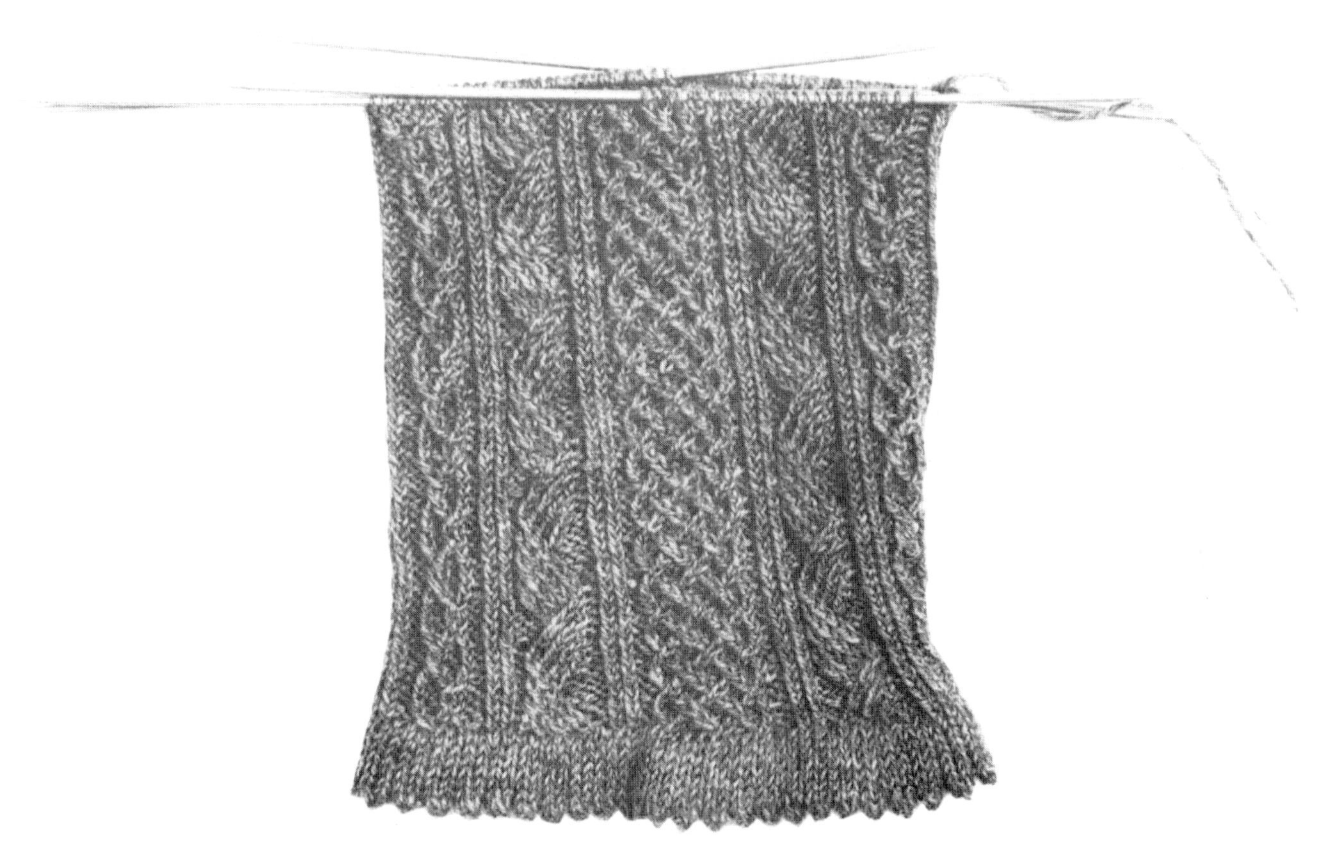

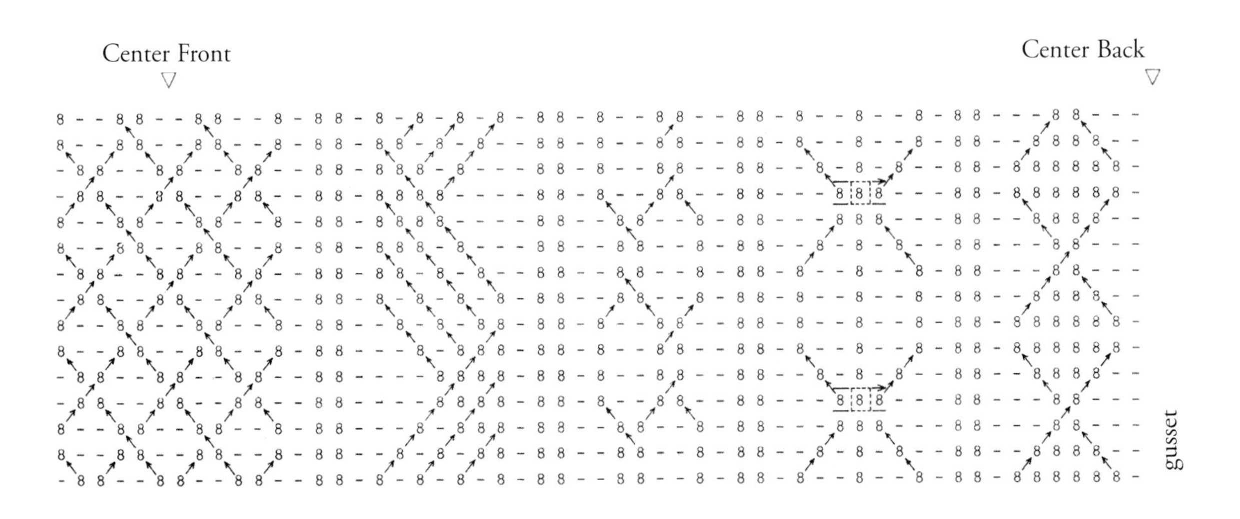

Center Front
Center Back
gusset

Calf Gusset: Window-Chain-Braid,
for stocking shown on
pages 114, 115

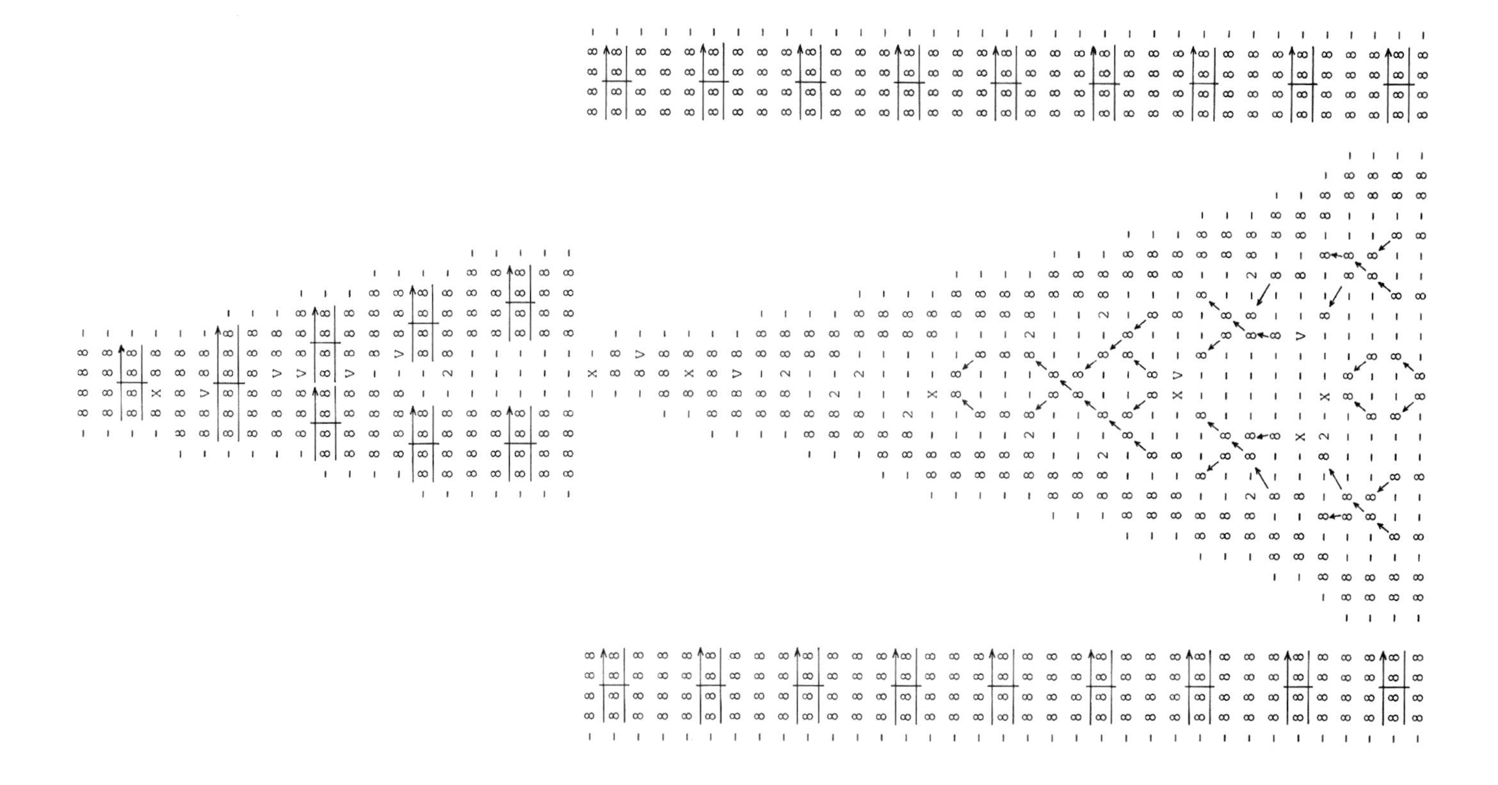

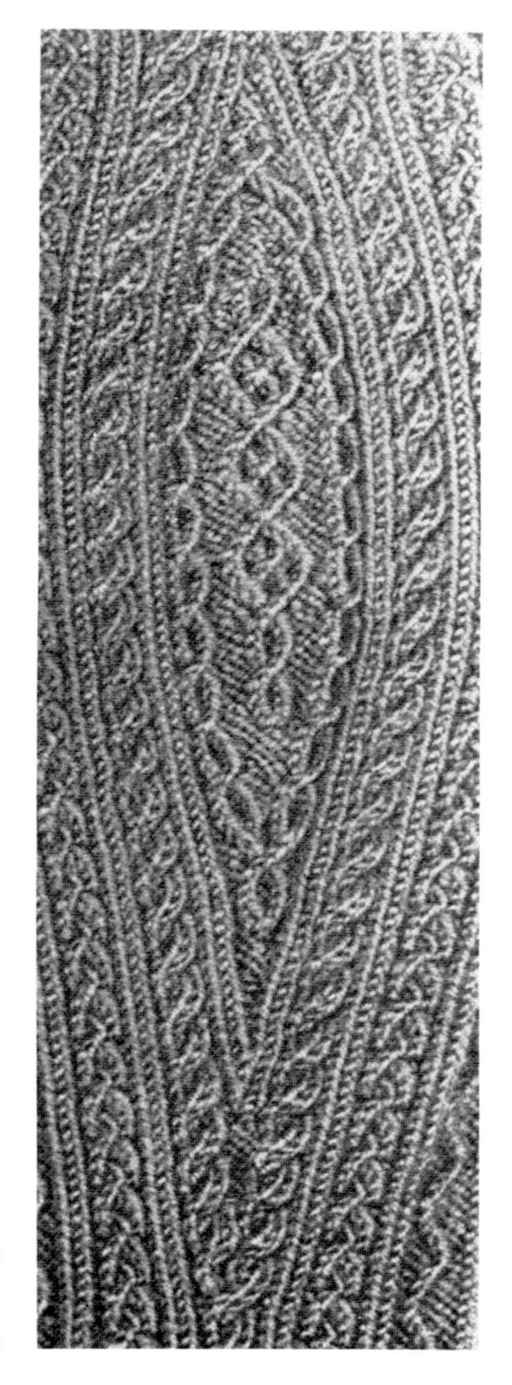

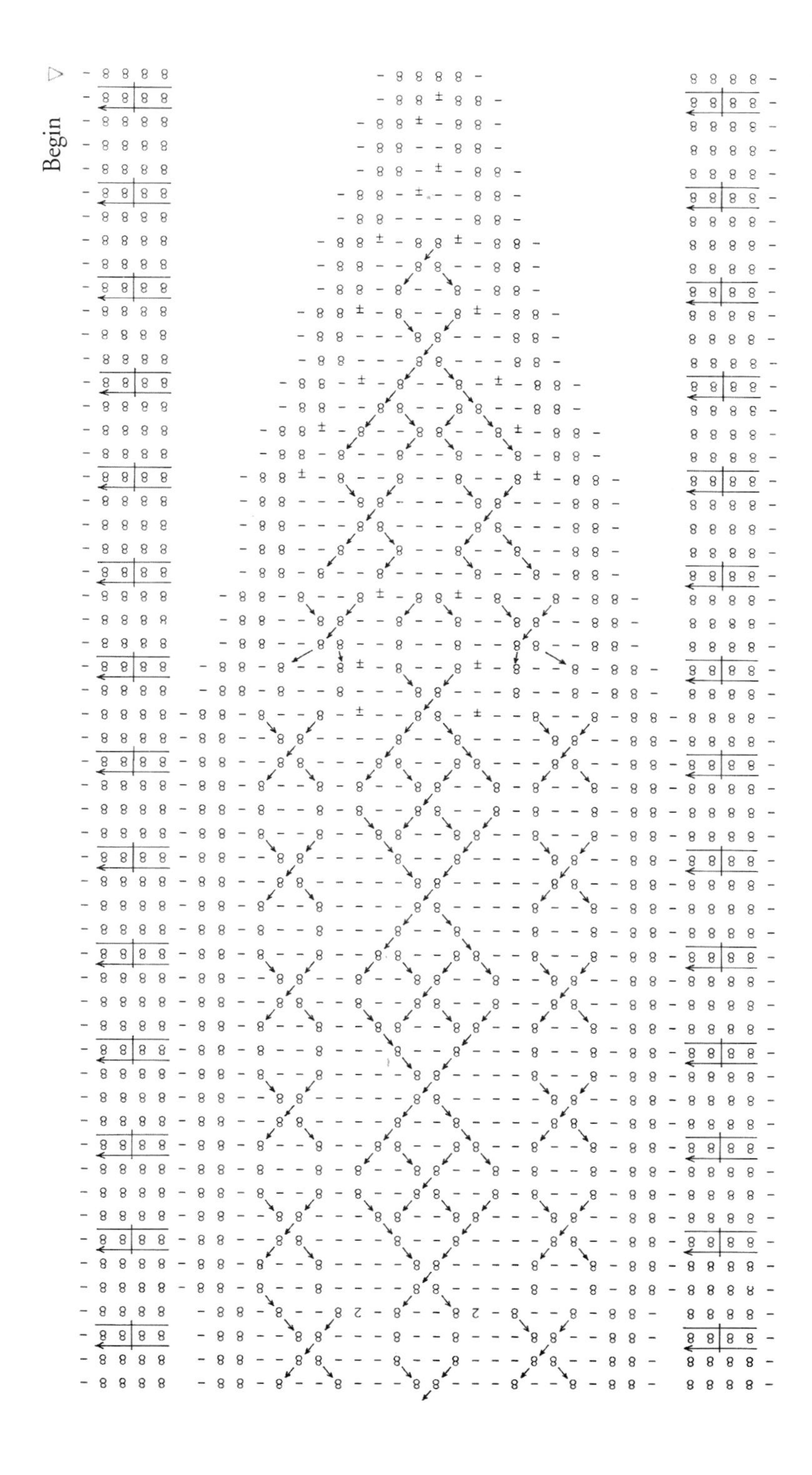
Begin

Calf Gusset: Little Tree with Chain

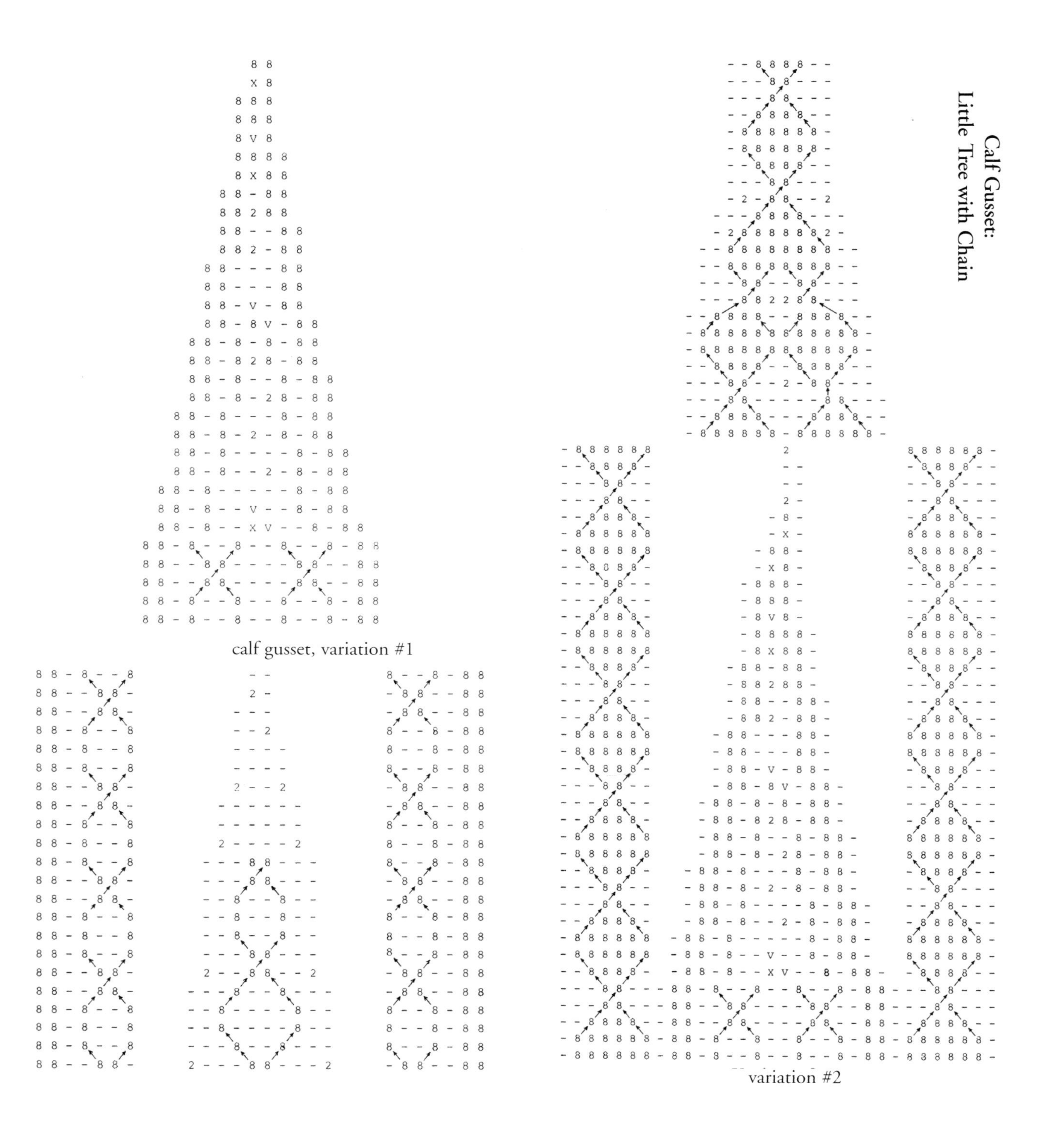

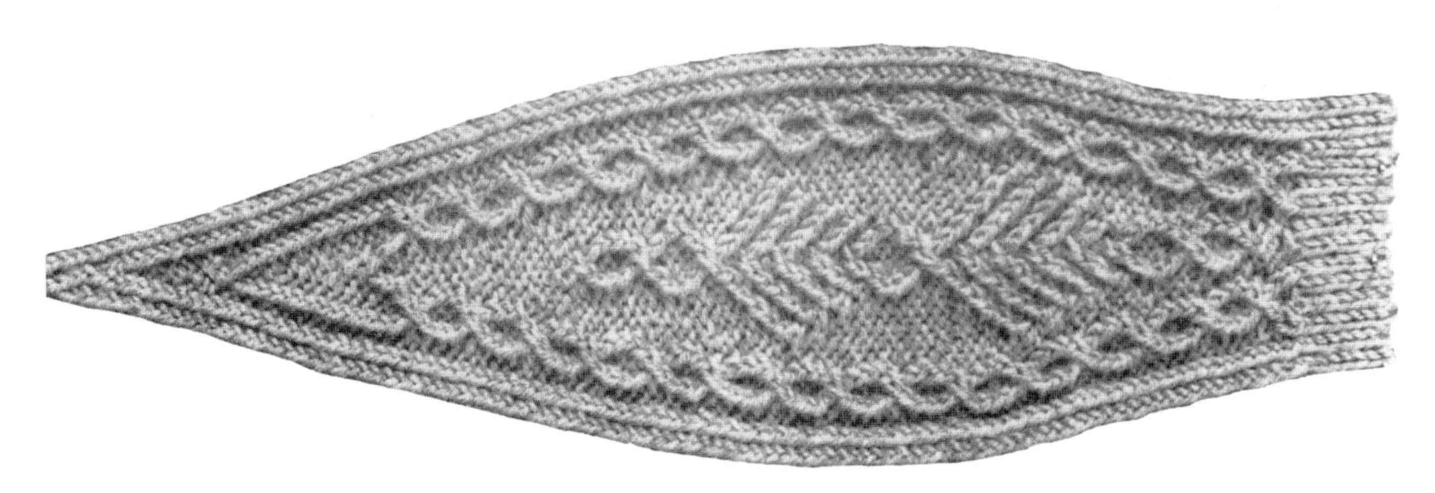

The calf gusset in this photo and chart is for a boy's size stocking. To increase to an adult size, add some edge patterns such as, Smooth Chain *(Glattes Ketterl),* to the variation #2 example, to widen the calf gusset.

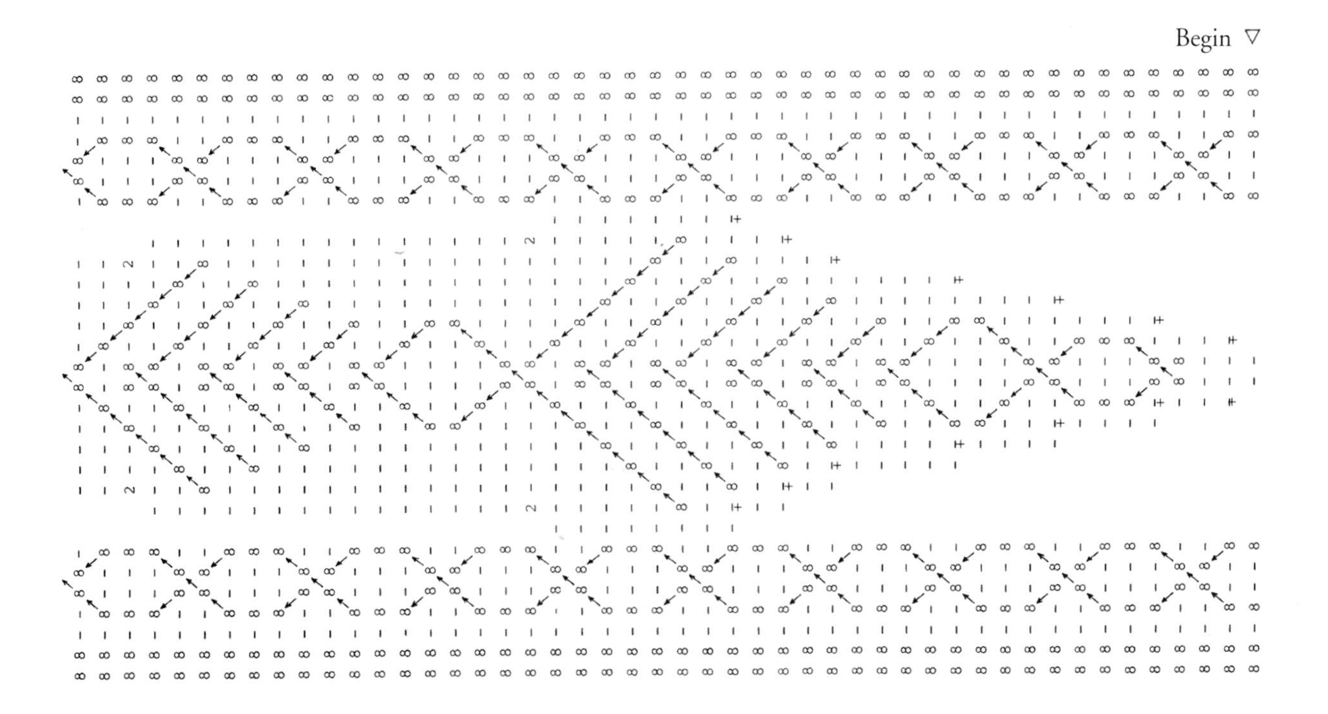

Center Back

```
8 - - 8               - - 8 - - 8 - -           8 8 8 8|8 8 8 8
8 - - 8               8 - - 8 8 - - 8           8 8 8 8|8 8 8 8
- 8 8 -               8 - - 8 8 - - 8           8 8|8 8|8 8|8 8
- 8 8 -               - 8 - 8 8 - 8 -           8 8 8 8|8 8 8 8
- 8 8 -               - - 8 8 8 8 - -           8 8 8 8|8 8 8 8
- 8 8 -               - - 8 8 8 8 - -           8 8 8 8|8 8 8 8
8 - - 8               - - 8 8 8 8 - -           8 8 8 8|8 8 8 8
8 - - 8               - - 8 8 8 8 - -           8 8|8 8|8 8|8 8
8 - - 8               - - 8 8 8 8 - -           8 8 8 8|8 8 8 8
- 8 8 -               - - 8 8 8 8 - -           8 8 8 8|8 8 8 8
- 8 8 -               - - - 8 8 - - -           8 8 8 8|8 8 8 8
- 8 8 -               - - - 8 8 - - -           8 8 8 8|8 8 8 8
- 8 8 - - 8 8 - - - 8 - - 8 - - - 8 8 - 8 8|8 8|8 8|8 8 - 8 8 -
8 - - 8 - 8 8 - - - 8 - - 8 - - - 8 8 - 8 8 8 8|8 8 8 8 - 8 8 -
8 - - 8 - 8 8 - 8 - - 8 8 - - 8 - 8 8 - 8 8 8 8|8 8 8 8 - 8 8 -
8 - - 8 - 8 8 - 8 - - 8 8 - - 8 - 8 8 - 8 8 8 8|8 8 8 8 - 8 8 -
- 8 8 - - 8 8 - - 8 - 8 8 - 8 - - 8 8 - 8 8 8 8|8 8 8 8 - 8 8 -
- 8 8 - - 8 8 - - - 8 8 8 8 - - - 8 8 - 8 8|8 8|8 8|8 8 - 8 8 -
- 8 8 - - 8 8 - - - 8 8 8 8 - - - 8 8 - 8 8 8 8|8 8 8 8 - 8 8 -
- 8 8 - - 8 8 - - - 8 8 8 8 - - - 8 8 - 8 8 8 8|8 8 8 8 - 8 8 -
8 - - 8 - 8 8 - - - 8 8 8 8 - - - 8 8 - 8 8 8 8|8 8 8 8 - 8 8 -
8 - - 8 - 8 8 - - - 8 8 8 8 - - - 8 8 - 8 8 8 8|8 8 8 8 - 8 8 -
8 - - 8 - 8 8 - - - 8 8 8 8 - - - 8 8 - 8 8|8 8|8 8|8 8 - 8 8 -
- 8 8 - - 8 8 - - - - 8 8 - - - - 8 8 - 8 8 8 8|8 8 8 8 - 8 8 -
- 8 8 - - 8 8 - - - - 8 8 - - - - 8 8 - 8 8 8 8|8 8 8 8 - 8 8 -
```

Center Front

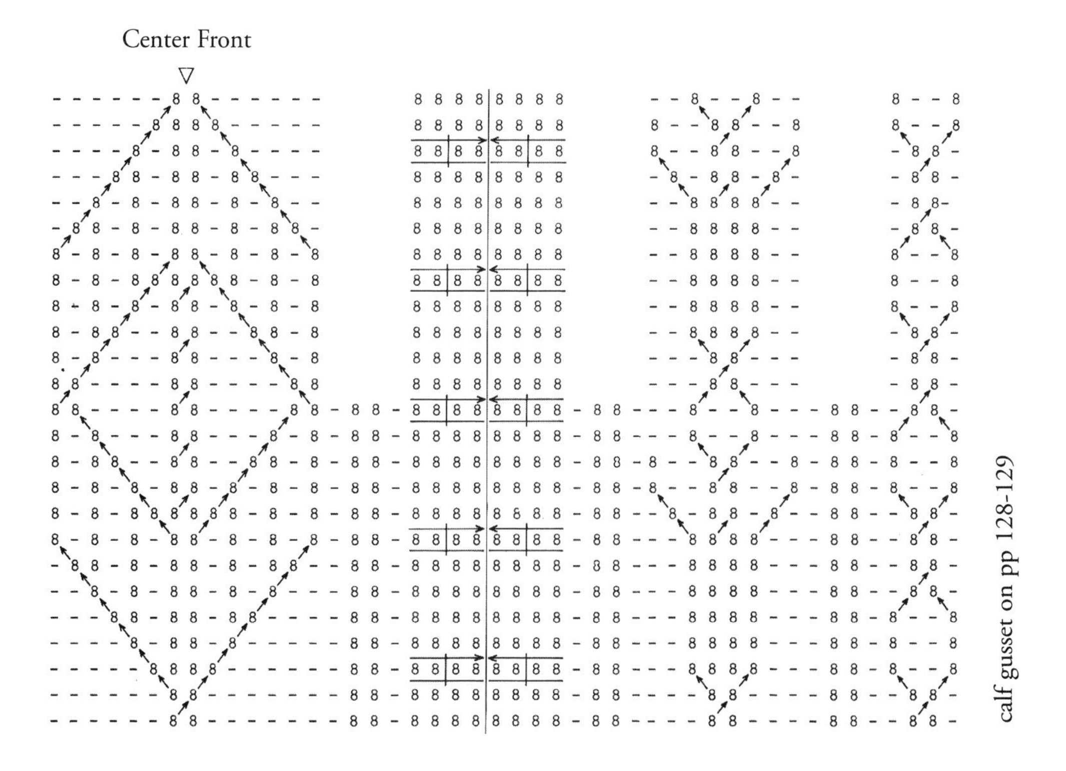

calf gusset on pp 128-129

Center Front

Center Front

▽

```
- - - 8           8 - - 8 8 - - 8       8 - - 8 8 - 8 - 8 8 -       8 8 - - 8 8 - - 8 8
- - - 8           8 - - 8 8 - - 8       - 8 8 - 8 - 8 - 8 8 -       8 8 - - 8 8 - - 8 8
- - 8 -           8 - - 8 8 - - 8       - 8 8 - 8 - 8 8 - - 8       8 8 - - 8 8 - - 8 8
- 8 - -           - 8 8 8 8 8 8 -       8 - 8 - 8 - 8 8 - - 8       8 8 - - 8 8 - - 8 8
8 - - -           - 8 - 8 8 - 8 -       8 - 8 - 8 8 - - 8 8 -       8 8 - - 8 8 - - 8 8
8 - - -           8 - - 8 8 - - 8       8 - 8 - 8 8 - - 8 8 -       8 8 - - 8 8 - - 8 8
- 8 - -           8 - - 8 8 - - 8       8 - 8 8 - - 8 8 - - 8       8 8 - - 8 8 - - 8 8
- - 8 -           8 - - 8 8 - - 8       8 - 8 8 - - 8 8 - - 8       - 8 8 - 8 8 - 8 8 -
- - - 8           8 - - 8 8 - - 8       8 8 - - 8 8 - - 8 8 -       - - 8 8 8 8 8 8 - -
- - - 8           - 8 8 8 8 8 8 -       8 8 - - 8 8 - - 8 8 -       - - 8 8 8 8 8 8 - -
- - 8 -           - 8 - 8 8 - 8 -       8 - 8 8 - - 8 8 - - 8       - 8 8 - 8 8 - 8 8 -
- 8 - -           8 - - 8 8 - - 8       8 - 8 8 - - 8 8 - - 8       8 8 - - 8 8 - - 8 8
8 - - -           8 - - 8 8 - - 8       8 - 8 - 8 8 - - 8 8 -       8 8 - - 8 8 - - 8 8
8 - - -           8 - - 8 8 - - 8       8 - 8 - 8 8 - - 8 8 -       8 8 - - 8 8 - - 8 8
- 8 - - - 8 8 -   8 - - 8 8 - - 8   8 8 - 8 - 8 - 8 - 8 8 - - 8 - 8 8 - 8 8 - - 8 8 - - 8 8 - 8 8 -
- - 8 - - 8 8 -   - 8 8 8 8 8 8 - - 8 8 - - 8 8 - 8 - 8 8 - - 8 - 8 8 - 8 8 - - 8 8 - - 8 8 - 8 8 -
- - - 8 - 8 8 -   - 8 - 8 8 - 8 - - 8 8 - - 8 8 - 8 - 8 - 8 8 - - 8 8 - 8 8 - - 8 8 - - 8 8 - 8 8 -
- - - 8 - 8 8 -   8 - - 8 8 - - 8 - 8 8 - 8 - - 8 8 - 8 - 8 8 - - 8 8 - 8 8 - - 8 8 - - 8 8 - 8 8 -
- - 8 - - 8 8 -   8 - - 8 8 - - 8 - 8 8 - 8 - - 8 8 - 8 - 8 - 8 - 8 8 - - 8 8 - 8 8 - 8 8 - - 8 8 -
- 8 - - - 8 8 -   8 - - 8 8 - - 8 - 8 8 - - 8 8 - - 8 8 - 8 - 8 - 8 8 - - - 8 8 8 8 8 8 - - - 8 8 -
8 - - - - 8 8 -   8 - - 8 8 - - 8 - 8 8 - - 8 8 - - 8 8 - 8 - 8 - 8 8 - - - 8 8 8 8 8 8 - - - 8 8 -
8 - - - - 8 8 -   - 8 8 8 8 8 8 - - 8 8 - 8 - - 8 8 - - 8 8 - 8 - 8 8 - - 8 8 - 8 8 - 8 8 - - 8 8 -
- 8 - - - 8 8 -   - 8 - 8 8 - 8 - - 8 8 - 8 - - 8 8 - - 8 8 - 8 - 8 8 - 8 8 - - 8 8 - - 8 8 - 8 8 -
- - 8 - - 8 8 -   8 - - 8 8 - - 8 - 8 8 - - 8 8 - - 8 8 - - 8 8 - 8 8 - 8 8 - - 8 8 - - 8 8 - 8 8 -
- - - 8 - 8 8 -   8 - - 8 8 - - 8 - 8 8 - - 8 8 - - 8 8 - - 8 8 - 8 8 - 8 8 - - 8 8 - - 8 8 - 8 8 -
```

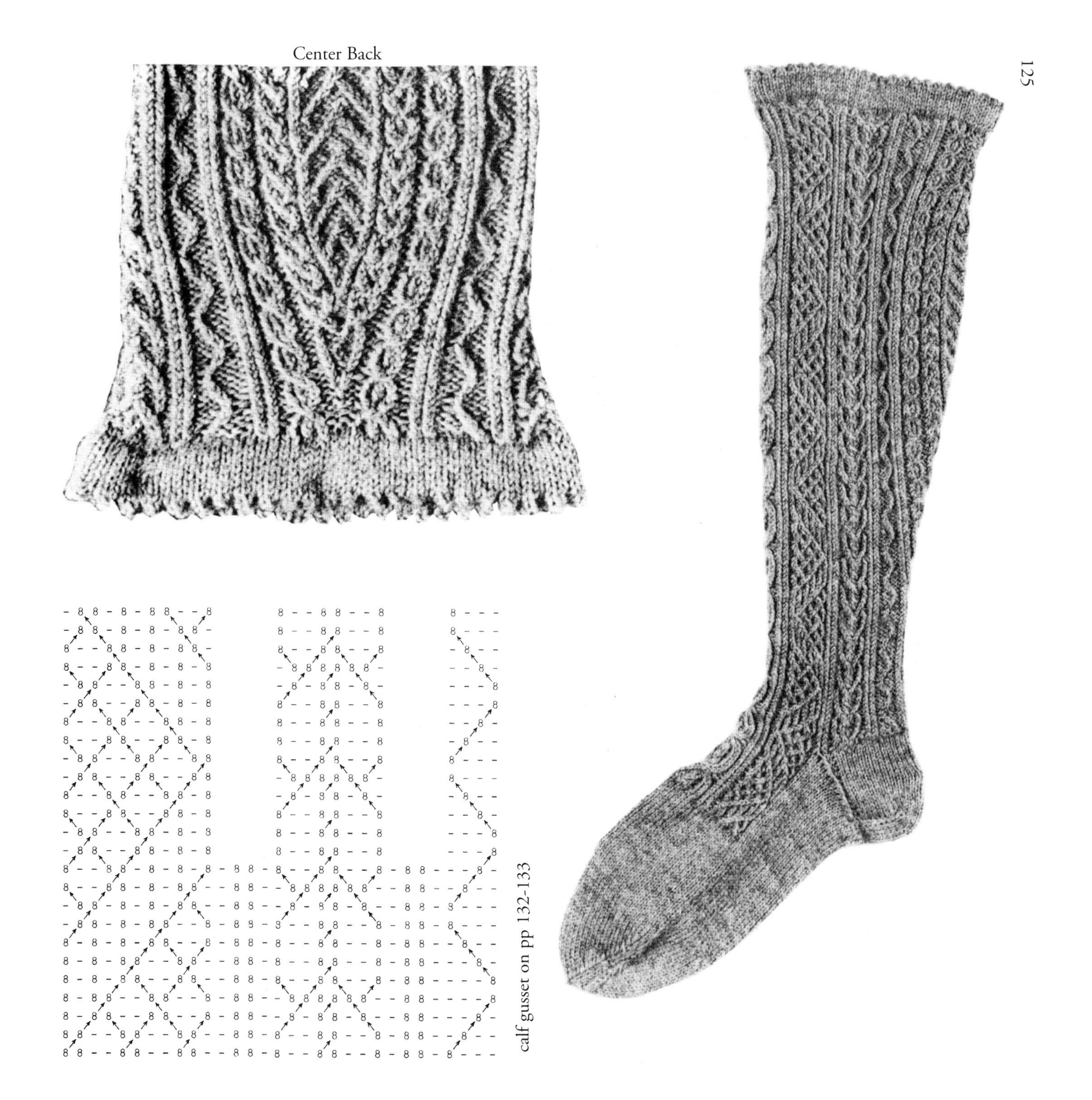
Center Back
calf gusset on pp 132-133

Center Front

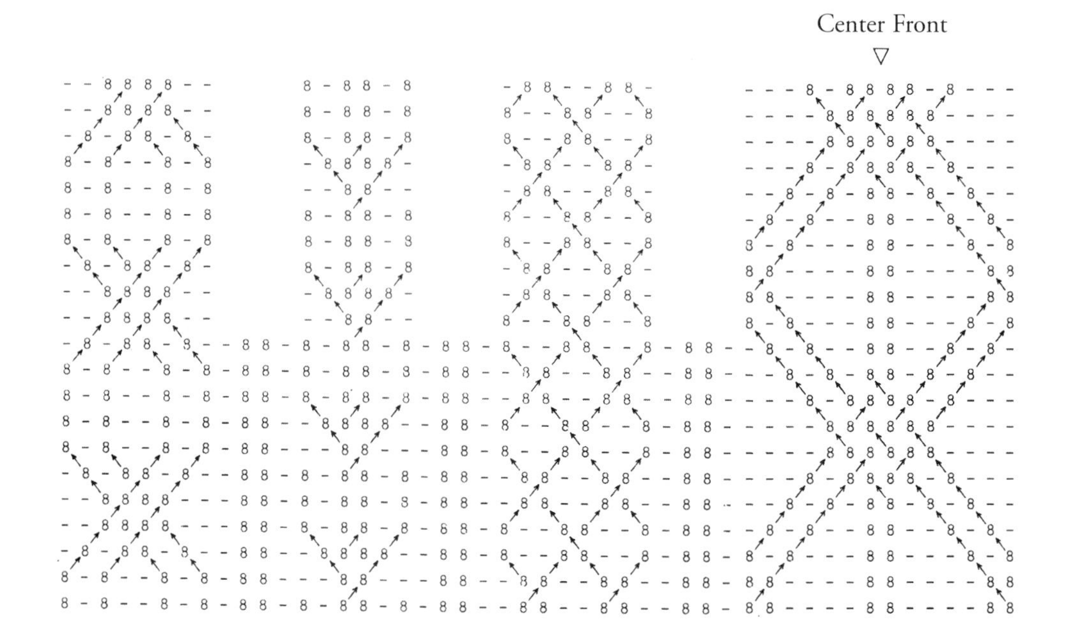

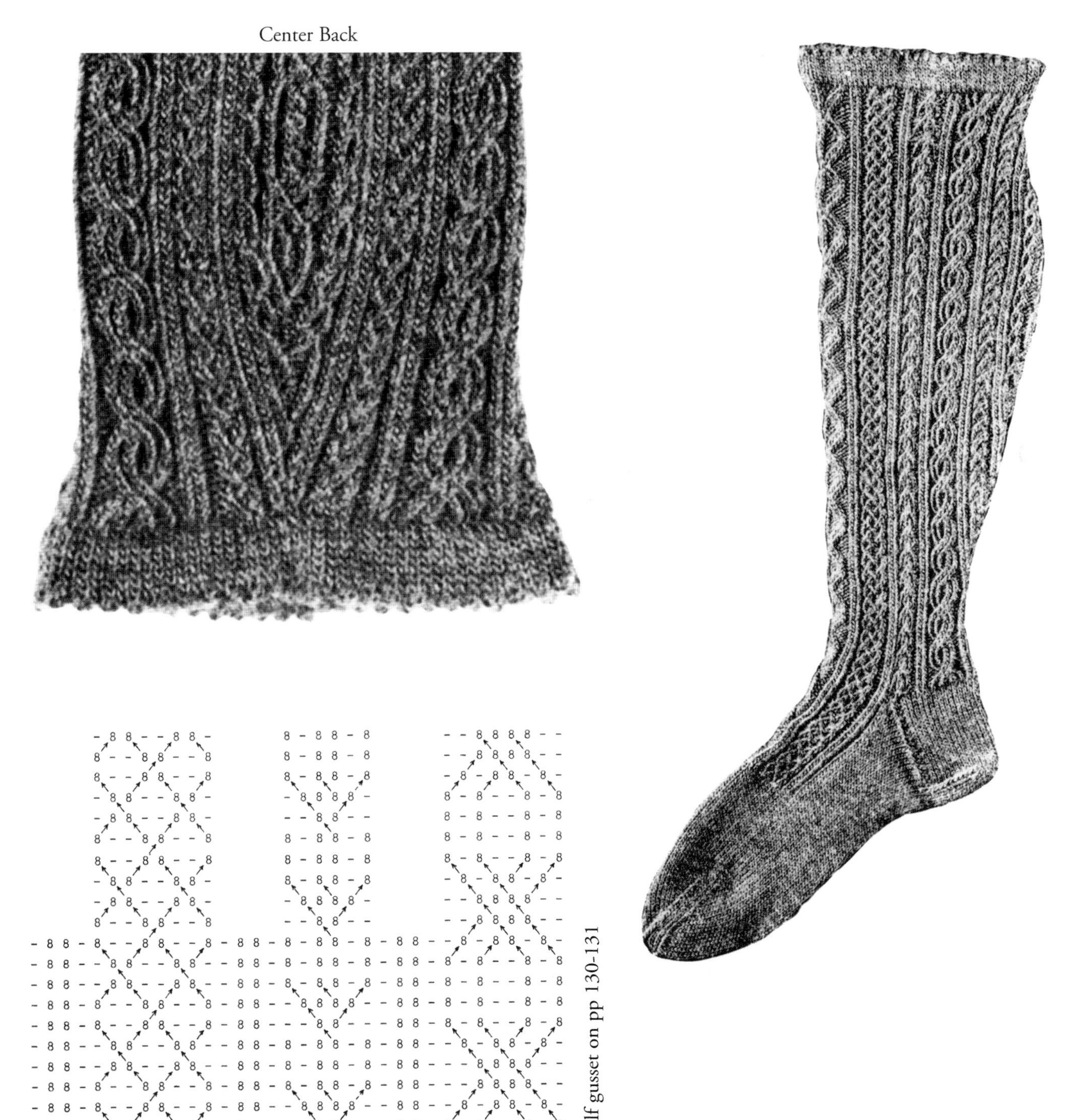

calf gusset on pp 130-131

Calf Gusset: Burning Love,
for stocking shown on
pages 122, 123

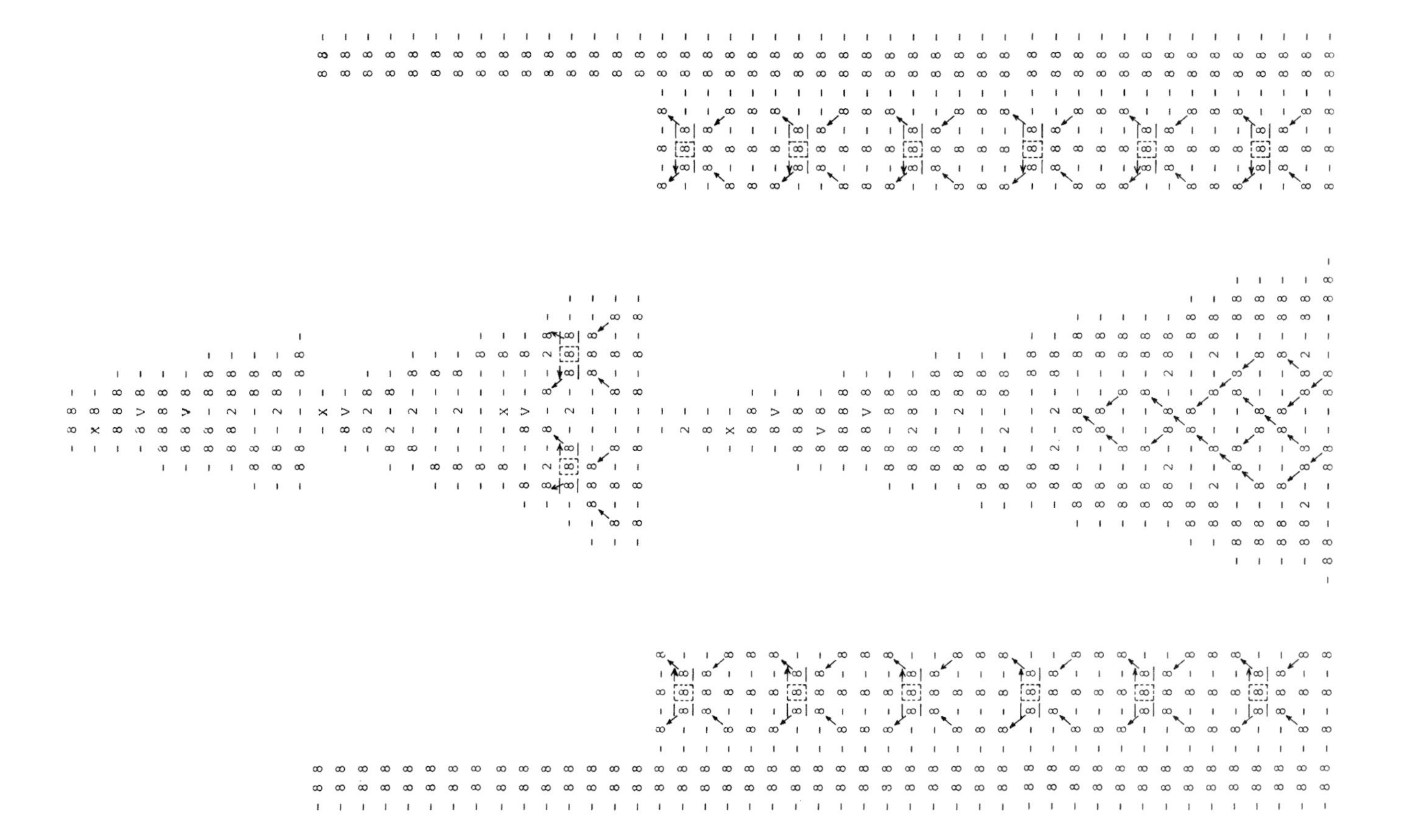

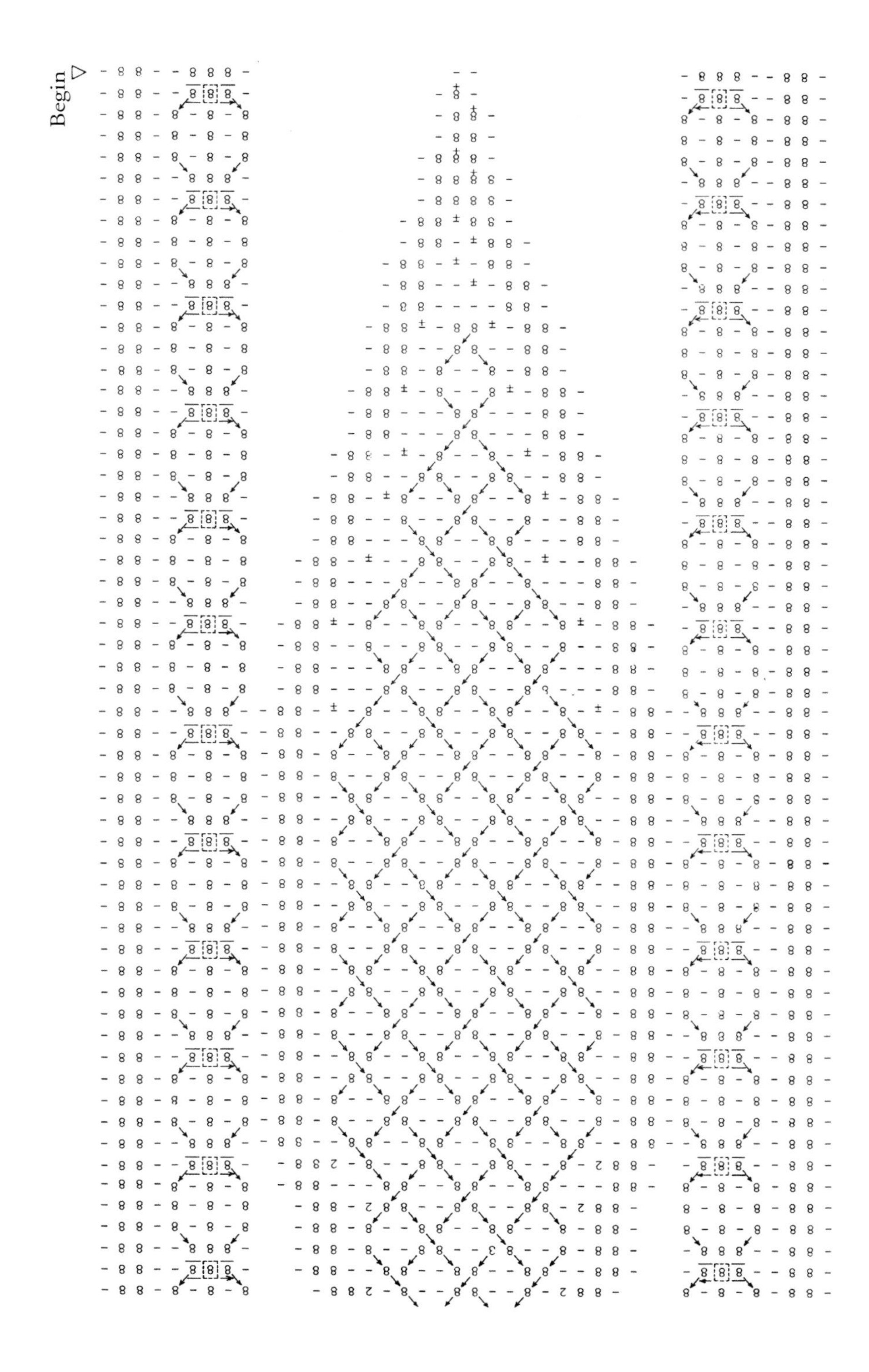
Begin

Calf Gusset: Little Tree,
for stocking shown on
pages 124, 125

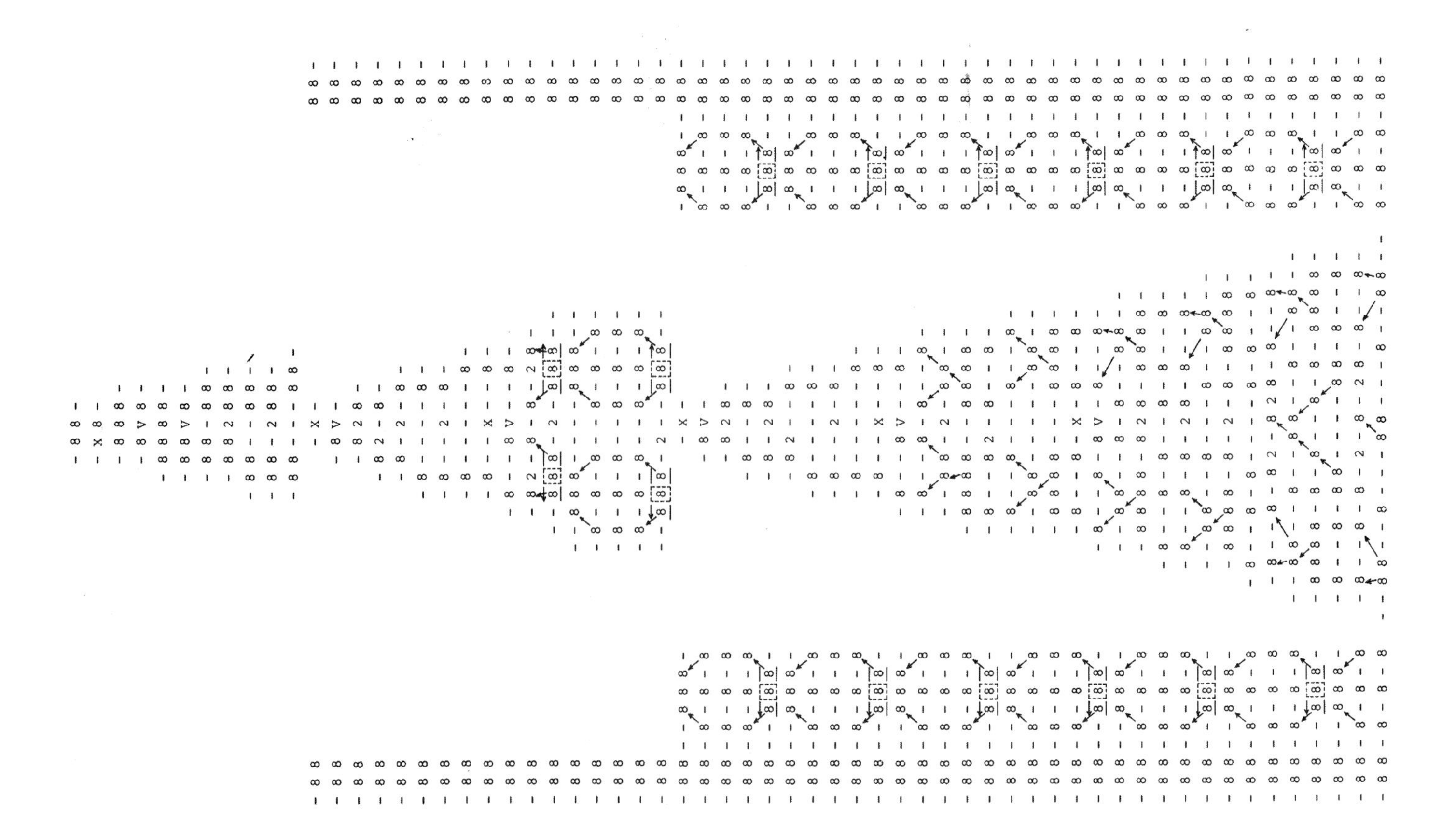

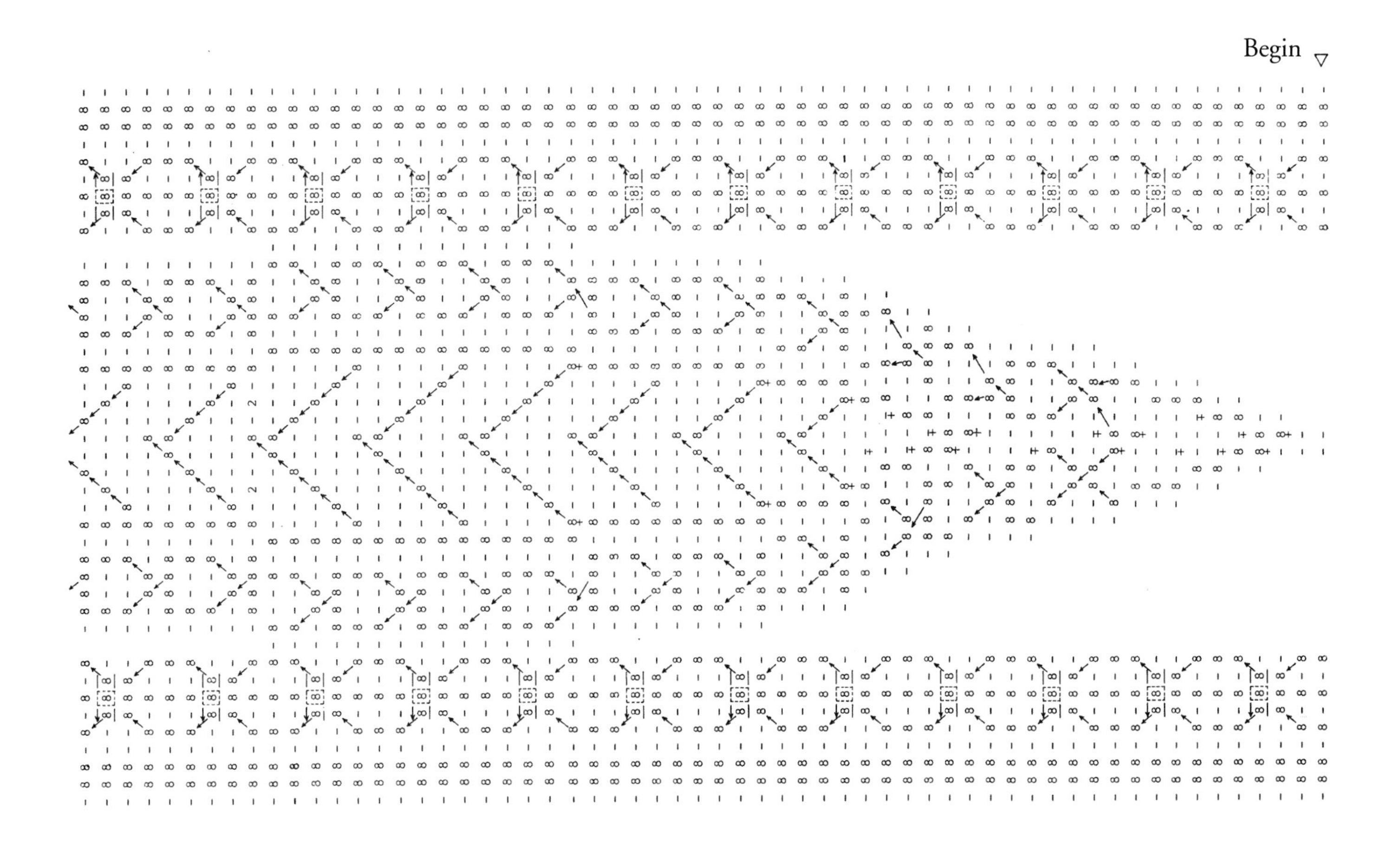
Begin

Calf Gusset: Double Chain,
for stocking shown on
pages 126, 127

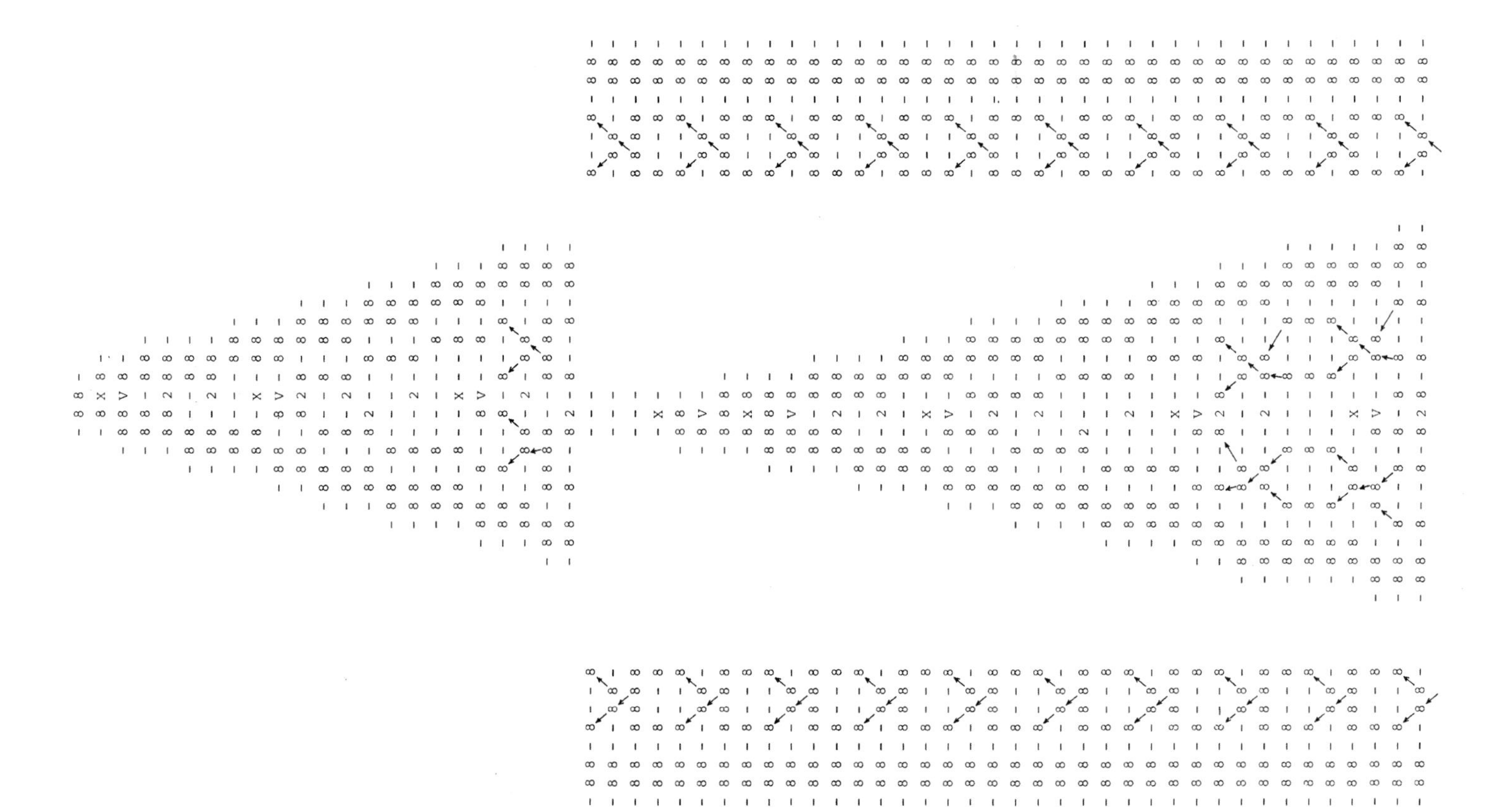

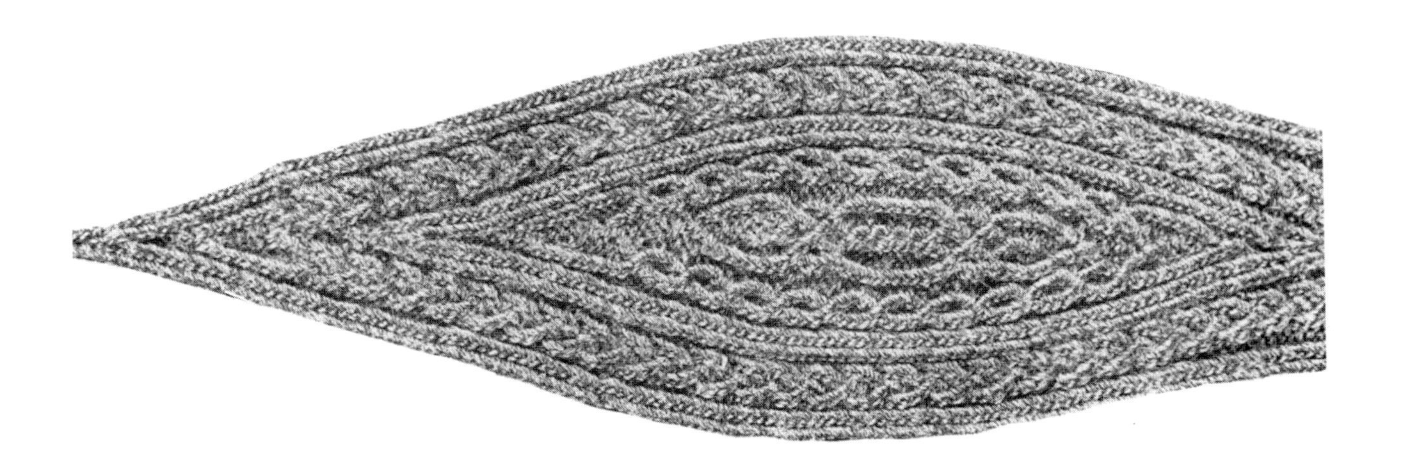

Begin

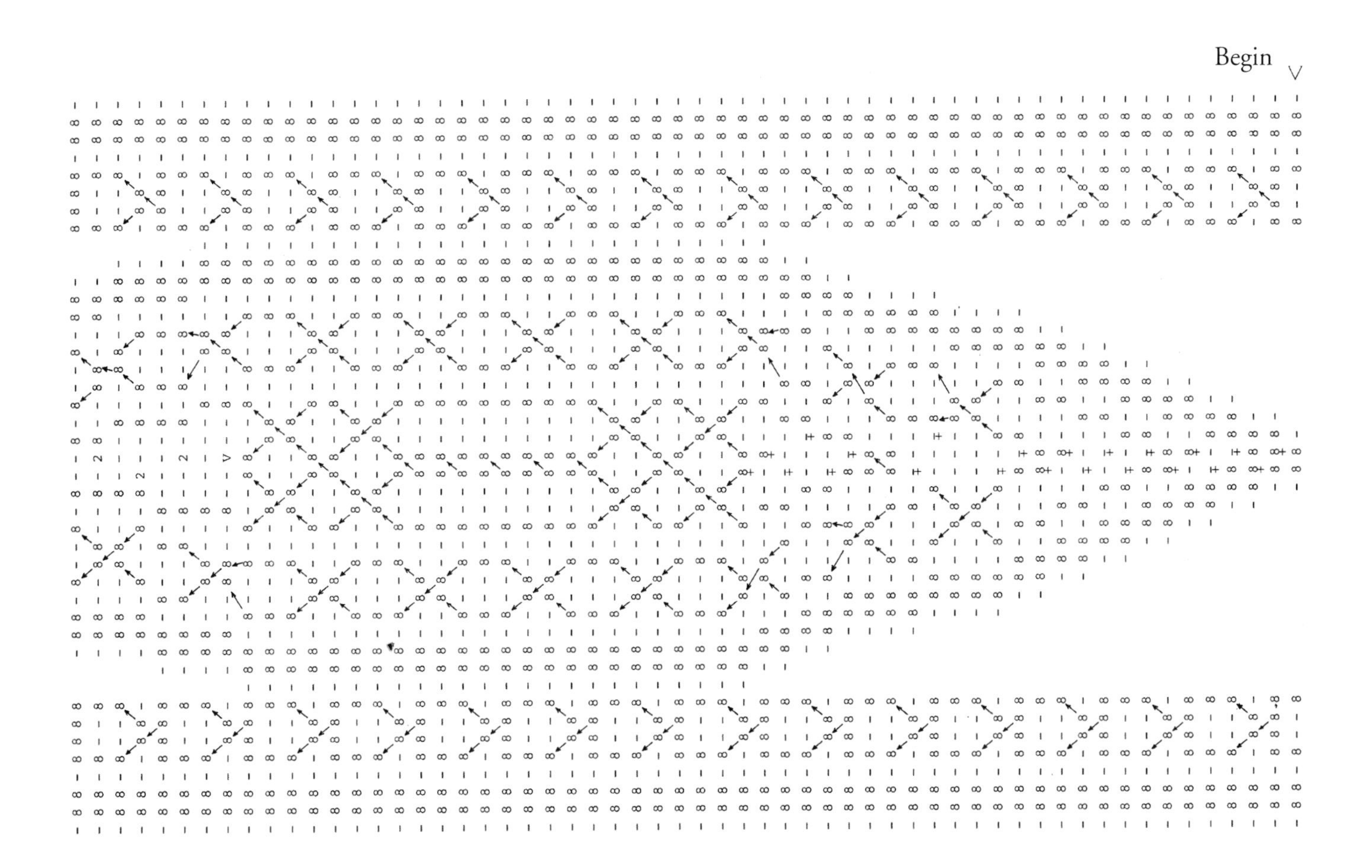

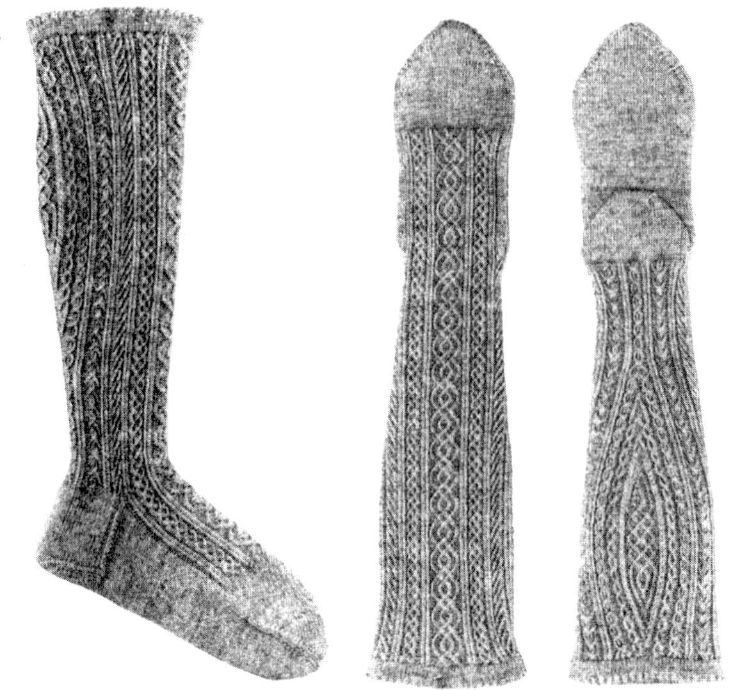

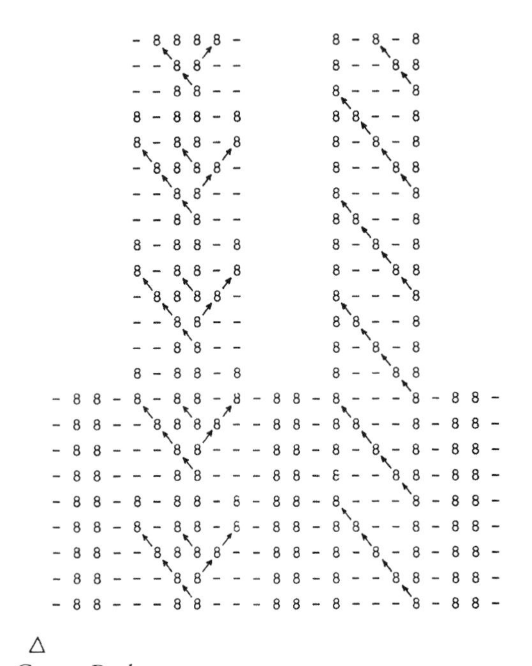

△
Center Back
▽

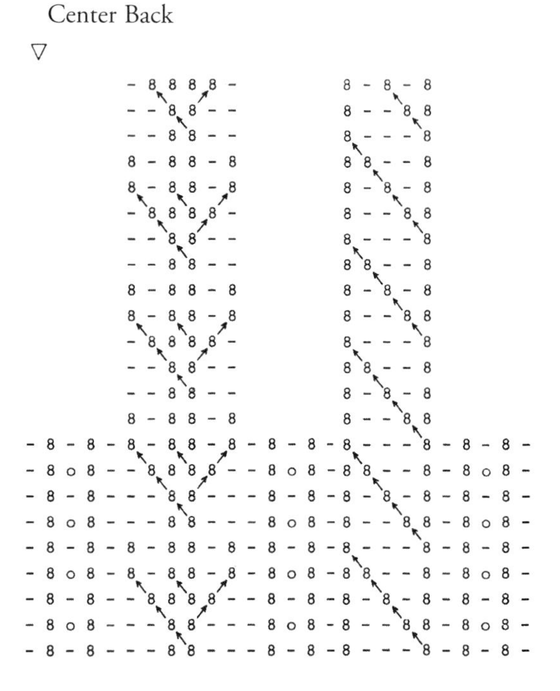

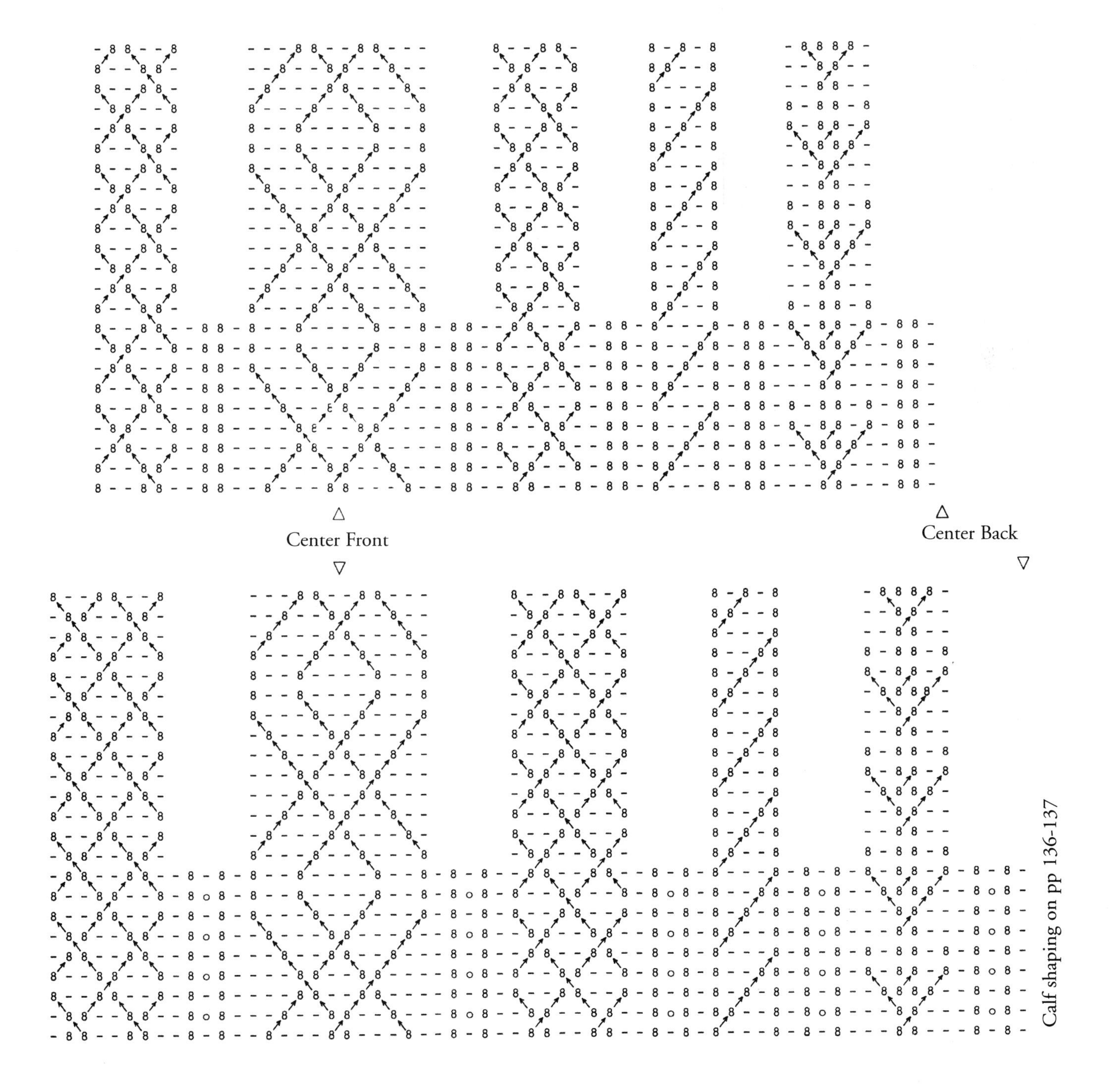

Calf shaping on pp 136-137

Calf Gusset: Large Burning Love,
for the stocking on pages 134, 135

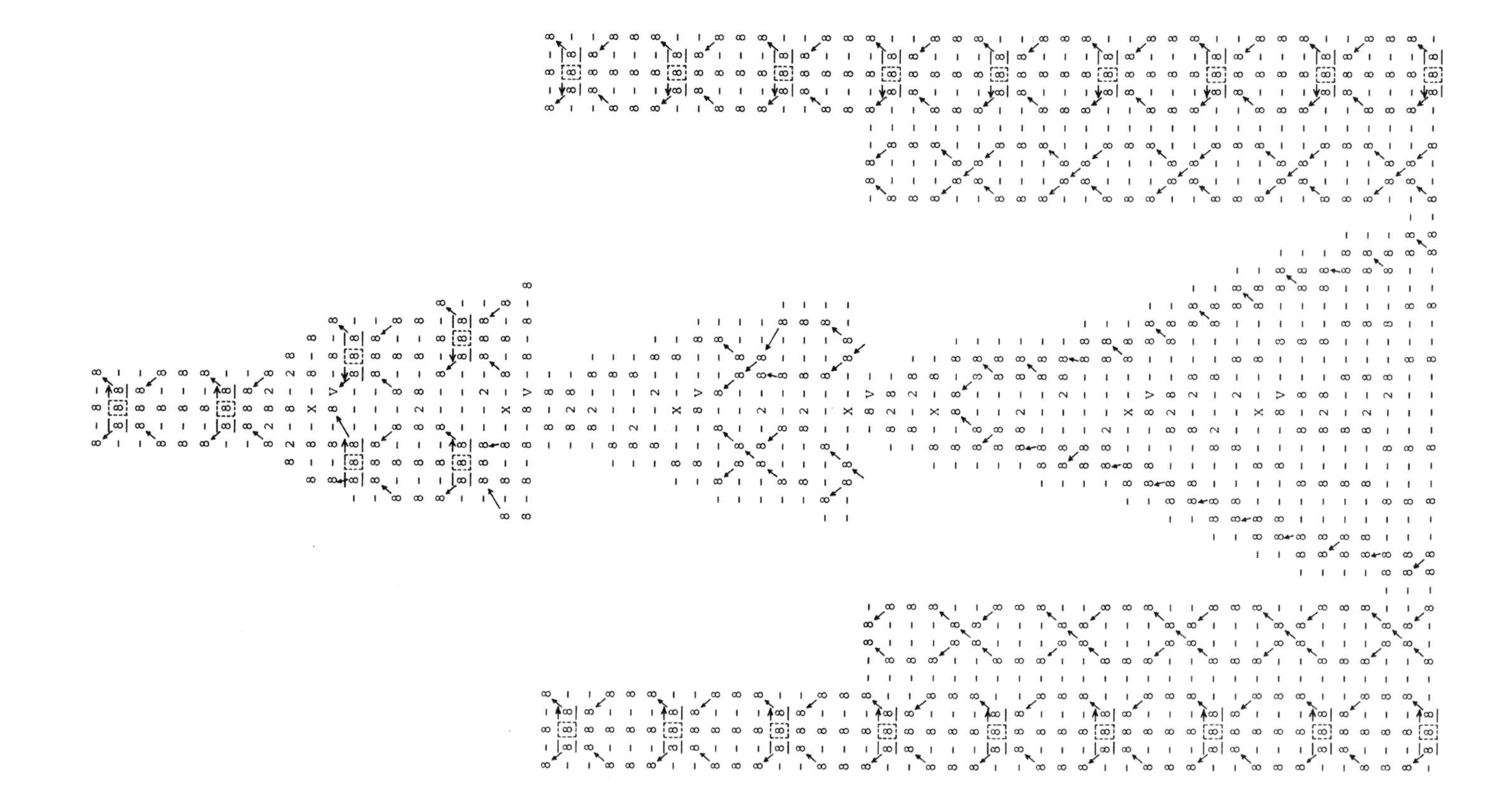

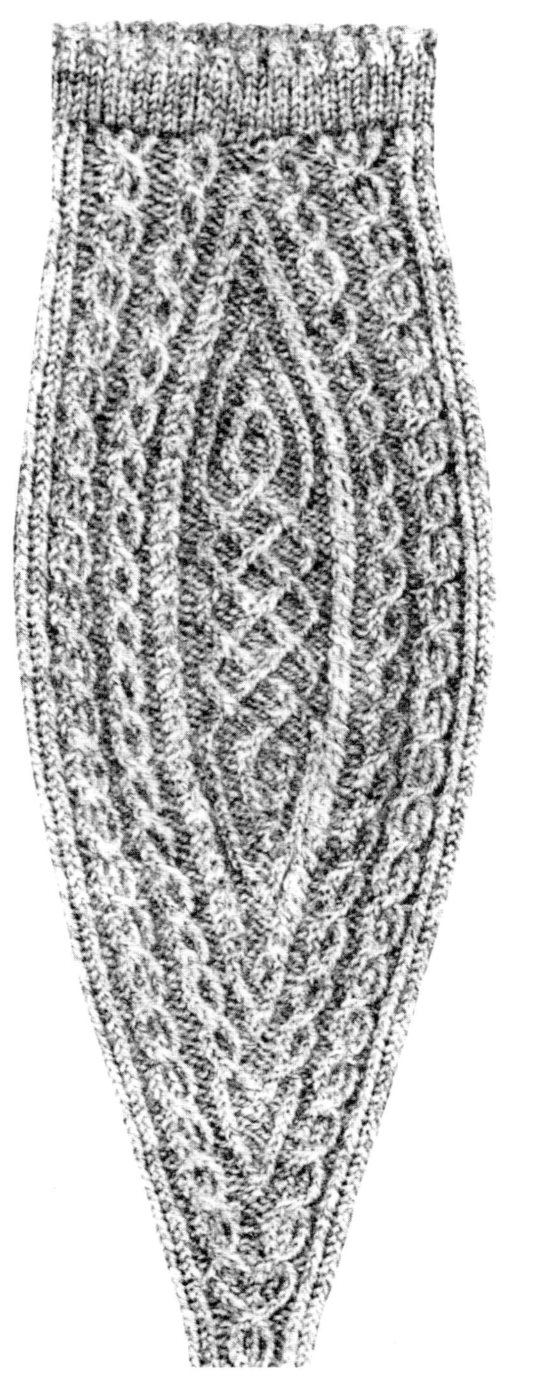

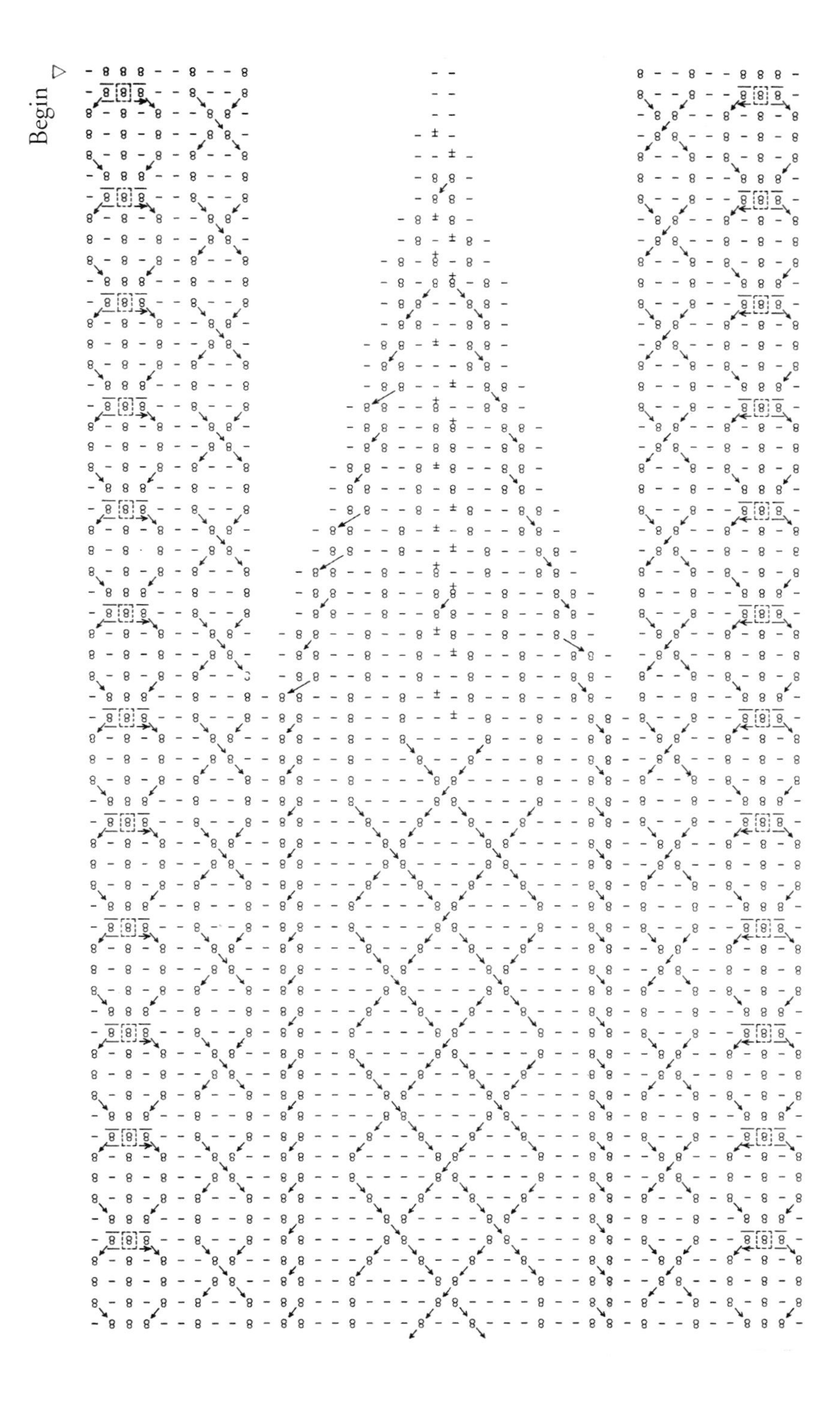
Begin

Boy's Stocking
Calf Gusset: Little Windows

Size 5- 6 years

Materials: 150 gram sock yarn (4- ply)
Needles size 2mm

Cast on 80 stitches,
Needed for patterned part: 94 stitches
Increase 14 stitches

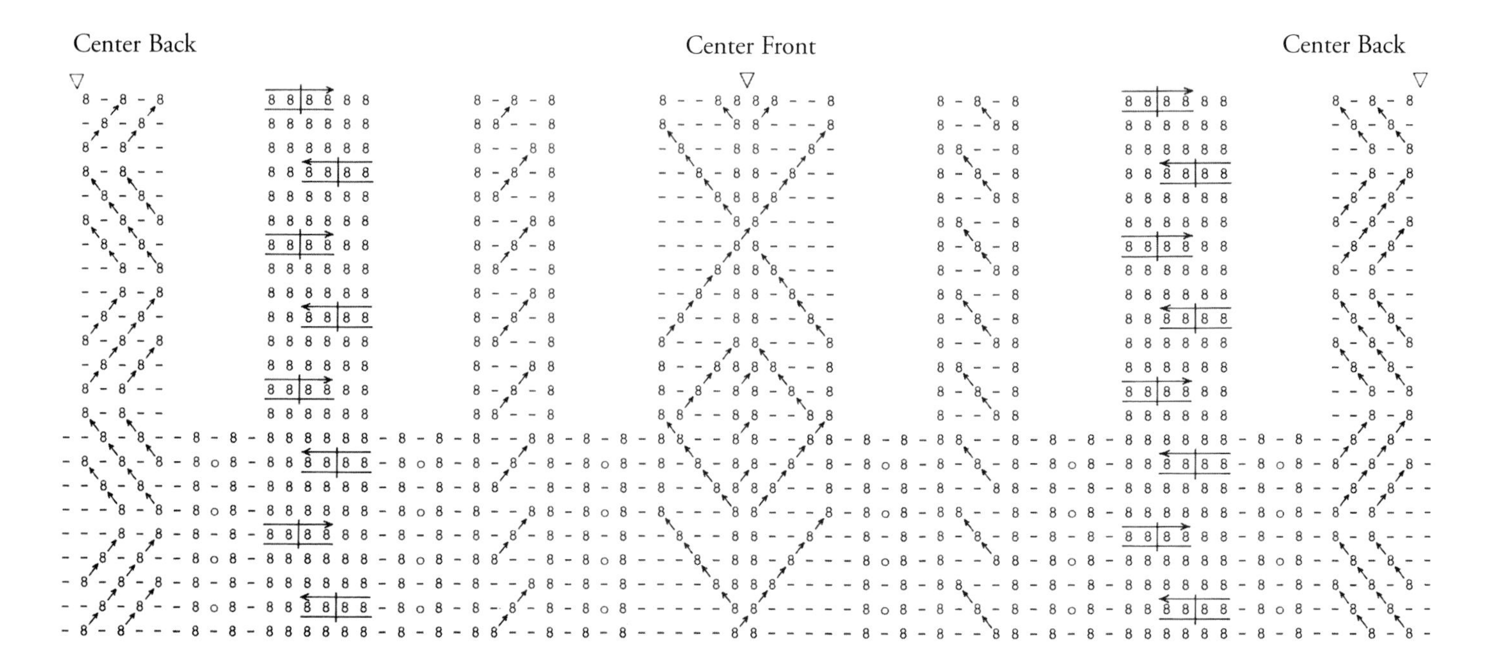

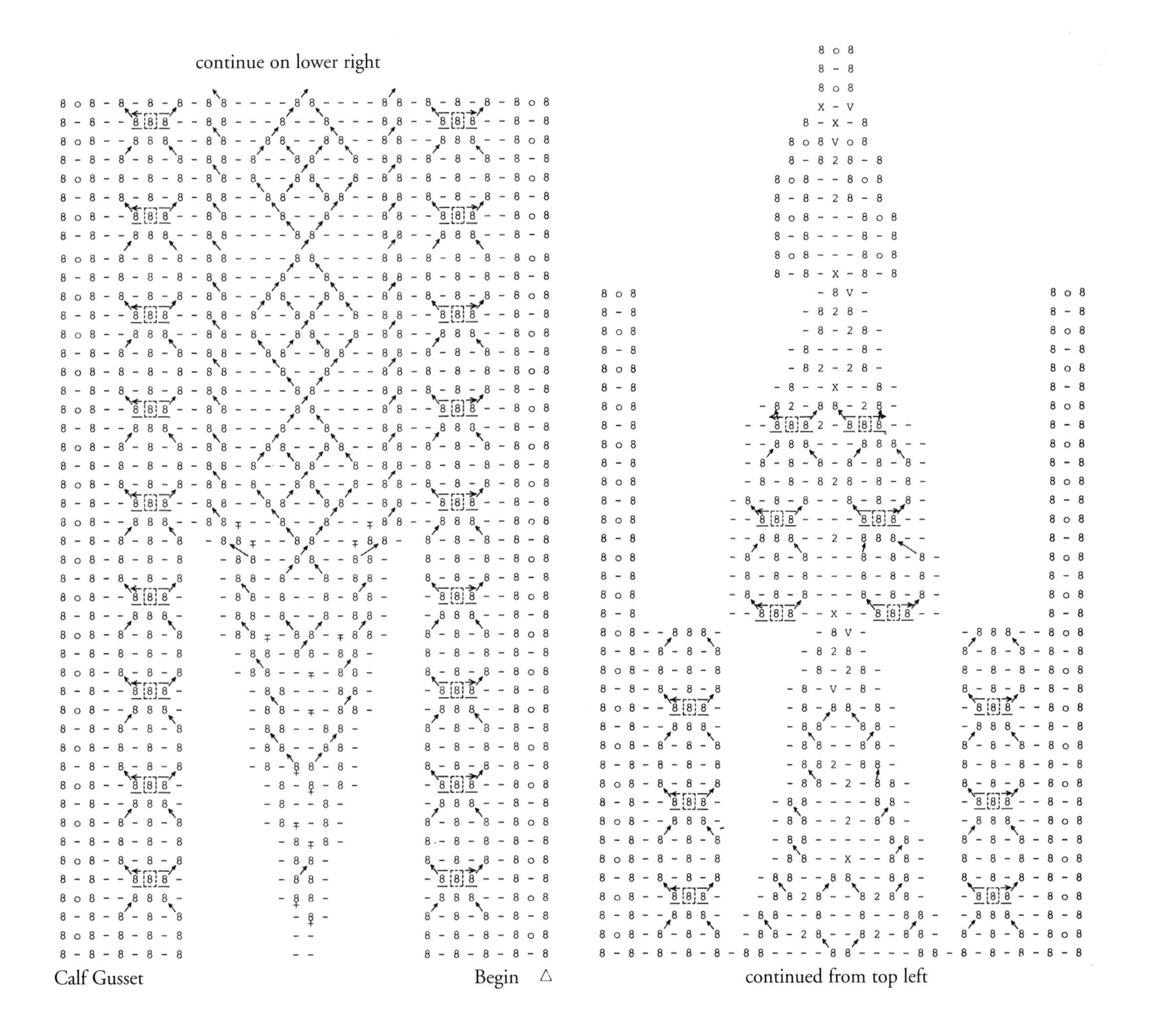
continue on lower right
Calf Gusset
Begin △
continued from top left

Women's Knee-Stockings

Shoe size 40 (German size)
Materials: 250 gram fine sock yarn,
Needle Size: 2mm

Cast on 104 sts for ribbing; increase 32 sts for patterned area: 136 stitches

Women's knee socks are constructed differently from men's in the calf and foot.

Please pay attention to the decreases, especially the ones on the right sides. The decreases are supposed to be part of the pattern and match up to the slant of the stitches. To achieve this, the right decreases should be done by taking the stitch to be decreased and pulling it across the next stitch. Knit both stitches together through the back loops.

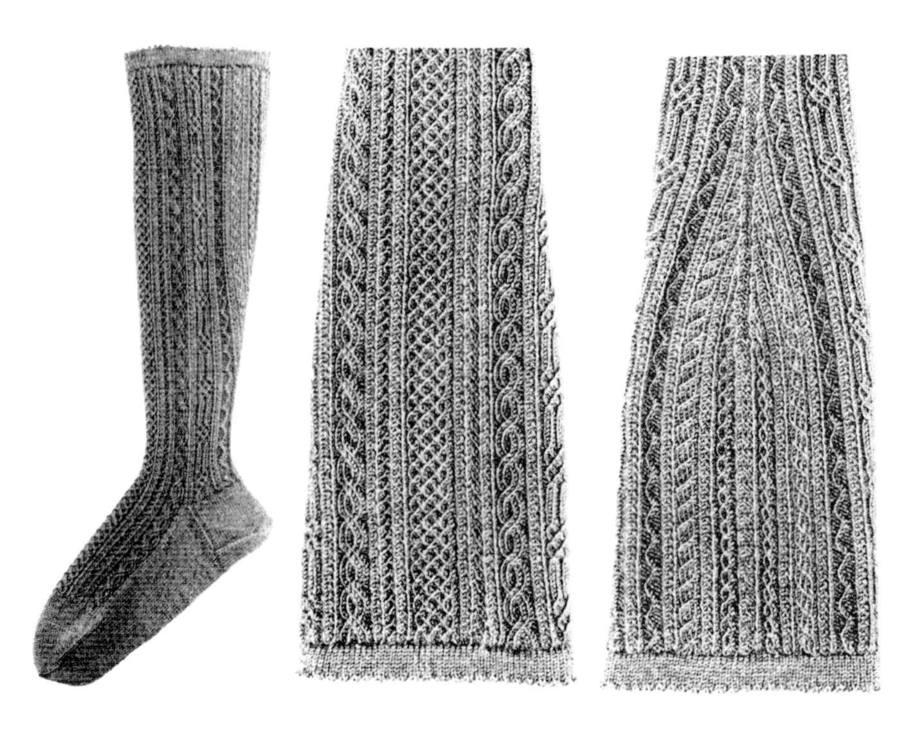

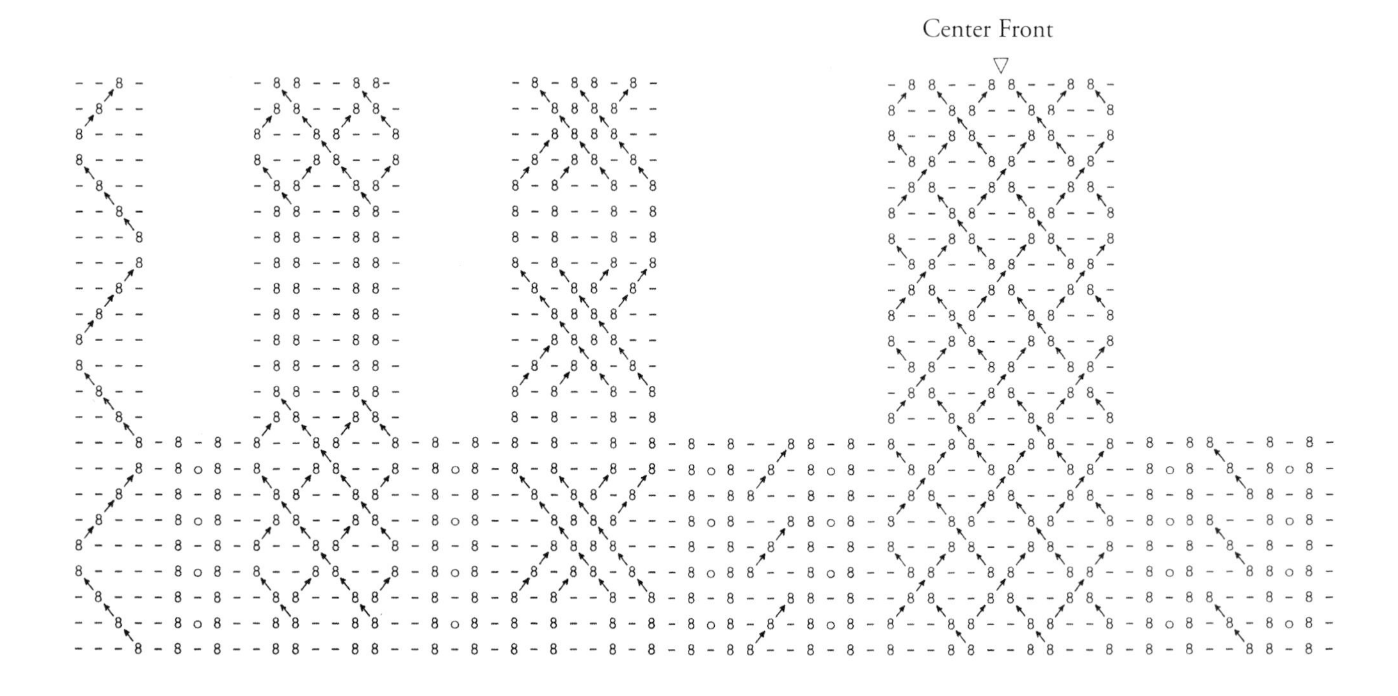

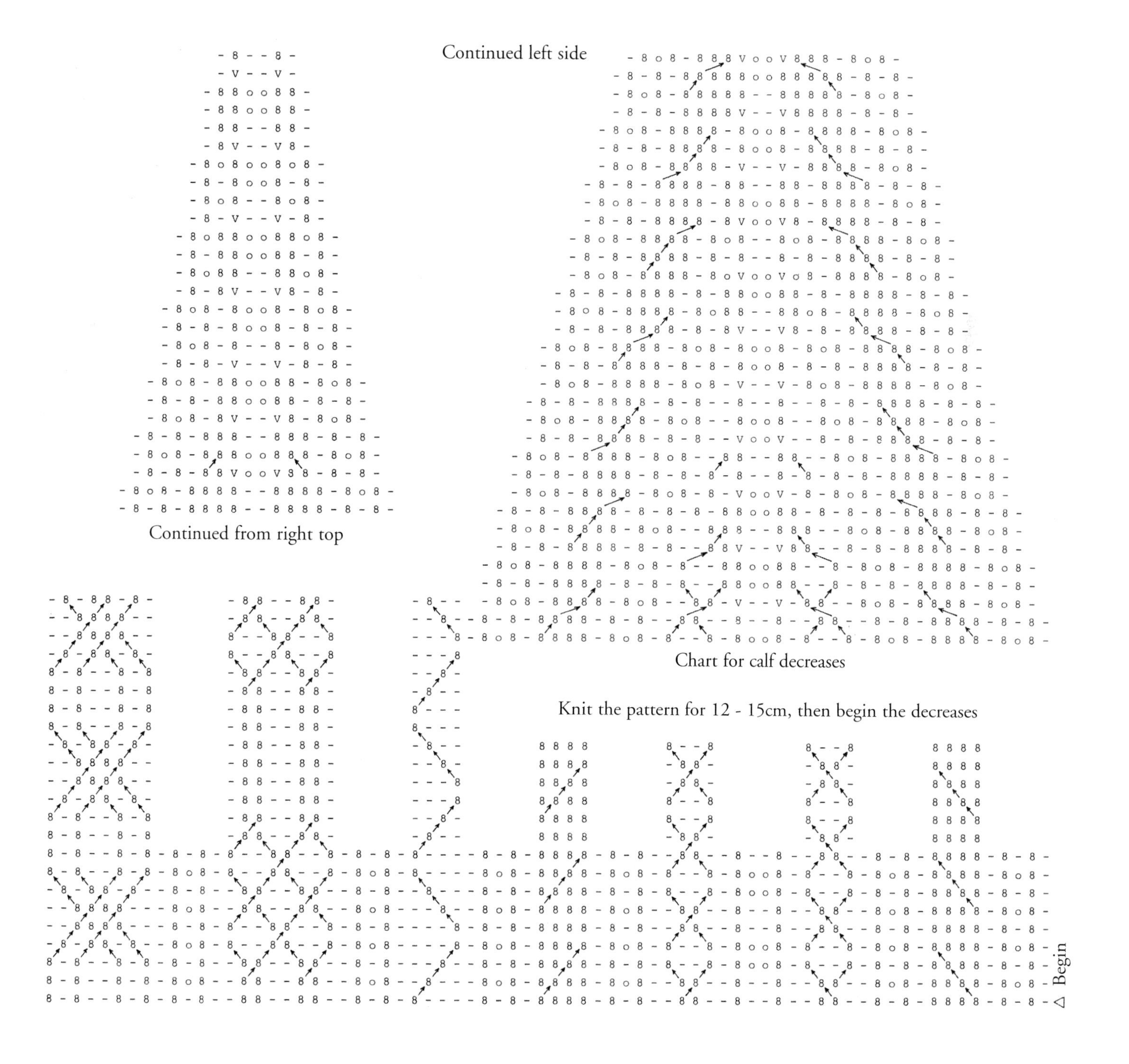
Continued left side
Continued from right top
Chart for calf decreases
Knit the pattern for 12 - 15cm, then begin the decreases
Begin

Jackets, Cardigans and Vests

Lady's Cardigan
From the Landschaftsmuseum, Schloss Trautenfels
Knitted by Mrs. Maria Erlbacher, Gröbming

Size 42 (German) Chest, 96 cm
Materials: 950- 1000 grams of wool Size 3 mm needles, or size needed to obtain optimal gauge

We have a wonderful assortment of wool available to us now. When knitting Twisted-Stitch patterns, the best fibers to work with are either a blend of 80% wool and 20% other fibers, or better yet, 100% wool. Use wool with a firm twist so the stitch pattern shows up nicely. Please don't be afraid to try these designs even though the instructions are for knitting back and forth with stitch patterns on both sides. *(See techniques for tips on working circular or back and forth.)*

Only by working pattern stitches every row will these designs be preserved in their original form. All too often the look is changed, because the knitter only does the pattern on the right side and uses plain knit and purl on the inside. Of course you will need practice in order to master patterning on the inside - or convert the flat pieces to circular.

It helps to be very familiar with the stitch patterns you use; it involves more effort to knit the pattern correctly, but in the end you will be happier with the finished garment.

General Notes on Patterns:

Gauge Swatch

It is very important to start with a gauge swatch. As some people knit tightly and others loosely, it will help you to cast on the exact amount of stitches you need for your measurements.
For example: cast on 30 sts + 2 edge sts = 32 sts. Using the pattern stitch that you have chosen for your project, knit for 10 cm. Stretch this a tiny bit, and measure how wide it is without the edge stitches on either side.

Let's pretend that your swatch measures 30 sts = 8.8cm, and the width of the back is 48 cm; divide 48 cm by 8.8 cm = 5.4. The width of the back equals to 5.4 times the width of the swatch, so you will need 5.4 times the number of stitches in the swatch. 5.4 x 30 = 162 sts plus the two edge sts. So you will need to cast on 164 sts.

Please note: Not all of the motif-repeats are the same number of rows high, so repeats start in different rows. Along the right side of the charts you will see a pair of dots to indicate one vertical repeat.

RM = Edge stitch: This selvedge is worked as follows: Knit to within last stitch. Slip last stitch, purlwise, to right-hand needle. Turn and knit (wool wraps around base of first stitch). This gives a pretty, knot - like appearance to the edge.

Sleeve charts: Most of the sleeves are knitted in the round until you reach the cap-shaping. There are usually two chart for each sleeves; one shows the main sleeve and the other is for the underarm increases.

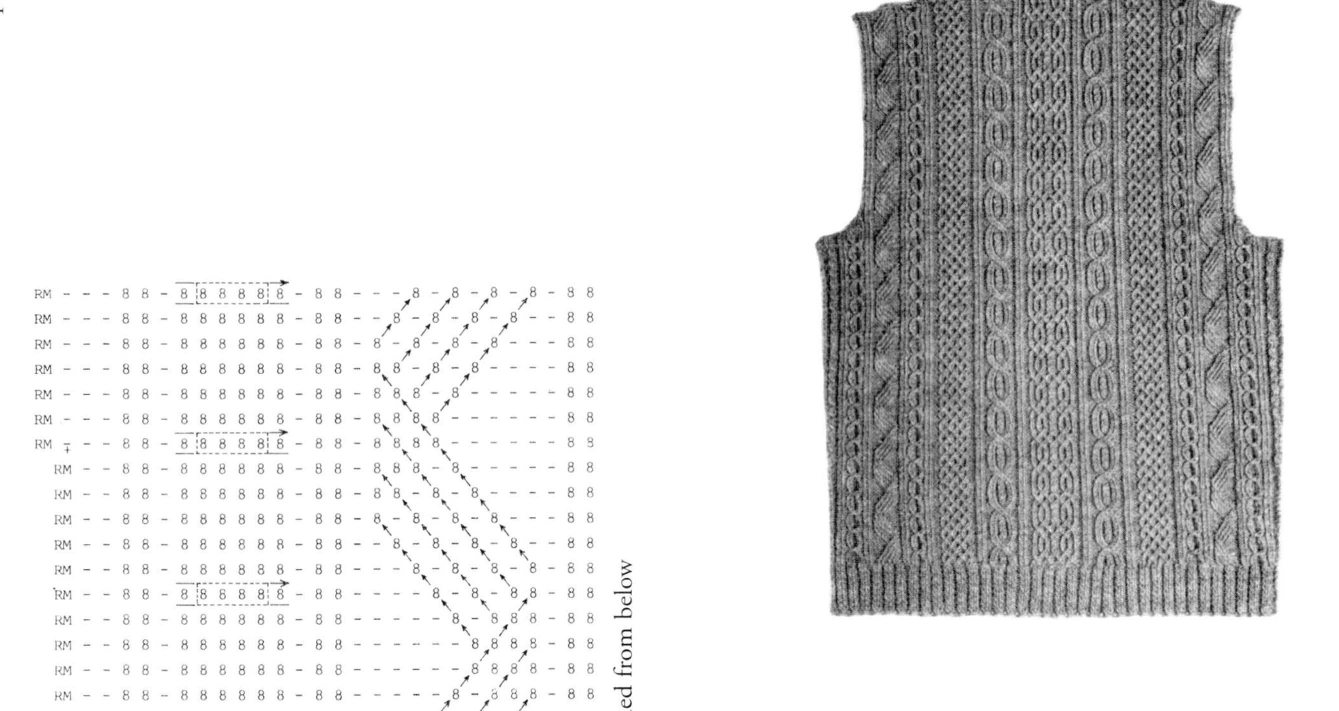

Continued from below

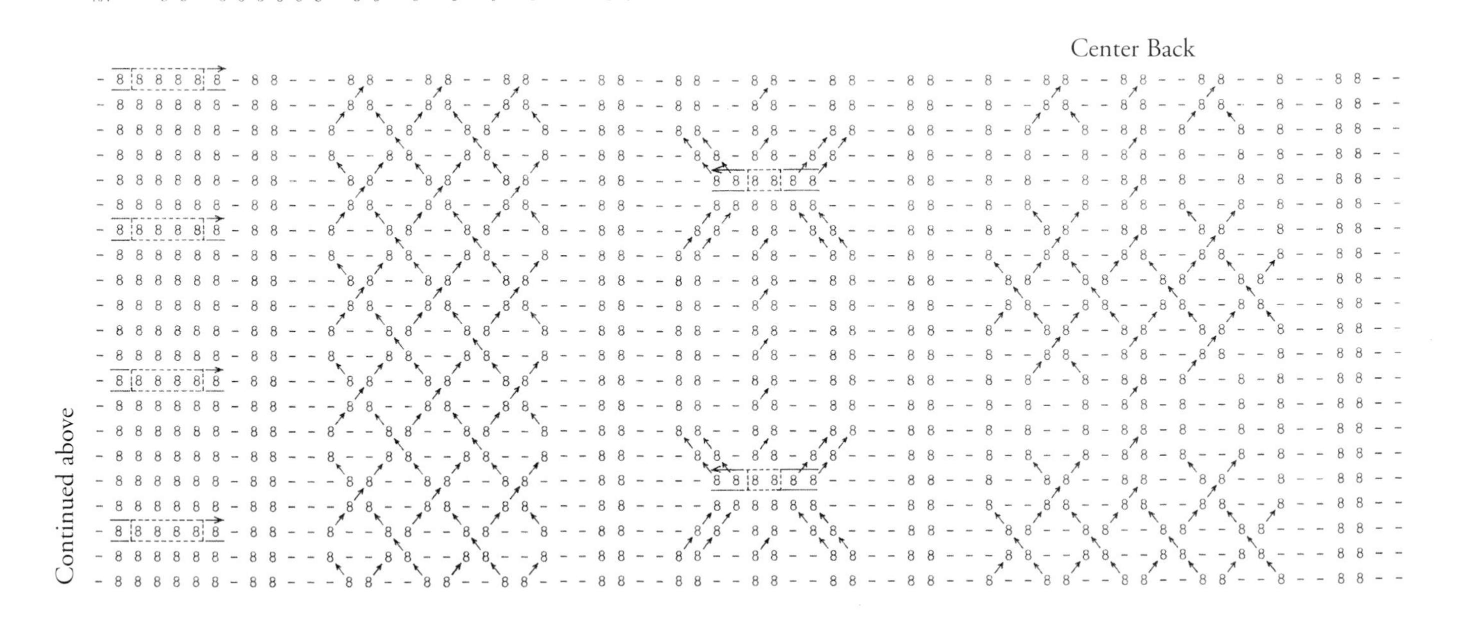

Continued above

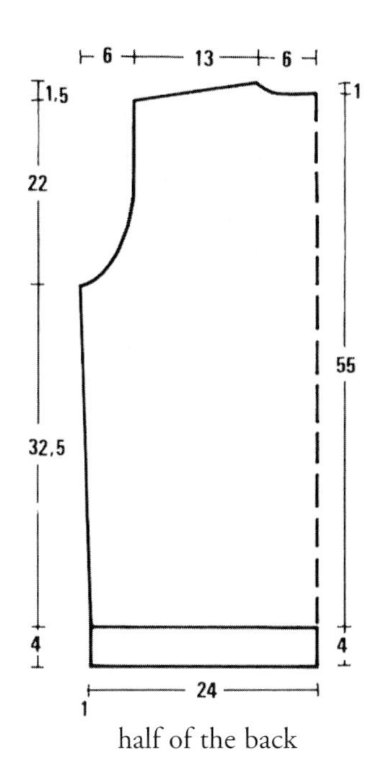

half of the back

Back: Cast on 150 sts + 2 edge sts.
The ribbing is knitted in p2, k2b (twisted) for 4 cm. After this, start the pattern. In the first row increase 12 sts evenly across the width; 164 sts. Any time you knit with patterns such as these, increases will need to be done above the ribbing, as Twisted-Stitch fabric has a tendency to pull in.

Follow the chart exactly, knitting the pattern forwards and back (see Techniques). After a few rows, the pattern becomes apparent and you won't have to look at the chart quite as often. Continue in pattern to the armholes, increasing 4 sts between the edge stitch and the first pattern on both sides, evenly spaced, vertically, between ribbing and armhole.

Armhole: Cast off sts on each side, every other row: (6 sts) x1, (3 sts) x1, (2 sts) x2, (1stitch) x2. When the armhole is 22 cm deep, start the neck decreases by casting off 34 sts in the center.

Shoulder Slope: Knit the shoulders individually. Cast off sts are worked on every other row; 13 sts at a time, three times. Cast off the remaining 15 sts. Repeat for the second shoulder.

Back Chart runs across these two pages

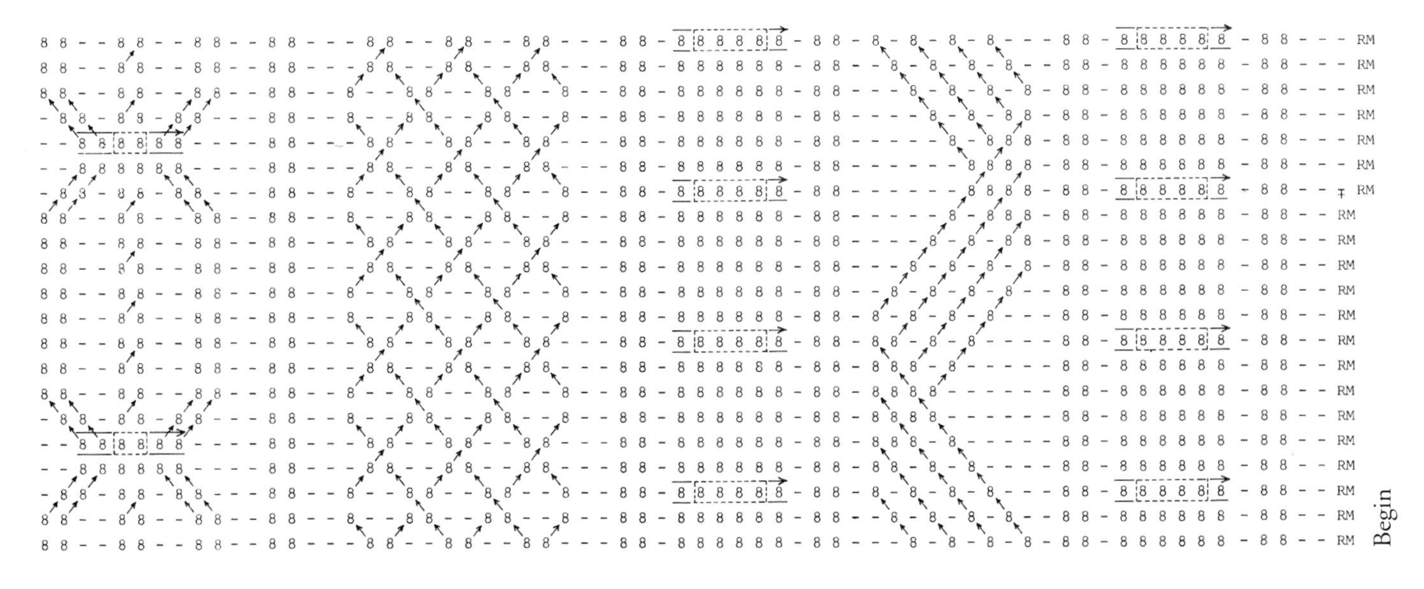

Left Front:
I recommend that you knit the left front first, so you can figure out the placement of the buttonholes on the right front.

Cast on 80 sts + 11 sts for the buttonhole strip + 2 edge sts = 93 sts. Knit the ribbing as for the back. In the first row after the ribbing, increase 11 sts, evenly across the front (104 sts).

Knit, following the charts up to the armholes, increasing 4 sts evenly spaced along the length of the front on the armhole side.

Edge Stitch: Work to last stitch (RM), slip last stitch p'wise to right-hand needle, turn. Take wool between needles to back (around the base of the slipped stitch) and knit. This gives a pretty, knot-like appearance to the edges.

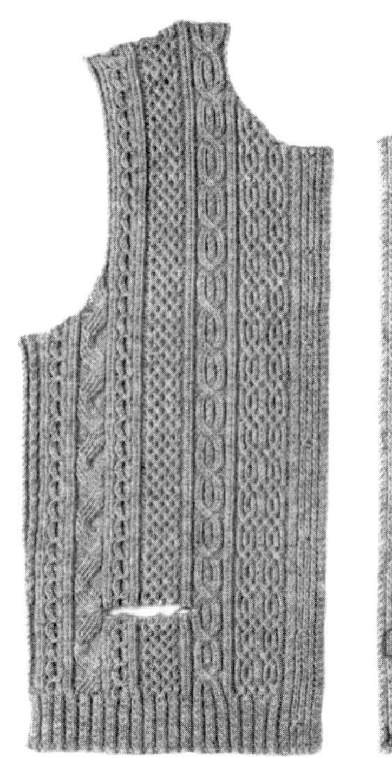

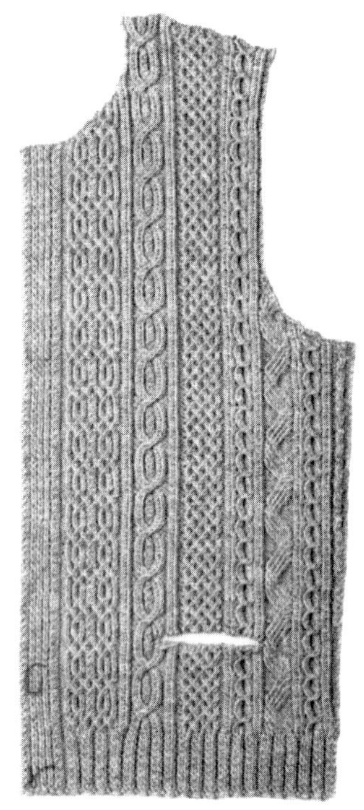

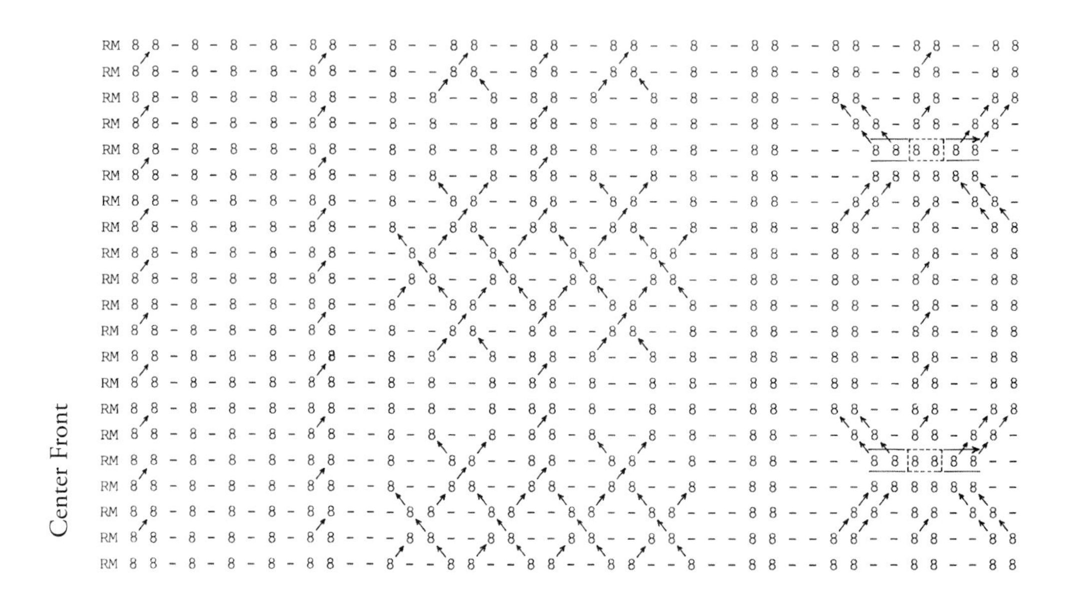

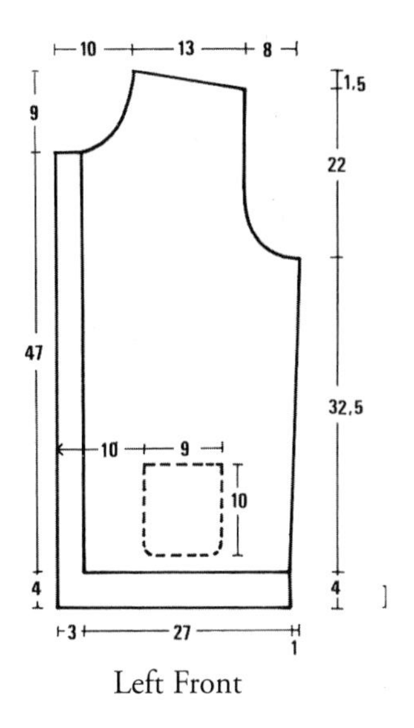

Left Front

Armhole: Work the front for as many rows as the back. Cast off for armhole shaping in every other row, on the side opposite the button band, as follows: (9 sts) x1, (4 sts) x2, (3 sts) x1, (2 sts) x2, (1 stitch) x4.

Shoulder Slope: Cast off 11 sts in every second row 4 times.

Right Front: Work the same as the left front, but add buttonholes, evenly spaced.

Buttonholes: Knitted horizontal: Figure out where to place the buttonholes, and how many stitches wide your buttons are. Make the buttonhole in the center of your button band. Knit a few stitches, cast off the required number of stitches and finish the row. Knit back to the point where you cast off and cast on the same number of stitches that you cast off. Finish the row.

Left Front Chart runs across these two pages; reverse charts for Right Front

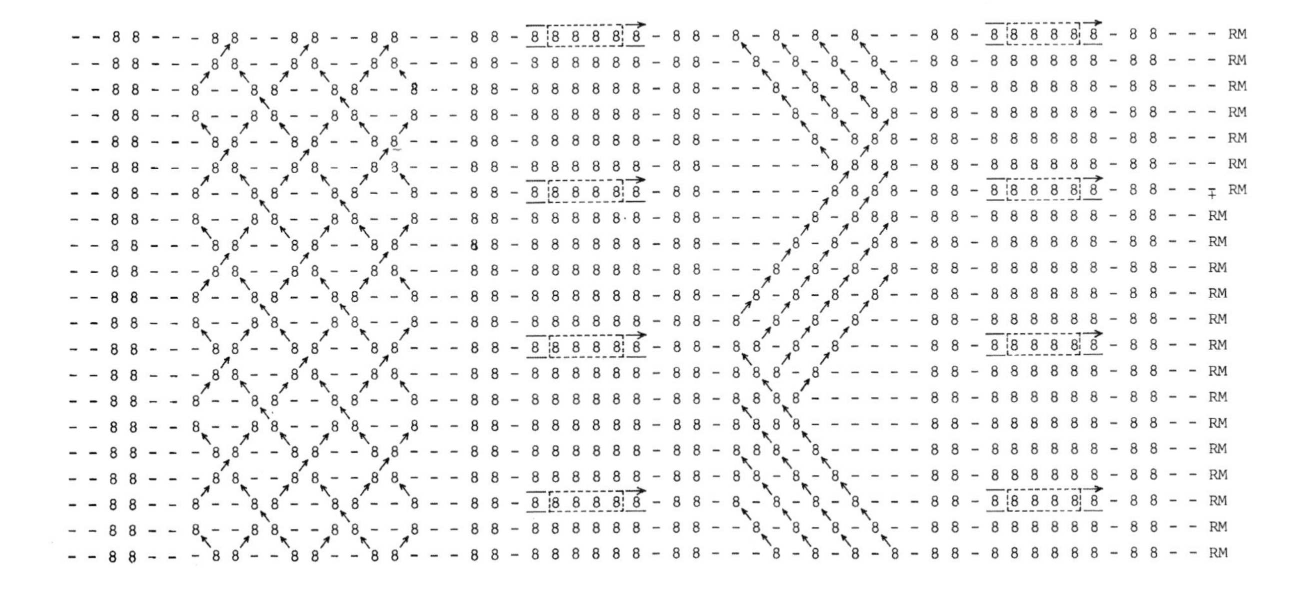

Sleeve: With dp needles, cast on 60 sts. Knit in ribbing for 4 cm. In the first row after the ribbing, increase 12 sts = 72 sts. Between this point and the top of the sleeve you need to increase 48 sts (24 pairs) on each side of the center underarm stitch - approximately 5 to 7 rounds apart: 120 sts. Add narrow patterns to fill increased stitch sections.

The top of the sleeve is knitted back and forth. The cast offs are done in every other row on both sides, as follows: (3sts) x1, (2 sts) x3, (1 stitch) x7.

Now decrease 1 stitch every 4th row, x 3.

After this, the decreases will once again be in every other row (1 stitch) x4, (2 sts) x4, (3 sts) x2 and (4 sts) x1. In the next row cast off the remaining 38 sts. Work the second sleeve the same way.

Finishing: Block all of the pieces by pinning them, lightly stretched, to a soft surface. Dampen them by spraying with water, or cover with a damp cloth. Let them dry. Sew the side seams and set in the sleeves.

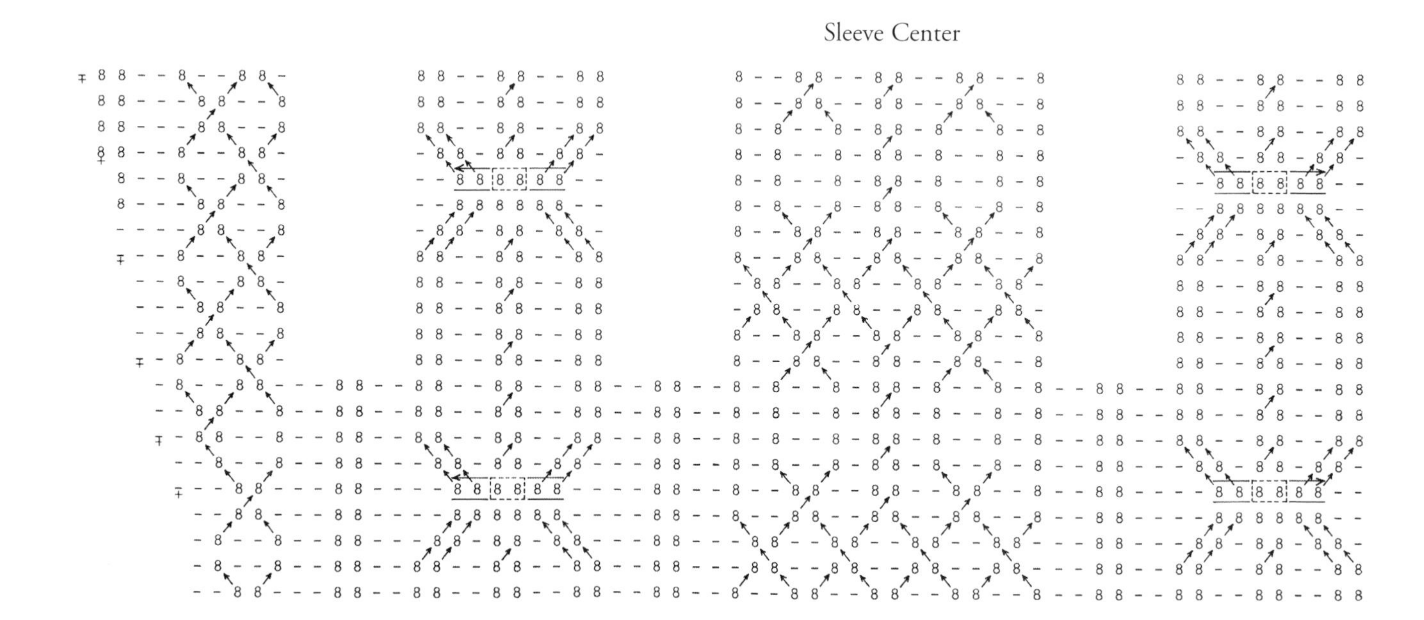

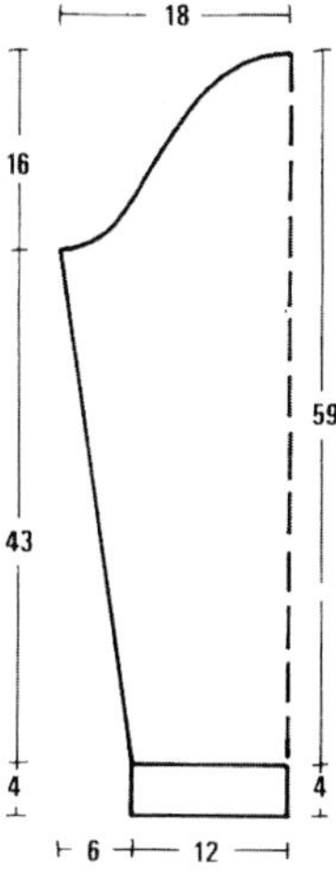

half of the sleeve

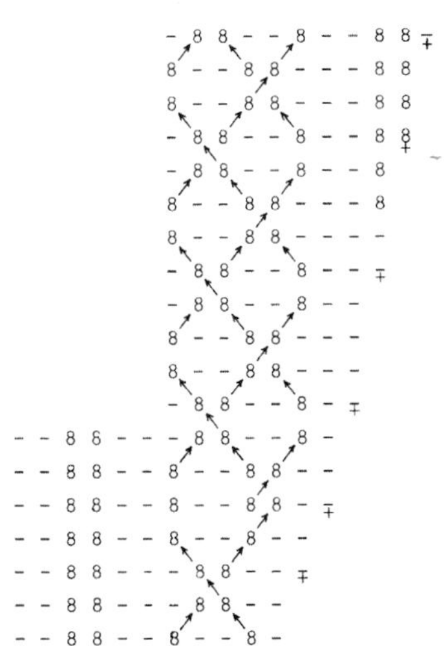

Neck Edge: Pick up about 94 sts from the previously cast off edges. Knitting from the front (outside) of the cardigan, make one row of twisted knit stitches. The following rows are worked in p1, k1 twisted for 6 cm. Cast off. This is double the width that is needed, as you will now fold it in half to the inside and fasten it down, using a seam stitch. Sew the buttons in the appropriate spots on the front.

Sleeve Chart runs across these two pages.

Men's Cardigan

From the Landschaftsmuseum Schloss Trautenfels
Knitted by Rosina Pilz from Jager, Ramsau

Back: Cast on 108 sts (106 pattern sts + 2 edge sts). Knit for 3 cm in garter stitch (knit each row), using green yarn. Switch to grey yarn in the next row (first pattern row) and increase 36 sts evenly across that row (144 sts). Follow chart to underarms.

Armhole: The cast offs for the arm hole are done on both sides in every other row as follows: (4 sts) x1, (3 sts) x2 times, (2 sts) x1 and (2 sts) x2. Continue in pattern until the total length of the arm hole is 22 cm. Cast off the 18 center stitches, and make the neck opening by casting off (2 sts) x3 in every other row. At the same time work the shoulder slope by casting off 11 sts, 3 times, and 10 sts, once in every other row. Repeat on other side.

Size 52 (German sizing)
Materials: 1000 to 1100 grams of grey wool, a little heavier than sport weight, 50 grams of green wool in the same weight.
Needle size: 3 mm

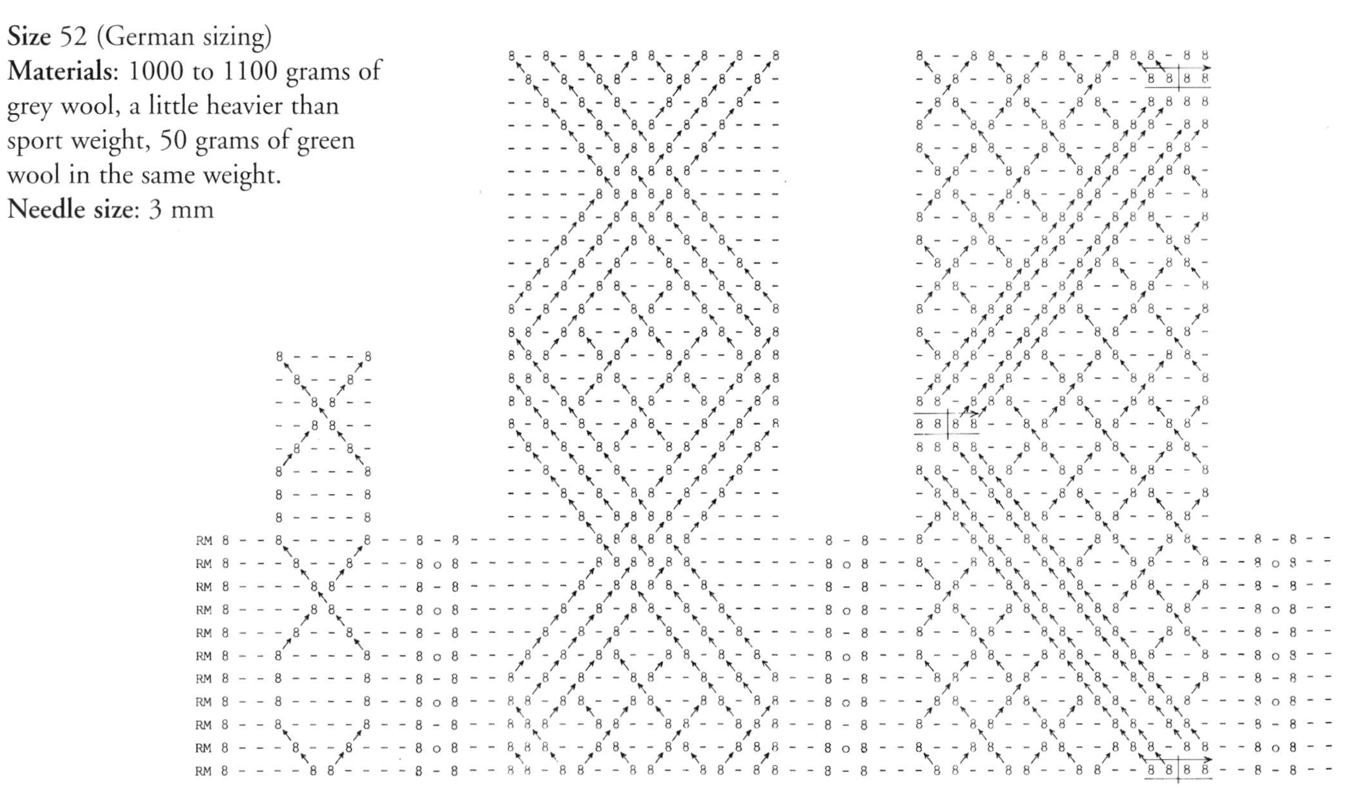

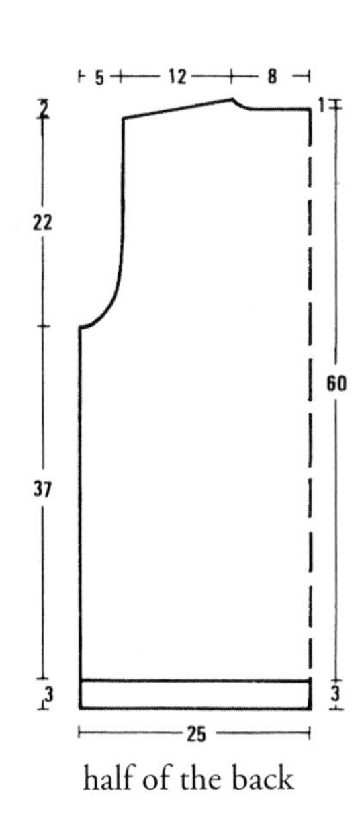

half of the back

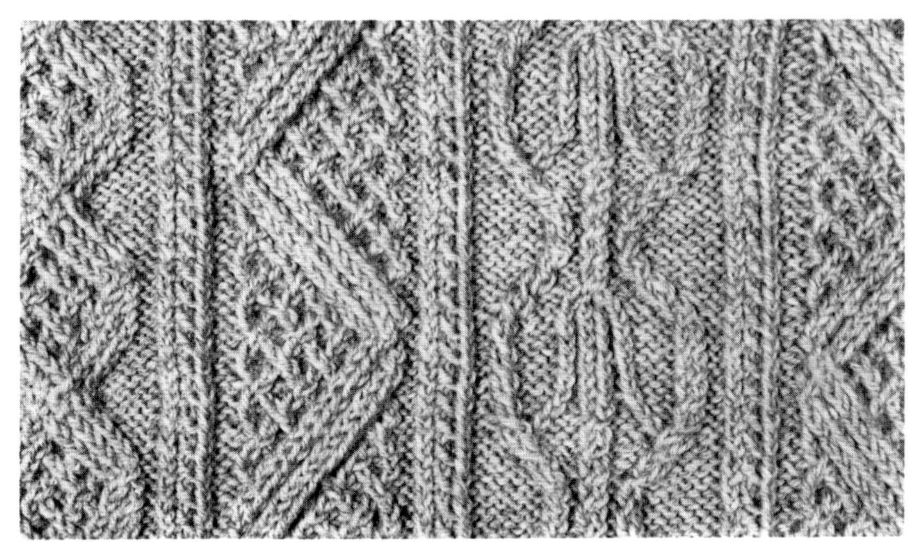

center back of Men's Cardigan

Center Back

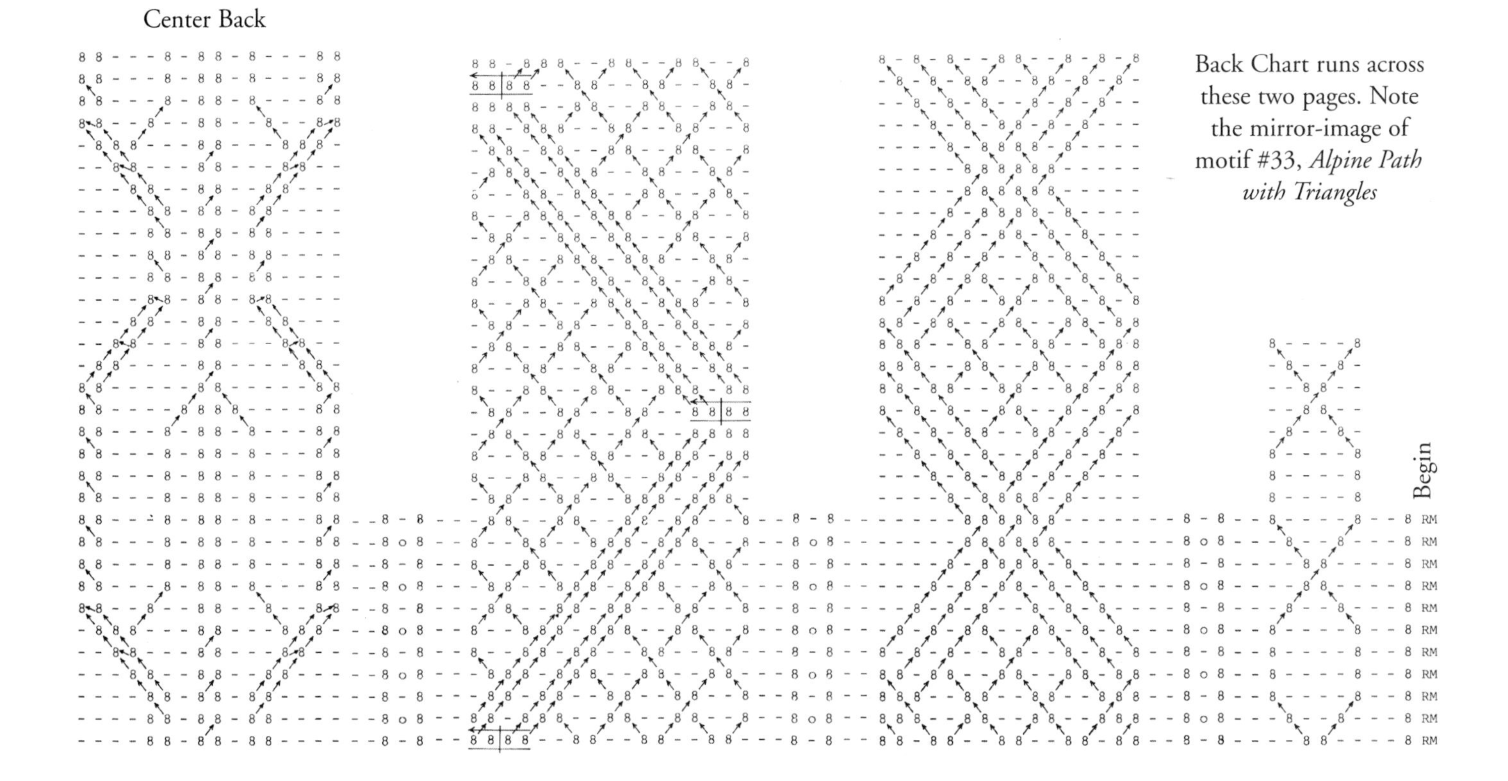

Back Chart runs across these two pages. Note the mirror-image of motif #33, *Alpine Path with Triangles*

Left Front: Cast on 60 sts (58 pattern sts and 2 edge sts) using green yarn. Knit 3 cm in garter stitch. Switch to grey yarn, and increase 17 sts evenly spaced across the first pattern row (77 sts). Work, following the graph, to the same length as the back up to the armhole.

Armhole: Cast off at armhole edge every other row as follows: (4 sts) x1, (3 sts) x2, (2 sts) x2, and (1 stitch) x2. Continue to the neck opening (56 cm). On the neck edge cast off every other row as follows: (4 sts) x2, (2 sts) x2 times and (1 stitch) x4. Knit until the piece measures 27cm from beginning of armhole shaping. Cast off on the armhole edge as follows: 11 sts, 3 times then 12 sts once.

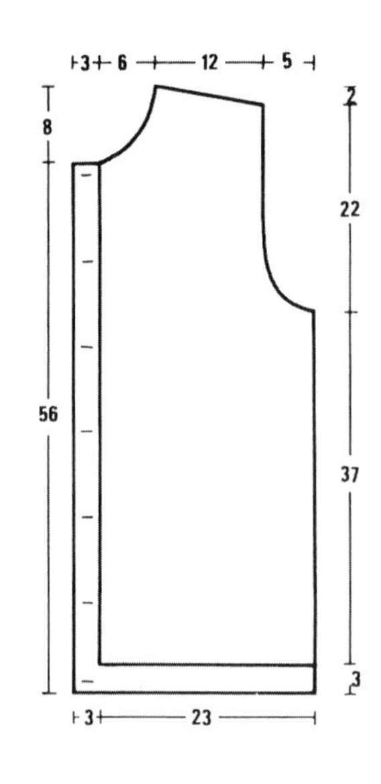

Left Front chart; reverse chart for Right Front

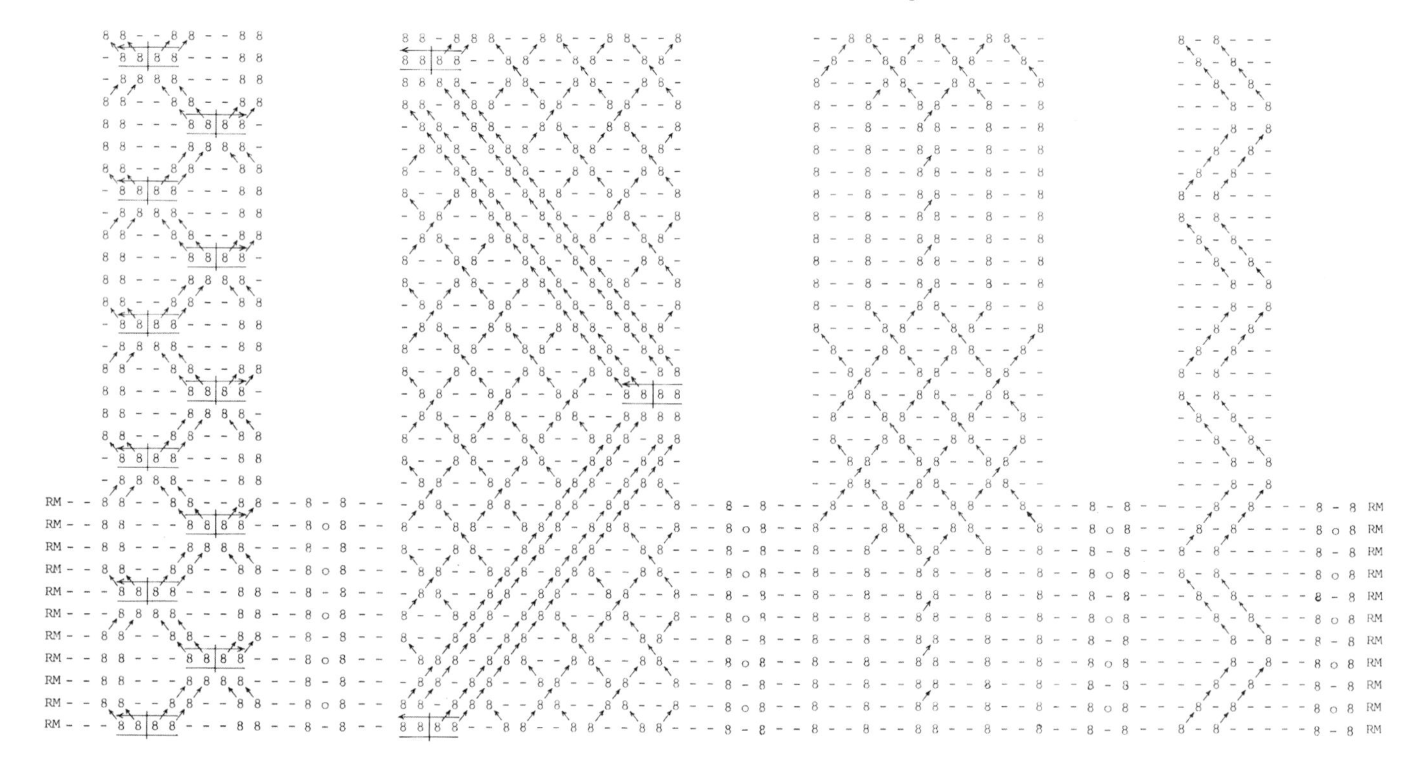

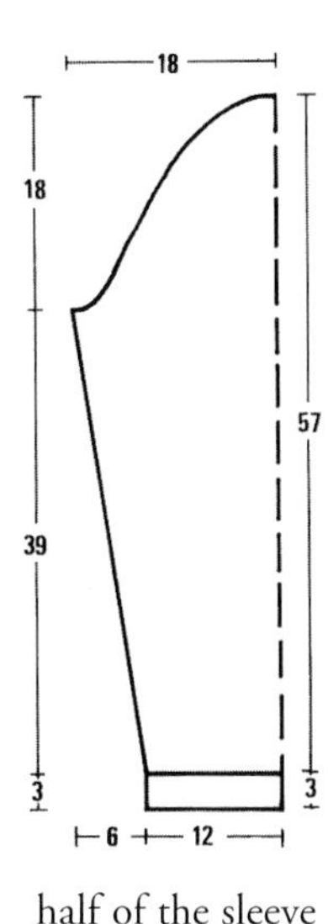

half of the sleeve

Sleeves: With green wool, cast on 48 sts (46 pattern sts + 2 edge sts). Work in garter stitch for 3 cm. Switch to grey yarn and increase 12 sts evenly across the first pattern row (60 sts). This sleeve is knitted flat (see Techniques). Knit 39 cm, increasing 15 sts evenly on each side (90 sts). Add small patterns to the increased sts.

Sleeve Top: Cast off each side of every other row as follows: (3 sts) x1, (3 sts) x2 and (1 stitch) x5. After this, decrease 1 stitch every 4th row, 5x. Now bind off every other row again as follows: (1 stitch) x4, (2 sts) x3, (3 sts) x1 and (4 sts) x1. Cast off remaining sts. Work second sleeve, reversing the crossed stitches in the center panel.

Finishing: Pin each piece, slightly stretched, to a soft surface. Cover with a damp cloth and let dry. Sew the side and sleeve seams. Sew in the sleeves.

Buttonband: With green wool, pick up 90 sts along one front edge. Knit in garter stitch for 3 cm and cast off. Repeat on the other side, working buttonholes evenly spaced along this band. Now pick up 100 sts evenly around the neckline, using the green wool and knit for 3 cm in garter stitch. Cast off and sew on buttons.

Sleeve Chart

Sleeve Center

Child's Sweater

Age: 3- 4 years
Materials: 350 gr. Wool
Needle Size:- 2 mm

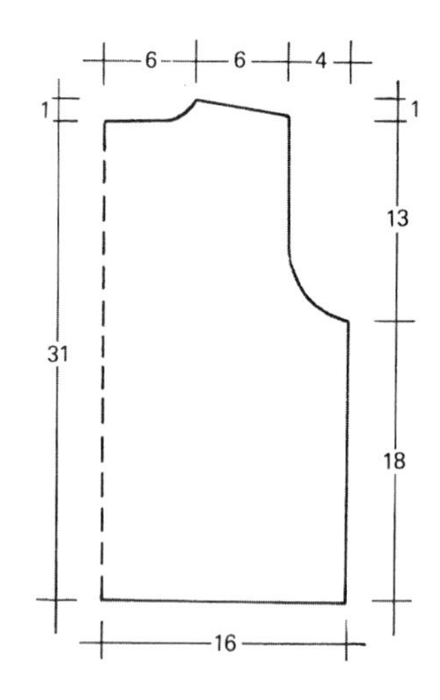

Back: Cast on 90 + 2 sts= 92 sts. Knit 11 rows in garter stitch. Increase 32 sts evenly spaced across the row (124 sts); begin chart. Knit for 18 cm.

Armholes: cast off on both sides, every other row: (3 sts) x1, (2 sts) x2 and (1 stitch) x3; 104 sts. When armhole is 13 cm long, shape neck by casting off 12 center sts, finishing the 2 sides separately, as follows:

First Shoulder: On the neck opening side, cast off in every other rows: (3 sts) x1, (2 sts) x1, and (1 stitch) x5 = 36 sts for shoulder. Cast off at the shoulder edge every other row as follows: (7 sts) x4 and (8 sts) x1.
Work other shoulder as above.

Left Front: Cast on 49 sts + 11 sts for the button band+ 2 edge sts = 92 sts. Knit 11 rows in garter stitch. Increase 13 sts spaced evenly across the first pattern row = 75 sts. When piece measures 18 cm, start the armhole: Cast off (4 sts) x1, (2 sts) x2, and (1 stitch) x3. Knit on 64 sts to the neck. When piece measures 26 cm, shape the neck: cast off 11 sts from the button band, then cast off (4 sts) x1, (3 sts) x1, (2 sts) x2 and (1 stitch) x6 = 36 sts. Continue front; work shoulder cast off the same as for back.

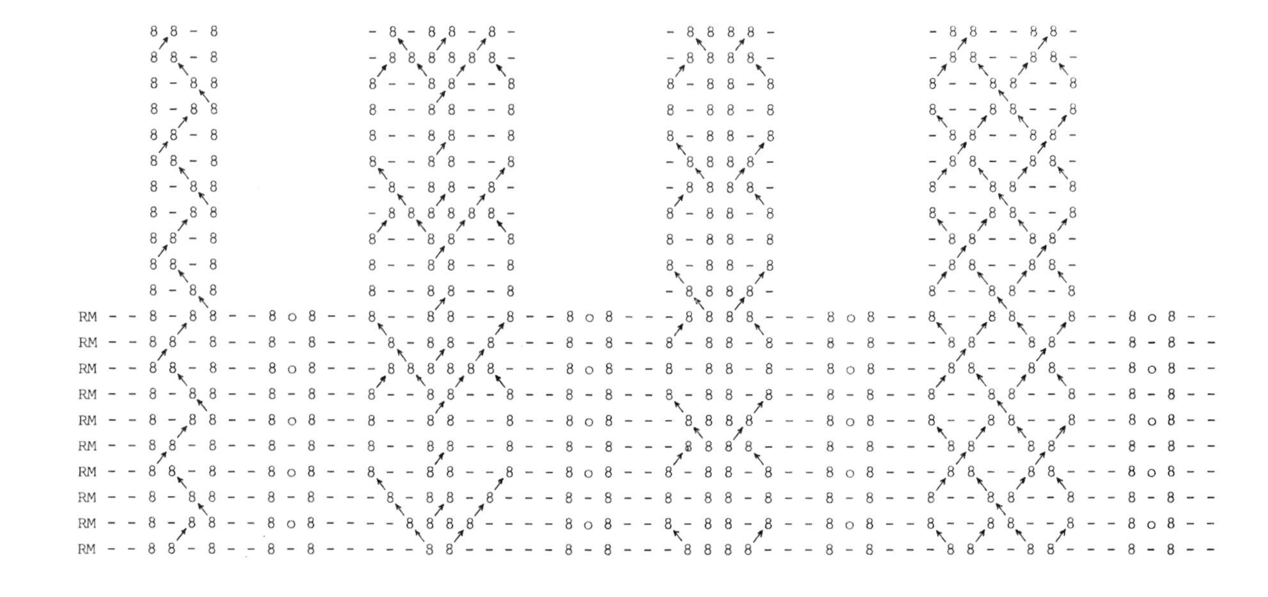

Child's Sweater
Knitted by Mrs. Erna Brunner, Gröbming

Back Chart runs across these two pages

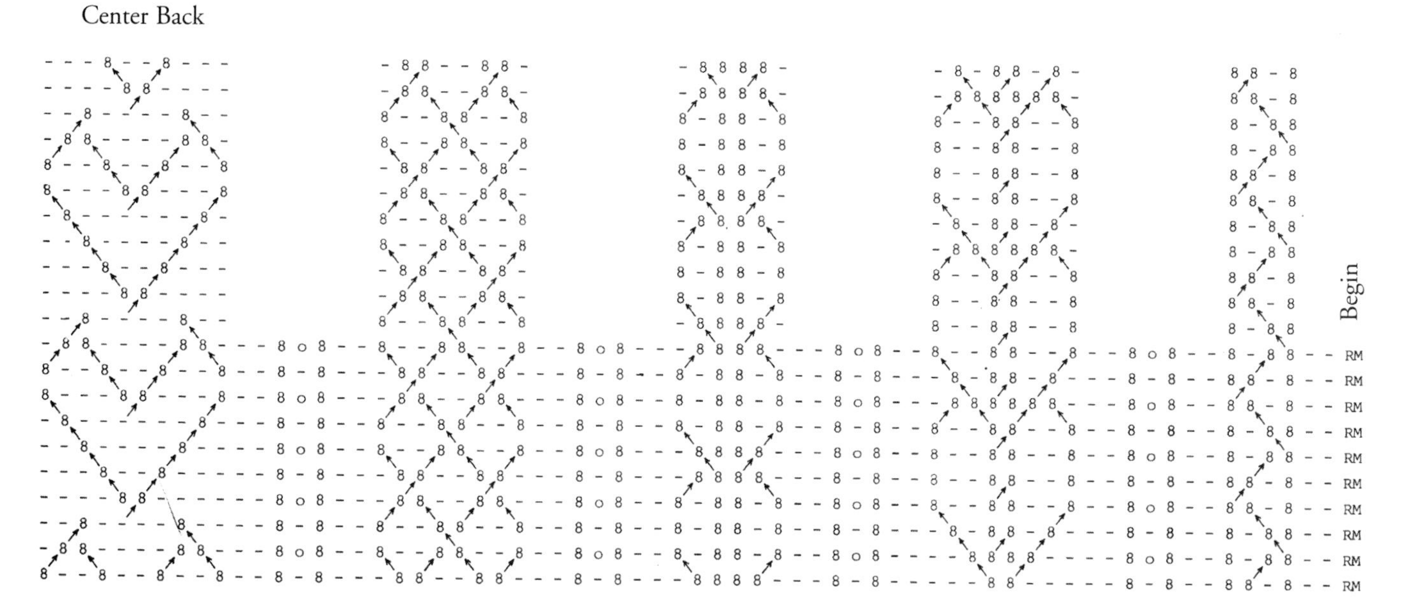

Right Front: Work as for left front, (reversing all shaping) and add 7 buttonholes evenly spaced in button band.

Sleeves: Cast on 48 sts and work 11 rows of garter stitch. Join and knit in the round; increase 12 sts evenly spaced in first round (60 sts). Knit sleeve, following the graph, and increase - evenly spaced over 26 cm - 35 sts each side of center underarm stitch. Fill in new stitches with some narrow motifs.

Chart for Left Front; reverse chart for Right Front.

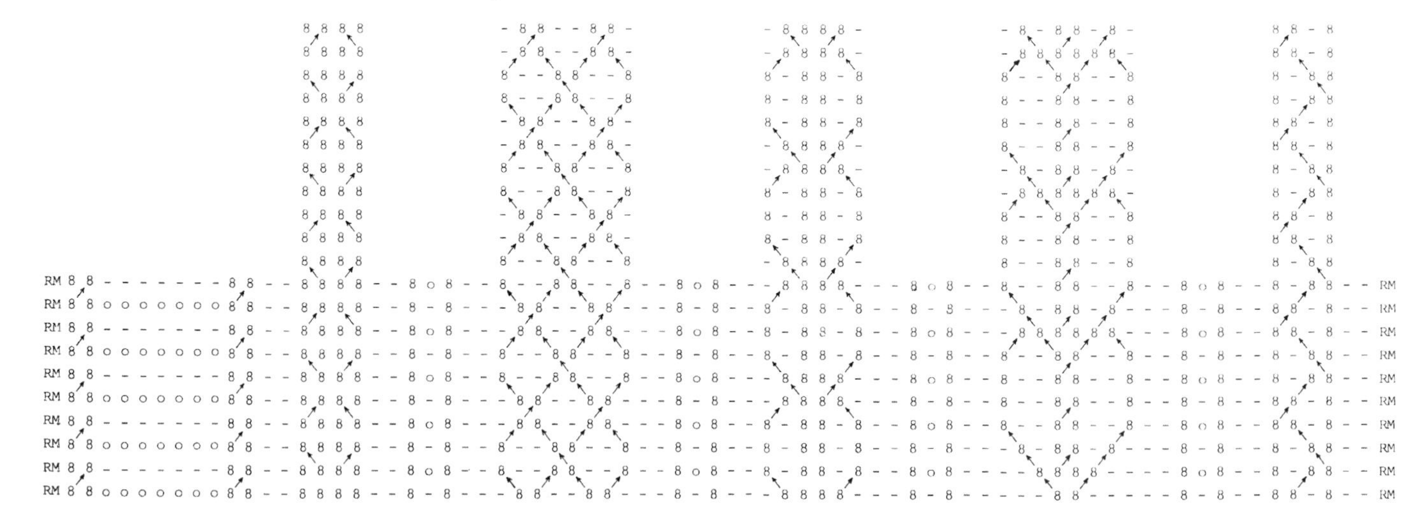

Top of Sleeve is knitted flat, so pattern has to be worked on inside and outside. Shape sleeve top as follows: decrease (3 sts) x1, (2 sts) x3, (1 stitch) x13 and (2 sts) x9. Cast off the remaining 15 sts.

Finishing: Pin the pieces, lightly stretched to a soft surface. Cover with a damp cloth and let dry. Sew the fronts and back together and set in the sleeves.

Neck edge trim: Along the neck edge, pick up 36 sts from the front, 32 sts from the back and 36 sts from the other front: 104 sts. Knit 5 rows by twisting the outside knit sts, and purling the inside.

Row 6: Knit 4 twisted knit sts. Do not work the 5th stitch yet. Insert the needle 4 rows below the 5th stitch and work a normal knit stitch. Drop the 5th stitch from the needle. Repeat this to the end of the row. Knit 5 more rows as before. The 5th row is knitted as before, but the needle is inserted 6 rows below each 5th stitch. In the next row cast off all sts. Fold to the inside and sew down. Sew on the buttons. If needed, sew around the buttonholes with buttonhole stitch.

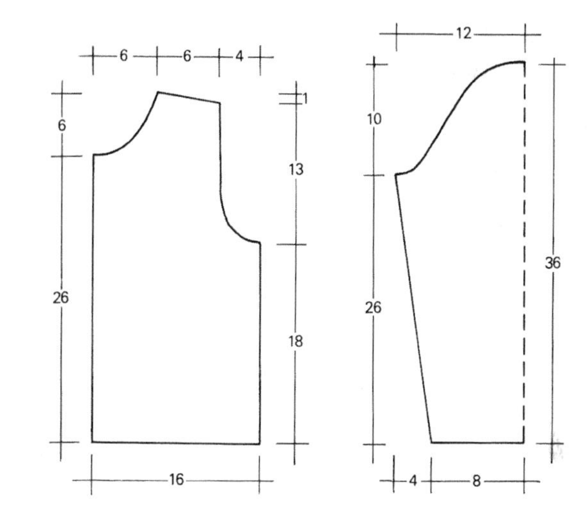

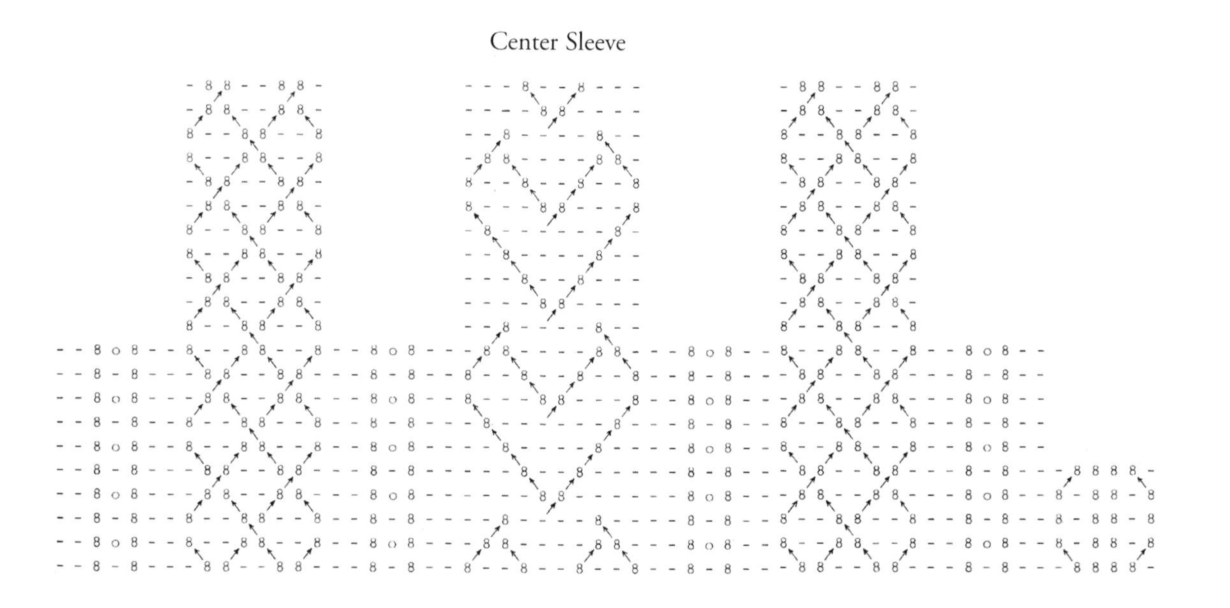

Example of Pattern Arrangement

This is a suggested combination for the back of a small child's vest

Knitted by Mrs. Hilda Stiegler, Gröbming

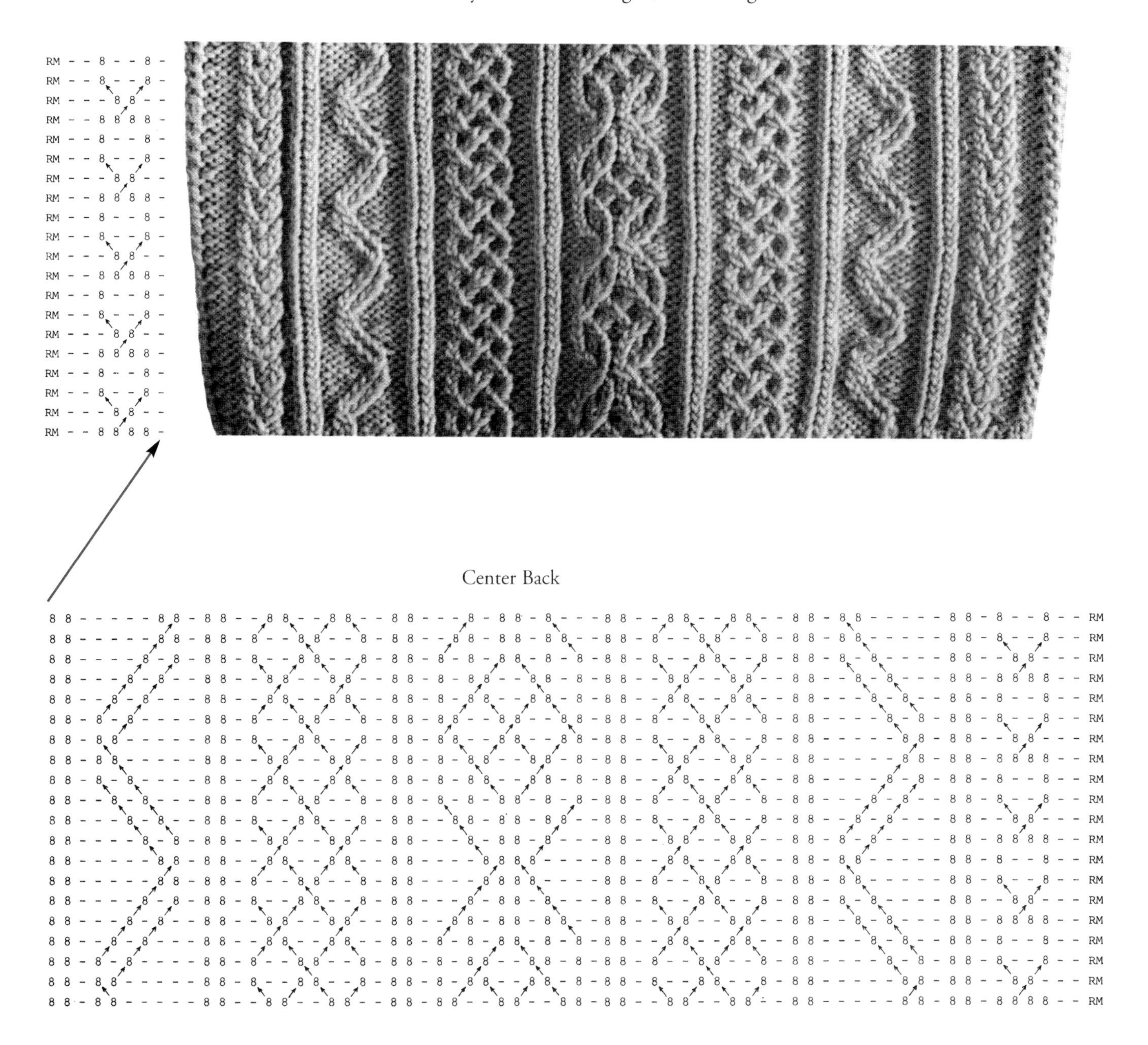

Alpine Cardigan
From the Landschaftsmuseum, Schloss Trautenfels
Knitted by Mrs. Maria Erlbacher

Size: 50/52 (German sizing)
Materials: 1000- 1100 gram wool
Needle Size: 3 mm
Gauge: see page 143

Back Chart for Alpine Cardigan

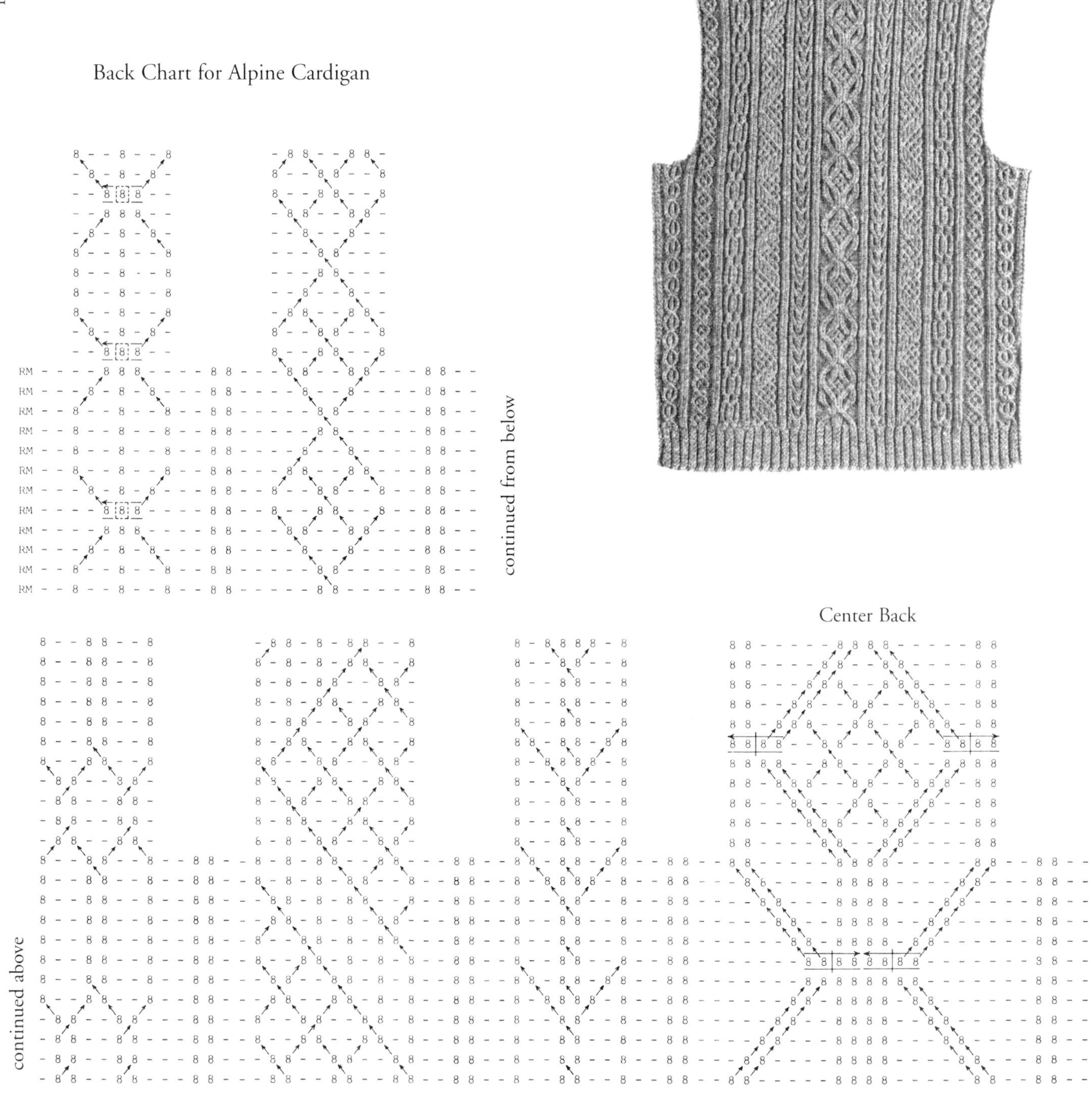

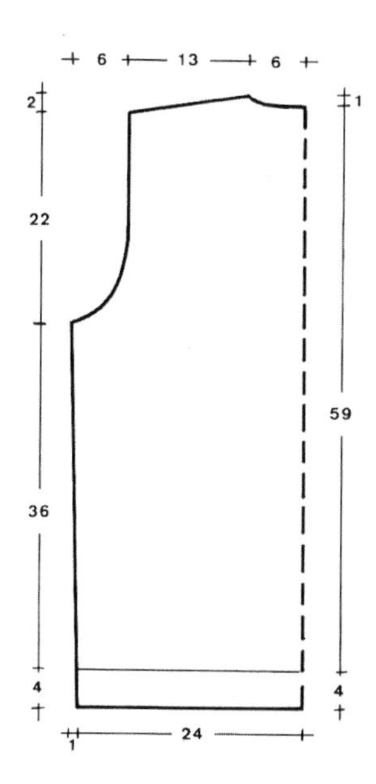

Back: Cast on 158 sts + 2 edge sts = 160 sts. Purl 2, knit 2b (twisted) ribbing for 4 cm, then start the pattern. In the first row increase 8 sts evenly spaced across the width = 168 sts.

Follow the charts and work the pattern on both sides. After a few rows, the pattern will become apparent and you won't have to look at the chart quite as often. Increase 3 sts between the edge stitch and the first pattern on both sides, evenly spaced between ribbing and armhole. Your stitch count at the armhole is 174.

Armhole: Decrease every other row on both sides, as follows: 8 sts, 5 sts, 2 sts, 1 stitch, and 1 stitch. When armhole is 22 cm deep, start neck and shoulder shaping.

Neck Opening: Cast off the center 34 sts, and finish each shoulder separately. Cast off 3 sts, 2 times next to the neck opening. At the same time slope the shoulder by casting off - every other row - 12 sts, 3 times, and 11 sts one time. Repeat the shaping in reverse on the second shoulder.

Back Chart runs across these two pages.

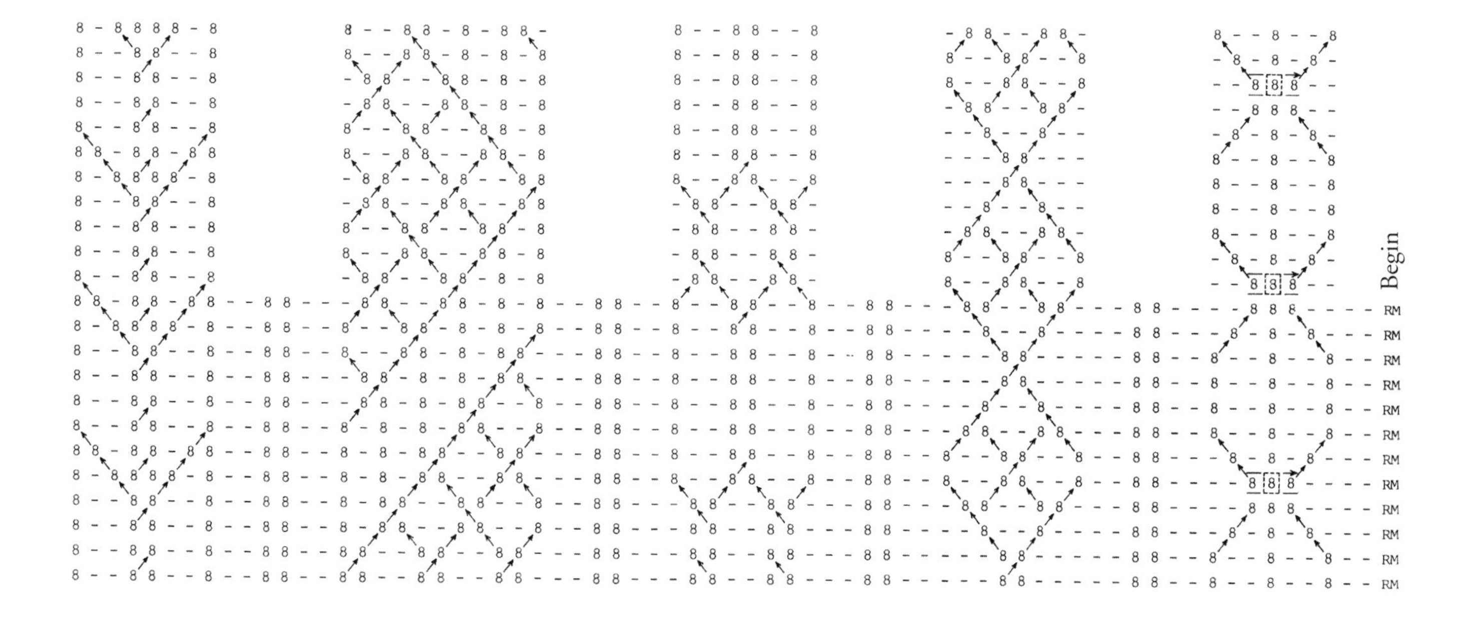

Right Front: On a men's garment, it is best to knit the right front first, as it is easier to space the buttons and make the placement of buttonholes on the left front easier.

Cast on 80 sts + 11 sts for the buttonhole strip + 2 edge sts = 93 sts. Knit the ribbing for 4 cm, the same as for the back. In the first row after the ribbing, increase 5 sts evenly across the front. You should now have 85 sts for the pattern, 11 sts for the button band and 2 edge sts = 98 sts. Knit, following the charts up to the armholes, increasing 5 sts evenly spaced the length of the front on the armhole side. This should give you 103 sts. Don't forget to knit the buttonhole strip on the side opposite this side.

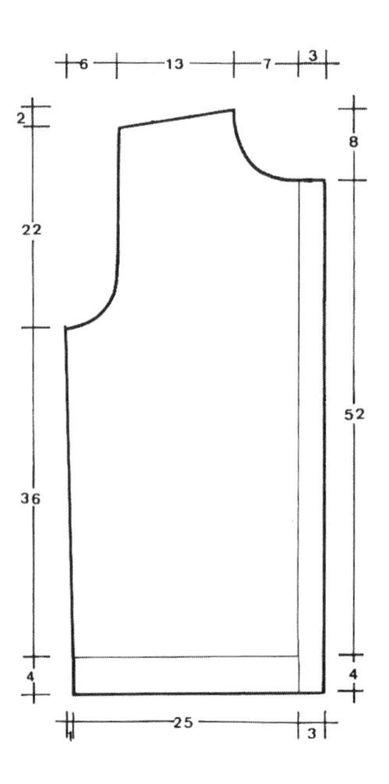

Armhole: Knit to the same height as the back. Cast off every other row as follows: 9 sts, 5 sts, 2 sts and 1 stitch 3 times. Continue in pattern to the neck opening. Cast off every other row as before: 12 sts, (4 sts) x1, (3 sts) x3, (2 sts) x4 and (1 stitch) x4.

Shoulder Shaping: Work as for back, on the side opposite the armhole opening.

Left Front: Knit as for right front, reversing the shaping.

Buttonholes: On appropriate side, work buttonholes in the center of the button band horizontally across the row as follows: Cast off the required number of stitches needed for the button to fit. Cast on the same number of stitches in the return row.

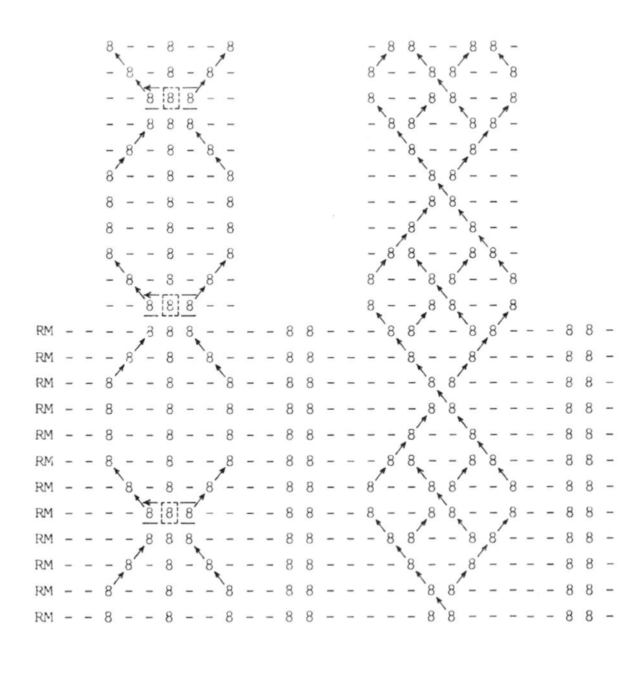

Center Front

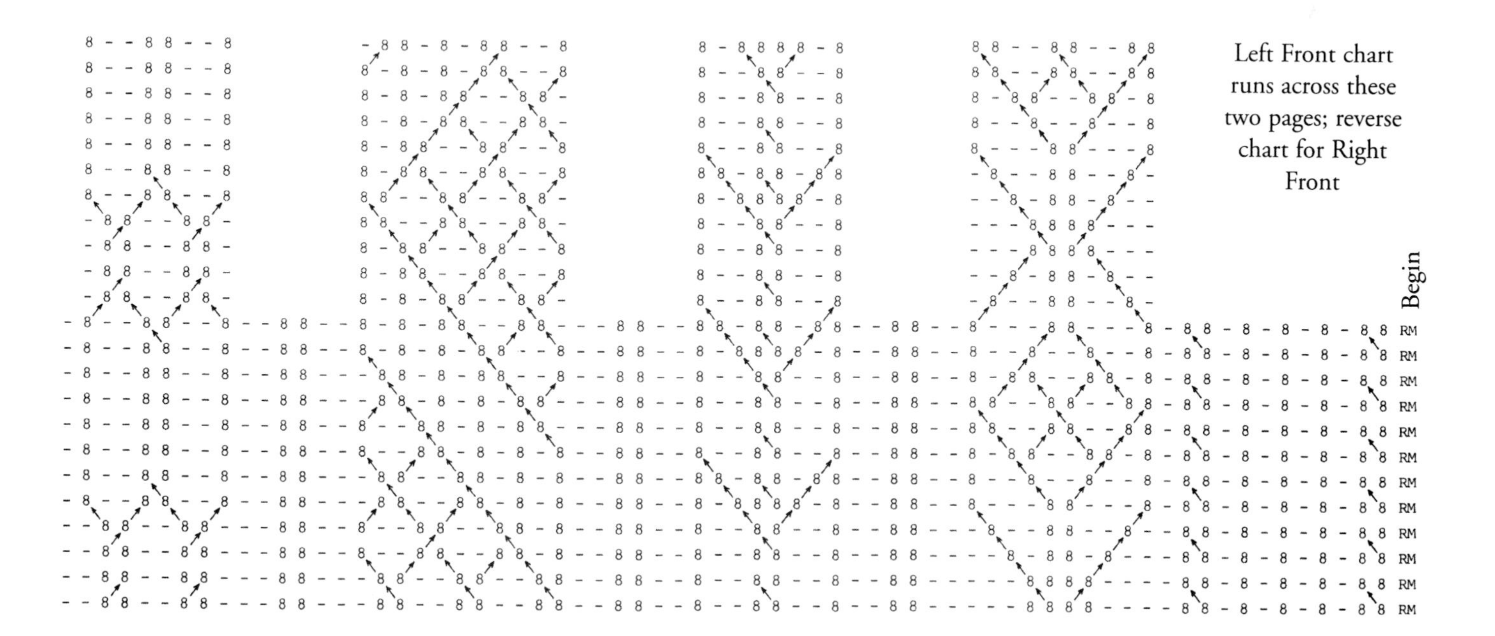

Left Front chart runs across these two pages; reverse chart for Right Front

Sleeves are worked in the round on dp needles: Cast on 64 sts; purl 2, knit 2b for 4 cm. In the first row after the ribbing, increase 10 sts evenly spaced = 74 sts. Continue following the chart (increases are shown; work them each side of the center underarm stitch), until the sleeve is long enough. There should be an increase of 54 sts. When you get to the top of the sleeve, your stitch count should be 128.

Sleeve Top: This part of the sleeve is knitted back and forth. Stitches will be bound off every other row, starting at the underarm. Place a marker on that spot, and work the bind offs **on both sides equally**. Cast off 4 sts on both sides of the marker, being careful they are done at the beginning of a row. After this, cast off (3 sts) x1, (2 sts) x3, (1 stitch) x7, (2 sts) x3, (1 stitch) x6, (2 sts) x4 and (3 sts) x 4 times. Cast off remaining 24 sts. Work second sleeve the same manner.

Finishing: Block all pieces by pinning them, slightly stretched, to a soft surface. Dampen with water, or cover with a damp cloth. Let them dry.

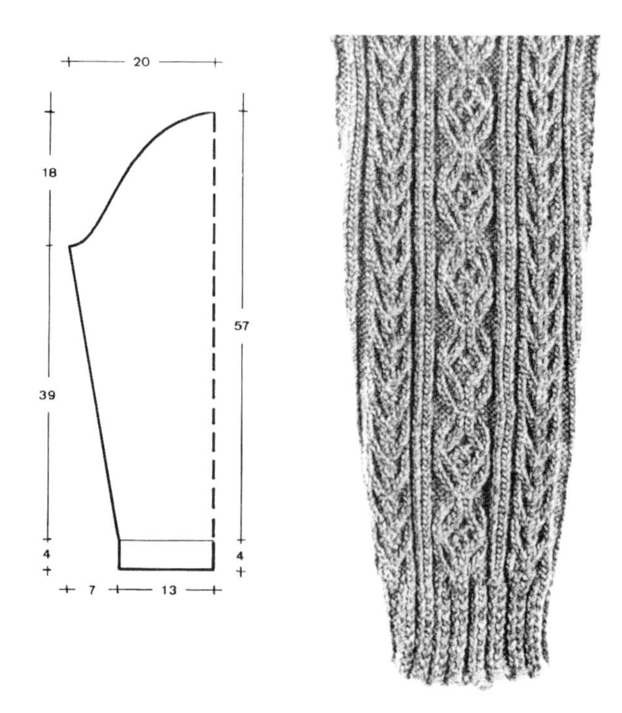

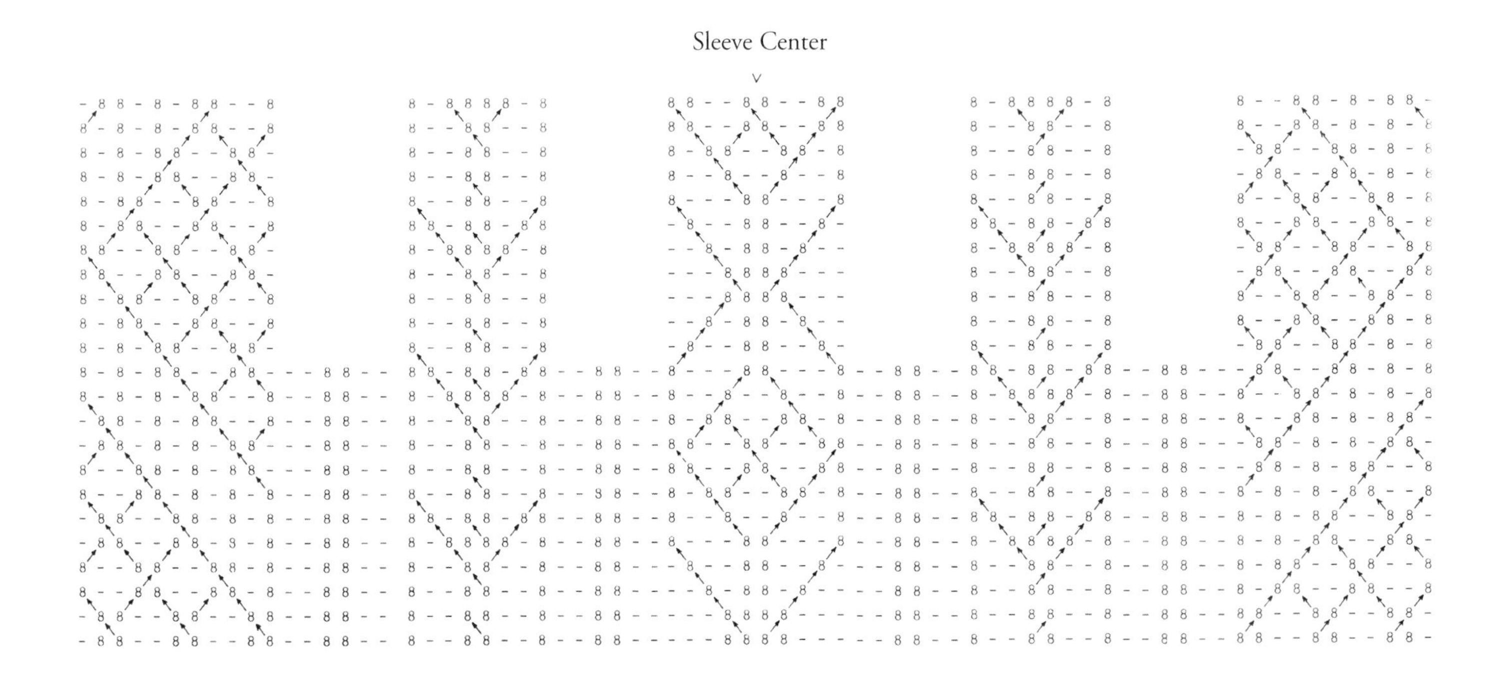

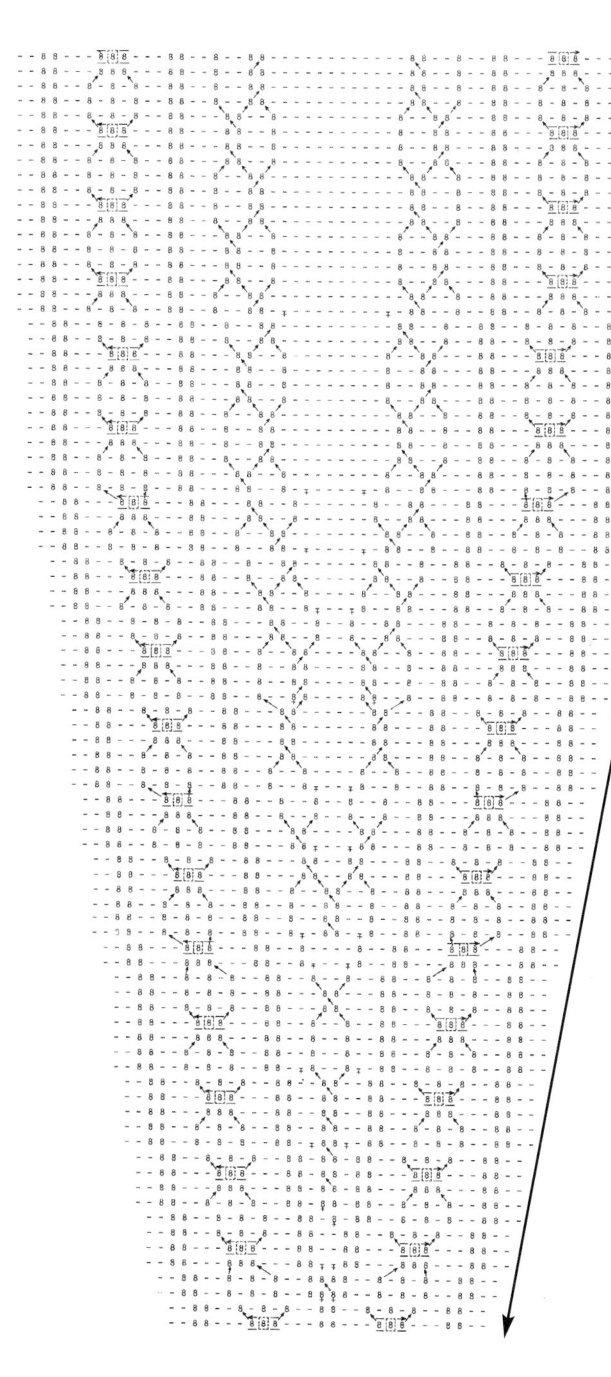

continue from top of chart on the right

continue at bottom of chart on the left

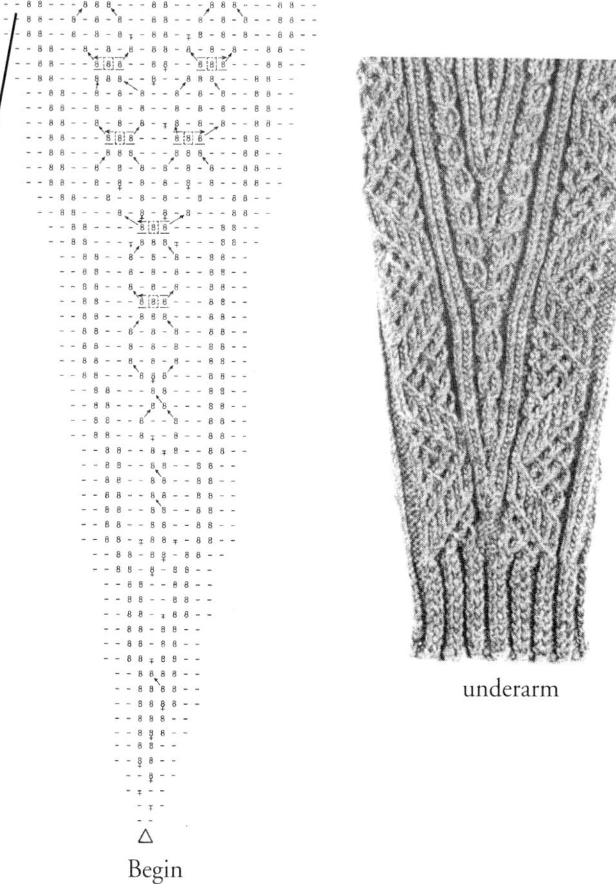

Begin

This chart shows sleeve increases.

underarm

Sew the side seams and set in the sleeves. The **neck edge** is finished by picking up about 110 sts from the cast off edges. Work from outside and make one row of twisted knit sts. The following rows are worked in p1, k1b for 6 cm. Cast off. This is double the width that is needed; fold it in half to the inside and tack it down.

Note: Knit the back half of the button band in plain knit (last 3 cm); this will make the band thinner. Sew on buttons.

Sleeveless Vest

Knitted by Mrs. Erna Brunner, Gröbming

Size 42 (German sizing)
Materials: 300- 350 gram wool
Needle Size: 2 mm
Gauge: see page 143

Back Chart

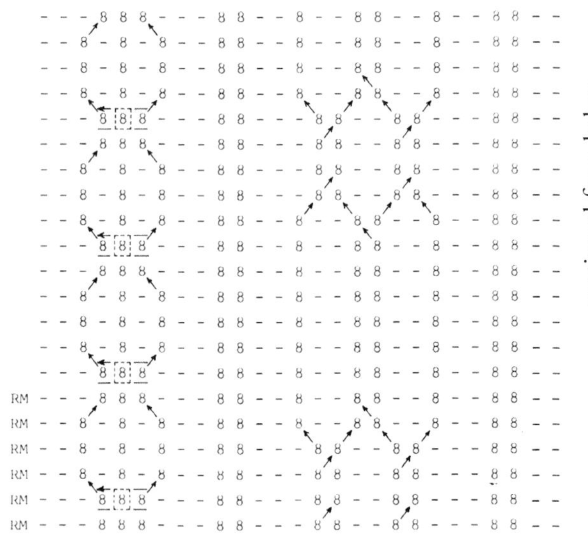

continued from below

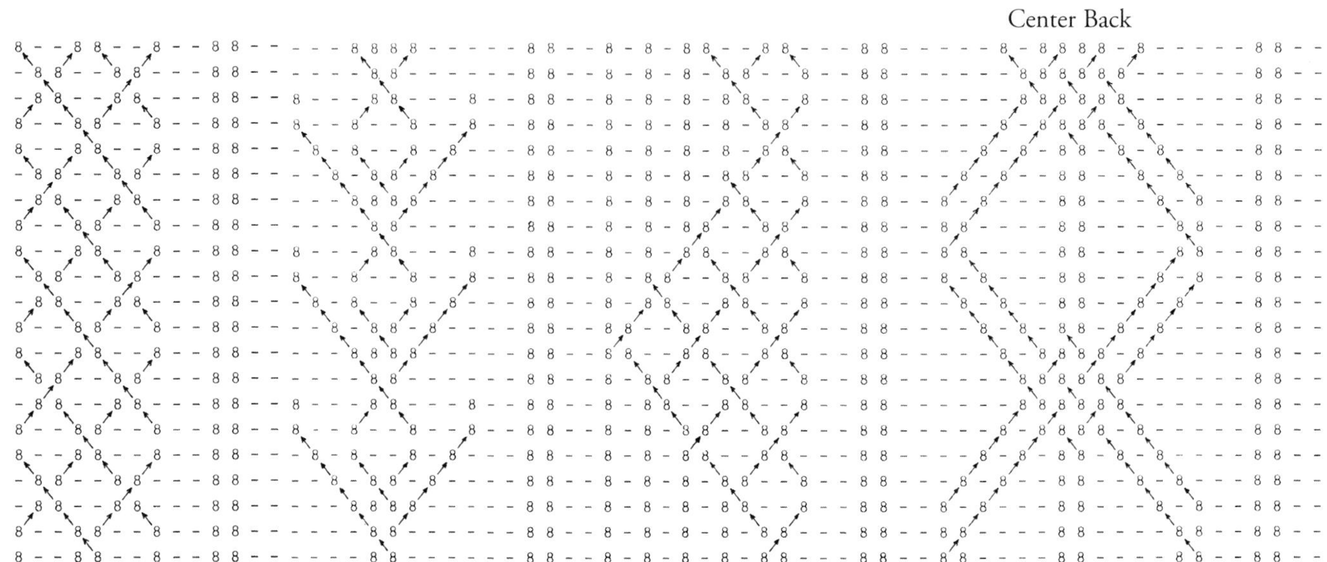

continued above

Back: Cast on 132 stitches + 2 edge stitches (RM) = 134 stitches. For a picot edge, Knit 4 rows in stockinette stitch. Row 5 will create the picot edging (called *mouse tooth edging* in German): *Knit 2 together twisted, yo (yarn over),* repeat to end of row. Knit 4 more rows in stockinette stitch. Fold the strip along the row of holes. Pick up loop from first stitch of the first row and knit it together with first stitch on the needle. Continue knitting together a loop of the cast-on row and a stitch until the row is finished. Purl back. Increase 30 stitches evenly spaced across the first pattern row. You should now have 164 stitches - the right amount for the pattern. Follow the chart and the measurements on the drawing. Decrease 1 stitch each side 3 times. Knit 2 cm in pattern. Increase 10 sts on both sides evenly divided between the next row and the armhole.

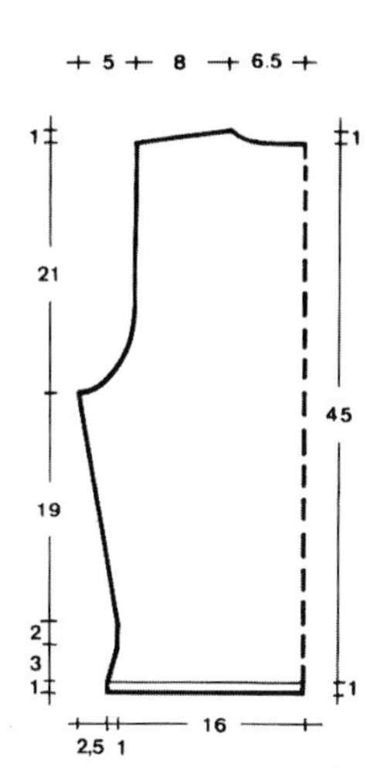

Armholes: Work the cast offs every second row at the beginning of the rows, as follows: 5 sts, (3 sts) x2, (2 sts) x3 and (1 stitch) x4. There should be 136 sts left. At 21 cm, start the neck opening and shoulder shaping.

Back Chart runs across these two pages. Note the mirror-imaged motifs.

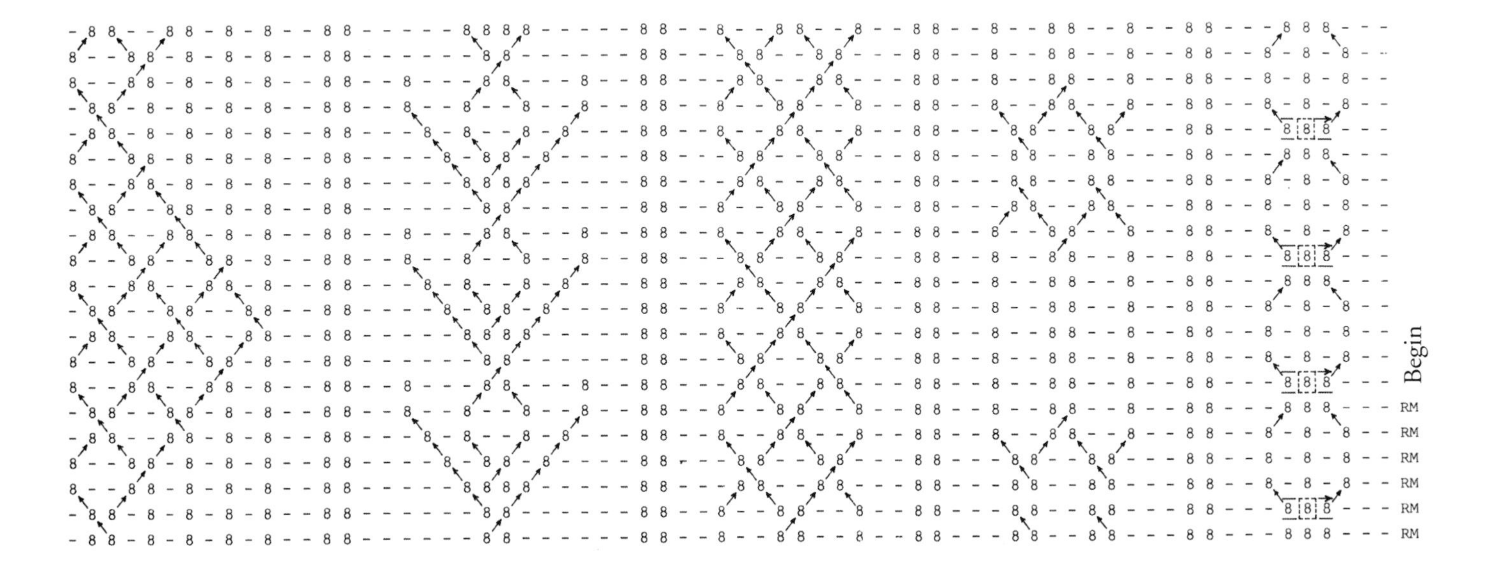

Neck opening: Cast off 24 center stitches and work each shoulder separately. On one side, cast off 5 sts, 3 times in every other row on the neck edge. At the same time the shoulder slope is worked (again in every other row - at the beginning of the row) by casting off 10 sts, 3 times and 11 sts once.

Left Front: Cast on 72 sts + 2 edge sts + 12 sts for the button band = 86 sts. Make a picot edging - same as on the bottom of the back. Increase 14 sts evenly spaced across the first pattern row. You should have 100 sts now. Work the next 5 cm the same as for the back. Increase by 10 sts evenly spaced in the rows of the armhole side between this point and the beginning of the armhole.

Armhole: Cast off in every second row 1 time 5 sts, 2 times 3 sts, 3 times 2 sts and 4 times 1 stitch = 86 sts. When the piece measures 33 cm, start the neck opening (opposite the armhole edge) by casting off 14 sts.
After that cast off in every other row as follows: (5 sts) x2, (3 sts) x2, (2 sts) x5 and (1 stitch) x5.

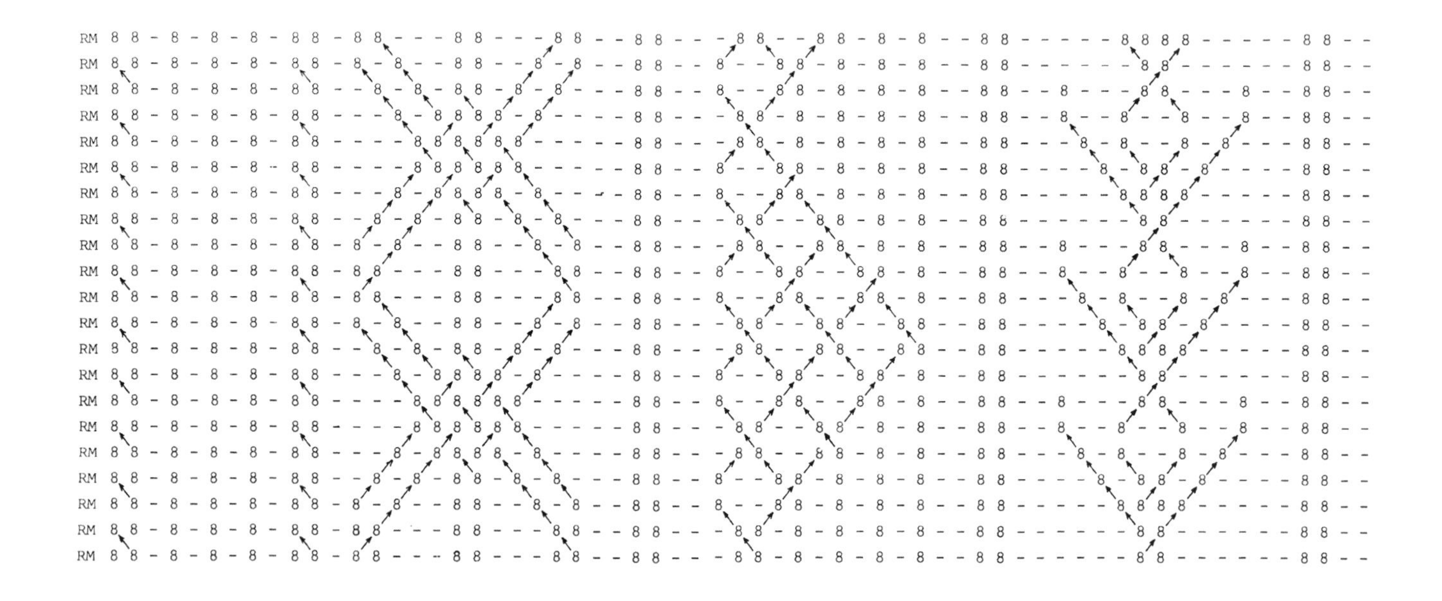

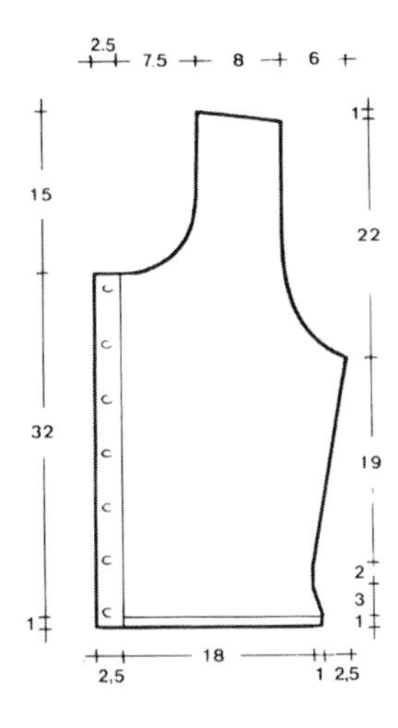

Left Front Chart runs across these two pages; reverse chart for Right Front.

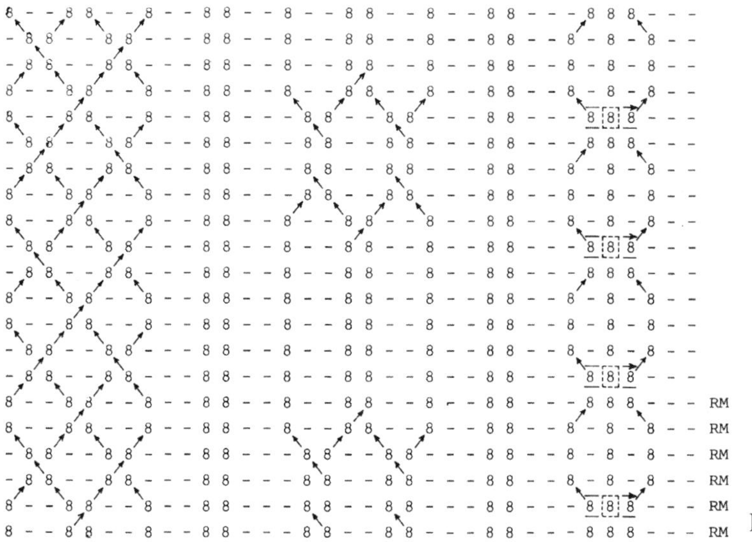

Begin

Shoulder Shaping: When the height of the armhole measures 22 cm, work the shoulder shaping the same as on the back.

Right Front: Work the same as the other front, reversing the shaping; add buttonholes, evenly spaced in the button band.

Finishing: Pin the pieces, lightly stretched to a padded surface. Cover with a damp cloth and let everything dry thoroughly. Sew the side seams and the shoulder seams.

Child's Cardigan (for 3 - 4 year old)

Materials: 350 grams natural color wool, suitable for knitting with 3 mm needles.
50 grams green wool in the same thickness, for borders

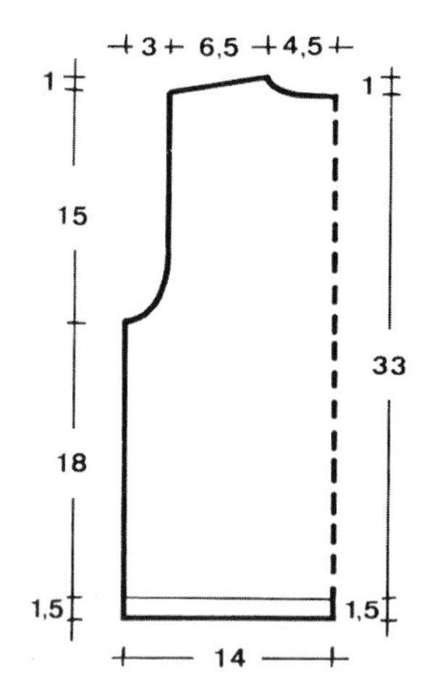

Gauge: see page 143

Back: With green wool cast on 60 sts, plus 2 edge sts = 62 sts
Knit in garter stitch (knit both sides) for 7 rows. In Cream wool, increase 26 sts evenly spaced across the row. Follow the pattern chart, knitting without any increases, up to the armholes.

Armholes: Cast off every other row, on both sides as follows: (4 sts) x1, (3 sts) x1, (2 sts) x1 and (1 stitch) x2. Knit until the armhole measures 15 cm.

Shoulder Shaping: Work one shoulder at a time. Start by casting off the center 14 sts. The shoulder shaping is done every other row, starting next to these bound off sts. It is worked as follows: (2 sts) x1, and (1 stitch) x1. There should be 23 sts left on each shoulder. Bind off 8 sts twice (every other row), and 7 sts once.

Right front: With green wool cast on 34 + 2 sts = 36 sts. Knit 7 rows in garter stitch. In the first pattern row increase 12 sts evenly spaced across the row. The button bands will be added when the pieces are finished. Work the same as for the back, without increasing any sts, following the chart for the right front, up to the armholes.

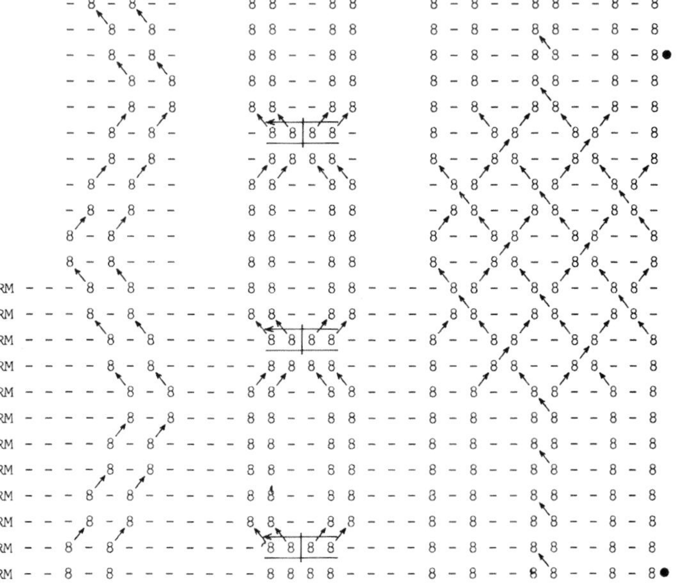

From the Landschaftsmuseum at Castle Trautenfels
Knitted by Mrs. Rosina Pilz nee Jager, Ramsau at the Dachstein

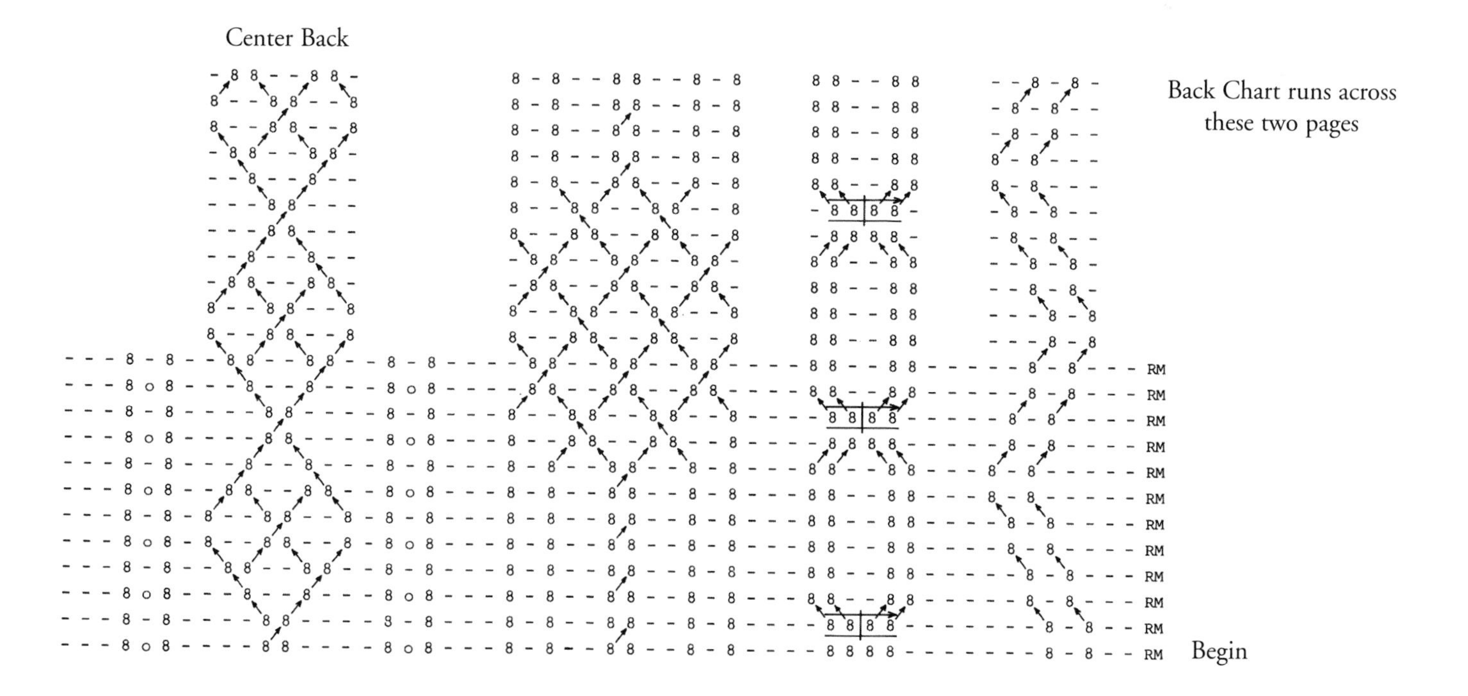

Armholes: cast off every other row, as follows: (4 sts) x1, (3 sts) x1, (2 sts) x1 and (1 stitch) x2. Knit on the remaining sts, until the front measures a total of 29.5 cm . Work the **neck opening** on the side opposite the armhole side. Cast off every other row as follows: 1 time 4 sts, 3 times 2 sts and 4 times 1 stitch.

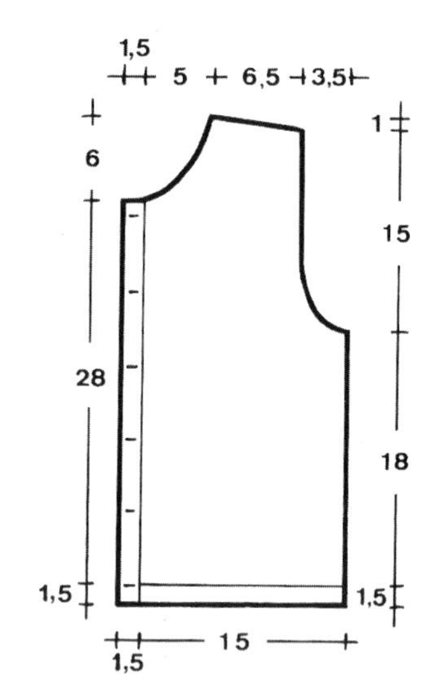

Work **shoulder shaping** the same as on back.

Left Front is worked as for right front. The armholes and neck shaping are done reverse to the right front.

Sleeves: With green wool cast on 36 + 2 sts = 38 sts, and knit in garter stitch for 7 rows. Increase 12 sts evenly spaced across the first pattern row. Follow chart, increasing a stitch on each side 10x about 2 cm apart = 70 sts. When sleeve measures about 20 cm, it is time to start ...

Sleeve Top Shaping: Work on both sides, every other row. Cast off (3 sts) x2 and (1 stitch) x2. Then decrease 1 stitch on both edges, every 4th row. Now cast offs are worked every other row again, still on both sides, as follows: (2 sts) x4 and (3 sts) x1. Cast off the remaining 12 sts. Work identical second sleeve.

Notice that Left and Right front motifs are mirror-imaged.

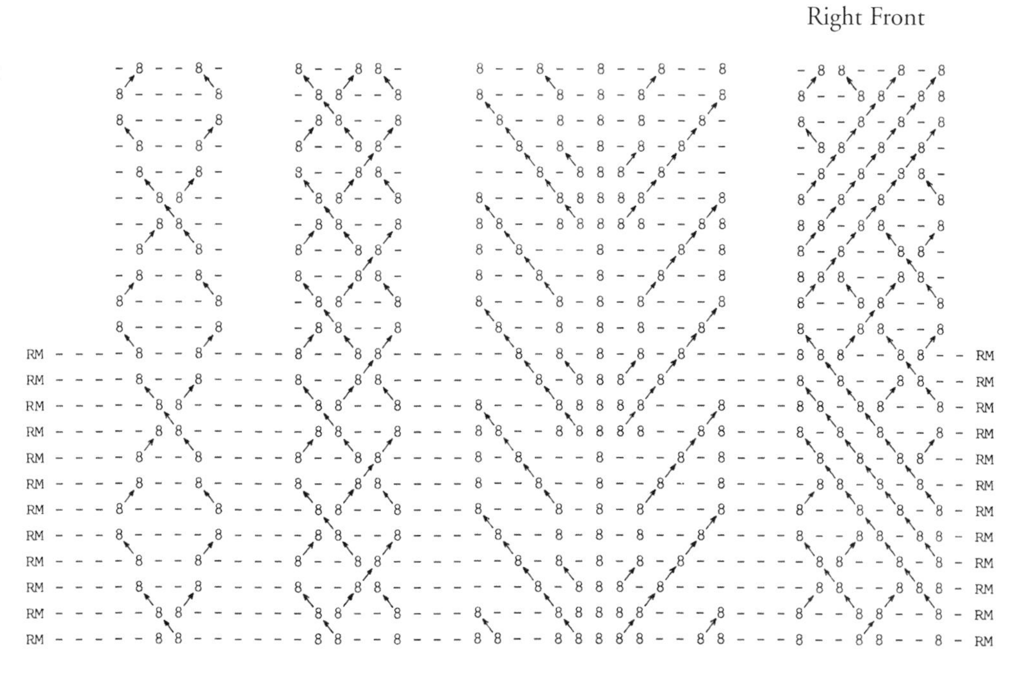

Left Front

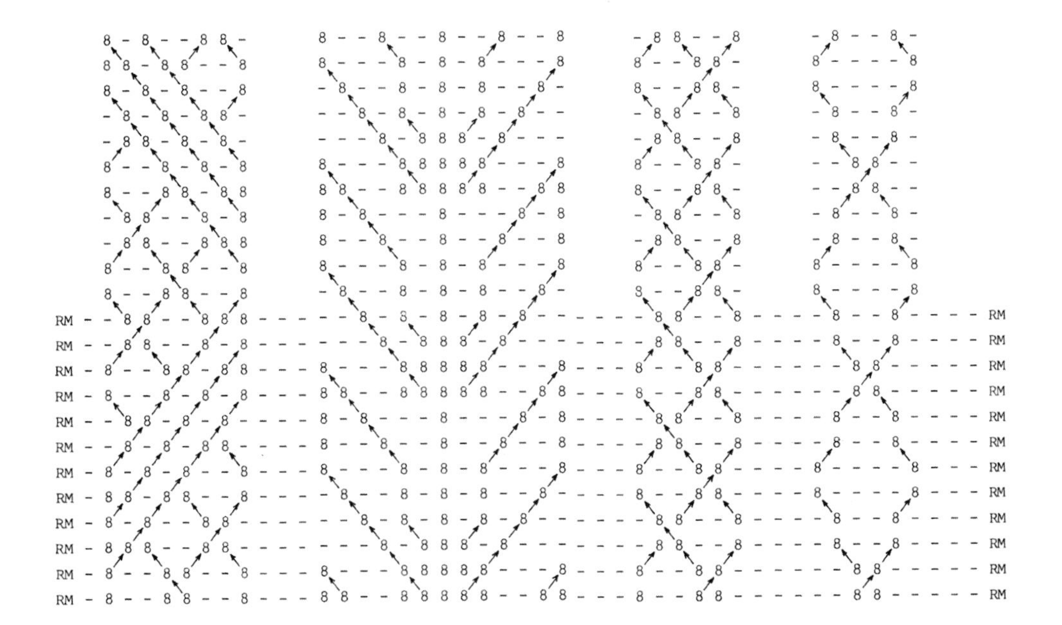

The pattern *Lebensbaum* (*Tree of Life*) was created by Mrs. Pilz.

Finishing: Pin the pieces, lightly stretched, to a padded surface. Cover with a damp towel, and let dry thoroughly. Sew all pieces together, and set in the sleeves. With green wool, pick up 65 sts along the edge of the right front. Work in garter stitch for 7 rows and cast off. Repeat on the left side; add 6 buttonholes, evenly spaced. Pick up 76 sts along the neck edge and knit 7 rows of garter stitch. Bind off loosely. Sew on buttons.

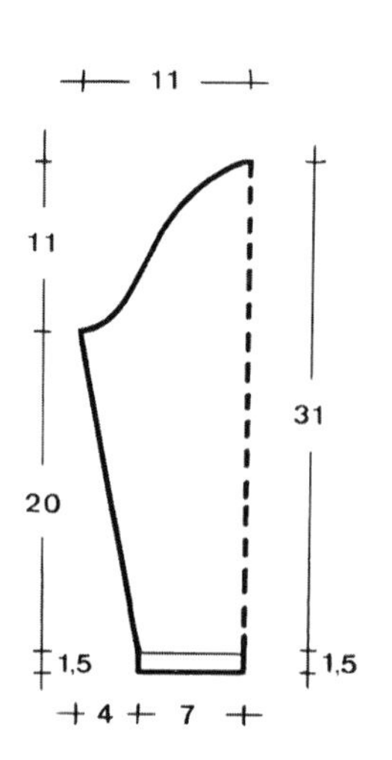

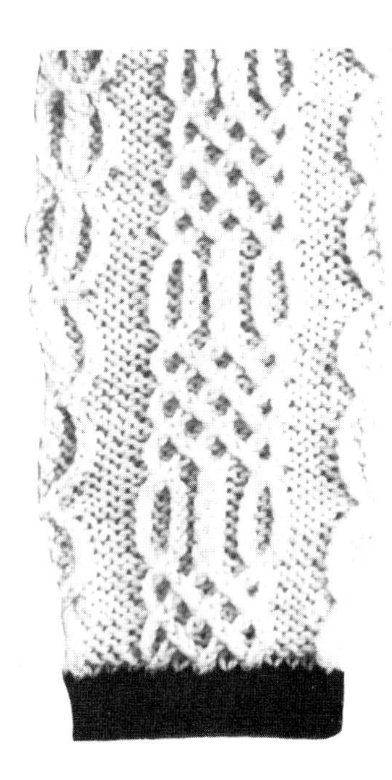

Sleeve Chart

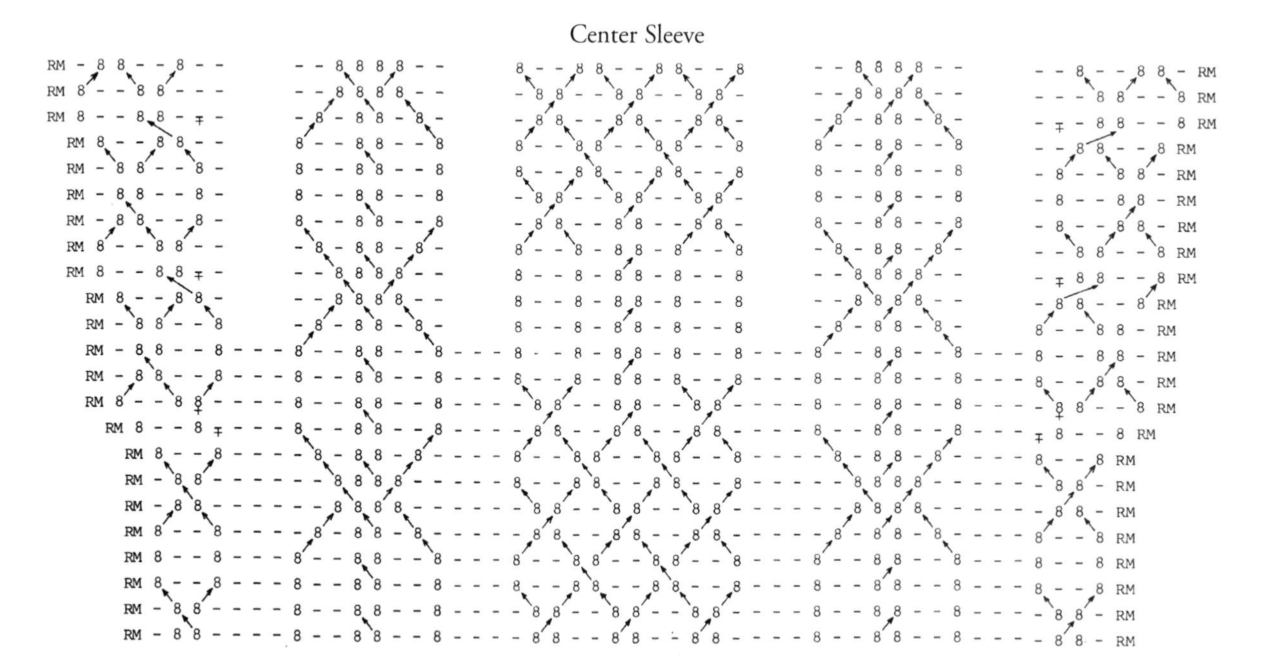

Ennstal Jacket

Size 50/ 52 (German sizing)
Materials: 1100 gram wool (sport weight)
Needles Size: 2.5mm
Gauge: see page 143

Back: Cast on 174 sts + 2 edge sts = 176 sts. Knit 4 cm of ribbing (purl 2, knit 2b) across the row. Increase 18 sts evenly spaced across the row: 192 sts + 2 edge sts = 194 sts. Follow charts to the armholes. Don't forget to knit in pattern even on the wrong side of the piece.

Armholes: When the back measures 42cm from the start, decrease for the armholes on both sides in every other row as follows. Decrease (7 sts) x1 (4 sts) x1, (2 sts) x 2, and (I stitch) x1. When the armhole measures 23 cm, start the shoulder sloping and neck opening.

Neck opening: Cast off the center 40 sts. The shoulders are worked separately. On the Neck opening cast off every other row (3 sts) x2 and at the armhole side, at the same time, (14 sts) x3 and (13 sts) x1

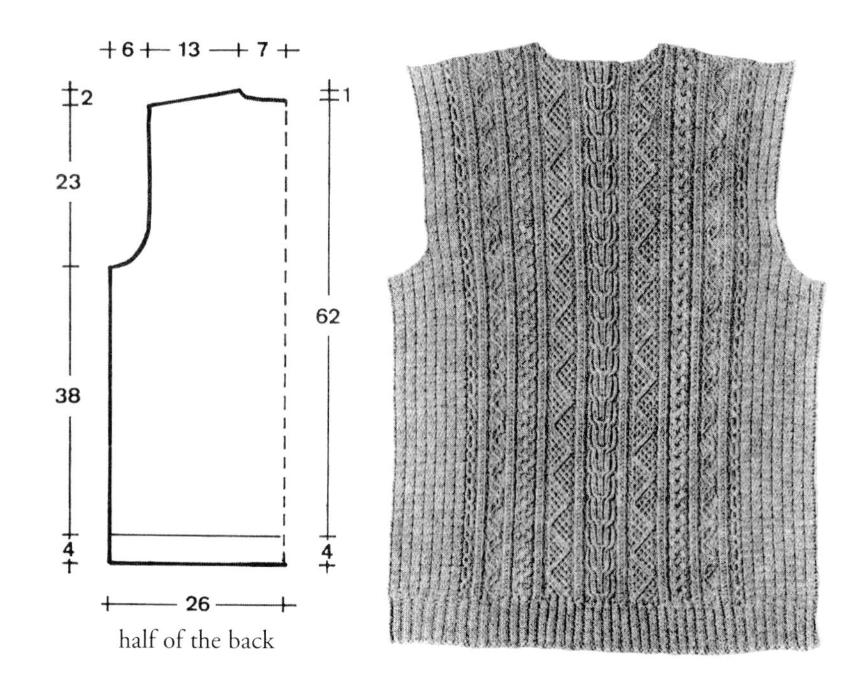

half of the back

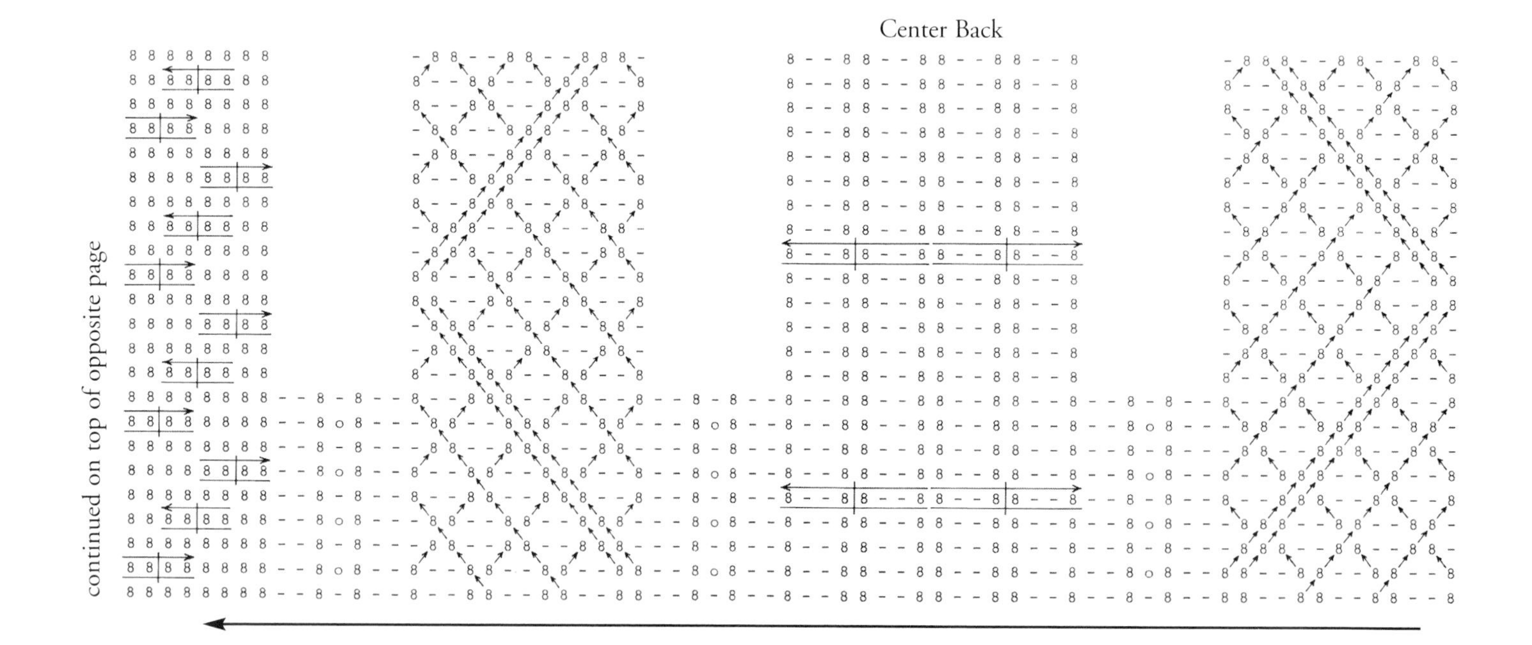

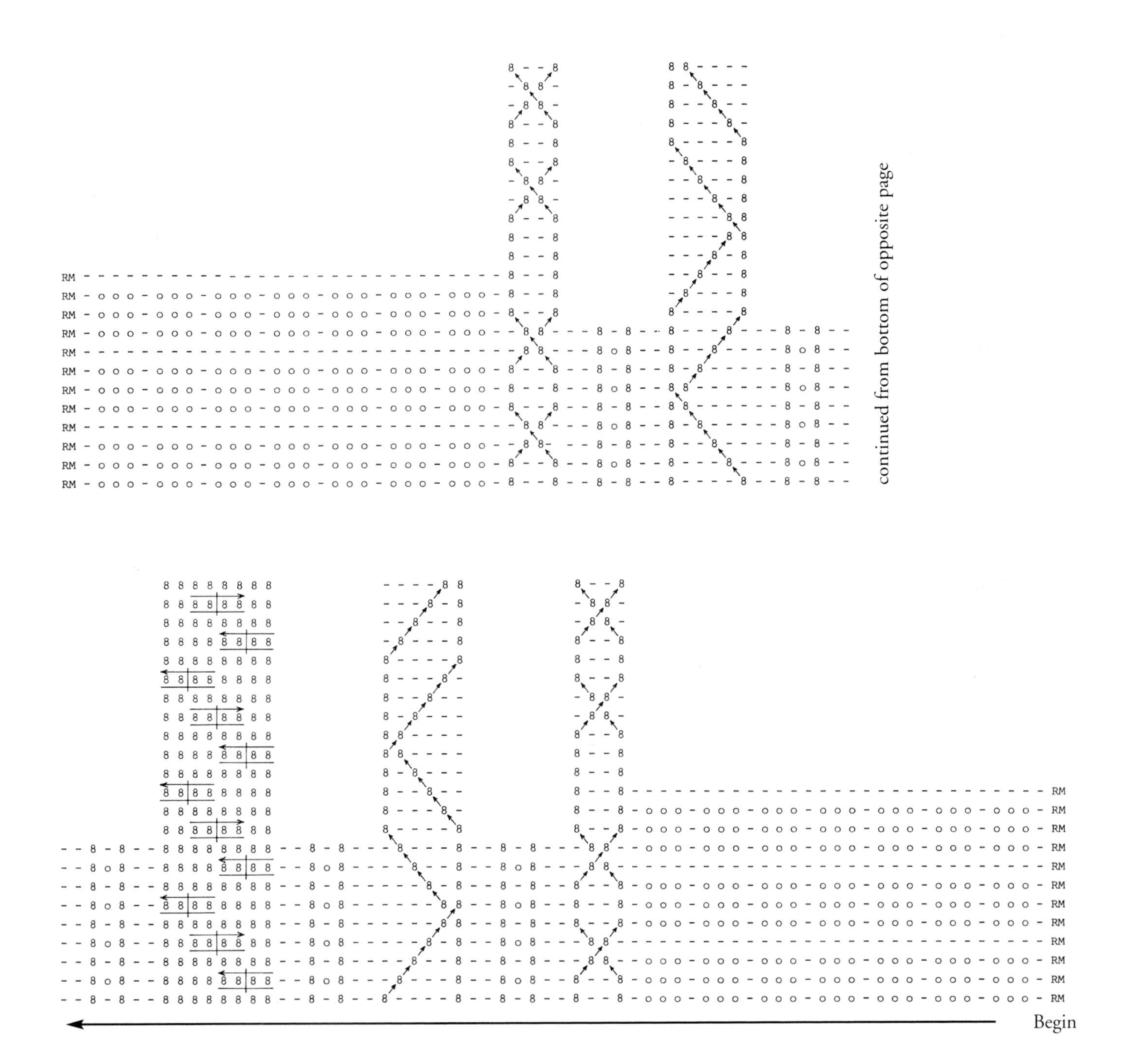
continued from bottom of opposite page
RM
Begin

Right Front: Men's garments have buttons on the right front. This is why it is better, to knit the right front first, so you can figure out where to place the buttons when the entire front is knitted. The buttonholes are knitted in the left front, and you won't have to guess where to put them.

Cast on 100 sts for the ribbing. 88 sts will be for the ribbing, knitted the same as on the back, 10 sts for the button band, and 2 edge sts. After knitting 4 cm, increase 13 sts, evenly spaced across the row = 113 sts. Knit in pattern to the armhole, without any increases.

Armhole: Work the same as the back, making sure it is on the correct side.

Neck Opening: When the front measures 59 cm from the start, cast off 14 sts on the side opposite the armhole. The other decreases are worked every other row: (6 sts) x1, (4 sts) x2, (3 sts) x2, (2 sts) x2 and (1 stitch) x4.

Shoulder Slope: At the same time, when the piece measures 23 cm from the beginning of the armhole, cast off every other row as follows (on the armhole side), (14 sts) x3 and (13 sts.) x1.

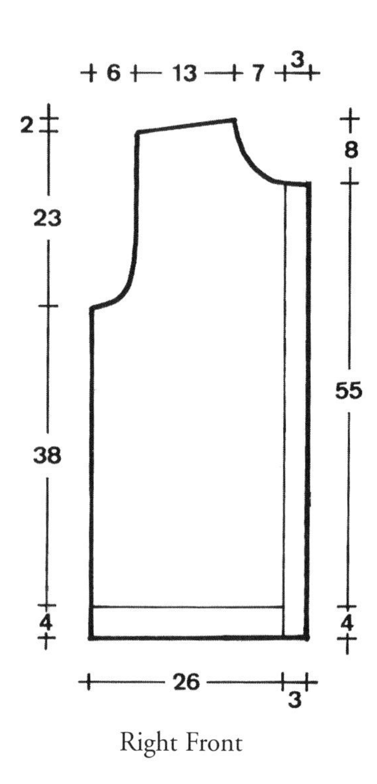

Right Front

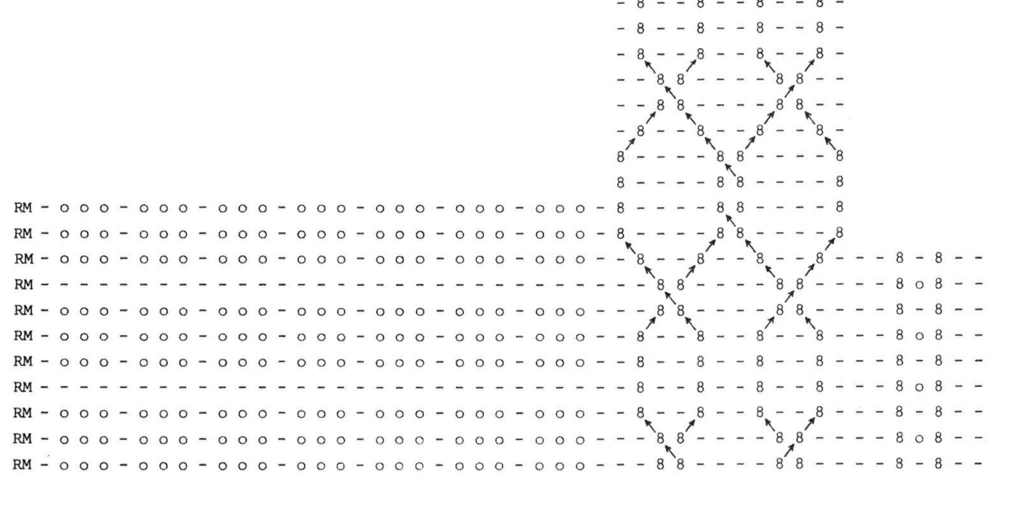

Left front: Work a mirror-image of the right front, but include buttonholes in the border.

Buttonholes: The buttonholes are knitted horizontally, evenly spaced the length of the front. In the center of the button band, cast off as many sts as you need for the size of the button. Finish knitting across the row. In the return row, cast on the same number of sts that you cast off and finish knitting to the end of the button band.

Right Front Chart runs across these two pages; reverse chart for Left Front.

Center Front

Sleeves: These are knitted in the round on dp needles.Cast on 84 sts and divide onto 4 needles. Knit 4 cm of ribbing as on the other pieces. In the next row increase 16 sts evenly spaced across the row, giving you 100 sts. Follow the chart - note the increases - until you reach the underarm. You should have 174 sts.

Sleeve top: This will be knitted back and forth. Cast Off in every other row as follows. (6 sts) x1, (2 sts) x5, (1 stitch) x21, (3 sts) x4, (4 sts) x4 and (5 sts) x1. Cast off the remaining 34 sts. Work an identical second sleeve.

Finishing: Pin all of the pieces to a padded surface, stretching slightly to measurements. Cover with a damp towel and let it dry. Sew all the seams and attach the sleeves.

Pick up 136 sts around the neck opening, and knit 1 row of twisted knit sts. Knit 6 cm of ribbing and cast off loosely. Fold in half to the inside and sew to the base of the band.

Tip: If you think this is too bulky around the neck, you can twist-knit the first 3 cm in the pattern, and work the last 3 cm in plain stockinette stitch. Sew on buttons.

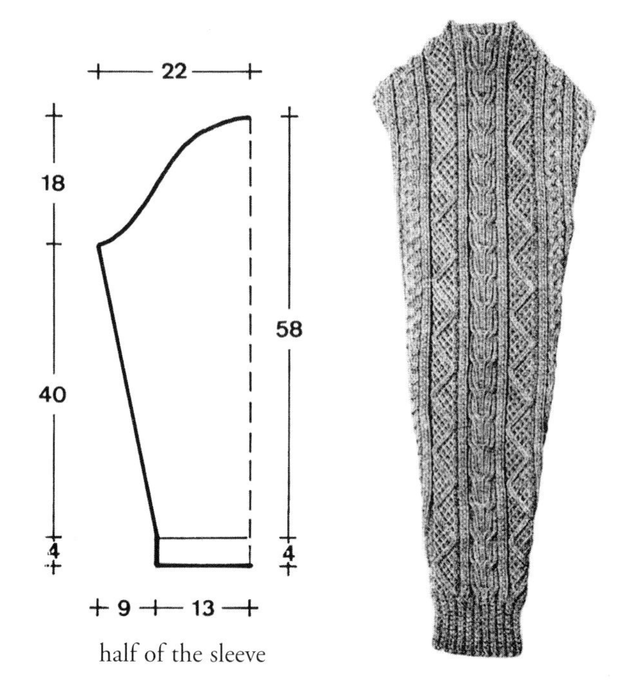

half of the sleeve

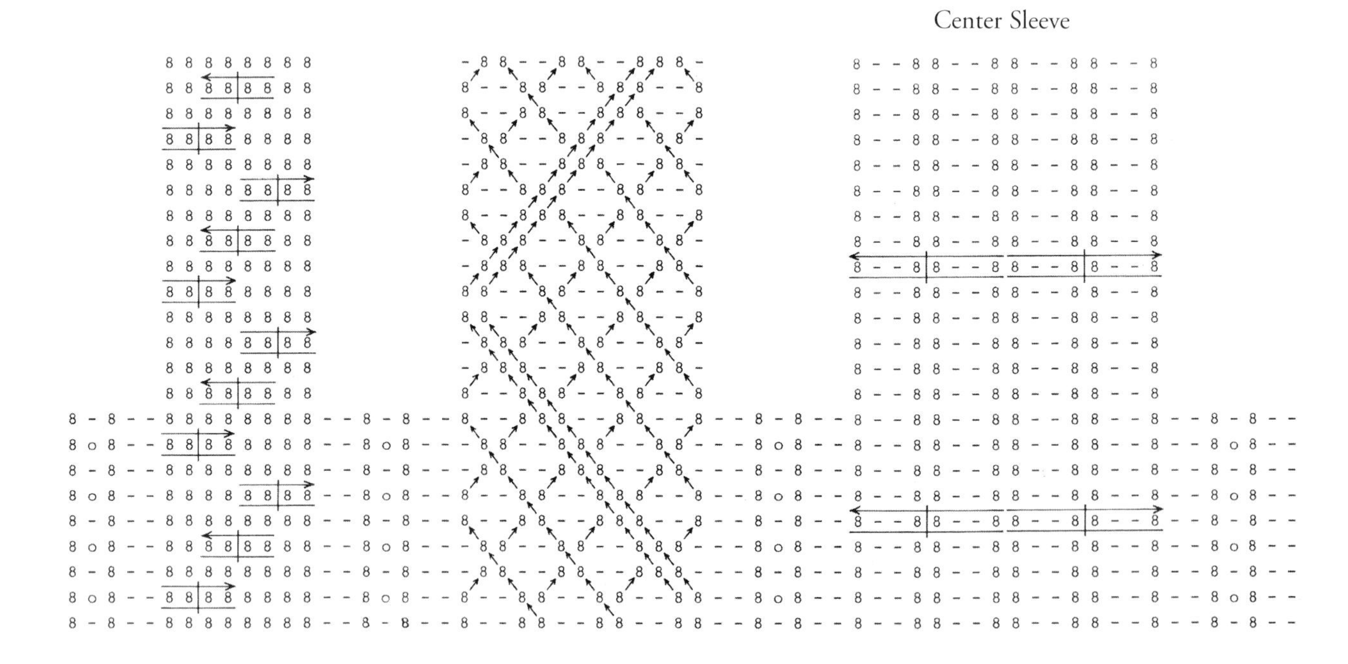

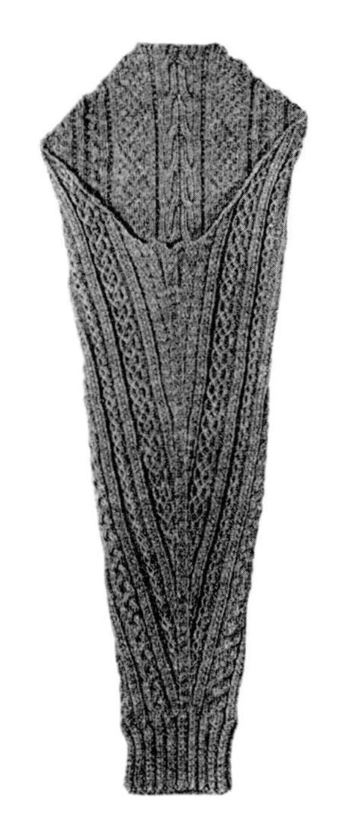

continued on page 182

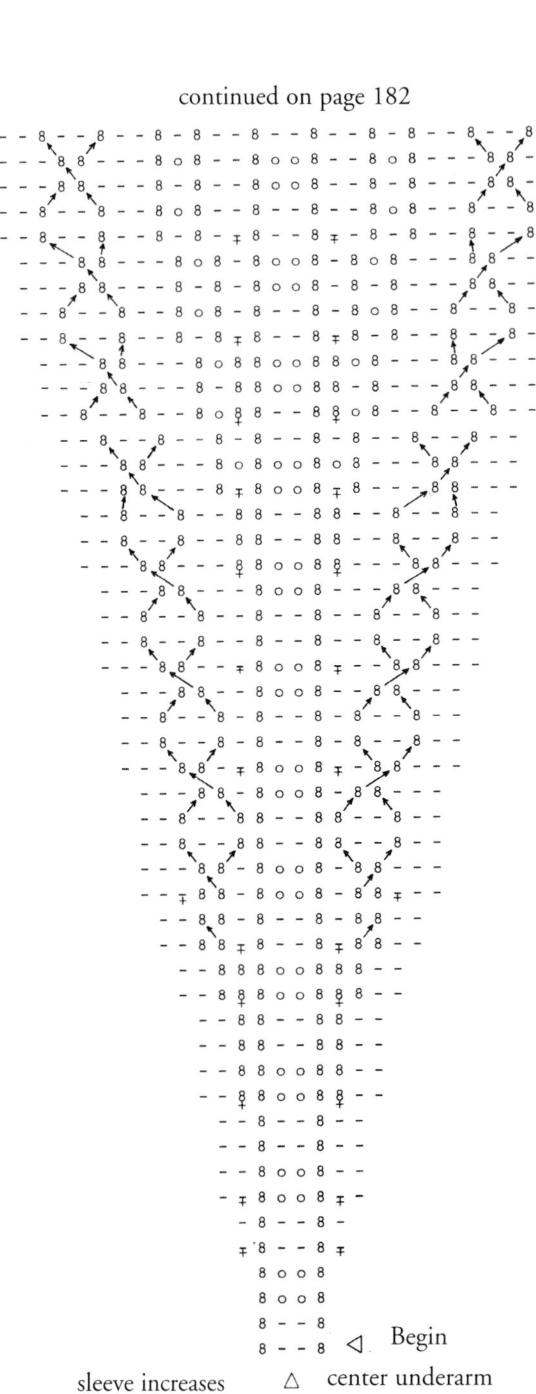

Continued on bottom of page 183

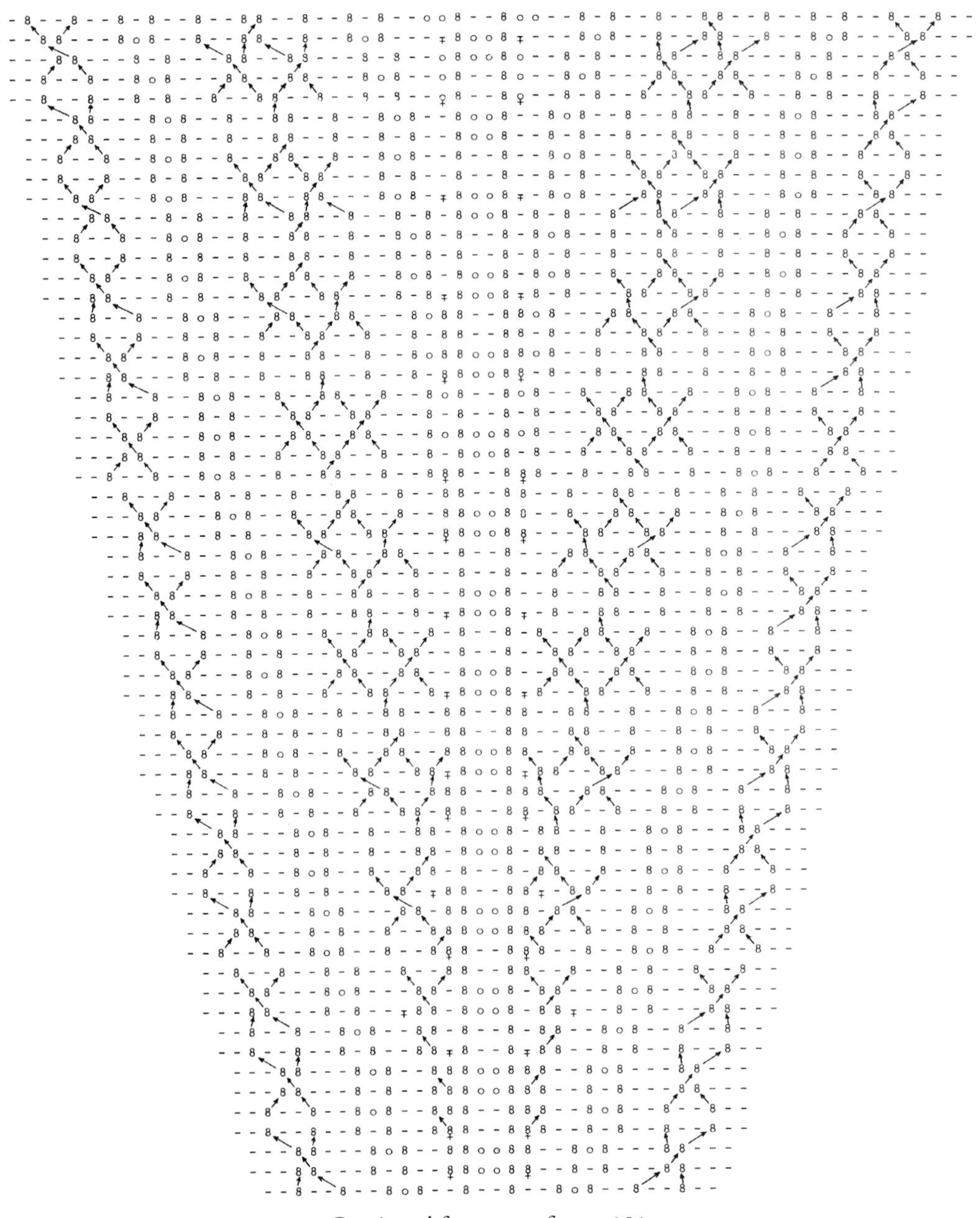

Continued from top of page 181

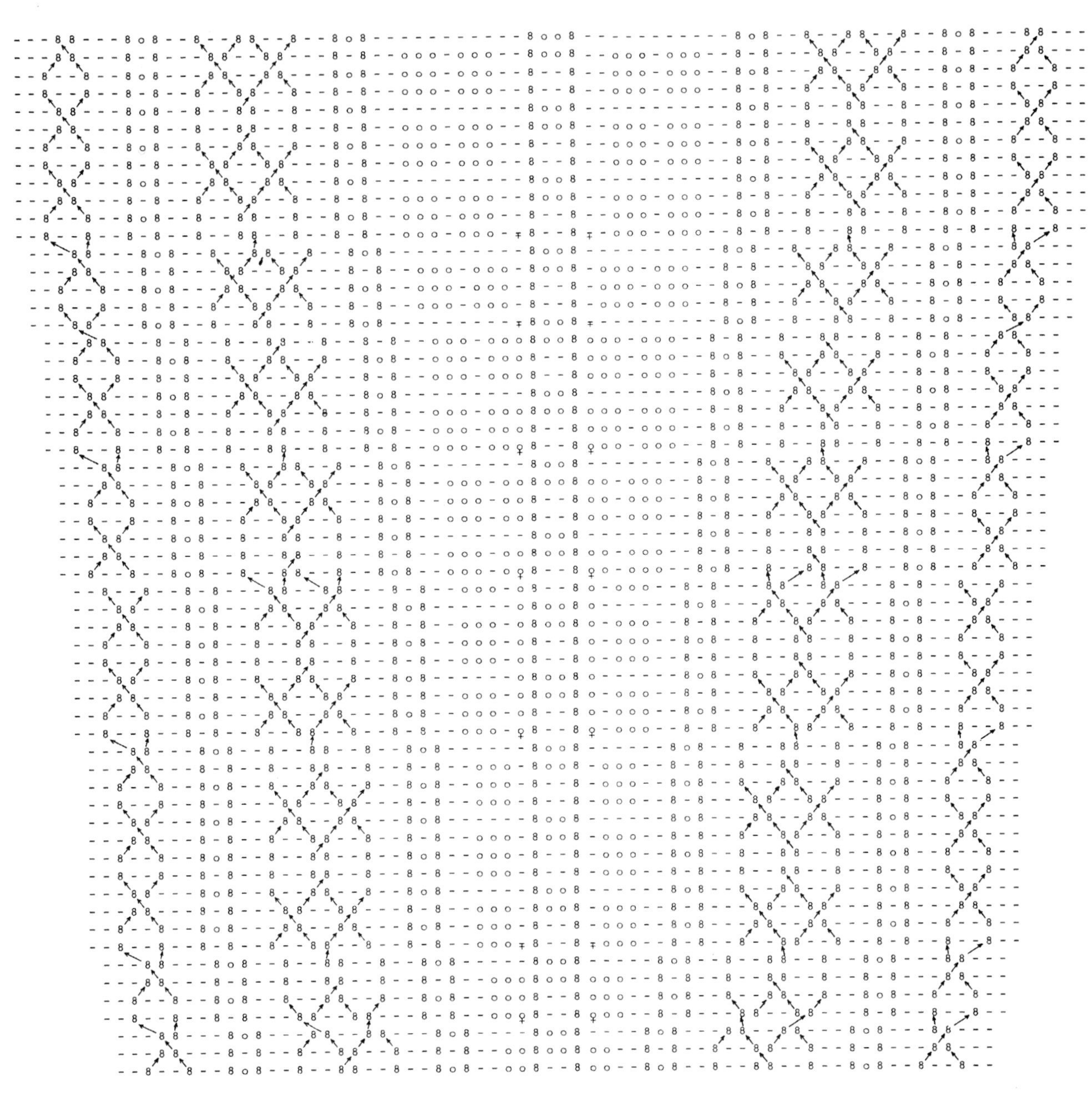

Continued from top of page 182

Women's Cardigan

Size:42 (German sizing)
Materials: 950 gr wool (fine 4- ply wool)
Needles Size: 2mm
Gauge: see page 143

Back: Cast on 170 sts plus 2 edge sts= 172 sts. Knit for 2 cm in garter-stitch. In the last row increase 38 sts evenly spaced across the row: 208 sts + 2 edge sts= 210 sts. Start pattern in the next row. Follow chart to the armholes. Increase 2 sts on both sides. There are now 214 sts in all.

Armholes: When the back is 30.5 cm long, start the armhole shaping. Cast off every other row on both sides, as follows: (7 sts) x1, (4 sts) x1, (3 sts) x3 and (2 sts) x2. When arm-hole measures 22 cm, work the neck opening and shoulder shaping.

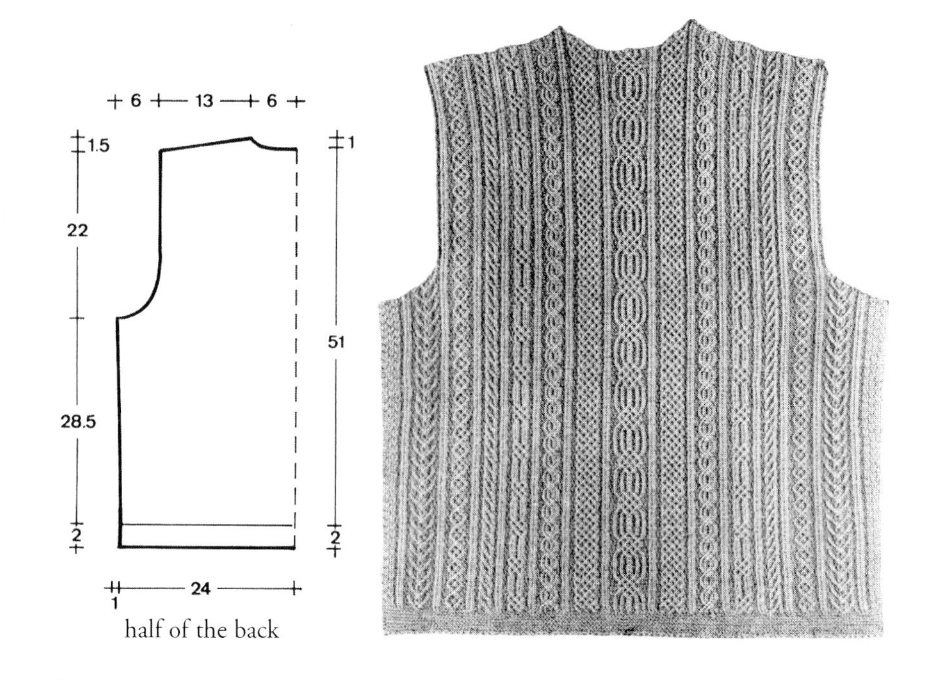

half of the back

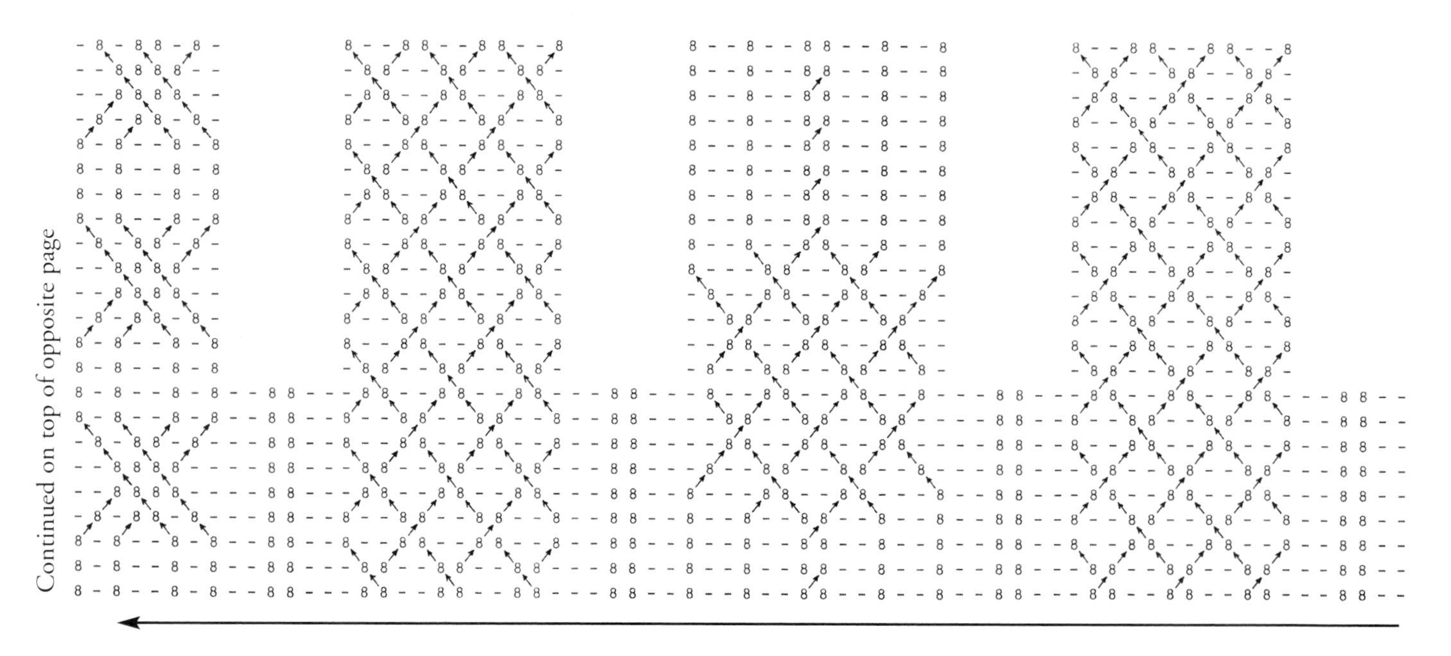

Continued on top of opposite page

Back Chart is on these two pages

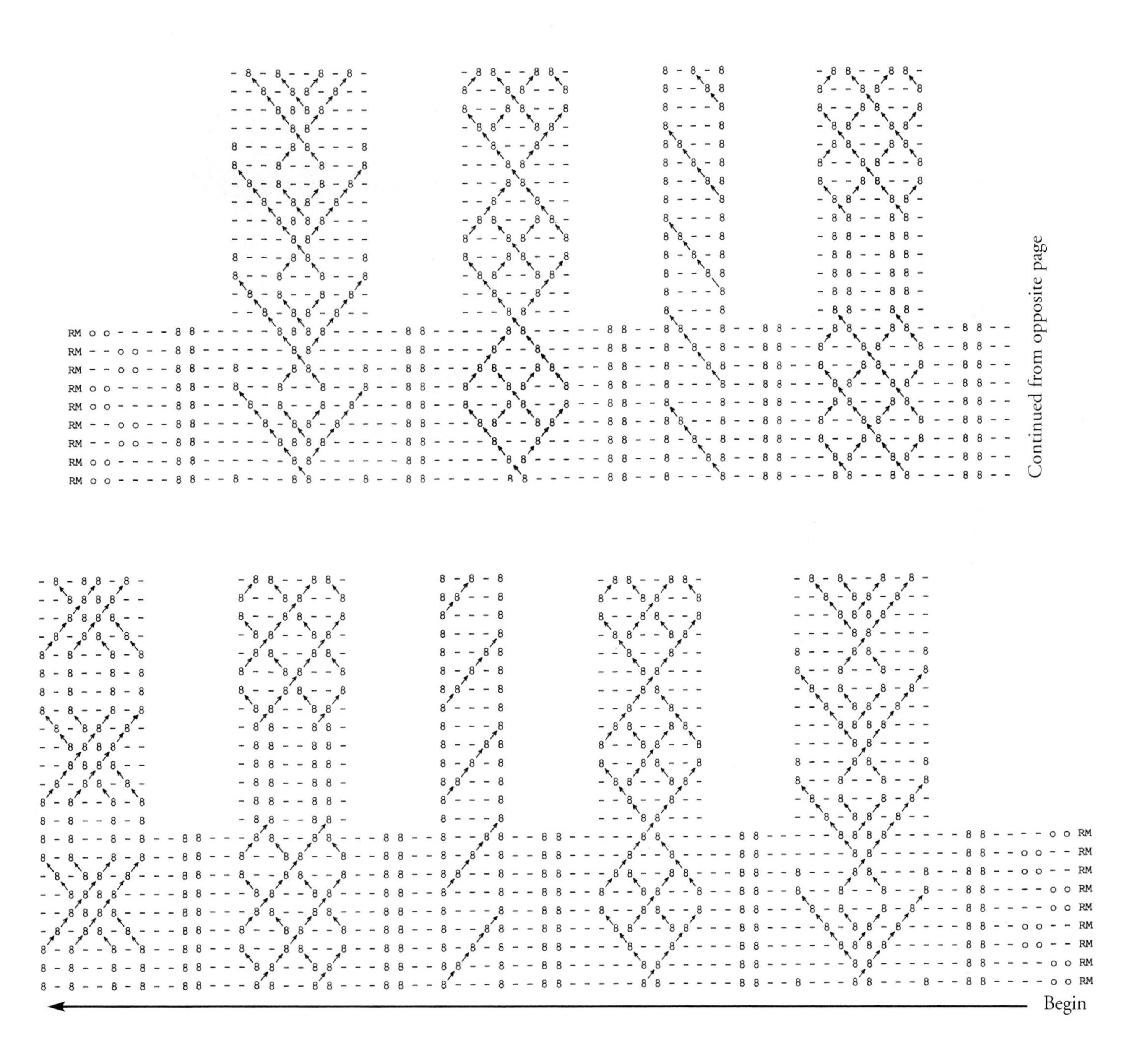

Neck opening: Cast off the center 26 sts, and finish shoulders separately. Cast off (6 sts) x2 for the neck opening. At the same, shape each shoulder by casting off (15 sts) x4 times, every other row.

Left front: When knitting a women's garment, work the left front first; it will be easier to place the button holes on the right side. **Cast on** 102 sts for the front: 89 sts for the ribbing, 11 sts for the button band and 2 edge sts. Knit 2cm in garter stitch. In the last row increase 17 sts evenly spaced across: 117 sts plus 2 edge sts = 119 sts. Follow chart. As you knit to the armholes, increase 2 sts on each outside edge between the ribbing and the armholes: 121 sts.

Armholes: Cast off every other row as for the back. (7st) x1, (4 sts) x1, (3 sts) x3 and (2 sts) x1.
Sleeve: Sleeves are worked in the round. Cast on 76 sts. Knit in garter stitch for 2 cm, increasing 14 sts in the last round. Divide these sts evenly onto dp

Neck opening: When front measures 45cm cast off 12 sts on side opposite armhole, every other row: (7 sts) x1, (4 sts) x1, (3 sts,) x2, (2 sts) x4 and (1 stitch) x2. Work even to the shoulder shaping. Every other row, cast off (15 sts) x4.

Right front: Work as for left front, reversing all shaping. Don't forget the button holes.

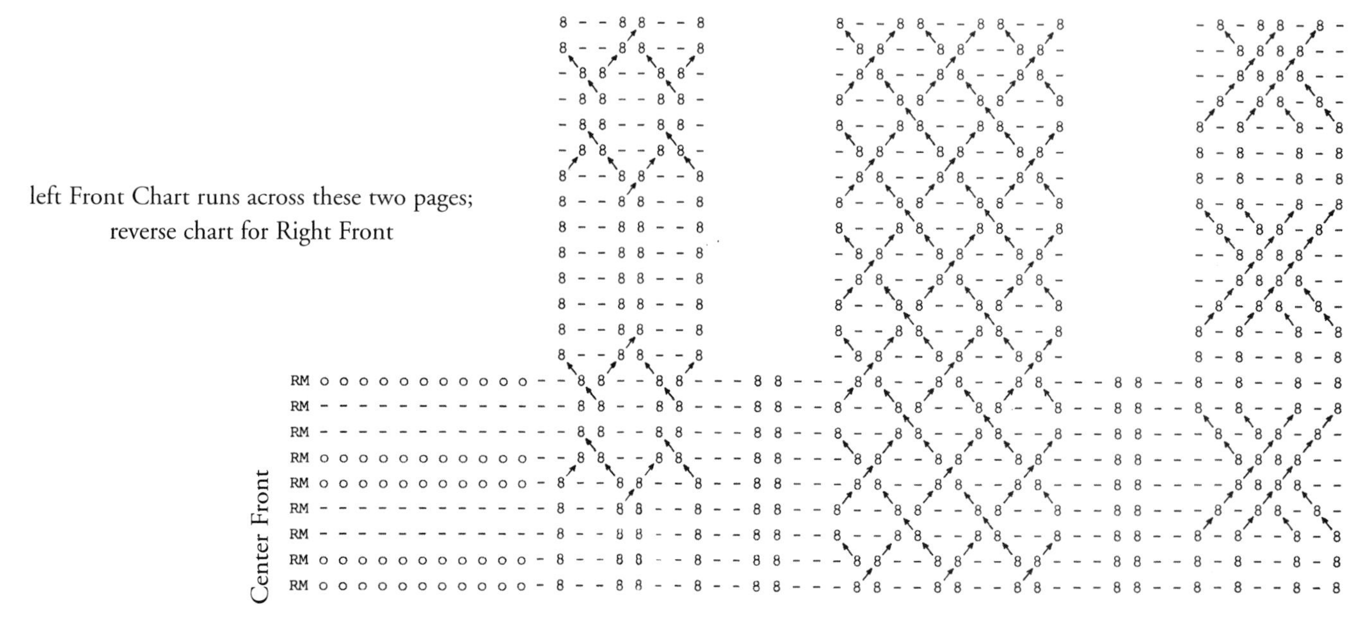

left Front Chart runs across these two pages; reverse chart for Right Front

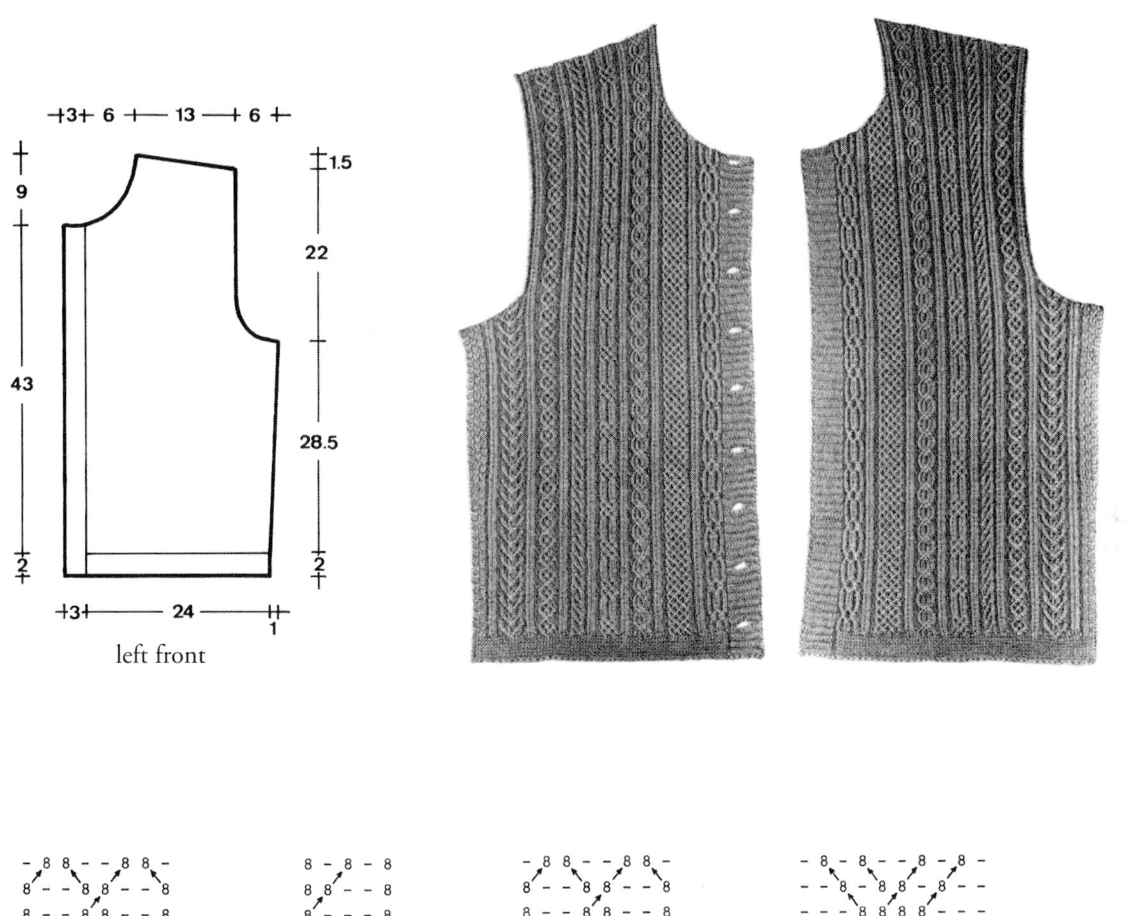

left front

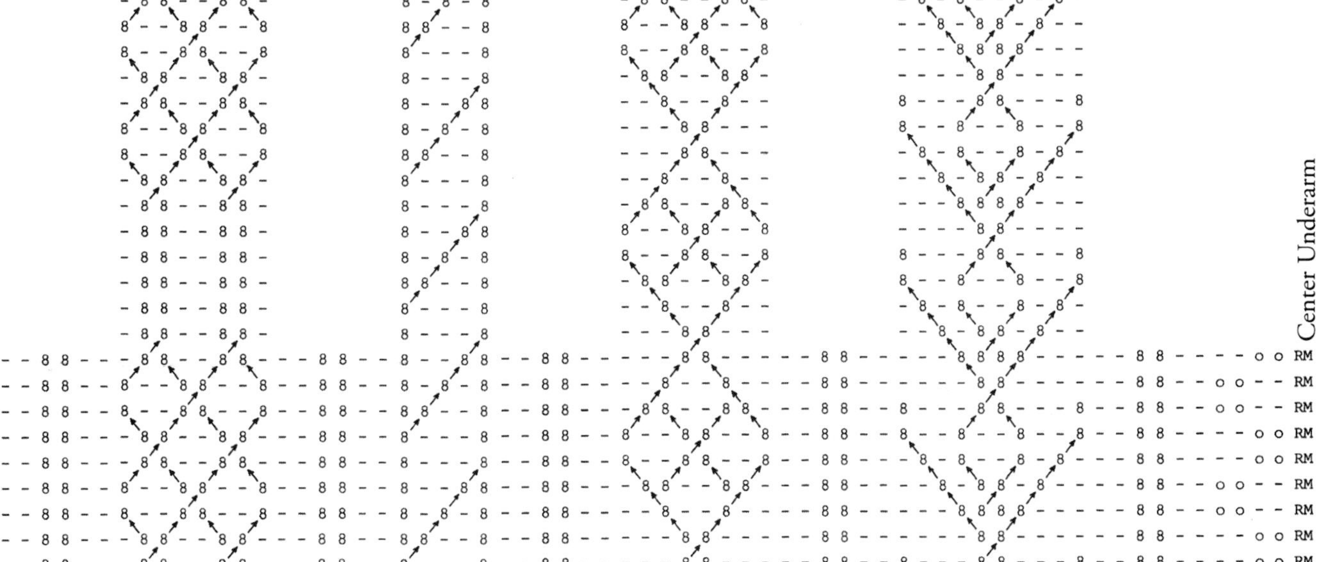

Sleeve: Sleeves are worked in the round. Cast on 76 sts. Knit in garter-stitch for 2 cm, increasing 14 sts in the last round. Divide these sts evenly onto dp needles. Follow the chart, including increases, to the underarm. You should have 194 sts.

Sleeve top: The top of the sleeve is worked back and forth on 2 needles. The shaping is done on both sides, every other row as follows. (5 sts) x2, (1 stitch) x10, (2 sts) x5, (1 stitch) x8, (2 sts) x10, (3 sts) x4, (4 sts) x1 and (5 sts) x1. Cast off the remaining 36 sts.

Work an identical second sleeve.

Finishing: Pin the pieces to a soft surfaces, lightly stretching them to size. Cover with a damp cloth and allow to dry. Sew seams and set in the sleeves. Pick up 136 sts evenly spaced around the neck opening for the neck band. Knit in garter stitch for 2 cm, decreasing by 3 sts on each front, to slant the neck-band a little. Cast off all of the sts. To give the edges a nice finish, 1 row of single crochet can be worked around the neck-band and both the button and buttonhole bands.
Sew buttons opposite button holes.

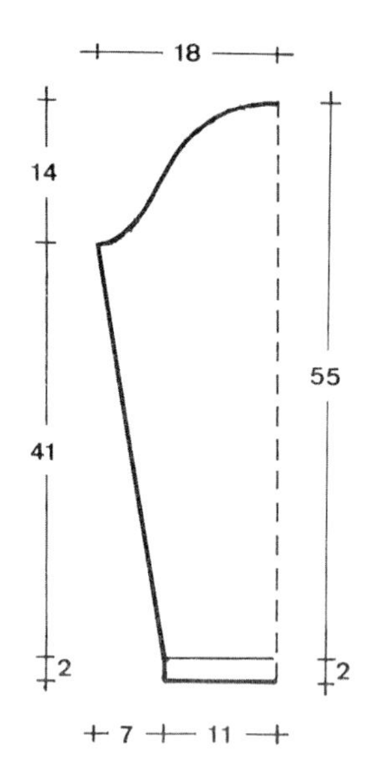

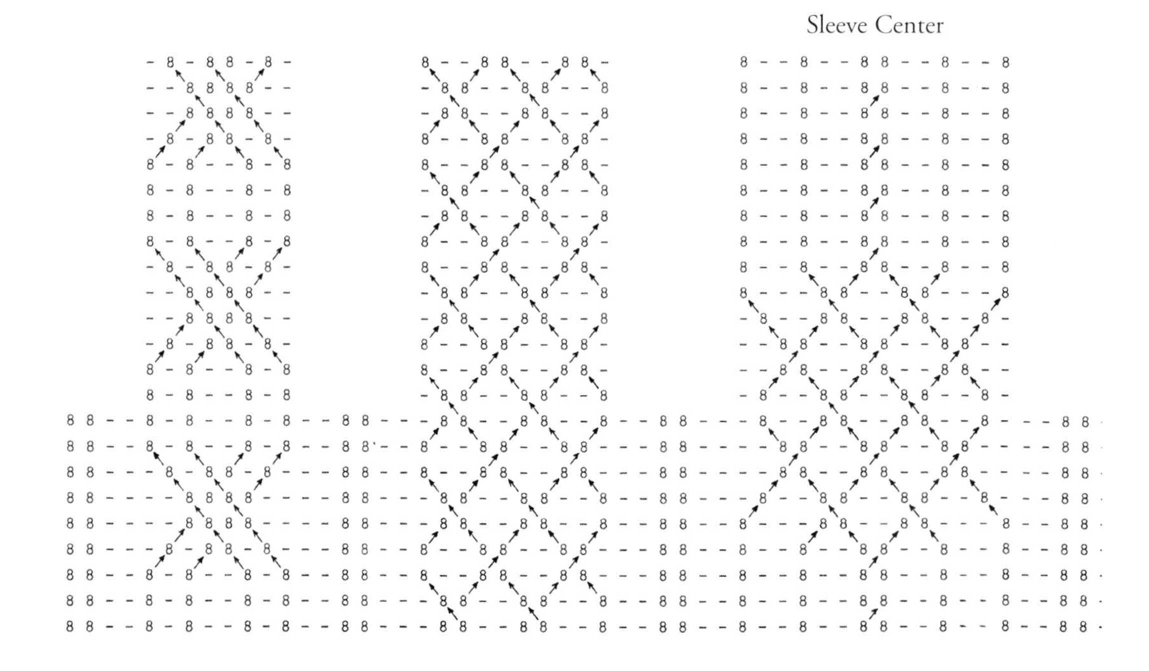

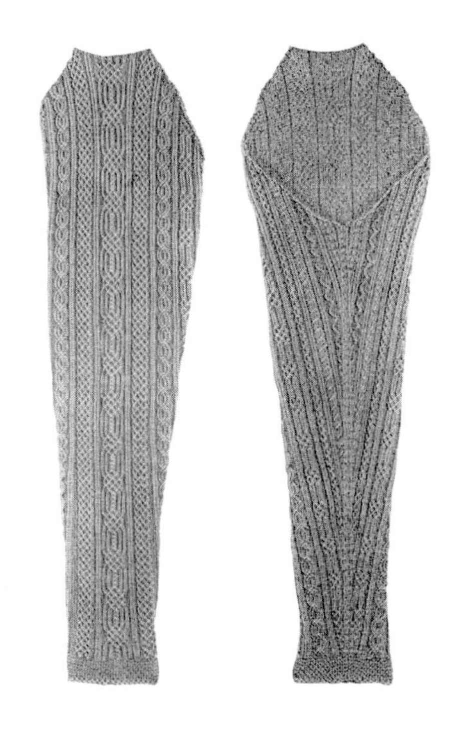

continued at bottom of page 190

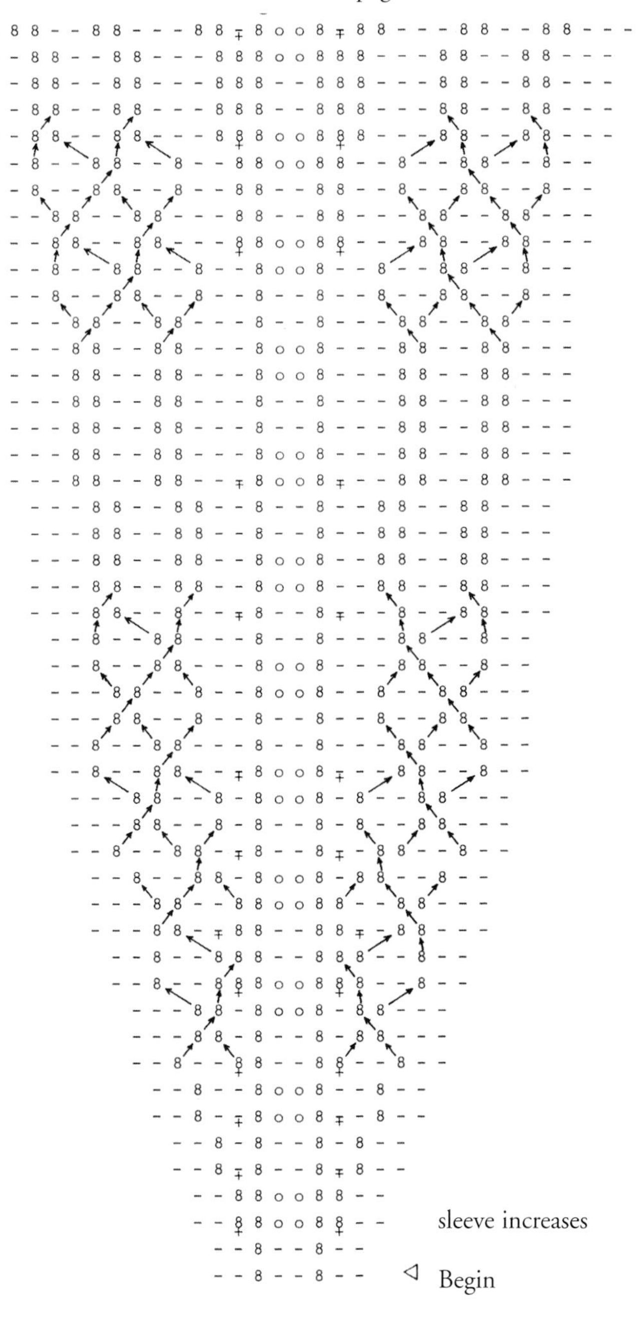

Sleeve Chart runs across these two pages

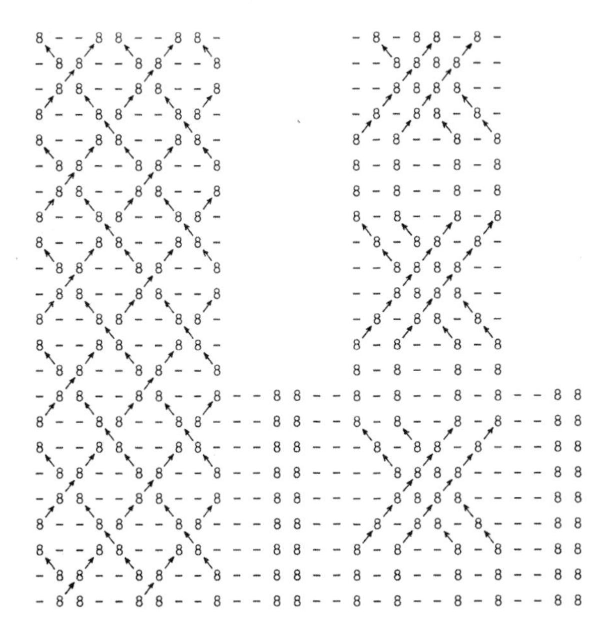

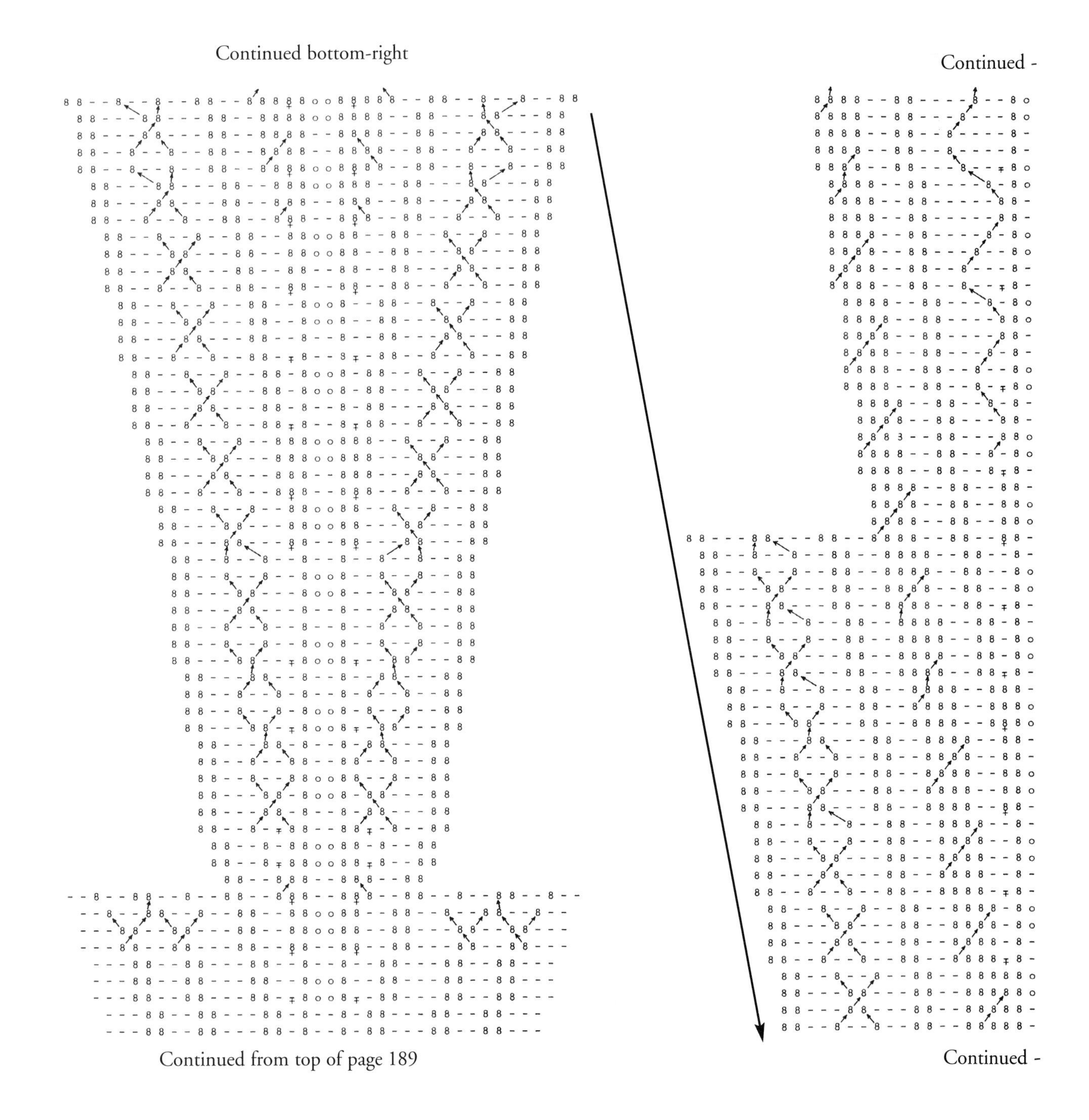
Continued bottom-right
Continued -
Continued from top of page 189
Continued -

- on bottom right

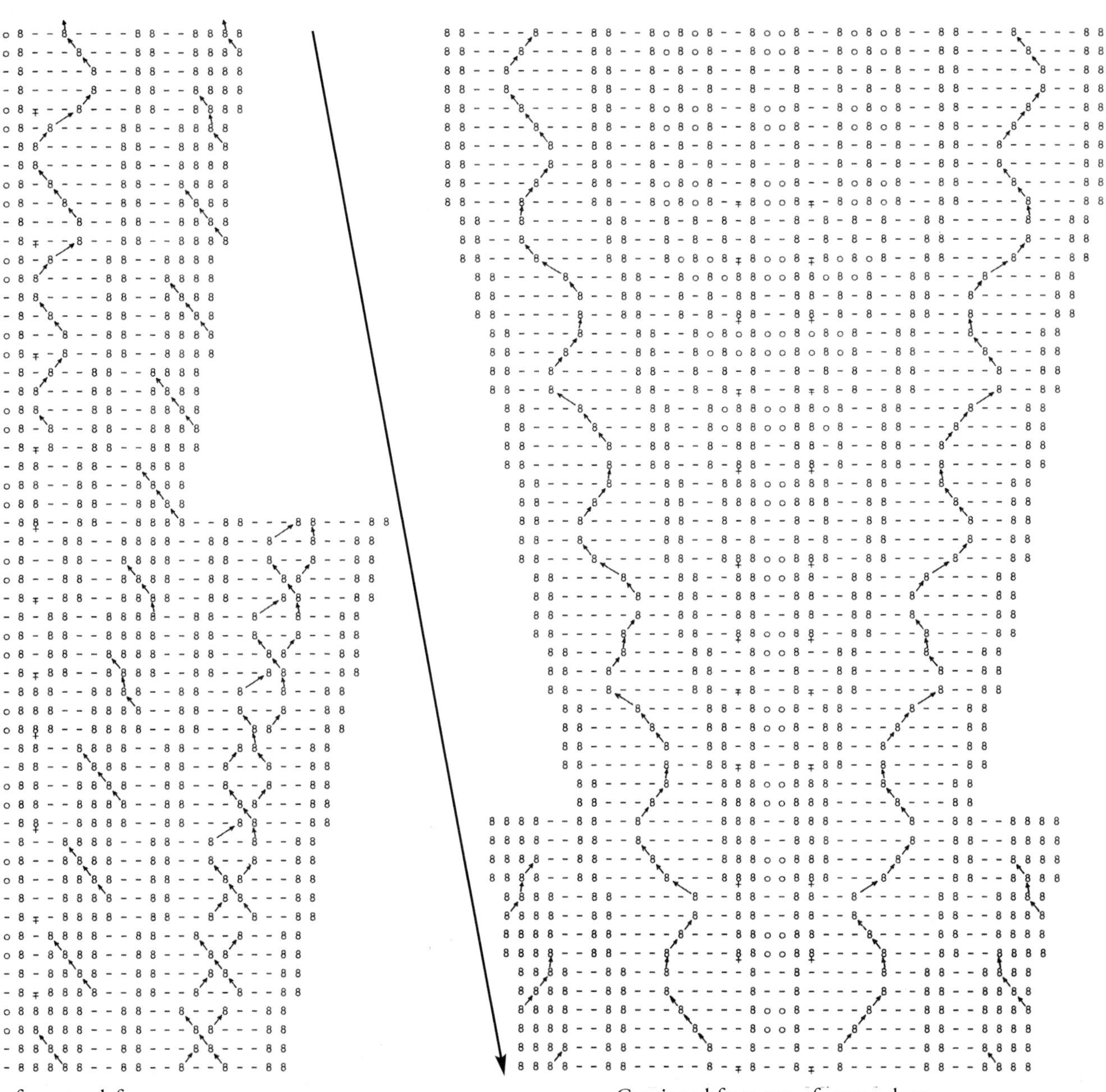

- from top left

Continued from top of center chart

Little Boys' Styrian Sweater

Size: 4- 5 years
Materials: 450 gram wool (sport weight)
Needles Size: 2.5mm

Gauge: see page 143

Back: Cast on 98 sts + 2 edge st s= 100 sts.
Work 10 rows in garter stitch. Increase 20 sts, evenly spaced across the next row (row 11): 118 sts + 2 edge sts= 120 sts. Follow the chart to the armholes.

Armholes: When the back measures 24 cm, cast off sts for the armholes. Work on both sides, every other row as follows: (5 sts) x1, (3 sts) x1, (2 sts) x1 and (1 stitch) x1. When the armhole measures 14cm, start the neck opening and shoulder shaping.

Neck Opening: Cast off the center 18 sts and work each side separately. Cast off (2 sts) x2 at the neck edge and at the same time cast off (12 sts) x3 for the shoulder shaping.

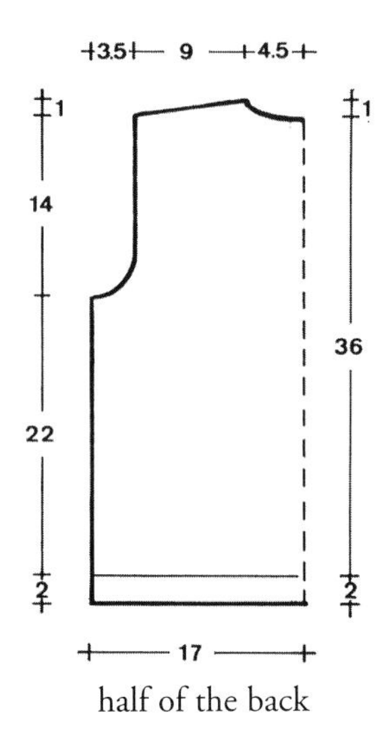

half of the back

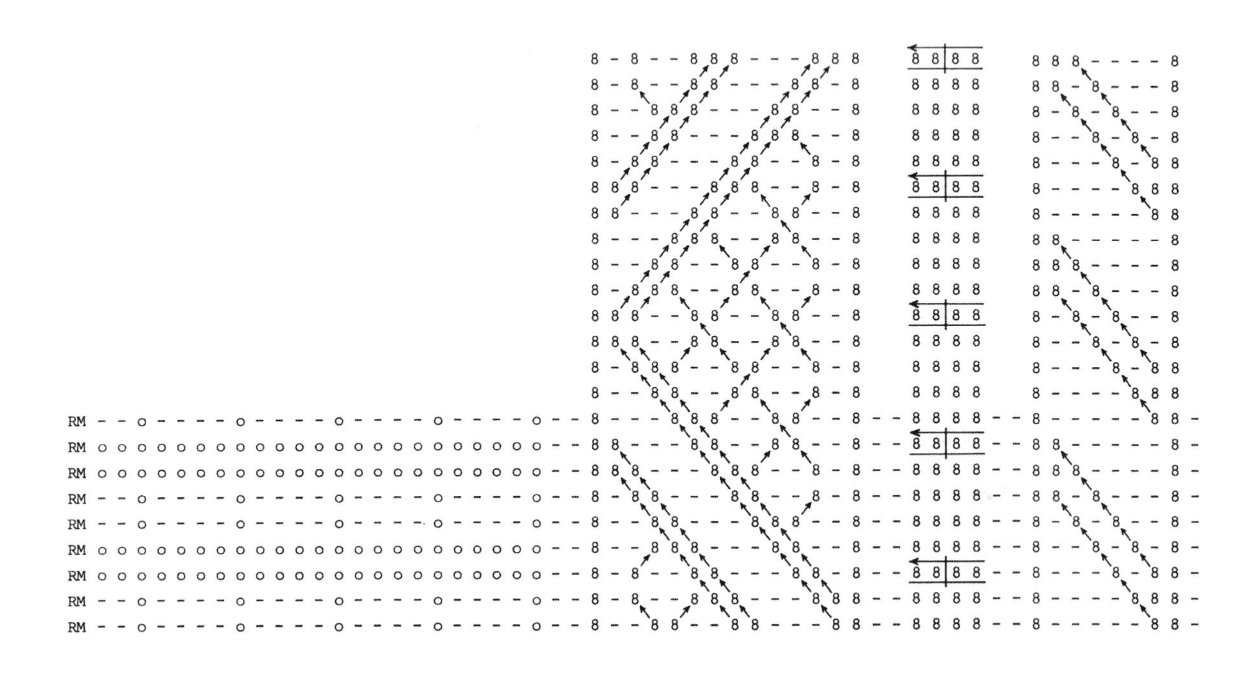

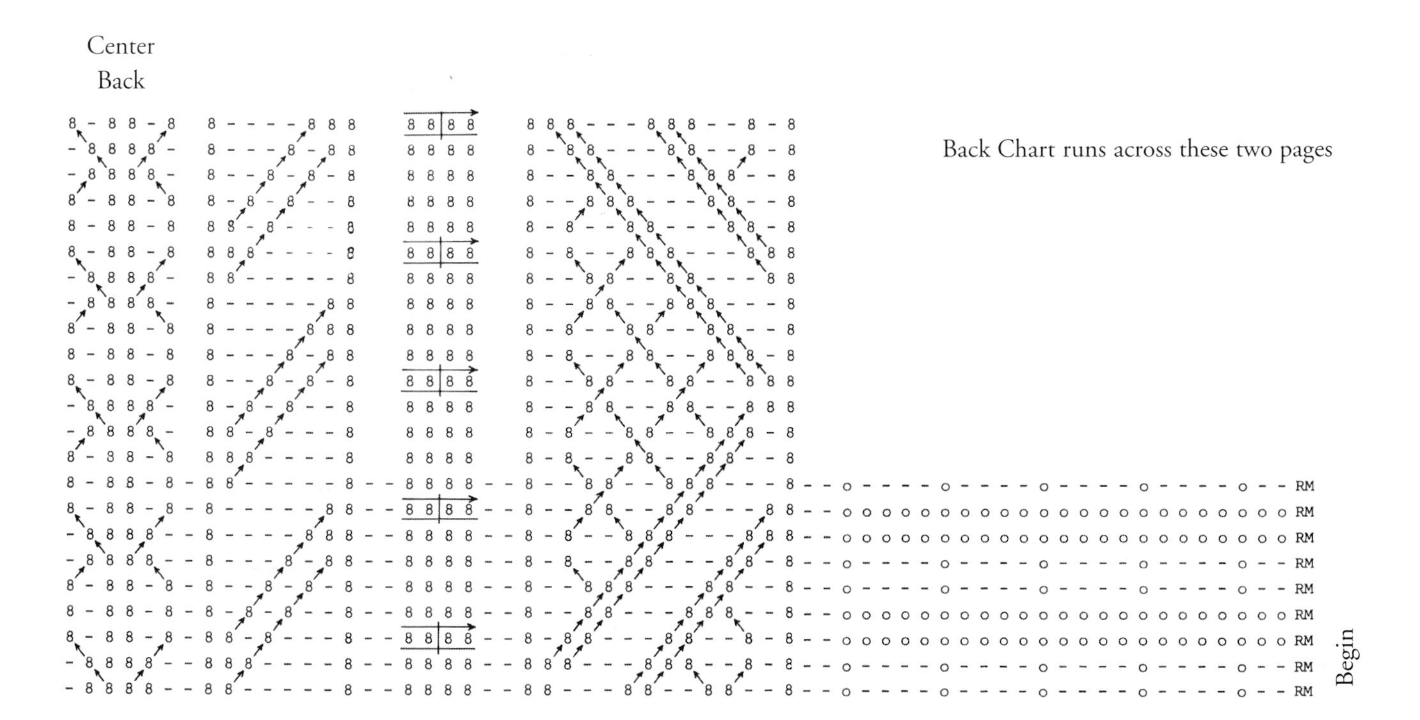
Center
Back
Back Chart runs across these two pages
RM
Begin

Right front: Cast on 56 sts. The ribbing uses 47 sts, 7 sts for the button band and 2 edge sts. Knit 10 rows in garter stitch and on the 11th row (wrong side row) increase 17 sts evenly spaced across. You now have 73 sts. Follow the chart and knit straight up to the armhole.

Armhole: Work the cast off sts same as on the back, every other row: (5 sts) x1, (3 sts) x1, (2 sts) x1 and (1 stitch) x1.

Neck opening: When the front measures 33cm, start the neck opening. Cast off 9 sts on the side opposite the armhole. After this, (in every other row) cast off (4 sts) x1, (3 sts) x1, (2 sts) x4 and (1 stitch) x2. Knit straight to the shoulder shaping: cast off (12 sts) x3 at armhole side.

Left front: Work as the right front, reversing the shaping. Don't forget to work the armholes.

Sleeve: Sleeves are knitted in the round to the armhole. Cast on 48 sts and knit 10 rows in garter stitch. Increase 15 sts evenly spaced across the round in row 11. In row 12, beginning with 63 sts, follow the chart, increasing 20 sts on each side of the center of the sleeve (underarm), the same as on the men's and the ladies' sweaters. There should be 103 sts at the top of the sleeve.

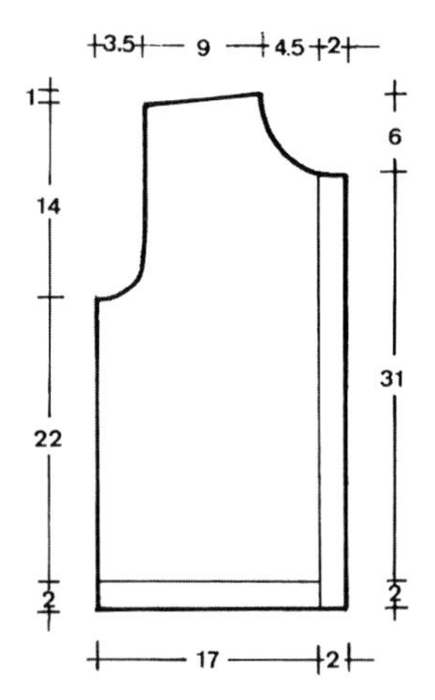

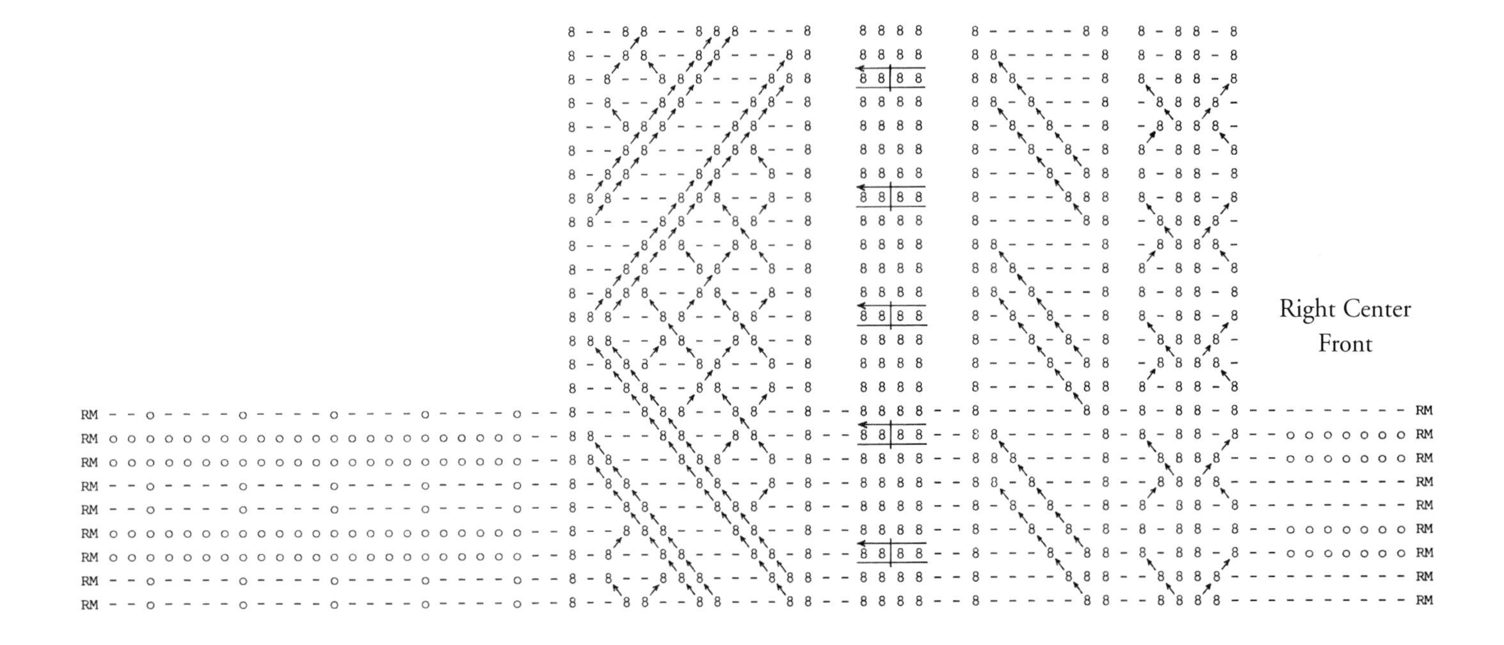

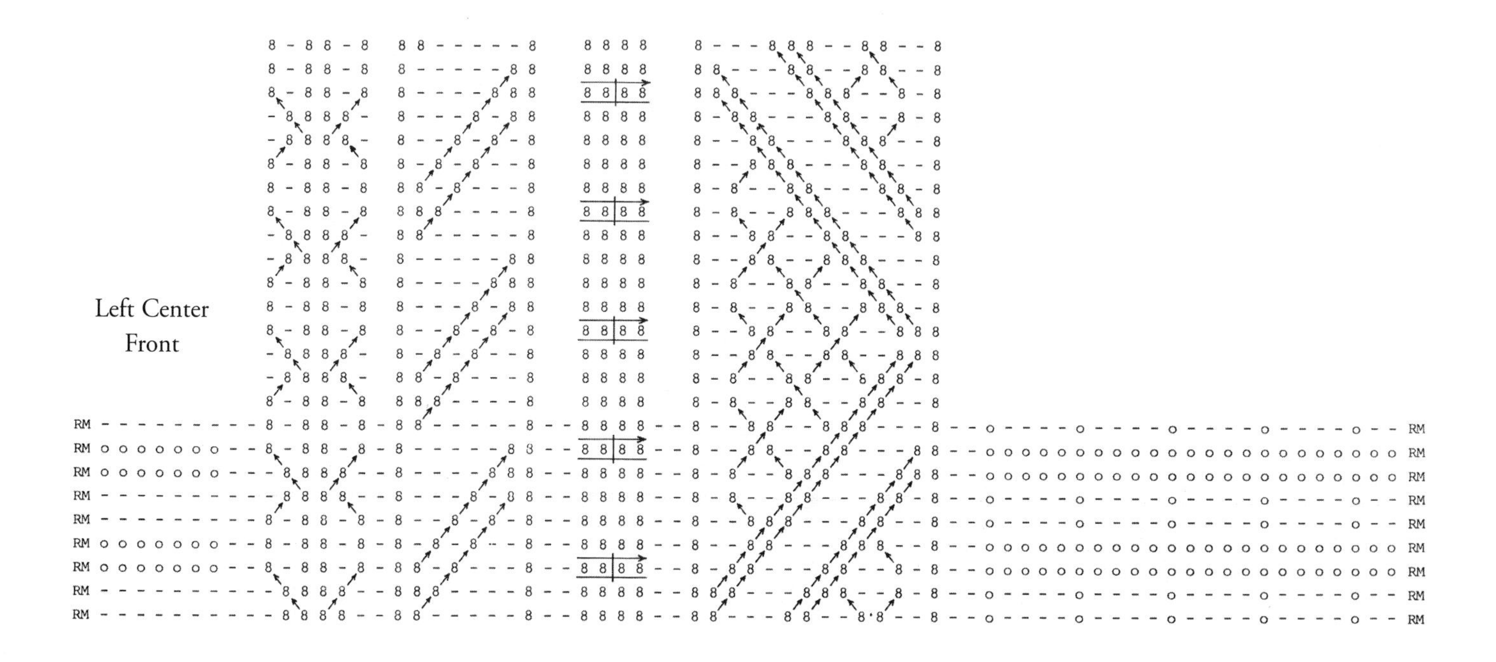
Left Center
Front

every second row as follows. (3 sts) x1, (2 sts) x1, (1 stitch) x15, (3 sts) x2 and (4 sts) x3. Cast off the remaining 27 sts.
Work the second sleeve identical to the first.

Finishing: Pin the pieces to a soft surface, stretching lightly to measurements. Cover with a damp cloth and allow to dry. Sew seams and set in sleeves.

Neck Band: Cast on 90 sts and knit in garter stitch for 10 rows, decreasing 2 or 3 sts on each end to slant the edges. Cast off loosely and sew the cast off edge to the neck edge.

If you want the sweater to look like the original Styrian sweaters, you can single crochet around all of the edges in green wool. In that case the main color of the sweater would be grey. Sew on buttons.

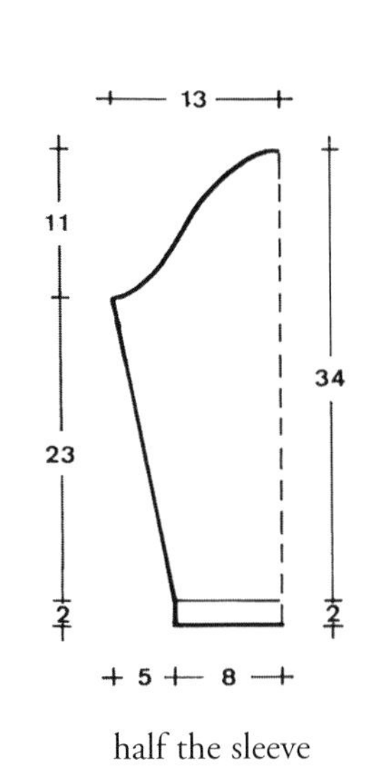

half the sleeve

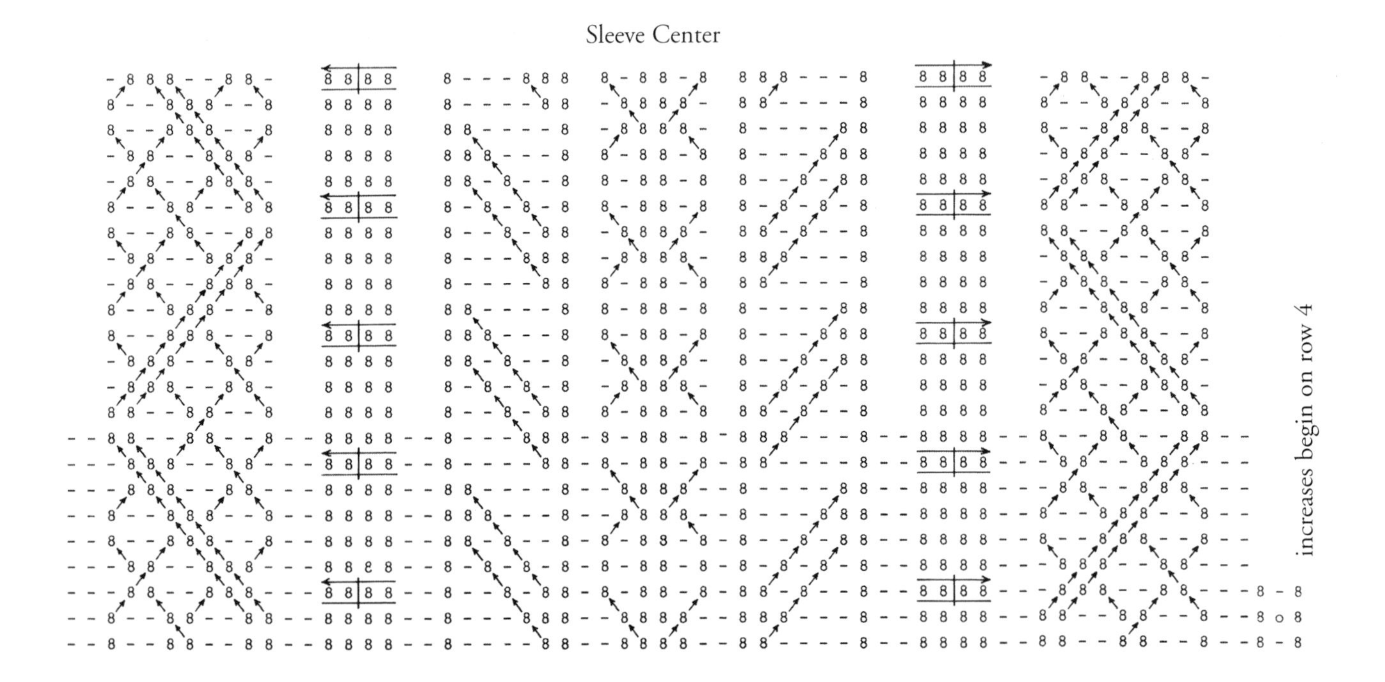

Im Frühjahr 1982 erschien das 1. Heft „Überlieferte Strickmuster aus dem steirischen Ennstal“ in der Reihe der *Kleinen Schriften* des Landschaftsmuseums Schloß Trautenfels. Das zweite Strickheft derselben Reihe, das eine Fortsetzung und Erweiterung des ersten Bandes ist, erschien im Spätherbst 1982. Zu unserer großen Freude wurden beide Ausgaben bei uns im Ennstal und weit darüber hinaus mit großer Begeisterung aufgenommen. Diese Freude und echte Begeisterung vieler Mädchen und Frauen ermunterte uns, in einem dritten Heft weitere Model aus dem Ennstal und Ausseerland im Rahmen dieser Schriftenreihe zu veröffentlichen. Nun ist auch diese Ausgabe fertig. Dieses 3. Strickheft stellt mit seinen 53 Modeln, ebenso wie der zweite Band, eine Erweiterung des gesammelten Musterschatzes dar. 30 Model davon stammen aus dem Nachlaß von Frau Thekla Zeiler, die übrigen sind Sammelergebnisse aus dem Ennstal und Ausseerland.

Das Heft ist ebenso aufgebaut wie die beiden ersten Hefte. Der 1. Teil enthält den erweiterten Musterschatz in Bild und Strickschrift, der 2. Teil praktische Anwendungsmöglichkeiten für Stutzen und Westen mit genauen Beschreibungen. Diese Arbeitsbeschreibungen werden Ihnen sicher sehr helfen, aber sie bürgen nicht zur Gänze dafür, daß Ihr Werkstück auch zu Ihrer vollsten Zufriedenheit ausfällt. Es hängt soviel von der persönlichen Strickart, der Wolle und der Nadelstärke ab. Daher die Bitte: Machen Sie immer vorher eine Maschenprobe (siehe S. 51). Nur auf Grund dieser errechnet man die richtige Zahl der Anschlagmaschen. Die Mühe lohnt sich! Waren Ihnen diese praktischen Arbeitsanleitungen und Musterzusammenstellungen zunächst eine Hilfe, wenn Sie zum erstenmal „gemodelte“ Stutzen oder Westen gestrickt haben, so sind wir sicher, wenn Sie mehr stricken, werden Sie selbst schöpferisch und voller eigener Ideen sein, wie das eben in der echten Volkskunst immer gewesen ist.

Herzlichen Dank sagen wir an dieser Stelle Frau Erna Brunner, die immer mit Freude bereit ist, beim Stricken helfend und ergänzend mitzutun. Ebenso herzlich bedankt sei Frau Anni Gruber für's helfende Stricken.

Für die Strickschrift werden wieder jene Symbole — durch einige Zeichen ergänzt — verwendet, die Frau Hildegard Rieger bereits 1944 in ihrem Werk „Deutsche Strickkunst“ eingeführt hat.

Im ersten Heft haben wir die Muster mit fortlaufenden Nummern versehen (1—59), diese Numerierung haben wir im 2. Heft fortgesetzt (60—121) und im 3. Heft setzen wir sie mit den Nummern 122—174 fort. Wir wünschen auch diesem 3. Strickheft, daß es gut aufgenommen wird, damit diese echte Volkskunst erhalten und lebendig bleibt.

Dr. Volker Hänsel

Über die Technik des Modelstrickens

Es ist eine Sache, die jeder interessierten und einigermaßen geübten Strickerin gelingt. In vielen Fällen sogar großartig gelingt! Die **glatte Masche** hat den **Model (= Muster)** zu bilden. Sie wird nicht normal glatt gestrickt, sondern **immer verschränkt** (= englisch); dadurch hebt sie sich aus dem Grunde heraus.

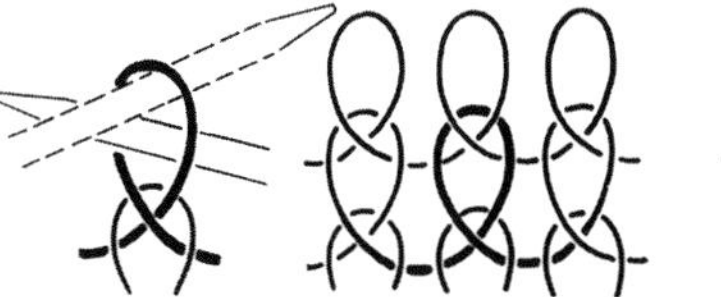

glatte verschränkte Maschen, links, wie sie gestrickt werden

verkehrte Maschen

Den Grund bilden die verkehrten Maschen. Folglich sind es die verschränkt glatt gestrickten Maschen, die zur Musterbildung nach rechts oder links **überhoben** (= gekreuzt) werden müssen.

Folgendes ist bitte zu beachten: Alle Strickschriften und Bilder zeigen den Model auf seiner Oberseite. Bei Arbeiten, zum Beispiel Stutzen, bei denen man rund stricken kann, wird Masche für Masche genau so gestrickt, wie sie die Strickschrift zeigt. Schwieriger wird es beim flachen Stricken, zum Beispiel bei Westen, hier gibt es Hin- und Rückreihen. Es muß auch in der Rückreihe „gemustert“ werden! Das ist zunächst mühevoll, aber diese Mühe lohnt sich — die Model werden nur so schön und richtig. (Nähere Erklärung siehe bei den Jacken, S. 50).

Strickschrift:

8	glatte verschränkte (= englische) Masche
–	verkehrte Masche
O	glatte Masche
X	2 Maschen glatt zusammenstricken
2	2 Maschen verkehrt zusammenstricken
V	2 Maschen glatt verschränkt zusammenstricken
∓	1 Masche verkehrt aufnehmen
8 mit +	1 Masche glatt verschränkt aufnehmen
•	Wiederholung des Musters

Abkürzungen:

R	Reihe(n)
M	Masche(n)
RM	Randmasche(n)
gl	glatt
verk	verkehrt
verschr	verschränkt
li	links
re	rechts

An folgenden Beispielen sollen die notwendigen Voraussetzungen für das Stricken der Model erläutert werden. Die Strickschrift beginnt immer rechts unten und ist daher von **rechts** nach **links** zu lesen. Wir empfehlen, die ersten Probeversuche unbedingt rund, d. h. in Form eines „Strumpfes" zu stricken. Dann ist jede der folgenden Musterreihen von **rechts** nach **links** zu lesen.

1. Überheben einer glatten verschränkten Masche über eine verkehrte Masche
Beispiel *Almwegerl*

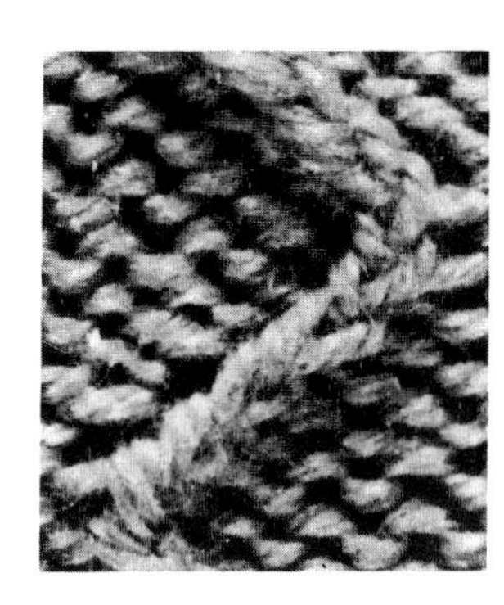

```
8.R.   - - 8 - -
7.R.   - - - 8 -
6.R.   - - - - 8
5.R.   - - - - 8
4.R.   - - - 8 -
3.R.   - - 8 - -
2.R.   - 8 - - -
1.R.   8 - - - -
```

1. R.: M so stricken, wie sie die Strickschrift zeigt.

```
- - 8 -
- 8 - -
- 8 - -
```

2. R.: Diese einfachen Überhebungen oder Kreuzungen können mit oder ohne Hilfsnadel durchgeführt werden.

a) Mit Hilfsnadel: 3 M nach Strickschrift verk stricken, die 4. verk M auf eine Hilfsnadel nach hinten legen, dann die gl verschr M gl verschr abstricken und dann die verk M von der Hilfsnadel verk abstricken.

b) Ohne Hilfsnadel: 3 M nach Strickschrift verk stricken, die nächsten 2 M (1 verk M, 1 gl verschr M) auf die re Nadel heben (ohne sie abzustricken), dann mit der li Nadel die verk M von hinten fassen, für einen Augenblick die gl verschr M fallen lassen und sie dann gleich wieder mit der re Nadel vor der verk M nach re ziehen, auf die li Nadel heben und gl verschr abstricken, dann die verk M verk abstricken.

Wiederholung in der 3., 4. und 5. R.

6. R.: M nach Strickschrift stricken (keine Kreuzung).

7. und 8. R.: Gegengleich, gl verschr M nach li überheben.

Kurzgefaßt bedeutet diese Strickschrift:

```
8 -
- 8
```

Glatte Masche der vorherigen Reihe nach **links überheben!**

Glatte Masche der vorherigen Reihe nach **rechts überheben!**

2. Kreuzen von 2 glatten verschränkten Maschen

Beispiel *Brennende Liab*

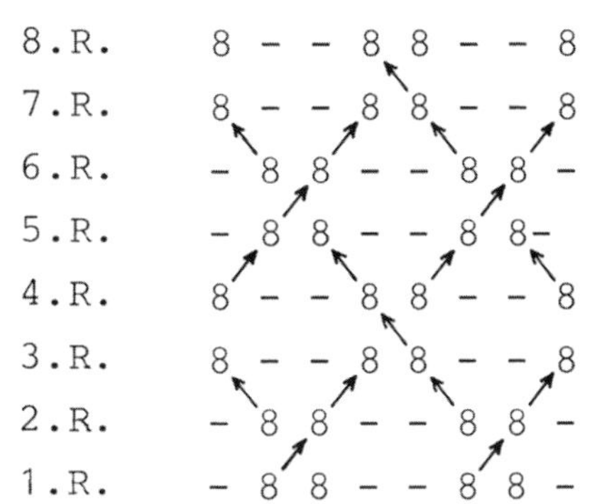

1. R.: Wie Strickschrift.

2. R.: a) Mit Hilfsnadel: verk M abstricken, die 1. gl verschr M auf eine Hilfsnadel hinter die Arbeit legen, die 2. gl verschr M verschr gl abstricken, dann die gl verschr M von der Hilfsnadel verschr gl abstricken.

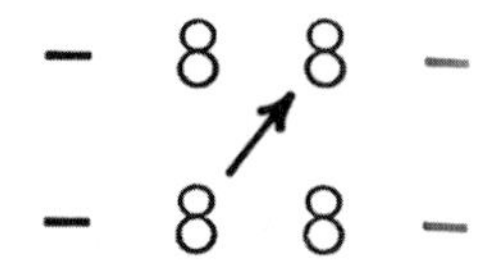

b) Ohne Hilfsnadel: verk M abstricken, die 2 gl verschr M auf die re Nadel heben, die 1. gl verschr M von hinten auf die li Nadel nehmen, die 2. gl verschr M einen Augenblick fallen lassen und gleich wieder mit der re Nadel aufnehmen, nach re vorne überziehen, auf die li Nadel heben und gl verschr abstricken, dann die andere gl verschr M gl verschr abstricken.

3. R.: Die 2 gl verschr M, die in der 2. R gekreuzt wurden, werden in der 3. R nach li bzw. re auseinander gehoben. Das sind Kreuzungen, wie sie unter 1 beschrieben sind.

4. R.: gl verschr M gegengleich kreuzen! Wiederholungen in den nächsten Reihen.

Kurzgefaßt bedeutet diese Strickschrift:

Linke Masche der vorherigen Reihe nach **rechts kreuzen** (nach rechts überziehen!).

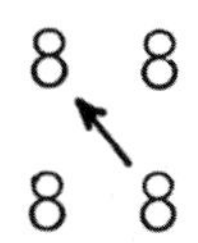

Rechte Masche der vorherigen Reihe nach **links kreuzen** (nach links überziehen!).

3. Überheben von 2 glatten verschränkten Maschen über eine verkehrte Masche
Beispiel *Almweg*

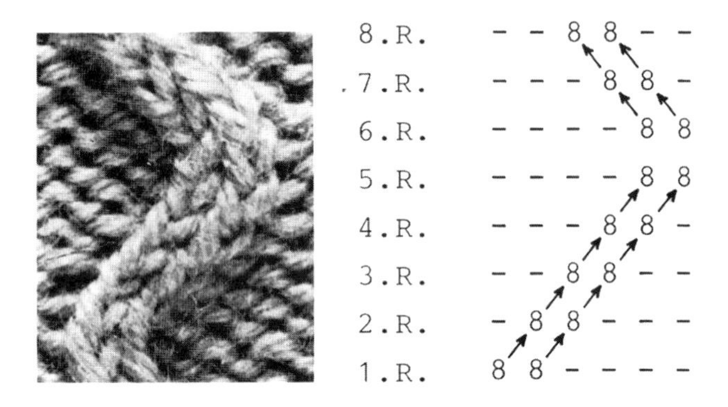

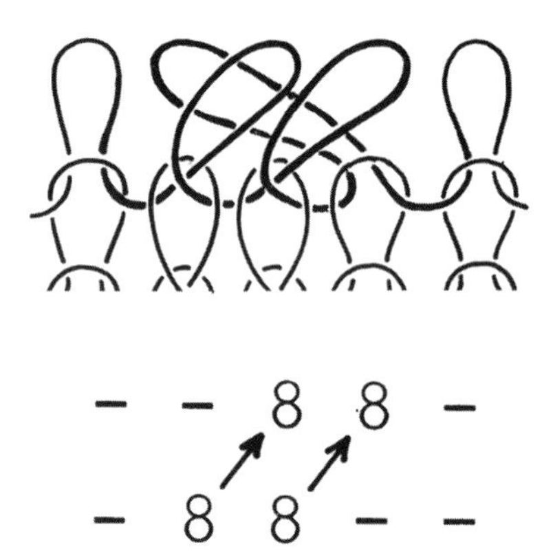

1. R.: M so stricken, wie sie die Strickschrift zeigt.
2. R.: a) Mit Hilfsnadel: 3 M nach Strickschrift verk stricken, die 4. verk M auf eine Hilfsnadel nach hinten legen, dann die 2 gl verschr M gl verschr abstricken und dann die verk M von der Hilfsnadel verk abstricken.

b) Ohne Hilfsnadel: 3 M nach Strickschrift verk stricken, die nächsten 3 M (1 verk M, 2 gl verschr M) auf die re Nadel heben (ohne sie abzustricken), dann mit der li Nadel die verk M von hinten fassen, für einen Augenblick die 2 gl verschr M fallen lassen und sie gleich wieder mit der re Nadel aufnehmen, nach re ziehen, auf die li Nadel heben und glatt verschr abstricken, zum Schluß die verk M verk abstricken.

3., 4. und 5. R.: Wiederholung.
6. R.: Wie Strickschrift.
7. und 8. R.: gegengleich, gl verschr M nach li überheben.

Kurzgefaßt bedeutet diese Strickschrift:

8 8 –
– 8 8

Die 2 glatten Maschen der vorherigen Reihe nach **links überheben!**

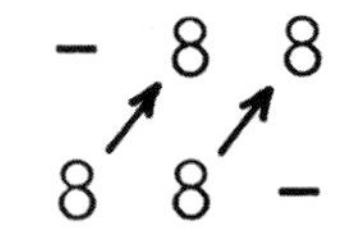

Die 2 glatten Maschen der vorherigen Reihe nach **rechts überheben!**

4. Kreuzen von 4 glatten verschränkten Maschen
Beispiel *4facher Zopf*

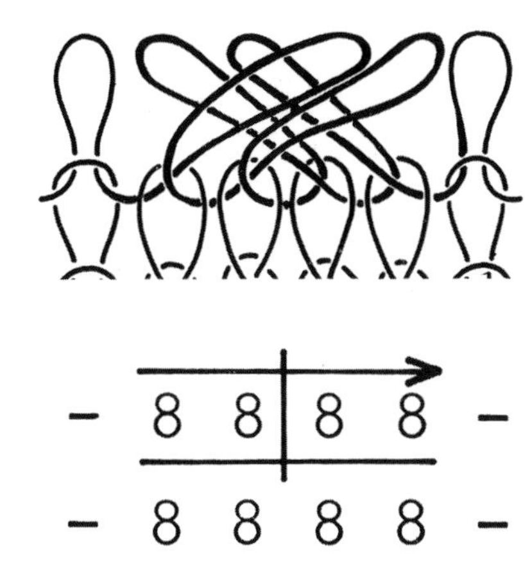

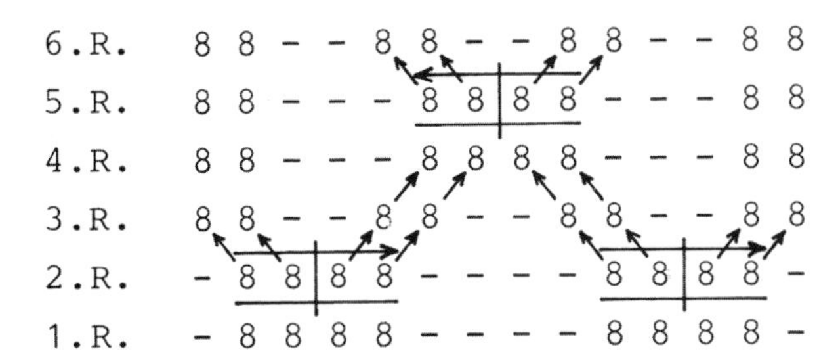

Der senkrechte Trennstrich in der Mitte bedeutet, daß jeweils die 2 re M bzw. die 2 li M zusammengehören und beim Kreuzen **nicht getrennt** werden. Der Pfeil oben zeigt immer an, in welche Richtung gekreuzt wird, das heißt, daß in dieser Richtung die 2 gl M oben = vorne liegen müssen.
Diese Kreuzung von 4 glatten Maschen ist im Prinzip mit und ohne Hilfsnadel gleich auszuführen, wie das Kreuzen von 2 glatten Maschen, nur daß man eben in diesem Falle die doppelte Maschenzahl hat.

Kurzgefaßt bedeutet diese Strickschrift:

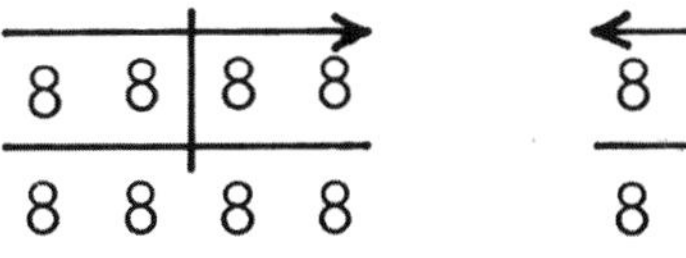

Die 2 linken glatten Maschen werden nach **rechts überhoben!**

Die 2 rechten glatten Maschen werden nach **links überhoben!**

Diese vier bis jetzt besprochenen Kreuzungen wiederholen sich immer wieder. Wenn Sie diese beherrschen, können Sie viele Model damit stricken.